Global Racing

The Complete Guide to the
Greatest Foreign Racecourses

ALAN SHUBACK

DRF Press
NEW YORK

Published by
Daily Racing Form Press
100 Broadway, 7th Floor
New York, NY 10005

ISBN: 978-1-932910-68-1
Library of Congress Control Number: 2008930963

Cover and jacket designed by Chris Donofry
Text design by Neuwirth and Associates

Printed in the United States of America

All entries, results, charts and related information provided by

C O M P A N Y

821 Corporate Drive • Lexington, KY 40503-2794 Toll Free (800) 333-2211 or

(859) 224-2860; Fax (859) 224-2811 • Internet: www.equibase.com

The Thoroughbred Industry's Official Database for Racing Information

Contents

Introduction

THE SOCIOECONOMIC CONCEPT of globalization that currently has the world in its grip was long preceded by the internationalization of the sporting world. The modern Olympic games got their start in 1896. The ABC television program *Wide World of Sports,* reflective of a planet that played games other than baseball, football, and basketball, debuted in 1960. Professional soccer is such a global game that an English club like Manchester United has more followers outside of England than it does inside, and most teams in the National Basketball Association have at least one foreign player these days.

But horse racing has long been the most international of sports. Beginning in 1865, when Gladiateur became the first French-bred, and the first non-British-bred, to win the Epsom Derby, the racing game has been played on a worldwide stage. Thoroughbred breeding on an international scale predates even that milestone event. The British had been sending horses to their colonies in America since the early 19th century, and would continue that trend in Australia, New Zealand, South Africa, and Hong Kong.

The great American economic boom of the late 19th century allowed wealthy Yankee businessmen to plunder some of the best British bloodstock. The net result of World War I saw America prospering and Britain floundering, enabling rich American sportsmen to consolidate their Thoroughbred gains at the expense of their across-the-pond cousins. The post-World War II era was even more conducive to American breeder-owners, leading to the golden age of American racing between 1950 and 1980.

That long-lived pro-American trend in Thoroughbred circles began to change during the 1970s when Europe, fully recovered from the ravages of the war, began to assert itself on the international bloodstock market. Aided, abetted, and frequently challenged by oil-rich sheikhs from the Middle East and by Japanese entrepreneurs, Europeans made unprecedented raids on yearling sales at Keeneland and Saratoga. In the meantime, improved transoceanic travel made sending horses around the world not much more difficult than shipping a horse from Belmont Park to Churchill Downs.

The inaugural Washington, D.C., International at Laurel in 1952 served to introduce Americans to international racing. From that point, turf racing became more and more popular in the United States. Broad-minded Americans such as Paul Mellon, John Galbreath, and Nelson Bunker Hunt all had stables in Europe from the 1960s onward. In 1984, the first Breeders' Cup at Hollywood Park proved to be one of the most important milestones in the evolution of the globalized racing industry.

It was during the 1980s that we began to see a steady trickle of ex-Europeans making their way to America, not in an effort to win a single race, but to complete their careers in a country that offered so many more opportunities for horses not up to Group 1 or Group 2 levels at home. By the early nineties that trickle had become a flood as European owners began to take advantage of the broad array of allowances and minor stakes races available on American turf courses.

American owners and trainers, having noticed how well ex-European horses—many of them from American families that had been whisked out of the country by Robert Sangster, the Maktoum brothers, Khalid Abdullah, and company—were running, began dipping into the European horses-in-training market. The results of all this transatlantic traffic had a revolutionary effect on American racing.

And so it became increasingly important for American racegoers to familiarize themselves with European form. The advent of Dubai World Cup Night, the Hong Kong International Races, and the Japan Cup-Japan Cup Dirt doubleheader brought Asia into the international arena. No longer was it good enough to have a grasp of domestic racing and breeding. Anyone who wanted to be successful in the sport, be it as an owner, a breeder, a trainer, a jockey, or a bettor, had to become well versed in foreign ways of doing things—no matter whether he or she lived in Kentucky, California, or New York; England, Ireland, or France; Hong Kong, Japan, or Australia.

In this book, I will attempt to sort out the mysteries of international racing from an American perspective, in the hope of providing readers with an overview of how things are done in the far-flung reaches of the racing world—and possibly steering them toward a few more winners as well.

And yet, the simple fact is that there is no substitute for being there. You can read this book, or any number of books about racing in foreign countries, and still not become completely familiar with the subject. This volume is offered merely as a guide to a much wider and richer world. For the real thing, a two-week racing holiday in England or France will go farther in your understanding of international racing, and result in more future winning wagers. Until then, it is hoped that this effort to whittle the great big world of horse racing into something more manageable will have a positive effect.

Outside of the Triple Crown, racing is no longer a part of America's cultural or social scene, and more's the pity. That is not the case in countries like England, Ireland, Australia, Hong Kong, or Japan, where jockeys and trainers can be as well known to the public as baseball players and football players are in America.

The connection between racing and the larger culture is a sign of the health, good or otherwise, of every nation's racing industry. To that end I have endeavored to relate the world's leading racecourses to their country's political and cultural background. After all, man does not live by racing alone.

Great Britain

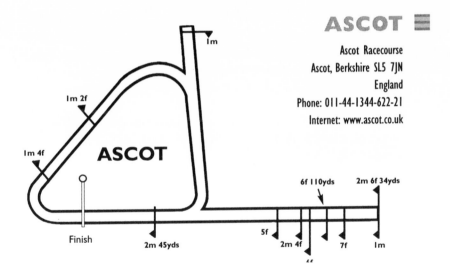

ASCOT ☰

Ascot Racecourse
Ascot, Berkshire SL5 7JN
England
Phone: 011-44-1344-622-21
Internet: www.ascot.co.uk

LOCATION: 36 miles west of London.

COURSE DESCRIPTION: Ascot is a right-handed, triangular track, 1¾ miles around with a stretch of 2½ furlongs. There is a one-mile straight course that joins the right-handed course at the head of the stretch.

Races at 1½ miles begin with a downhill run of a half-mile to Swinley Bottom, a right-hand bend at the lowest point of the track. From the mile pole it is stiffly uphill to the 90-degree turn into the stretch, which is mildly uphill until the final furlong, which is level.

Races at 1¼ miles have a shorter run to Swinley Bottom, but are just as much a test of endurance.

One-mile races are run on both the right-handed course (the Old Mile) and the straight course. Those run over the Old Mile (St. James's Palace Stakes, Coronation Stakes, Queen Elizabeth II Stakes) start from a chute at Swinley Bottom and are entirely uphill until the eighth pole.

Straight miles (Queen Anne Stakes, Royal Hunt Cup) are mildly undulating until reaching the head of the stretch. All races between five and seven furlongs are run on the straight course, where balance and stamina are of equal importance.

The 2½-mile Ascot Gold Cup, which was first run under its current conditions in 1807, has been the Thursday centerpiece of Royal Ascot for decades. It begins on the straight course with a six-furlong run to the line prior to a complete loop around the track. The Queen Alexandra Stakes, at 2⅝ miles, 34 yards, is the longest flat race in the world and traditionally the last race on the last day of the Royal Meeting. It begins at the head of the straight course in front of the Golden Gates, through which the Royal Family arrives at Ascot to begin the Royal Procession at the start of each day of the Royal Meeting. After passing the finish line the first time, it then winds its way once around the right-handed track.

Ascot places a premium on stamina and is ideal for long-striding gallopers. The Old Mile, over which the Queen Elizabeth II Stakes is run, is hardly an ideal prep for the Breeders' Cup Mile or any other American mile, since its uphill nature makes it a stayers' mile as opposed to the near sprint that is the BC Mile. No winner of the Queen Elizabeth II has ever won the BC Mile, though horses such as Banks Hill, winner of the Coronation Stakes, have been successful going 1¼ miles, as that filly's subsequent victory in the Breeders' Cup Filly and Mare Turf at Belmont Park proved.

As testing as Ascot can be, it becomes even more difficult for the endurance-challenged in soft or heavy ground, especially in the nether regions of Swinley Bottom. There was no greater evidence of this than in the 1997 running of the King George VI and Queen Elizabeth Diamond Stakes.

One hour before the first race that day the ground was good to firm and every sign pointed to a rip-roaring battle between Helissio, Pilsudski, and Singspiel. A torrential downpour not only turned the track into a quagmire but also played havoc with the form. Those three floundered in the heavy going while the mud-loving Swain turned the tables at odds of 16–1.

Duke of Marmalade (Johnny Murtagh up) prevails in the Prince of Wales's Stakes at Royal Ascot 2008.

HISTORY: Ascot was founded in 1711 by the last of the Stuart monarchs, Queen Anne, after she had decided during a stag-hunting party that the grounds would make a nice racecourse. The history of racing has been and will forever be indebted to her presence of mind.

Since its inception, Ascot has operated under the auspices of Britain's ruling monarch. Its first meeting, held on August 13, 1711, would eventually develop into a four-day August meeting in 1749. In 1766 this affair was moved to the third week in June, a place on the calendar it has held ever since as Royal Ascot. The four-day Royal Meeting was expanded to five days in 2002.

A number of extracurricular activities during the 19th century have helped give Royal Ascot a particular charm. On June 19, 1832, King William IV was hit in the head by a rock thrown by a disgruntled one-legged sailor. Two years later, Princess Victoria, in an effort to get a better look at the horses as they turned into the stretch, put her Royal Forehead through the window of the Royal Box, smashing the glass to smithereens. The future queen emerged from the mishap unscathed.

The 1850 Gold Cup victory of The Flying Dutchman was the first by the previous year's Derby winner. From that point until World War II it became customary for Derby winners to test their stamina in the 2½-mile Gold Cup.

Fourteen horses would go on to match The Flying Dutchman's feat, among them British Triple Crown winners West Australian, Gladiateur, and Isinglass, with Blue Gown (1868) and Triple Crown winners Gay Crusader (1917) and Gainsborough (1918) managing it in the same year when the Gold Cup was still open to 3-year-olds. The last horse to pull off the famous double was Ocean Swell in 1944–45.

The declining influence of stamina has led to a decline in the influence of the Gold Cup, although a number of multiple winners, chief among them the Francois Boutin-trained Sagaro and the Aidan O'Brien-trained Yeats, each a three-time winner, kept the great race in the forefront. It remains the official centerpiece of the Royal Meeting, although it has long since been displaced in racing value by a handful of races run at distances between five furlongs and 1½ miles.

But stamina will always have a place at Ascot, and there is no greater example of that quality to have paraded itself before the lords and ladies of the British nobility than Brown Jack.

Although he could never be classified as a member of the Thoroughbred kingdom's elite, Brown Jack was as professional a race-horse as any who ever lived, winning the Queen Alexandra Stakes six years in a row from 1929 through 1934. All of this came after he had concluded his jump-racing career by winning Cheltenham's Champion Hurdle in March 1928. That he had won the 2½-mile Ascot Handicap in June 1928 made him a winner at the Royal Meeting seven years in succession, a sporting record that rates as perhaps the safest in the world.

His statue, by the renowned artist Alfred Munnings, is put on display at Ascot just twice a year: on the last day of the Royal Meeting, when the Queen Alexandra Stakes is run, and on the Friday of the King George VI and Queen Elizabeth Stakes meeting in late July, when they run the race named after him, the two-mile Brown Jack Handicap.

Royal Ascot itself is as much a garden party as it is a race meeting. It has always been the key stop on Britain's summer social scene, where ladies are given the opportunity to show off their latest fashions, a custom that has inspired equivalents in French Oaks Day at Chantilly and Kentucky Derby Day at Churchill Downs.

Hats are de rigueur for women at Royal Ascot. The only female who ever got round that unwritten rule was the young lady who in 1984 did her hair up in the shape of a bowler hat. A more ostentatious millinery display was always made by the legendary—some might say notorious—Gertrude Shilling, whose 1960s headgear ranged from a five-foot-wide feathered boa to a five-foot-high giraffe to a soccer field.

But it was Edwardian Ascot that forever set the tone of the Royal Meeting in the eyes of the public at large. Ascot's fashion influence

Shades of the Edwardian Era? Ladies and gentlemen in the Royal Enclosure at Royal Ascot 2008.

reached its peak between 1902 and 1909 under the patronage of King Edward VII.

As the Prince of Wales, Edward had been the most visible member of the Royal Family at Ascot or anywhere else since his mother, Queen Victoria, had disdained racing after the death of her husband, Prince Albert, in 1861.

Edward ascended to the throne in 1901 as arguably the most popular monarch in British history. A devoted horseman, he owned two Derby winners as the Prince of Wales, Persimmon and Diamond Jubilee, and one, Minoru, as the king. His presence was always a cause for celebration at Royal Ascot.

During his reign the great fillies Sceptre and Pretty Polly both won at the Royal Meeting, and his own Minoru followed his Epsom Derby triumph with victory in the St. James's Palace Stakes in 1909. It was also the period that saw the ascension of the two American riders, Tod Sloan and Danny Maher, who introduced a new, more streamlined riding style to British jockeys.

When Edward died on May 6, 1910, barely a month before the Royal Meeting, racegoing ladies had to make some quick changes to their wardrobes. Mourning was the order of the day and black the color of all four days. The 1910 Royal Meeting would be forever known as Black Ascot.

By the next year women went back to wearing whatever was the current fashion, but it is curious to note that gentlemen have ever since worn very much the same costume that was au courant in 1909, the last Royal Ascot attended by Edward.

The Edwardian Ascots served as inspiration, in part at least, for Lerner and Loewe's hit 1956 musical *My Fair Lady*. The "Ascot Gavotte" is set at the racecourse itself and Cecil Beaton's black-and-white race-day costume for Audrey Hepburn in the film version was a match for anything any gentlewoman has ever worn at the Royal Meeting.

Royal Ascot was abandoned from 1915 through 1918 in deference to the hostilities in which Great Britain was involved across the English Channel. The period between the wars was not a particularly great one in British racing as British owners were beginning to feel the financial pinch caused by a declining empire and the rising American economic juggernaut.

Artistically, however, Ascot was in its fullest flower between 1919 and 1939. Painters such as Munnings and Raoul Dufy captured the color and pageantry of the Royal Meeting as it has not been seen on canvas before or since. But color—and racing—was absent from the royal scene during the horrors of World War II between 1940 and 1945.

Following close on the heels of the inaugural King George VI and Queen Elizabeth Stakes in July 1951 was the coronation of Queen Elizabeth II two years later. In 1954 the young queen's Aureole won the race named after her father and mother. The King George, as it soon became known, quickly developed into one of the world's most important mile-and-a-half contests, giving way only to the Prix de l'Arc de Triomphe, and in some years even surpassing the quality of the great French race.

And well it should rate so highly, as its winners include the likes of Ribot, Ballymoss, Nijinsky, Mill Reef, Brigadier Gerard, Dahlia, Shergar, Dancing Brave, Generous, Lammtarra, Swain, Daylami, Montjeu, and Galileo.

In 1961, at a cost of 1 million pounds ($2 million), the new Queen Elizabeth II Stand was opened, creating more space for racegoers just in time for the swinging sixties. The decade saw an increase in attendance at Royal Ascot with a concurrent rise in hemlines. Gone were the attitudes of the Victorian Era that had held sway since the former grandstand had been erected in 1839.

The winds of change extended to more than miniskirts. On April 30, 1965, Ascot conducted its first jump races, a steeplechase and a hurdle, over a new course constructed inside the flat track. Although the great Arkle would easily win the SGB Handicap Chase on December 14,

1966, while spotting four outclassed rivals 35 to 38 pounds, jump racing has never sat well with certain elements of the Ascot hierarchy. With the death in 2003 of the Queen Mother, a great and influential jump-racing enthusiast, the future of the discipline at Ascot is not crystal clear.

The 1970s have emerged as racing's most recent golden age on both sides of the Atlantic, and Ascot was not excluded from that decade's cavalcade of stars. The great influx of Kentucky-breds, largely through the efforts of Robert Sangster and the four Maktoum brothers, added wealth to British racing. But an even bigger star emerged in the 1990s, and he was one who rewrote racing's record books at Ascot on September 28, 1996.

On that day, Frankie Dettori, already a household name in England as the world's most famous jockey, ran the seven-race card at Ascot's Festival of Racing. Among his victories were Mark Of Esteem in the Group 1 Queen Elizabeth II Stakes, Diffident in the Group 2 Diadem Stakes, and Wall Street in the Group 3 Cumberland Lodge Stakes. A $2 wager carried over onto each of Dettori's mounts that day would have resulted in a payoff of $55,338.

As crowds at Royal Ascot swept past the 60,000 mark late in the century (and in excess of 75,000 on the Thursday, Ladies Day, the day of the Ascot Gold Cup), it became clear that another new grandstand was needed.

And so after racing on Sunday, September 26, 2004, Ascot closed. Two weeks later the wrecking crews moved in to dismantle the Queen Elizabeth II Stand and soon thereafter the builders arrived to begin work on the new Millennium Stand. At a cost of $95 million, Ascot reopened on June 20, 2006, the first day of the Royal Meeting, with the latest state-of-the-art grandstand. It accommodated 80,000 people in a style to which racegoers at the world's classiest racecourse have become accustomed.

ANALYSIS: Almost every race at Ascot contains a touch of class. While it must be remembered that a good maiden, a good handicap, or a good Group 3 can pop up at any British racecourse, such races at Ascot are almost always run at a level deserving of their published status. Occasionally they surpass that rating.

And what goes for Ascot in general goes especially for Royal Ascot and the last weekend in September, when the track runs the Queen Elizabeth II Stakes, the Fillies Mile, the Royal Lodge Stakes, and the Diadem Stakes.

The Royal Meeting is especially important. Not only do owners and trainers point many of their horses to the five-day festival, but also, foreign invaders from Ireland, France, and in recent years, Australia, are seen much more at Royal Ascot than at any other time of the year in England. All of this makes for racing at the very highest level.

Take, for example, the St. James's Palace Stakes and the Coronation Stakes. Both are Group 1 miles—the St. James's for 3-year-old colts, the Coronation for 3-year-old fillies.

Although the 1000 and 2000 Guineas in England, Ireland, and France have classic cache, these two Royal Ascot fixtures have emerged in recent years as a kind of championship final for 3-year-old milers who have won or placed in the assorted Guineas. In any given year, they may have a championship status that any of the Guineas lacks.

The one-mile Queen Elizabeth II Stakes has emerged as a key prep for the Breeders' Cup Classic. Giant's Causeway parlayed a second-place finish in 2000 into a narrow defeat to Tiznow in the Classic. In 2008, Raven's Pass and Henrythenavigator repeated their QEII one-two in the Classic at the expense of Curlin in what was the first start for all three horses on a synthetic surface.

Run on a largely uphill course, the Queen Elizabeth II is a stamina-inducing mile that perfectly suits horses stretching out to an American mile and a quarter.

However, in gauging the Ascot performances of horses that have been imported to America, it is important to remember that factors such as the state of the ground and the particular quality of the competition in a given race must be taken into account. Never assume that just because a horse has won at Ascot that he should be able to win at Santa Anita or Belmont, or even Gulfstream or Churchill Downs.

TRACK RECORDS (Since 2006)

DISTANCE	RECORD TIME	HORSE	DATE	MEDIAN TIME
5f	57.44	Miss Andretti	June 19, 2007	1:00.50
6f	1:12.46	Henrythenavigator	June 19, 2007	1:14.40
7f	1:25.89	Dabbers Ridge	July 29, 2006	1:28.00
1m (Str)	1:37.21	Ramonti	June 19, 2007	1:40.60
1m (RH)	1:38.70	Henrythenavigator	June 17, 2008	1:40.80
1¼m	2:04.15	I'm So Lucky	June 23, 2006	2:09.80
1½m	2:27.40	Linas Selection	June 23, 2006	2:35.50
2m	3:25.52	Tungsten Strike	May 2, 2007	3:32.60
2½m	4:18.29	Full House	June 19, 2007	4:20.60
2⅝m, 159y	4:56.25	Enjoy The Moment	June 23, 2007	—

TRACK RECORDS (Pre-2006)

DISTANCE	RECORD TIME	HORSE	DATE
5f	59.10	Orient	June 21, 1986
6f	1:12.18	Fayr Jag*	June 21, 2003
		Ratio*	June 21, 2003
7f	1:25.83	Master Robbie	Sept. 27, 2003
1m (Str)	1:38.07	Colour Sergeant	June 17, 1992
1m (RH)	1:38.51	Russian Rhythm	June 20, 2003
1¼m	2:02.76	First Island	June 18, 1996
1½m	2:26.53	Doyen	June 19, 2004
2m, 45y	3:25.29	Landowner	June 17, 1992
2½m	4:15.30	Royal Gait (DQ'd)	June 16, 1998
2¾m, 34y	4:47.89	Cover Up	June 21, 2003

* Finished in a dead heat in the Wokingham Handicap.

MAJOR RACES (Chronological Order)

RACE	CONDITIONS
Sagaro Stakes-G3	2m 4yo+
Paradise Stakes (Listed)	1m (Str) 4yo+
Pavilion Stakes (Listed)	6f 3yo
ROYAL ASCOT	
St. James's Palace Stakes-G1	1m (RH) 3yo c
Queen Anne Stakes-G1	1m (Str) 4yo+
King's Stand Stakes-G1	5f 3yo+
Coventry Stakes-G2	6f 2yo
Windsor Castle Stakes (Listed)	5f 2yo
Prince of Wales's Stakes-G1	1¼m 4yo+
Windsor Forest Stakes-G2	1m (Str) 4yo+ f&m
Queen Mary Stakes-G2	5f 2yo f
Jersey Stakes-G3	7f 3yo
Sandringham Handicap (Listed)	1m (Str) 3yo f
Royal Hunt Cup Handicap	1m 3yo+
Ascot Gold Cup-G1	2½m 4yo+
Ribblesdale Stakes-G2	1½m 3yo f
Norfolk Stakes-G3	5f 2yo
Hampton Court Stakes (Listed)	1¼m 3yo
Coronation Stakes-G1	1m (RH) 3yo f
King Edward VII Stakes-G2	1½m 3yo c&g

RACE	CONDITIONS
Queen's Vase-G3	2m 3yo
Albany Stakes-G3	6f 2yo f
Wolferton Handicap (Listed)	1¼m 4yo+
Golden Jubilee Stakes-G1	6f 3yo+
Hardwicke Stakes-G2	1½m 4yo+
Chesham Stakes (Listed)	7f 2yo
Wokingham Handicap	6f 3yo+
KING GEORGE MEETING	
Valiant Stakes (Listed)	1m (Str) 3yo+ f&m
King George VI and Queen	
Elizabeth Diamond Stakes-G1	1½m 3yo+
Princess Margaret Stakes-G3	6f 2yo f
Winkfield Stakes (Listed)	7f 2yo
BRITISH FESTIVAL OF RACING	
Princess Royal Stakes-G3	1½m 3yo+ f&m
Queen Elizabeth II Stakes-G1	1m (RH) 3yo+
Fillies Mile-G1	1m (RH) 2yo f
Royal Lodge Stakes-G2	1m (RH) 2yo c&g
October Stakes (Listed)	7f 3yo+ f&m
Rosemary Handicap (Listed)	1m (RH) 3yo+ f&m
Diadem Stakes-G2	6f 3yo+
Cumberland Lodge Stakes-G3	1½m 3yo+
Fenwolf Stakes (Listed)	2m 3yo+
Autumn Stakes-G3	1m 2yo
Bengough Stakes-G3	6f 3yo+
Cornwallis Stakes-G3	5f 2yo

DAYS OF RACING: Fifteen days of flat racing, chief among them the five-day Royal Meeting, held from Tuesday through Saturday in the third week of June; the two-day King George Meeting on the third or fourth Friday and Saturday of July; and the three-day Queen Elizabeth II Stakes Meeting on the last weekend of September. There are also nine days of jump racing between November and March.

HOW TO GET THERE: When staying in London, the fastest, most efficient, and most comfortable way to get to Ascot is via train. They leave hourly from London's Waterloo Station, a 55-minute journey leaving one off at Ascot Station, after which there is a pleasant, mostly uphill 10-minute walk to the racecourse (downhill, thankfully, back to the station). The pre-race train ride affords an excellent opportunity to study the form in the *Racing Post,* Britain's estimable racing daily. There is even a pub across the way from Ascot Station, providing a good way to get the day's festivities off to a fast start.

SURROUNDING AREA: The town of Ascot was built up, if that phrase can be used, around the racecourse. It consists of little more than a main road, called in England the High Street, which extends half a mile past the front of the track. It contains a few pubs not far from the grandstand entrance.

There are also a number of golf courses, including Sunningdale, in the area. These have attracted Grand Slam-winning golfers like Nick Faldo and Nick Price, who live nearby. But if you plan on attending the full five days of Royal Ascot, or any other day of racing at the track, you are best advised to stay in London and make the daily commute, as there is nothing to do in Ascot Town after racing has ended.

CHESTER

Chester Racecourse
The Racecourse
Chester, Cheshire CH1 2LY
England
Phone: 011-44-304-600
Internet: www.chester-races.co.uk

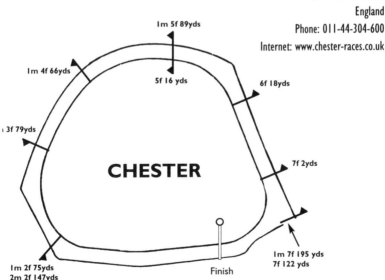

LOCATION: 207 miles northwest of London, 19 miles south of Liverpool.

COURSE DESCRIPTION: Chester is a level, virtually round left-handed course that bears close—but not too close—comparison with most North American tracks. Measuring one mile, 73 yards around, it is also one of Britain's smallest racecourses.

Horses at Chester are rarely off the turn, since there is not a straightaway measuring farther than a single furlong. That said, most of the bends are quite mild by American standards.

As Chester is the second-oldest racetrack in Britain after York, the distances of its races never fall precisely upon a given furlong, because measuring devices were far from accurate in days of old. A 1¼-mile, 75-yard race starts at the head of the two-furlong stretch, makes its first turn just past the finish line, and travels about a furlong down the side straight before embarking on a wide, sweeping turn of nearly half a mile. The quarter-mile stretch has a slight left-hand bend at the furlong marker.

An inside draw is important at Chester, as horses tend to drift to the outside, given the tight nature of the place. Long-striding gallopers are at the mercy of compact, close-coupled types, but athleticism is even more important than size.

Chester Racecourse is squeezed in between the medieval city wall and the River Dee. Because of a lack of room, the paddock is located on the infield just behind the finish line, offering grandstanders a clear, if distant, view of the preliminaries.

In theory, the track should be a perfect test for Epsom's Derby, Oaks, and Coronation Cup—all 1½-mile tests held a month after Chester's early May Festival—since balance and athleticism are at an even greater premium at Epsom than at Chester.

Chester has at least one prep race for each of those Epsom contests. The 1½-mile, 66-yard Chester Vase and the 1¼-mile, 75-yard Dee Stakes are trials for the Derby. The 1⅜-mile, 79-yard Cheshire Oaks is a prep for the Oaks, while the 1¼-mile, 75-yard Huxley Stakes and the 1⅜-mile, 89-yard Ormonde Stakes are prelims for the Coronation Cup.

Chester proved the perfect venue for a Derby prep when the great foundation sire Hyperion followed his Chester Vase victory with a triumph in the 1933 Derby. In 1952, the Aga Khan's Tulyar beat older horses in the Ormonde on the way to winning his Derby. The mud-loving Henbit and Shergar, a great athlete by any standard, pulled off the same double in 1980 and 1981, Shergar following his 12-length Vase score with a magesterial 10-length triumph at Epsom. Although good horses such as Law Society, Unfuwain, future Irish Derby winner Old Vic, Luso, and Millenary have won the Vase since then, Chester has faded as a key venue for Derby hopefuls, perhaps because of its great distance from England's major training centers at Newmarket and Lambourn.

HISTORY: Nicknamed the Roodee for the twin reasons that the track occupies a plot of land once known as Rood Eye while the River Dee parallels the sweeping backstretch, Chester's first day of racing was held in 1539 during the reign of Henry VIII. The Silver Ball was run until 1609, when it was renamed St. George's Race after England's patron saint. From 1624 the race was run at a distance of five miles, or five dizzying times around the course, but during the 1660s Oliver Cromwell's puritanical Protectorate put an end to the proceedings, as well as to riders' anxiety at having to remember which lap they were on.

The first meeting at Chester under rules we would now recognize was held in 1729. The tight confines of the track were emphasized in 1775 when a horse named Mine-Ass-In-A-Band-Box won the Grosvenor Gold Cup for his owner, Lord Grosvenor.

By 1870, the May Festival had become so popular that it was decried by one William Wilson, an uncompromising non-Conformist who declared that "brawling, drunkenness, gambling, theft, fornication, suicide and every vice denounced by the divine authority are invariably the results of the present racing system" in Chester. Not much different than Saratoga or Del Mar, really.

In 1899, the Prince of Wales, later to become King Edward VII, made his first appearance at Chester at a time when prize money there was second only to Ascot, and when the track was referred to as the Ascot of the North—this despite the fact that it ran just three days of racing a year, all of them at its prestigious May Festival.

The Ormonde Stakes, named for the 1886 British Triple Crown winner, was first run at its present distance of 1⅝ miles, 89 yards in 1936 when it was won by Quashed, who a month later would defeat 1935 American Triple Crown winner Omaha in one of the most memorable Ascot Gold Cups.

In 1985, a fire set by an arsonist, who was never apprehended, destroyed the charming Victorian-era, Tudor-style grandstand that had been built in 1900. For the next two years, Chester operated with a temporary stand, much like Arlington Park between 1985 and 1987, until a new $4.5 million structure was opened in 1988.

In 1987, Chester made history in becoming the first British track from which pictures were beamed live into betting shops, all two of them in Bristol and Colchester!

Racing at Chester is a unique experience. The old City Wall envelops the racecourse from the sixteenth pole to the half-mile marker, and fans crowd atop it for a free view of the races. Racegoers are closer to the action at Chester than at almost any other track in the world, while residents of the town have a shorter walk from home to the track than anywhere in the world—even Saratoga. The Roodee literally abuts the downtown area, one reason why Chester routinely attracts near-capacity crowds of more than 10,000.

ANALYSIS: It is a myth that horses that run well at Chester must necessarily run well in America. Just because the Cheshire track is a left-handed affair with tight turns, that does not mean that anything that runs there will transport his form to Gulfstream Park, Churchill Downs, or Del Mar.

Of greater importance for Americans seeking to interpret Chester form is the quality of the racing there. At the May Festival it is high, if not as high as it once was. That surmise must, however, be taken with a grain of salt vis-à-vis America, because most of the better horses running in the Ormonde, the Dee, the Chester Vase, and the Cheshire Oaks need a minimum of 10 furlongs.

With the number of races run at 1¼ miles or farther in the U.S. ever dwindling, we do not see as many of Europe's middle-distance horses, as 10-to-12-furlong types are called across the Atlantic, being imported. Any horse that is imported that has done well in the above-named races would have to be considered, as long as his more recent form has held up.

A perfect example of good Chester form translated into even better American form was My Memoirs. The Richard Hannon-trained son of the good miler Don't Forget Me won the 1992 Dee Stakes, then a listed race, before traveling to New York, where he closed with a rush to split A.P. Indy and Pine Bluff in the Belmont Stakes. When switched to a new American trainer, he failed to reach the winner's circle in five subsequent outings.

Such clear-cut examples emerging from Chester are rare. Moreover, the horses that run in the summer and autumn meetings at the Roodeye are rarely in the class of My Memoirs, much less Shergar or Old Vic, two of the very best horses who have run there in recent times.

Most of Chester's better races outside of the May Festival are good handicaps or low-end listed events. If, however, you see a horse from Chester who has shown speed in winning a sprint around those tight turns, he should be able to win an American race at any distance up to a mile on turf—if he is properly placed.

TRACK RECORDS

DISTANCE	RECORD TIME	HORSE	DATE	MEDIAN TIME
5f, 16y	59.20	Althrey Don	July 10, 1964	1:01.00
6f, 18y	1:12.70	Play Hever Golf	May 4, 1993	1:13.80
	1:12.70	Stack Rock	June 23, 1993	
7f, 2y	1:23.75	Three Graces	July 9, 2005	1:26.50
7f, 122y	1:30.91	Cupid's Glory	Aug. 18, 2005	1:33.80
1¼m, 75y	2:07.15	Stotsfold	Sept. 23, 2006	2:12.20
1⅜m, 79y	2:22.50	Rockerlong	May 9, 2001	2:26.60
1½m, 66y	2:34.20	Old Vic	May 9, 1989	2:41.00
1⅝m, 89y	2:45.40	Rakaposhi King	May 7, 1987	2:55.70
1⅞m, 179y	3:24.50	Moonlight Quest	July 30, 1995	3:29.90
2¼m, 147y	3:59.59	Greenwich Meantime	May 9, 2007	4:10.90

MAJOR RACES (Chronological Order)

RACE	CONDITIONS
Cheshire Oaks (Listed)	1⅜m, 79y 3yo f
Chester Cup Handicap	2¼m, 147y 4yo+
Chester Vase-G3	1½m, 66y 3yo c&g
Huxley Stakes-G3	1¼m, 75y 4yo+
Ormonde Stakes-G3	1⅝m, 89y 4yo+
Dee Stakes-G3	1¼m, 75y 3yo c&g
Queensferry Stakes (Listed)	6f, 18y 3yo+
Chester Handicap (Listed)	1⅝m, 89y 3yo+
Henry Gee Stakes (Listed)	6f, 18y 2yo
Stand Cup (Listed)	1½m, 66y 3yo+

DAYS OF RACING: There are 13 days of racing at Chester, chief among them the three-day midweek May Festival beginning the Wednesday after Newmarket's Guineas Meeting. Then there are two single days in June, a two-day meeting in mid-July, and two single days in August followed by a two-day weekend August Festival late in the month. The year concludes with two more single days of racing in September.

HOW TO GET THERE: From London by train from Euston Station to Chester General Station.

SURROUNDING AREA: Founded by the Romans, who built the City Wall and who used the place as a buffer against the wild tribes of Wales and the north of England, Chester is steeped in history. From gothic Chester Cathedral to the Rows, a series of half-timbered houses dating from the 13th century connected by long covered galleries that resemble medieval shopping centers, the city is flush with charming nooks and crannies.

Now a city of 80,000 inhabitants just a stone's throw from the Welsh border, Chester abounds in pubs with names like the Pied Bull and the supposedly haunted George and Dragon.

No less an authority than Samuel Johnson's biographer James Boswell wrote that "Chester pleases my fancy more than any town I know of." Racegoers with a taste for history might agree.

DONCASTER

Doncaster Racecourse
Leger Way
Doncaster, South Yorkshire DN2 6BB
England
Phone: 011-44-1302-304-200
Internet: www.doncaster-racecourse.co.uk

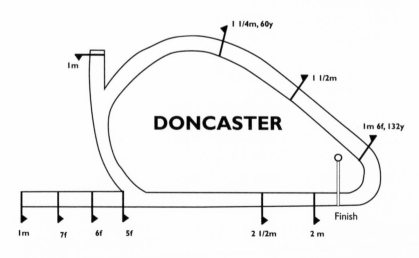

LOCATION: 173 miles north of London, 75 miles east of Liverpool, 30 miles south of York.

COURSE DESCRIPTION: Doncaster is a pear-shaped, left-handed course measuring 1¹⁵⁄₁₆ miles around, ending with a 4½-furlong stretch that forms the last part of the one-mile straight course.

One-mile races are also run out of a chute that joins the long, sweeping left-hand turn about five furlongs from the finish.

Virtually level, Doncaster is a classic galloping track upon which stamina is at a premium. The 1¾-miles, 132 yards of the St. Leger Stakes require a horse to reach down deeply for whatever staying power he may possess, especially given the very long homestretch.

The St. Leger course starts at the beginning of the half-mile straight that leads into the long and wide left-hand turn that empties into the 4½-furlong stretch. There are slight undulations on that part of the turn farthest from the finish, but the course is otherwise level.

All races between five furlongs and seven furlongs are run on the straight course, and these are generally run on the stands side to preserve the ground along the inner rail for the longer races run on the left-handed course.

HISTORY: Doncaster has been conducting race meetings since about 1600, although no written records exist prior to 1728. Those early races were run at Cantley Common, an area adjacent to the site of the present course on the Town Moor.

More importantly, the town was the 18th-century home of Colonel Anthony St. Leger, a cultured ex-soldier and sportsman who had the happy idea—in an age of grueling three- and four-mile heats for older horses—that single-heat events restricted to 3-year-olds would be the ideal way to test a Thoroughbred's true caliber.

St. Leger's initial concept was a race of two miles for 3-year-old colts and fillies. On September 24, 1776, barely 2½ months after Thomas Jefferson and company had declared their new nation's independence from Great Britain, six horses lined up for what would soon after be recognized as the world's first classic race.

All six were unnamed at the time, although the winner, Lord Rockingham's filly by Sampson, was eventually named Allabaculia. Rockingham, who was also Britain's prime minister at the time, proposed in 1777 that the 1778 running should be named for its founder, St. Leger, whose name in those days was pronounced Sellinger.

George Strawbridge's Lucarno takes Doncaster's classic St. Leger Stakes in 2007 with Jimmy Fortune aboard.

Appropriately, the 1778 renewal was the first run on the present Doncaster course on the Town Moor. In 1800, the aptly named Champion became the first to pull off the Derby-St. Leger double. The St. Leger was on the racing map, once and for all.

In 1813 the distance of the race was reduced to 1¾ miles, 193 yards, and there have been periodic minor alterations since then. The event has been run for one reason or another at Newmarket, Manchester, and Thirsk (war), Ayr (a hole in the Doncaster stretch), and York (Doncaster closed for reconstruction), but it always returns to its original home.

Hambletonian, no relation to the Standardbred foundation sire, won it in 1795. A grandson of Eclipse, he won the 2¼-mile Doncaster Cup the very next day. It was, after all, the age of stamina.

A filly version of the St. Leger was inaugurated in 1839. Called the Park Hill Stakes after the home of Colonel St. Leger, it was won in 1857 by the Derby and Oaks winner Blink Bonny, but the best fillies have almost always opted for the St. Leger itself, as evidenced by the victories of immortal 20th-century distaffers such as Sceptre, Pretty Polly, Sun Chariot, Dunfermline, Sun Princess, Oh So Sharp, and User Friendly.

In fact, the St. Leger has always been the most filly friendly of the classics, with 20 of its 232 runnings through 2007 having fallen to females.

The first Triple Crown winner in history was crowned at Doncaster when West Australian followed his 2000 Guineas and Derby triumphs with a victory in the 1853 St. Leger.

Since the end of World War II, however, the great race has been criticized as being increasingly irrelevant, at least in classic terms, because of its 1¾-mile, 132-yard length.

In an age of speed, the St. Leger no longer commands the respect of breeders, as do the Guineas and the Derby.

Yet the race continues to produce more than the occasional top-class winner. Since 1970, the year Nijinsky won it to become the last British Triple Crown winner, the St. Leger has been won by Bustino, Touching Wood, Derby winner Reference Point, the excellent stayer Millenary, and Grand Prix de Paris winner Scorpion, as well as the aforementioned fillies Dunfermline, Sun Princess, Oh So Sharp, and User Friendly.

Still, it cannot be denied that the St. Leger no longer attracts the type of horse it did before World War II, in part due to its proximity on the calendar to the Prix de l'Arc de Triomphe. If the tyranny of the commercial breeder ever wanes, the St. Leger might yet reclaim its deserved place as a genuine classic horse race, one befitting the old racing proverb that "the fittest horse wins the 2000 Guineas, the luckiest horse wins the Derby, but the best horse wins the St. Leger."

That was certainly the case in 1849 when The Flying Dutchman won it and a year later when it was taken by Voltigeur in a run-off against Russborough, with whom he had dead-heated just an hour earlier. Two days later, Voltigeur bested The Flying Dutchman in the Doncaster Cup, another example of what stamina can bring out in a Thoroughbred.

Doncaster is also the site of the Flying Childers Stakes, a five-furlong juvenile Group 2. The race commemorates the Thoroughbred who may have been the first to lay claim to the title "the fastest horse in the world."

A son of the Darley Arabian himself, Flying Childers was named for his breeder, Leonard Childers, a man who lived just a few miles from Doncaster. Sold to the Duke of Devonshire, Flying Childers never ran at Doncaster, having earned his reputation in but two outstanding performances at Newmarket.

Although the race named for him has been won by champion sprinter Marwell and the outstanding sire Green Desert, it was downgraded to Group 2 status in 1979, but has for the last 20 years rarely attracted fields better than Group 3 quality.

At a cost of $64 million, a new grandstand, along with new stables and office buildings, opened for the St. Leger meeting in 2007. The new stand replaced the bland concrete structure erected in the 1980s, which in turn had replaced a fading Victorian building that had long since outlived its usefulness. Racing at Doncaster may not be as much fun as it is at Ascot or Epsom, but it does possess a grand sense of history.

ANALYSIS: While many of the better horses that run at Doncaster are attracted by staying races like the St. Leger, the Park Hill, and the Doncaster Cup, the track's St. Leger Festival includes a number of seven-furlong and one-mile events that always have a marked influence.

The listed Doncaster Mile in March was used in 1986 by Bold Arrangement as a prep for his Bluegrass Stakes third and Kentucky Derby second. That, however, was not indicative of the race's general quality and, anyway, the Mile is now restricted to 4-year-olds and up.

The seven-furlong Park Stakes has of late become a pointer to the Breeders' Cup Mile. The first two home in the 2005 Park, Iffraaj and Sleeping Indian, were both headed to the 2006 Mile. Iffraaj missed it with an injury, while Sleeping Indian finished a most unlucky fourth.

Horses that run in the St. Leger can in theory be competitive in any of the late-season mile-and-a-half events around the world, although they rarely are. Even the great Nijinsky was unable to cut back from his 1970 St. Leger victory to win the Arc four weeks later, failing to run down Sassafras by a neck.

User Friendly ran a similar race in the 1992 Arc, losing by a neck to Subotica three weeks after her St. Leger score. Snurge followed his 1990 St. Leger victory with a good third behind Saumarez in the Arc, but he did use his staying power to win the 1992 Canadian International on soft ground. In 2003, St. Leger third-place finisher Phoenix Reach won the Canadian International in his next start. The success, however, of St. Leger runners at Woodbine as opposed to Longchamp may have more to do with the fact that the Canadian International is a low-end international Group 1 while the Arc just may be the best race in the world.

The 2001 St. Leger winner, Milan, followed with a decent fifth in Sakhee's Arc, then was a fast-closing second to Fantastic Light in the Breeders' Cup Turf, performances that come close to defining the relative merits of all three of those races.

In 2005 Scorpion set a Longchamp track record for 1½ miles in the Grand Prix de Paris before winning his St. Leger, but injury prevented him from living up to his considerable potential. He returned to form to win Epsom's 1½-mile Coronation Cup as a 5-year-old, after which he developed into an outstanding stayer.

Suffice it to say that any horse that finishes in the first three in the

St. Leger should not be considered in any American graded stakes shorter than 1½ miles.

On a day-in, day-out basis, horses with Doncaster form that wind up in America are not really hot prospects unless they have run well at the St. Leger Festival. Being located in the north of England, it is far removed from the main southern training centers at Newmarket and Lambourn, so the majority of horses that run there in the spring, summer, and late fall are generally not among the leaders of any division.

The exception is the Racing Post Trophy, a Group 1 contest for 2-year-olds run on the straight mile in late October.

Originally called the Futurity Stakes, the Racing Post is one of the most important juvenile races in Europe. Its 1986 winner, Reference Point, went on to win both the Derby and the St. Leger the following year, and 1995 winner Celtic Swing won the '96 French Derby. In 2001, winner High Chaparral went on to win the Epsom Derby, the Irish Derby, and two Breeders' Cup Turfs, while the 2004 winner, Motivator, won the 2005 Epsom Derby.

TRACK RECORDS

DISTANCE	RECORD TIME	HORSE	DATE	MEDIAN TIME
5f	57.20	Celtic Mill	Sept. 9, 2004	1:00.50
5f, 140y	1:05.60	Halmahera	Sept. 8, 2004	1:07.40
6f	1:09.60	Caesar Beware	Sept. 8, 2004	1:13.60
6½f	1:17.42	Royal Confidence	Sept. 12, 2007	1:20.48
7f	1:21.60	Pastoral Pursuits	Sept. 9, 2004	1:26.30
1m (Str)	1:36.50	Singhalese	Sept. 9, 2004	1:39.30
1m (LH)	1:35.40	Playful Act	Sept. 9, 2004	1:41.00
1¼m, 60y	2:04.81	Red Gala	Sept. 12, 2007	2:11.10
1½m	2:27.70	Takwin	Sept. 9, 2000	2:35.10
1¾m, 132y	3:01.07	Hi Calypso	Sept. 13, 2007	3:06.70
2¹⁄₁₆m	3:34.40	Farsi	June 12, 1992	3:35.50
2¼m	3:48.41	Septimus	Sept. 14, 2007	3:58.20

MAJOR RACES (Chronological Order)

RACE	CONDITIONS
Lincoln Handicap	1m (Str) 4yo+
Doncaster Mile (Listed)	1m (LH) 4yo+
Cammidge Trophy (Listed)	6f 3yo+
Scarborough Stakes (Listed)	5f 2yo+

ST. LEGER MEETING

Race	Conditions
Doncaster Cup-G2	2¼m 4yo+
Park Hill Stakes-G2	1¾m, 132y 3yo+ f&m
May Hill Stakes-G2	1m (LH) 2yo f
Park Stakes-G2	7f 3yo+
Sceptre Stakes (Listed)	7f 3yo+ f&m
Troy Stakes (Listed)	1½m 3yo+
Portland Handicap	5f, 140y 3yo+
Champagne Stakes-G2	7f 2yo c&g
Flying Childers Stakes-G2	5f 2yo
St. Leger Stakes-G1	1¾m, 132y 3yo c&f
Racing Post Trophy-G1	1m (Str) 2yo c&f
Doncaster Stakes (Listed)	6f 2yo
Wentworth Stakes (Listed)	6f 3yo+
Gillies Stakes (Listed)	1¼m, 60y 3yo+ f&m
Serlby Stakes (Listed)	1½m 3yo+
November Handicap	1½m 3yo+

DAYS OF RACING: Twenty days of flat racing between late March and early November and seven days of jump racing from mid-December to early March.

The British flat season's traditional opening meeting (on turf at least), the Lincoln Festival, is a two-day affair on the third or fourth weekend in March. There is a two-day bank-holiday meeting on the first Monday and Tuesday in May. Single-day meetings are held periodically throughout the summer with the prestigious four-day St. Leger Festival beginning on the second Wednesday in September, the St. Leger itself always run on the Saturday.

A two-day meeting featuring the Racing Post Trophy is held on the last weekend in October. The final meeting of the British turf flat season is traditionally run on the second weekend in November.

HOW TO GET THERE: By train from London's Kings Cross Station to Doncaster Station, which is two miles from the racecourse.

SURROUNDING AREA: Sadly, Doncaster is a nondescript town of 125,000 with little to recommend it culturally. TV fans may be interested to know that it is the 1938 birthplace of actress Diana Rigg, who earned worldwide fame for her portrayal of Emma Peel in the tongue-in-cheek 1960s spy series *The Avengers*. Outside of the racing and the St. Leger Ball on the eve of the big race itself, not much has happened in Doncaster since then.

EPSOM

Epsom Racecourse
Epsom Downs
Surrey KT18 5LQ
England
Phone: 011-44-1372-726-311
Internet: www.epsom.derby.co.uk

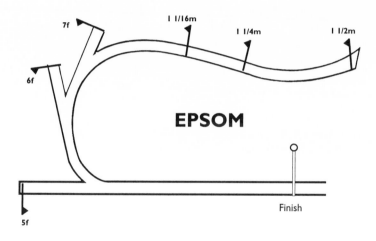

LOCATION: 17 miles southwest of central London.

COURSE DESCRIPTION: A 1½-mile horseshoe-shaped, left-handed course, Epsom is probably the most difficult flat track in the world. And well it should be, since it is the home of the Derby, the Blue Riband of the Turf, a race that reigned as the world's most important Thoroughbred contest from its inception in 1780 until World War II.

The Derby course begins at the bottom of the Downs, from which there is a mild right-hand bend through the first furlong and a half. The steep, steady rise continues through a mild left-hand bend until the highest ground is reached at the halfway point, six furlongs from home.

The left-hand bend then becomes a steep, unbanked left-hand turn that continues through Tattenham Corner, the famous turn into the 3½-furlong stretch. The stretch continues downhill but is also sloped toward the rail, making it difficult for tired horses to hold a straight line, a problem that not infrequently traps stronger horses that have been saving ground along the rail behind them.

The final sixteenth of a mile is slightly uphill, rising barely two feet through the last 110 yards. The famous head-on pictures of the Derby finish make it appear as if horses are climbing a mountain at the end, but that is an optical illusion caused by the downhill leading into the final uphill half-furlong.

Epsom also has two short chutes at the top of the hill from which races at six and seven furlongs start. The five-furlong straight course meets the stretch 3½ furlongs from home and is entirely downhill except for the last 110 yards. With a track record of 53.60 seconds, it can claim to be the fastest five-furlong course in the world, although the horses that run on it would never be described as the world's fastest horses.

The Derby course, used for the Oaks as well, requires horses to possess staying power, balance, and athleticism in equal measures. It was for these reasons that the Derby became the most important test for breeders for more than 150 years. The entire Thoroughbred breed is built upon horses that have been able to handle its rises, falls, and switchbacks as well as thoroughly seeing out the complete 12-furlong trip.

HISTORY: No racecourse in the world can compare with Epsom when it comes to the influence on the Thoroughbred breed. Newmarket, Longchamp, Churchill Downs, and Belmont Park have all had their considerable input, but it is at Epsom where the foundation for the Thoroughbred as we know it today has been formed over the last two and a quarter centuries.

The first recorded race meeting at Epsom was held on March 7, 1661, and was attended by the recently restored Stuart king, Charles II, but it was not until 1779 and the first running of the Oaks that things picked up on what is officially known as the Banstead Downs.

The inaugural St. Leger Stakes in 1776 had introduced the idea of a single-heat contest to determine 3-year-old supremacy. The Oaks was probably the idea of General John Burgoyne, the British officer who surrendered to American forces at the Battle of Saratoga, widely regarded as the turning point of the American Revolution, a difference of opinion the British still refer to as the American War for Independence.

The Oaks, named for the house in which Burgoyne had become a permanent guest following his ignominious return to England, was a success right off the bat. At the first-night celebrations, Burgoyne and his host and father-in-law, the 12th Earl of Derby (ancestor to Ouija Board's owner, the current Lord Derby), came to the conclusion—along with Jockey Club headman Sir Charles Bunbury, playwright Richard Brinsley Sheridan (author of *The Rivals* and *The School for Scandal*), and raconteur and Member of Parliament Charles Fox, who, along with Bunbury, was a leader in the anti-slave trade movement—that what Epsom needed was a similar race for colts.

Whether Lord Derby prevailed over Sir Charles in a draw of lots or drew the highest card to determine the name of the new race will never be known. We can only thank our lucky stars that it was not called the Bunbury Stakes, in which case the famous race run on the first Saturday in May at Churchill Downs might have become known as the Kentucky Bunbury.

The initial Derby Stakes in 1780 was run at a distance of one mile and was won, fittingly enough, by Bunbury's colt Diomed. Lord Derby won the race named after him for the first time in 1783 with Sir Peter Teazle. A year later, when Sir Thomas, owned by the Prince of Wales (the future King George IV), was victorious, the Derby's future was made.

Like any great sporting event, the Derby has a rich and colorful history. There have been betting scandals, fixed races, deaths on the racecourse, in the stands, and on the way to the track. The famous as well as the infamous have graced its stage. The Derby is part of British folklore in precisely the same way that the Kentucky Derby is pure Americana.

Milestones in early Derby history are synonymous with milestones in the sport in general.

The historic reputation of Eclipse was established primarily through his influence on the Derby. Three of its first five winners—Young Eclipse, Saltram, and Serjeant—were his sons. Highflyer, perhaps the greatest of 18th-century stallions and the horse after whom Tattersalls' major yearling sale is named, also sired three early Derby winners in Noble, Sir Peter Teazle, and Skyscraper.

Sir Peter Teazle was the first Derby winner to become a prolific sire of Derby winners. There were four of them. Waxy, the 1793 winner, sired four of his own, among them the 1810 winner, Whalebone, who would sire two himself—or three, if you count 1822 winner Moses, whose parentage is disputed and may have been the son of a rival stallion, Seymour.

The 1811 winner, Phantom, sired two Derby winners, but as time wore on and the pool of Thoroughbreds increased, the number of Derby-winning sires of Derby winners decreased.

Sir Charles Bunbury's Eleanor was the first filly to land the Derby in 1801. There have been just five female winners since: Blink Bonny (1857), Shotover (1882), Signorinetta (1908), Tagalie (1912), and Fifinella (1916), the last-named winning in the second of four years when the race was run at Newmarket during World War I. The victories of the 100–1 Signorinetta and the 11–2 Fifinella came just two days after each had won the Oaks.

But fallout from the Derby was not always positive. Thanks to some lax stewardship, betting scandals had become all too commonplace in the 1840s. The 1844 Derby brought matters to a head when a horse named Running Rein was exposed as a 4-year-old named Maccabeus. Lord George Bentinck, chief steward of the Jockey Club, exposed the cheaters and led the fight to clean up racing's act. To this day he is widely regarded as the savior of 19th-century racing in England.

The Derby has always been the lynchpin of the British Triple Crown—the 2000 Guineas, Derby, and St. Leger. West Australian was the first to complete the hat trick in 1853, but it was Gladiateur's 1865 Derby triumph and subsequent Triple Crown that provided perhaps the most historically important Derby of them all.

Until that year, the British had believed that Thoroughbred racing was their own plaything. The sport might be practiced in Ireland, France, Germany, and America, but that wasn't the genuine article. Or so they thought.

Gladiateur, bred in France by his owner, Comte Frederic de Lagrange, may have been trained in England by Tom Jennings, but he was every inch a Frenchman. As such he became the first French horse to win the Derby, earning the nom de guerre the Avenger of Waterloo, after the battle at which Wellington had ended Napoleon's career 51 years earlier, not long enough for the French to have forgotten their national disgrace at British hands.

The Derby victory of Gladiateur was the first step in the evolution of Thoroughbred racing as an international sport. It was followed in

The 2003 Epsom Derby field approaches Tattenham Corner, four furlongs from the finish.

1881 by the first Derby victory by an American horse, Iroquois, owned and bred by Carolina tobacco magnate Pierre Lorillard. In 1897 Galtee More became the first Irish-bred winner. Five years later his half-brother Ard Patrick won it, but history was made in 1907 when Orby became the first Irish-trained Derby winner, an event that prompted an Irishman with a keen sense of history to shout, "Thank God! A Catholic horse has finally won the Derby."

Not that the British were about to relinquish the reins of the sport they had invented. The Prince of Wales, who would become King Edward VII in 1901, won a pair of Derbies with Persimmon in 1896 and Diamond Jubilee in 1900, both of them by the outstanding sire St Simon. In 1909 he reinforced the old adage that racing was the Sport of Kings when he became the only reigning British monarch in history to win the Derby, courtesy of Minoru, but the times they were a-changin'.

Edward graciously sent Minoru to his second cousin Nicholas II, Czar of All the Russias, in an effort to buck up the Russian breeding program. But the 1917 revolution put an end to racing in the new Soviet Union and Minoru ended his life like a proper proletarian, pulling a cart.

There were social rumblings on the home front in England as well, and they were tragically reflected in the so-called Suffragette Derby of 1913, a race that is memorable for all the wrong reasons, one in which the harsh realities of the world came crashing down on a seemingly innocent sporting event.

At the time in Britain, women were agitating for the vote. A group of activists came to Epsom on June 4 to protest their cause in a manner that would end in disaster and put a serious dent in the move to full suffrage.

Emily Davison was selected to be the woman who would bring the feminist cause to the eyes of the world that day. As the Derby runners rounded Tattenham Corner, she slipped under the rails and targeted the horse owned by King George V, Anmer. Grabbing his reins as he raced near the back of the pack, she fell under the horse's full weight, her ribcage crushed.

Anmer escaped unscathed, while his rider, Harry Jones, suffered minor injuries, but the 40-year-old Davison died four days later. She was given a hero's funeral by the suffragette movement but most Britons viewed her senseless behavior as an act of folly, if not terrorism. Only five years later, women over the age of 30 got the right to vote. Full female suffrage was not granted until 1928.

The 1913 Derby also produced the most dismaying result in the race's history, none of it having to do with the trouble at the back of the pack. Craganour, the 3–2 favorite, crossed the line in front by a head but was disqualified and replaced in the winner's circle by the 100–1 runner-up, Aboyeur, much to the delight of the bookies.

In 1924, Lord Derby won the race named for his forebear for the first time in 137 years with his homebred Sansovino, but his lordship had greater cause for celebration in 1933 when the race was won by Hyperion. By the 1918 Derby winner, Gainsborough, Hyperion would sire just one Derby winner himself—Owen Tudor in 1941—but he would go on to top the British/Irish sire standings six times, establishing himself as a leading foundation sire. His son Pensive won the Kentucky Derby and the Preakness in 1944, and Hyperion is also the damsire of Nearctic, the sire of Northern Dancer.

The 1930s introduced the Aga Khan to racing, as the grandfather of the current Aga won three of his five Derbies with Blenheim in 1930, Bahram in 1935 and, perhaps most notably, Mahmoud in 1936. The diminutive gray broke Hyperion's track record for 1½ miles that day with a time of 2:33.80, a mark that would stand for 59 years until Lammtarra won the 1995 running in 2:32.31.

The Aga Khan would also win the 1948 Derby with My Love, who followed by two days the Aga's Oaks win with Masaka. And he took the 1952 renewal with Tulyar. After a 29-year hiatus, his grandson would return the famous name to the winner's circle with the ill-fated Shergar, who would ultimately be killed by his Irish Republican Army kidnappers. The current Aga Khan has since won three more Derbies with Shahrastani (1986), Kahyasi (1988), and Sinndar (2000).

American influence has been present in the Derby ever since Iroquois' 1881 triumph. Yankee riders dominated during the first decade of the 20th century. Tod Sloan caused a second American revolution with what the British termed his monkey-on-a-stick riding style. Although Sloan never won the Derby, his country-men won six of them from 1901 through 1912, the great Danny Maher taking three with Rock Sand (the eventual broodmare sire of Man o'War), Cicero, and Spearmint. The American brothers Reiff also took three Derbies: John was aboard Orby and Tagalie, and Lester became the first American jockey to win the Derby, piloting Volodyovski in 1901.

Riding Hawaiian Sound in 1978, Bill Shoemaker was nosed out of a Derby triumph by Greville Starkey on Shirley Heights. That was the year Affirmed was being ridden to the American Triple Crown by Steve Cauthen, the teenager who would end America's Epsom Derby drought with victories aboard Slip Anchor in 1985 and Reference Point two years later.

But the biggest American influence on the Derby may belong to Paul Mellon and his great son of Never Bend, Mill Reef. His 1971 victory followed those of the Sir Gaylord colt Sir Ivor in 1968 and the Canadian-bred son of Northern Dancer, Nijinsky, in 1970.

It was the age of the American in Europe. Derby victories by Kentucky-breds Roberto, The Minstrel, and Secreto followed in short order, and while Nijinsky may have had a more profound effect on the breed, the decision by the generous Anglophile Mellon to keep Mill Reef in Britain led to him becoming champion British/Irish sire in 1978 and 1987.

In recent years the Derby spotlight has shone most brightly on the world's two leading Thoroughbred outfits, Godolphin and Coolmore, run by Sheikh Mohammed bin Rashid Al-Maktoum and by John Magnier, respectively. Godolphin's Lammtarra not only set the course record in 1995, but he also did it off an incredible 10-month layoff, while the victories of the Magnier-controlled Galileo in 2001 and High Chaparral a year later confirmed Aidan O'Brien's Ballydoyle yard as the world's most powerful.

The study of the history of Thoroughbred racing in any country closely parallels that country's history in general. A study of the Epsom Derby alone reflects the history of England since 1790—its folly, trag-edy, and glory all wrapped up in a single horse race.

ANALYSIS: Any horse who acquits himself well in any of Epsom's three 12-furlong Group 1 contests—the Derby, the Oaks, or the Coronation Cup—must be considered a strong contender for any race at or about the same distance in the United States or anywhere else, as long as he has held his form or improved since then.

That said, the quality of the Derby, like that of its Kentucky namesake, has been spotty in recent years. From 1996 through 2007, eight of the 12 Epsom Derby winners— Shaamit, Benny the Dip, High-Rise, Oath, Kris Kin, North Light, Motivator, and Sir Percy—had a combined post-Derby record of just 1 for 27, High-Rise providing their lone victory in a Nad Al Sheba allowance.

Only during a three-year spell of Irish-trained winners from 2000 through 2002 have Derby victors lived up to their credentials. Sinndar went undefeated in three subsequent starts in the Irish Derby, the Prix Niel, and the Prix de l'Arc de Triomphe. Galileo won the Irish Derby and the King George VI and Queen Elizabeth Diamond Stakes. And High Chaparral landed the Irish Derby, the Irish Champion Stakes, and two Breeders' Cup Turfs.

Ten Group 1 victories garnered by the last 12 Derby winners do not stand up well to the eight Group 1 wins corralled by Derby runner-ups or the 14 Group or Grade 1 triumphs chalked up by Derby third-place finishers.

Derby runner-ups such as Sakhee have won the Juddmonte International and the Arc, Golan has won the King George, Rule of Law the St. Leger, and Hawk Wing the Eclipse Stakes and the Lockinge, a victory that earned him the European mile championship.

Recent Derby thirds who went on to win at the highest level include Beat Hollow in the Grand Prix de Paris, the Turf Classic, the Manhattan, and the Arlington Million; Alamshar in the Irish Derby and the King George; Dubawi in the Prix Jacques le Marois; Dylan Thomas in the Irish Derby, Irish Champion, Prix Ganay, King George, and the Arc; and Moon Ballad in the Dubai World Cup.

All of this may lend credence to the old saw that the luckiest horse wins the Derby. So does it follow that in most years there are better horses chasing the Derby winner home?

From an American point of view, this is difficult to judge, since few of the first three Derby finishers make it to the U.S. This is very likely because there are not enough worthwhile races run in North America beyond 1¼ miles, or farther than 1⅛ miles, for that matter, and because Europeans may be loath to run some of their best horses in America, where the use of legal medications presents a predicament for trainers of imports: If they use the same drugs as American horses in order to level the playing field, it might taint the perception of their horses' quality in the eyes of European breeders.

Oaks winners fare a little better in America than their Derby counterparts. Ouija Board duplicated High Chaparral's achievement in winning a pair of Breeders' Cup races, while Kazzia took Belmont's Flower Bowl Handicap. The only other Oaks winners to be seen in the U.S. in the last 20 years have been Casual Look, Intrepidity, and User Friendly, who won one of three American starts going shorter than her required minimum of 1½ miles.

The Coronation Cup is as good as any 12-furlong race for older horses in Europe outside of the Arc and the King George, with winners such as Exceller (who later beat Seattle Slew in an unforgettable Jockey Club Gold Cup); Time Charter; Rainbow Quest; Triptych (twice); subsequent Breeders' Cup Turf winner In the Wings; Swain; Singspiel (later a Dubai World Cup winner); future Man o' War and Breeders' Cup Turf winner Daylami; and Shirocco, who won a BC Turf of his own the autumn before his Coronation Cup victory.

In theory, winners of the two Group 3 races run at Epsom's Derby Meeting should do well in America, as the Diomed Stakes and the Princess Elizabeth Stakes are both run at the very American distance of 1¹⁄₁₆ miles. They are also run over a course requiring an athleticism typical of the American Thoroughbred.

That is the theory, but like the horses who compete on Epsom's seven annual days of racing outside of the Derby Meeting, few of them have been successful in America. In fact, outside of the Derby Meeting itself, Epsom is generally shunned by trainers with good horses, precisely because of the extreme difficulty of the course, not to mention the suspect quality of the races.

TRACK RECORDS

DISTANCE	RECORD TIME	HORSE	DATE	MEDIAN TIME
5f	53.60	Indigenous	June 2, 1960	55.70
6f	1:07.30	Loyal Tycoon	June 7, 2003	1:19.40
7f	1:20.10	Capistrano	June 7, 1972	1:23.30
1¹⁄₁₆m	1:40.70	Sylva Honda	June 5, 1991	1:46.10
1¼m	2:03.50	Crossbow	June 7, 1967	2:09.70
1½m	2:32.31	Lammtarra	June 10, 1995	2:38.90

MAJOR RACES (Chronological Order)

RACE	CONDITIONS
English Oaks-G1	1½m 3yo f
Coronation Cup-G1	1½m 4yo+
Princess Elizabeth Stakes-G3	1⅟₁₆m 3yo+ f&m
Surrey Stakes (Listed)	7f 3yo
Epsom Derby-G1	1½m 3yo c&f
Diomed Stakes-G3	1⅟₁₆m 3yo+
Woodcote Stakes (Listed)	6f 2yo
Fortune Stakes (Listed)	7f 3yo+

DAYS OF RACING: Epsom generally has 14 days of flat racing a year, starting with the theoretical Derby prep meeting in late April at which is run the Blue Riband Stakes, a 1¼-mile conditions race that has not provided a viable Derby candidate for many years. The Derby Meeting is held on either the first or second Friday and Saturday in June, with the Oaks and the Coronation Cup on Friday, the Derby on Saturday. Single evening meetings are run each Thursday in July, followed by six day meetings from late August through early October.

With the exception of the two-day Derby Meeting, crowds are sparse and the quality of the racing rarely rises above average.

HOW TO GET THERE: Train travelers are advised to begin their trip from London at either Victoria or London Bridge, arriving at Tattenham Corner Station, from which it is a one-mile walk between the racecourse and the temporary amusement park set up across the street during the Derby Meeting. There are also trains leaving London Victoria arriving at Epsom Downs on the opposite side of the track. Alternatively, there are trains from London Waterloo that deposit one at Epsom Station, about two miles from the racecourse.

SURROUNDING AREA: With a population of 27,000, Epsom is hardly a tourist town. Named for the salts that became famous around the world as a sort of medicinal cure-all, Epsom is a sleepy if rather prosperous place these days. Besides the racetrack, it has a small training center, one of whose tenants is Philip Mitchell of Running Stag fame.

If you are planning a day or two at the races at Epsom, it is wise to stay in London and commute to the track. If you can make a prompt railway connection after the last race, you can be back in London in time for dinner, if not for a show.

Goodwood Racecourse Ltd.
Goodwood
Chichester, West Sussex PO18 0PX
England
Phone: 011-44-1243-755-022
Internet: www.goodwood.co.uk

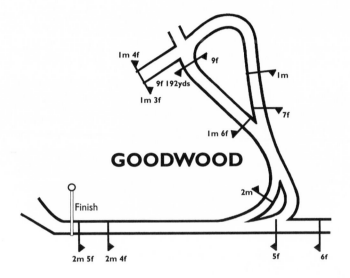

LOCATION: 66 miles west-southwest of London, 32 miles west of Brighton, 20 miles east of Portsmouth.

COURSE DESCRIPTION: Goodwood is a racecourse difficult to describe in words. Indeed, it seems improbable that a racetrack could even be built on the steep ridges and deeply rolling terrain that make up the area. There is an undulating six-furlong straight course that meets the stretch of what might be described as the largely right-handed, L-shaped main course over which all races between seven furlongs and 2½ miles are run.

The two-mile Goodwood Cup and other staying races begin on the stretch in front of the stands and make a left-hand turn out into the fields before swinging right near the 1½-mile chute. Races from that chute start with a two-furlong straight and then turn right preceding a half-mile straight before turning right on the upper spur into what is from there a 3½-furlong straight run to the finish.

Races at 1¼ miles start adjacent to the 1½-mile chute but proceed along the lower spur, turning right-handed into a three-furlong stretch.

Races at seven furlongs and a mile begin on the upper spur but take the lower turn into the three-furlong stretch.

Goodwood is what the British refer to as a sharp track, meaning that it is one that has relatively tight turns. The bends into the stretch are downhill, while the start of the 1½-mile course is uphill. More importantly, it is a fair track in that it does not disadvantage any type of horse, long-striding or close-coupled.

Even with binoculars it is difficult to follow the action on the turning course, so far does it lie from the grandstand. As the track is built on a ridge, there is a sharp fall just inside the inner rail to the rolling farmland that fills the gap between the stands and the furthest point of the track nearly a mile away beyond the 1⅛-mile start. The view from the grandstand is breathtaking, one that has earned the course the well-deserved sobriquet Glorious Goodwood.

HISTORY: Set on the Duke of Richmond's estate on the Sussex Downs, Goodwood has been the site of racing since 1802 when the third duke staged a meeting for the officers of the Sussex Militia to replace one that had been held at nearby Petworth Park. The first three-day meeting was an immediate success and led eventually to the five-day "Glorious" meeting, which remained the only racing at Goodwood until the mid-1950s.

The first Goodwood Cup was run in 1812. The first recorded flag start in the history of racing was held at Goodwood sometime in the

Glorious Goodwood

GLOBAL RACING

1830s, apparently because the starter had a speech impediment and could not clearly pronounce the word "Go!"

Comte Frederic Lagrange, owner of the 1865 Epsom Derby winner, Gladiateur, introduced himself to English racing with Goodwood Cup winner Monarque in 1857, but the most famous foreign invader at Goodwood was the great Hungarian mare Kincsem, who won the Cup in 1878. Unbeaten in 54 career starts, Kincsem would win the Grand Prix de Deauville and the Grosser Preis von Baden on her triumphant way back to Budapest, where the local track, Kincsem Park, is named after her.

The great racehorse and stallion St Simon, frequently the mount of the legendary Fred Archer, is inextricably linked to Goodwood. Foaled in 1881, St Simon had been bred and owned by the Hungarian nobleman Prince Batthyany, who died a year later. Under the old rules of the Jockey Club, his death automatically canceled St Simon's classic entries, and so, barred from the Guineas and the Derby, St Simon won his first two races at Goodwood for his new owner, the Duke of Portland. After a 20-length cakewalk in the Ascot Gold Cup at 4, he concluded his perfect 11-race career with a 20-length victory in the Goodwood Cup, after which he sired 10 classic winners.

The Sussex Stakes, a one-mile event for 3-year-olds and up that has long been the most prestigious race on the modern Goodwood calendar, was first run in 1878 for 3-year-olds only and was not opened to older horses until 1975. Since then it has been won by many of Europe's best milers, among them Kris, Kings Lake, Soviet Star, Warning, Zilzal, Marling, Giant's Causeway, Rock of Gibraltar, and Ramonti, as well as Dick Duchossois' Second Set, who won it in 1991.

The Stewards' Cup is relatively unknown in America, but in England the six-furlong handicap is one of the year's biggest betting races. Handicap racing in America is now reduced to a handful of graded races in which the weights are ridiculously compressed to encourage the participation of the best horses. In England, astute handicappers parlay their knowledge of form and the discrepancies of weight assignments into big winnings—or losings. The Stewards' Cup is perhaps the most contentious contest of the British racing season between punter and bookie, the winner rarely paying less than 10–1. In 1982, fan favorite Soba stunned the bookies at 18–1 on her way to 11 victories, an unheard-of annual total for an all-winning handicapper who was constantly being encumbered with higher and higher weights.

First run in 1877, the Richmond Stakes was the occasion of one of the most bizarre stewards' rulings in history in 1983. The six-furlong juvenile Group 2 was won that year by the 1–3 favorite, Vacarme, with Crag-An-Sgor second and Godstone third. But Lester Piggott aboard Vacarme had blasted his way out of trouble, banging into both Crag-An-Sgor and Godstone, while Crag-An-Sgor was judged to have interfered with Godstone as well.

The stewards, in their sagacity, moved Godstone up from third to first, demoting Vacarme from first to third. They also disqualified second-place finisher Crag-An-Sgor, but allowed him to keep second place, reasoning that Crag-An-Sgor had to be placed behind Godstone because he interfered with him—but given that Vacarme had interfered with Godstone *and* Crag-An-Sgor, he had to be placed behind them both. Thus Crag-An-Sgor remained in second, although officially dq'd.

During the late Victorian era, Glorious Goodwood secured its place on Britain's summer social/sporting calendar. Today it is the closing event on the tour, following Epsom's Derby Meeting, the Henley Regatta, Royal Ascot, Wimbledon, and the British Open.

Crowds reached the overflow point in the post-World War II period with 55,000 showing up on Goodwood Cup Day in 1953, an amazing number considering Britain's postwar austerity and Goodwood's out-of-the-way location. New grandstands for both members (clubhouse) and the general public were opened in 1991, by which time crowds at the Glorious meeting had dwindled to a more manageable 15,000 or so.

ANALYSIS: As the quality at Goodwood's five-day Glorious meeting in late July-early August is so high, any horse that does well there must be considered in America if he is running at the same level, or even one level above. In general, a horse acquitting himself well in a British Group 3 should be competitive in an American Grade 2; a good British Group 2 performer should be competitive in most American Grade 1 events.

The 1¼-mile Nassau Stakes for fillies and mares has proven to be a key race for future American runners in recent years. Its 1990 winner, Kartajana, finished a neck third in the Arlington Million a year later. In 1997, Ryafan vaulted from her Nassau victory to win Keeneland's Queen Elizabeth II Cup, then shipped to California to take the Yellow Ribbon and the Matriarch to earn an Eclipse Award as best filly or mare on turf.

In 2001, Nassau winner Lailani flew to Belmont a month later to take the Flower Bowl. A year later the Nassau was won by Islington, who could manage only third as the favorite three races later in the Breeders' Cup Filly and Mare Turf. She would, however, make amends in 2003 by taking that Cup race.

Ouija Board, who had won the Filly and Mare Turf in 2004 and finished second in 2005, won the 2006 Nassau. Later that autumn she added a second Filly and Mare Turf title. All of this makes the Nassau Stakes a European race to which American racegoers should pay close attention.

In theory, the Sussex Stakes, the first of four major Group 1 weight-for-age miles on the European circuit, should be a midsummer pointer to the Breeders' Cup Mile. In reality, that hasn't been the case.

Giant's Causeway won it in 2000 before ultimately just missing in the Breeders' Cup Classic. Two years later, Rock of Gibraltar's Sussex score did eventually lead to his heartbreaking second in the Mile, a race in which he was surely the best horse on the day.

In 1983, Tolomeo followed his fourth-place Sussex finish behind Noalcoholic with a victory over John Henry in the Arlington Million, a perfect example of a European miler stretching his speed to an American mile and a quarter, a theory European trainers should apply more frequently.

More recently, 2006 Sussex fourth-place finisher Aussie Rules would win Keeneland's Shadwell Turf Mile two months later, while 2005 Sussex seventh David Junior would improve to win the 2006 Dubai Duty Free.

The 1½-mile Gordon Stakes is of scant importance in America, but it does serve as a key prep for the classic St. Leger Stakes. Its 2003 winner, Phoenix Reach, finished third in his St. Leger, but later embarked on an international career that would bring him victories in the Canadian International and the Dubai Sheema Classic. He is, however, an exception to the Gordon rule from an American point of view.

The Group 2 Celebration Mile at the late-August meeting has been won by the likes of Kris, Known Fact, and Cape Cross, but also by Milligram, Selkirk, and Mark Of Esteem, all of whom flopped in the Breeders' Cup Mile.

Although it holds just Group 3 status, the mid-September Select Stakes has been won by Dancing Brave as a prep for his 1988 Arc triumph. Two years later, Mtoto followed his Select score with an Arc second. Singspiel vaulted from his 1996 Select victory to win the Canadian International and finish second in Pilsudski's Breeders' Cup Turf. Mutamam took the 1998 Select and would later finish fourth in the 2000 BC Turf and win the 2001 Canadian International, so there is good reason to keep an eye on future Select winners.

There is also good reason to watch maiden winners coming out of the Glorious Goodwood Meeting, as trainers with good horses there will frequently ship some of their better untried juveniles along with them. As a general rule, the same cannot be said of most of Goodwood's maiden races away from the late July-early August meeting, when the quality of the racing is not usually quite up to its "Glorious" standard.

TRACK RECORDS

DISTANCE	RECORD TIME	HORSE	DATE	MEDIAN TIME
5f	56.00	Rudi's Pet	July 27, 1999	59.40
6f	1:09.18	Tax Free	Sept. 9, 2006	1:12.20
7f	1:23.80	Brief Glimpse	July 25, 1995	1:27.40
1m	1:35.61	Spectait	Aug. 4, 2006	1:39.90
1⅛m	1:52.80	Vena	July 27, 1995	1:56.30
1¼m	2:02.81	Road To Love	Aug. 3, 2006	2:08.00
1⅜m	2:23.00	Asian Heights	May 22, 2001	2:28.30
1½m	2:31.50	Presenting	July 25, 1995	2:38.40
1¾m	2:58.50	Mowbray	July 27, 1999	3:03.60
2m	3:21.55	Yeats	Aug. 6, 2006	3:30.20
2½m	4:11.70	Lucky Moon	Sept. 2, 1990	—

MAJOR RACES (Chronological Order)

RACE	CONDITIONS
Conqueror Stakes (Listed)	1m 3yo+ f&m
Cocked Hat Stakes (Listed)	1⅜ m 3yo c&g
Height of Fashion Stks (Lstd)	1¼m 3yo f
Festival Stakes (Listed)	1¼m 4yo+
Tapster Stakes (Listed)	1½m 4yo+
GLORIOUS GOODWOOD	
Lennox Stakes-G2	7f 3yo+
Gordon Stakes-G3	1½m 3yo
Molecomb Stakes-G3	5f 2yo
Sussex Stakes-G1	1m 3yo+
Vintage Stakes-G2	7f 2yo
Goodwood Cup-G2	2m 4yo+
King George Stakes-G3	5f 3yo+
Lillie Langtry Stakes-G3	1¾m 3yo+ f&m

GLOBAL RACING

RACE	CONDITIONS
Richmond Stakes-G2	6f 2yo c&g
Oak Tree Stakes-G3	7f 3yo+ f&m
Glorious Stakes (Listed)	1½m 4yo+
Stewards' Cup Handicap	6f 3yo+
Nassau Stakes-G1	1¼m 3yo+ f&m
Thoroughbred Stakes (Lstd)	1m 3yo
Celebration Mile-G2	1m 3yo+
Prestige Stakes-G3	7f 2yo f
March Stakes (Listed)	1¾m 3yo+
Select Stakes-G3	1¼m 3yo+

DAYS OF RACING: Goodwood has 22 days of racing annually: four in May, four in June, and one in early July prior to the prestigious five-day Glorious Goodwood Meeting, which usually begins on the last Tuesday in July. These are followed by a two-day weekend meeting in late August, four days in September, and two in October.

HOW TO GET THERE: Trains taking a painfully slow one hour and 40 minutes leave from London Victoria for Chichester, which is about four miles east of the racecourse. Open-top double-decker buses await your arrival at Chichester Station to take you to the racecourse, a white-knuckle ride over tree-lined roads that line the very edge of some of the steepest ridges in the south of England.

SURROUNDING AREA: Chichester is a charming medieval town founded by the Romans in A.D. 70. Its centerpiece is the 900-year-old gothic cathedral. One of the most ancient churches still in use in Europe, it boasts a stained-glass window designed by 20th-century Russian artist Marc Chagall.

The May-to-September Chichester Festival attracts theater lovers from around the English-speaking world as well as fans of classical music.

Goodwood House, the historic seat of the Duke of Richmond, is the center of the vast estate on which the racecourse lies. Its art collection includes works by Van Dyck and Canaletto, as well as George Stubbs's *Horse Racing on the Downs at Goodwood.*

Automobile fanciers might be interested in the Goodwood Festival of Speed, a 1.16-mile hill climb held on the three-day weekend following Glorious Goodwood. The Goodwood Revival on the first weekend in September features races over the same course for vintage racing cars.

HAYDOCK PARK ≡

Haydock Park Racecourse
Newton-le-Willows, Merseyside WA12 0HQ
England
Phone: 011-44-1942-725-963
Internet: www.haydock-park.co.uk

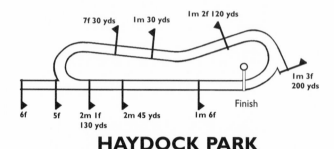

HAYDOCK PARK

LOCATION: 198 miles northwest of London, 17 miles east of Liverpool, 18 miles west of Manchester.

COURSE DESCRIPTION: Haydock is a virtually level, kidney-shaped, left-handed track that measures 1⅝ miles around. There is a six-furlong straight course that meets the main course at the head of its 4½-furlong stretch. There is also a chute at what Americans would call the clubhouse turn from which 1½-mile races are started.

Haydock is a dual-purpose course, used for flat racing from April through October and jump racing from November to March. The jumps course, with its steeplechase course outside of the hurdle course, is approximately 1½ miles long.

Races of 1¾ miles and longer start in front of the five-sectioned grandstand, making a sharp 200-degree left-hand turn onto the backstretch. A quarter-mile straight is followed by a slight right-hand bend that is followed by another straight about 2½ furlongs in length.

A second left-hand turn, even tighter than the first, empties into the lengthy stretch, which ends with a very mild uphill finish.

In spite of its American-like tight turns, Haydock is a galloping track conducive to long-striding types thanks to its long, decidedly un-American straights.

HISTORY: Racing in Newton-le-Willows commenced in 1807 with the first running of what would eventually become Haydock's premier handicap, the Old Newton Cup. At the time it was a four-mile event worth 100 guineas, about one-tenth the value of the inaugural 1000 Guineas in 1814.

That track was situated about two miles from the present race-course, which closed in 1898 and was replaced the following year with the current Haydock Park, which at the time was the latest word in "park" racetracks.

We have in America a number of such tracks. Belmont Park, Monmouth Park, Hollywood Park, and Santa Anita Park all owe their names to the British concept of park tracks, the first of which was Sandown Park.

Before Sandown, which opened in 1875, the public was given free admission to all areas of the racecourse, many of which had been built on public lands, save for the grandstand itself. The enclosure of the grounds and the charging of admission to all areas was what marked park courses from their predecessors.

Haydock is a 127-acre "park" that was originally leased from local Lord Newton. For decades it shared area prominence with the track in nearby Manchester.

Situated as close as it is to what was then Europe's most important port city, the frequently bombed Liverpool, Haydock abandoned racing during World War II. It reopened on August 14, 1946, under an economy vastly different from the prewar model.

The north of England struggled during this period of austerity. As a result, Manchester Racecourse closed its doors in 1963, leaving Haydock its midsummer fixture, the Lancashire Oaks.

But pride of place at Haydock belongs solely to the Haydock Sprint Cup, a race whose origins are deeply tied to two of British racing's most enduring legends, Robert Sangster and Peter O'Sullevan.

Heir to the fortune provided by the Vernons Football Pools, a money-spinning endeavor by which Britons attempted to figure the winners of each weekend's English League soccer matches, Sangster had parlayed his wealth into a racing and breeding empire.

Flush with cash, he sponsored a new race in 1966 at his local track, Haydock Park. The Vernons Sprint Cup, initially run on the first Saturday in November, was designed to become Britain's championship sprint. Its first two runnings went to Be Friendly, a sprinter owned by the man widely regarded as England's greatest race caller, Peter O'Sullevan.

In an age of corporate race sponsorship, Ladbrokes in 1989 took over the race that had been moved to early September to avoid the mists and heavy ground that so often plagued Haydock in mid-autumn. Since then the race has been run both with and without a sponsor. It is currently and officially called the Betfred Sprint Cup for as long as that bookmaking firm puts up the money, but will always be known in parlance as the Haydock Park Sprint Cup. As such it has been won by sprinting luminaries Moorestyle, Habibti, Green Desert, Danehill, Dayjur, and Sheikh Albadou.

The Victorian grandstand opened in 1899 was demolished to make way for a new stand in 1990, enabling Haydock Park to maintain its position as the leading flat track in the north of England.

ANALYSIS: An appreciation of the names of the best winners of the Haydock Sprint Cup must be tempered by the fact that there has not been a really outstanding winner of the race since Sheikh Albadou in 1992, one year after his Breeders' Cup Sprint triumph at Churchill Downs.

Subsequent winners Diktat, Nuclear Debate, and Somnus were all very good sprinters in their heyday, but no one would ever rate them as first-class international types. The most obvious reason for the Sprint Cup's relative decline goes hand in hand with the decline of sprint racing in England and in Europe in general. The emphasis on breeding in Europe is for horses to stay between a mile and a mile and a half. Longer distances have always been more important in Europe than in America, and with the bloodstock market being what it is today, classy sprinters are thin on the European ground.

Moreover, the Sprint Cup is not infrequently run on soft ground or worse. Such going stopped the outstanding speedster Oasis Dream, who was upset by Somnus in 2003.

The last Sprint Cup winner who went straight to the Breeders' Cup Sprint was Iktamal in 1996. He finished sixth at Woodbine behind the formerly French-trained Lit de Justice.

It must also be noted that as a northern track, Haydock does not receive a great many entries from the major training centers in the south of England at Newmarket and Lambourn. Trainers based there—for instance, Michael Stoute, Saeed bin Suroor, and John Gosden—will send horses up to Haydock for black-type races, but generally speaking, the fare at Haydock is meat-and-potatoes compared to Newbury's coq au vin and Newmarket's caviar.

That said, racing at Haydock is superior to that of all other tracks in the northern part of England or anywhere in Scotland, with the exception of York and, on its big race days, Doncaster and Chester.

In 2008, the five-furlong Group 2 Temple Stakes was moved from the all-uphill straight course at Sandown to Haydock. Its first winner at the new venue was the 3-year-old filly Fleeting Spirit, who smashed the old course record by 1.05 seconds. While Fleeting Spirit was a very talented sprinter, the ease with which she broke the record had more to do with the fact that there had never been such a good five-furlong race run at Haydock. In fact, the first seven finishers in that year's Temple Stakes all broke the old track record.

The Temple was moved to Haydock to serve as a late-May pointer to the six-furlong Haydock Park Sprint Cup in early September in an effort to make the latter race even more lucrative.

TRACK RECORDS

DISTANCE	RECORD TIME	HORSE	DATE	MEDIAN TIME
5f	57:15	Fleeting Spirit	May 24, 2008	1:00.50
6f	1:09.90	Iktamal	Sept. 7, 1996	1:14.00
7f, 30y	1:27.20	Indian King	June 5, 1982	1:30.20
1m, 30y	1:40.10	Untold Riches	July 11, 1999	1:43.80
1⁵⁄₁₆m	2:08.50	Fahal	Aug. 5, 1995	2:16.70
1½m	2:26.40	New Member	July 4, 1970	2:33.20
1¾m	2:59.50	Castle Secret	Sept. 30, 1989	3:04.30
2m, 45y	3:27.00	Prince of Peace	May 26, 1984	3:37.00
2⁵⁄₁₆m	3:55.00	Crystal Spirit	Sept. 8, 1990	—

MAJOR RACES (Chronological Order)

RACE	CONDITIONS
Spring Trophy (Listed)	7f, 30y 3yo+
John of Gaunt Stakes-G3	7f, 30y 4yo+
Cecil Frail Stakes (Listed)	6f 3yo+ f&m
Lancashire Oaks-G2	1½m 3yo+ f&m
Old Newton Cup Hcp	1½m 3yo+
Rose of Lancaster Stakes-G3	1⁵⁄₁₆m 3yo+
Haydock Park Sprint Cup-G1	6f 3yo+
Superior Mile (Listed)	1m, 30y 3yo+

DAYS OF RACING: Haydock Park conducts 24 days of flat racing per year and seven days of jump racing. There are two flat days in April, four each in May and June, and five in July, with the Lancashire Oaks on the first Saturday of that month. August has four days of racing with the Rose of Lancaster Stakes on the second Saturday. The Haydock Park Sprint Cup is held on the first Saturday in September and is one of five days of racing that month.

HOW TO GET THERE: Travelers by rail from London embark at Euston Station and disembark at Warrington Bank Quay, six miles from the racecourse. Change there for Newton-le-Willows.

SURROUNDING AREA: Haydock Park lies halfway between Liverpool and Manchester, and a trip for the racing there is best spent in one of those two intriguing cities rather than in tiny Newton-le-Willows.

Manchester, England's working-class hub since the start of the Industrial Revolution, is a city of 440,000, although greater Manchester, including Bolton, Oldham, and Wigan, has a population of 2.5 million. The city is crammed with classic Victorian architecture, of a quality that nearly puts London to shame.

Of greater interest to sports fans, the city is the home of the world-famous soccer club Manchester United. Perennial champions in one competition or another—if not in the Premiership, then the FA Cup or the European-wide Champions League—they are arguably the world's most popular and valuable sports team.

Their cross-town competition comes from the gallant-hearted but generally outgunned Manchester City club.

Tours of Manchester United's stadium, Old Trafford, are available on non-game days, but tickets to see the team coached by Alex Ferguson, himself part-owner with Mrs. John Magnier of Rock of Gibraltar in his racing days, are very difficult to come by.

Liverpool is a deliciously historic city. Throughout the 19th century it was the world's most important port, but will always be remembered as the birthplace of the Beatles. The Cavern Club, where they honed their talent, is long gone, replaced by a tacky replica. Anyone seeking an authentic hint of the Beatles in Liverpool should visit their favorite pub, the Grapes, where a picture of the Fab Four hangs on the wall above their favorite corner.

KEMPTON PARK ≡

Kempton Park Racecourse
Staines Road East
Sunbury-on-Thames
Middlesex TW16 5AQ
England
Phone: 011-44-1932-782-044
Internet: www.kempton.co.uk

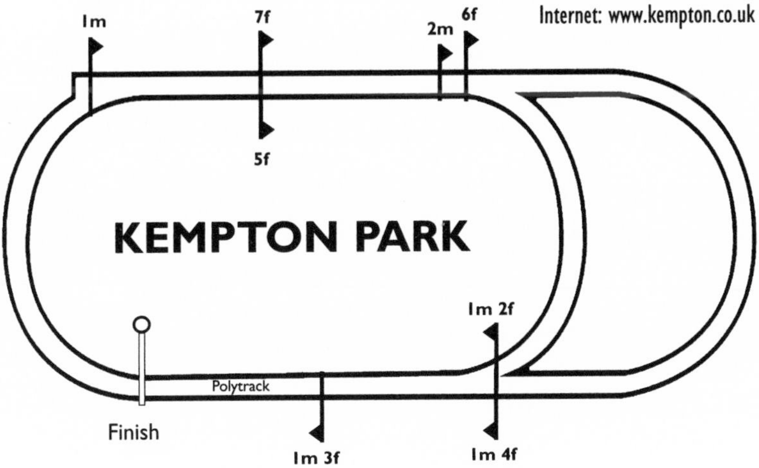

LOCATION: 18 miles southwest of central London.

COURSE DESCRIPTION: Kempton is a level, right-handed Polytrack oval 1¼ miles in length. This course is used for races at six furlongs, seven furlongs, one mile, 1⅜ miles, 1½ miles, and two miles. A six-furlong inner Polytrack course is used for races of five furlongs and 1¼ miles.

As a dual-purpose track, Kempton also has a turf course used for hurdle and steeplechase racing. It is a level, 1⅝-mile triangular course and lies outside the Polytrack course.

HISTORY: Kempton Park opened for business on July 18, 1878, as the second, after Sandown Park, of England's so-called park courses—completely enclosed tracks to which admission was charged to all areas. One of the ideas behind such tracks was to make the racing experience more attractive to women. At racecourses that were wide open and free to the public—for example, Ascot and Epsom, at the time—ladies were thought to be uncomfortable rubbing shoulders with ruffians from the lower classes. Park courses thus served the function of increasing track attendance by attracting larger numbers of women.

Flat racing at Kempton has always been of a rather tasty meat-and-potatoes variety. While conveniently situated midway between England's two major training centers, Lambourn to the west and Newmarket to the northeast, as the track closest to the center of London it has always been one whose first purpose has been to serve the paying public. The flat racing is frequently good at Kempton Park, but rarely great.

There have, however, been some memorable races there. Bendigo, winner of the first Eclipse Stakes at nearby Sandown Park in 1886, won Kempton's inaugural and now defunct Grand Jubilee Handicap a year later in honor of Queen Victoria's 50th anniversary on the throne. As a 2-year-old, Mill Reef won the Imperial Stakes, but the emphasis on quality at Kempton has always belonged to the jumpers.

Kempton's Boxing Day fixture—the race meeting held on the day after Christmas—is one of British jump racing's biggest days. The King George VI Chase ranks second in quality in the British steeple-chasing world only to the Cheltenham Gold Cup. Desert Orchid, argu-ably England's most popular Thoroughbred since World War II, won it four times between 1986 and 1990. Another Gold Cup winner, the French invader The Fellow, won it in 1991 and 1992. The 1965 King George went to Arkle, the three-time Cheltenham Gold Cup winner who is widely regarded as the greatest jumper in history.

The track was closed during World War I and World War II to serve as a clearinghouse for German and Italian prisoners of war. The postwar period saw the demise of two nearby tracks, Hurst Park and Alexandra Park, better known as Ally Pally, as it stood within shouting distance of the famed Crystal Palace left over from the 1896 World's Fair. Kempton was in danger of closing in the 1960s but was bailed out by United Racecourses, a subsidiary of the Jockey Club that was also in charge of Epsom and Sandown.

A modern grandstand was opened in 1990 and refurbished in 1997, but the introduction of a Polytrack course in 2006 made Kempton a track to be reckoned with by American observers, if still only on the handicap, allowance, and listed-race levels.

Kempton runs a pair of Guineas trials on either the week before or the week after Easter—the Easter Stakes for colts and the Masaka Stakes for fillies—but these rarely produce a Guineas contender, espe-cially now that these listed races are run on Polytrack. The two Group 3 races on the Kempton schedule, the September Stakes and the Sirenia

Stakes, have also been transferred to the Polytrack, as the turf course is now used exclusively for jump racing.

ANALYSIS: The 2006 change from a turf course to a Polytrack course gave England the fourth of its five artificial-surface tracks, in addition to the Polytracks at Lingfield, Wolverhampton, and Great Leighs and the Fibresand track at Southwell. While so-called all-weather racing on "the sceptre'd isle" is still greatly inferior to the turf product, the number of listed and group races on the artificial stuff is slowly increasing. More importantly, trainers are no longer loath to try horses on artificial surfaces. Conditioners with experience in America, such as John Gosden and Jeremy Noseda, as well as Clive Brittain, Richard Hannon, Ed Dunlop, Brian Meehan, Barry Hills, and Mark Johnston, do not hesitate to run horses in the better Polytrack maidens and allowances, most of which are run on the southern artificial surfaces at Kempton and Lingfield.

Most of Kempton's races, however, are handicaps of dubious reputation. In trying to gauge the quality of British imports that have run at Kempton, it is important to remember that handicaps there worth less than $20,000 rate among the weakest races in Britain. Of course, if a horse wins at that level with a certain frequency, he must be considered in U.S. allowance races other than those at the better tracks in New York, Kentucky, southern California, and at Gulfstream Park. At those venues, however, such a horse is more likely to find his proper level in the claiming ranks.

Since the increase in the number of synthetic-surface tracks in America in 2006–07, more than half of the horses imported to the United States from Britain have had some experience on one or another of England's artificial surfaces. The best of these, such as Eccentric, have had as much success on turf as on Polytrack or Cushion Track.

In England, most of the horses that run on artificial surfaces are switched back and forth to turf tracks as well. This practice seems to support the widely held belief that Polytrack, Cushion Track, and the other synthetic surfaces are much closer to turf tracks than they are to traditional dirt.

Synthetic surfaces are softer than dirt but not quite as easy as turf. Perhaps more importantly, these new surfaces have far less kickback than traditional dirt. American jockeys are already realizing that, as in turf racing, there is no need to dash out at a breakneck pace as in dirt racing. This is leading to races on artificial surfaces being run in much the same style as turf races—that is, back-to-front, or slow early and fast late, just like races in Europe, be they on turf or Polytrack.

Fifteen or 20 years ago, Britain's all-weather runners would have stood little chance on either turf or dirt in America. Now, they are a factor in America on synthetic surfaces and on turf, adding further credence to the notion that there has been an alarming decrease in the quality of the American Thoroughbred over the last 20 years.

TRACK RECORDS

DISTANCE	RECORD TIME	HORSE	DATE	MEDIAN TIME
5f	59.11	Hadaf	Oct. 6, 2007	1:00.50
6f	1:11.13	Rabbit Fighter	Dec. 12, 2007	1:13.10
7f	1:23.91	Bomber Command	Nov. 24, 2006	1:26.00
1m	1:36.82	Gentleman's Deal	Feb. 4, 2007	1:49.80
1¼m	2:04.44	Stotsfold	Sept. 6, 2006	2:08.00
1⅜m	2:18.15	Al Tharib	Aug. 27, 2007	2:21.90
1½m	2:30.48	Dansant	Nov. 3, 2007	2:34.50
2m	3:25.83	Featherlight	Sept. 29, 2007	3:30.10

MAJOR RACES (Chronological Order)

RACE	CONDITIONS
Ladybird Stakes (Listed)	1m 4yo+
Dragonfly Stakes (Listed)	1½m 4yo+
Easter Stakes (Listed)	1m 3yo
Masaka Stakes (Listed)	1m 3yo f
Magnolia Stakes (Listed)	1¼m 4yo+
Snowdrop Stakes (Listed)	1m 4yo+ f&m
Achilles Stakes (Listed)	5f 3yo+
September Stakes-G3	1½m 3yo+
Sirenia Stakes-G3	6f 2yo
King George VI Chase-G1	3m 6yo+
Christmas Hurdle-G2	2m 5yo+

DAYS OF RACING: Through 2005, when it was strictly a turf course, Kempton generally had no more than 14 days of flat racing. In 2007, its first full year back in operation with a Polytrack flat course, it ran 58 flat meetings spread throughout the year, 45 of those at night. There were also six days of jump racing during the winter, chief among them the prestigious two-day Christmas Meeting on December 26–27.

HOW TO GET THERE: Trains leave London Waterloo every half-hour for the 40-minute ride to Kempton Park Station. One of the world's great train terminals, Waterloo is worth a visit by itself. A classic early example of an indoor environment meant to provide a seemingly outdoor experience, as well as a lesson in how to arrive in and depart from a great city in style, it contains shops, newsstands, cafes, fast-food joints, a restaurant, and a pub. It is a good idea when heading out to any of the racetracks served by Waterloo—Ascot, Salisbury, Sandown, and Windsor, as well as Kempton—to arrive at least 45 minutes early to sample some of its many pleasures. That the train from Waterloo deposits one virtually on the doorstep of the Kempton Park entrance is another example of a country with a civilized racing culture.

SURROUNDING AREA: Sunbury-on-Thames is a typical English village, the sort in which Agatha Christie's Miss Marple might discover a dead body under the tea table. As close as Kempton Park is to London, there is good sense in staying in the big city and commuting to the track for the races.

LINGFIELD PARK ☰

Lingfield Park Racecourse
Lingfield, Surrey RH7 6PQ
England
Phone: 011-44-1342-834-800
Internet: www.lingfield-racecourse.co.uk

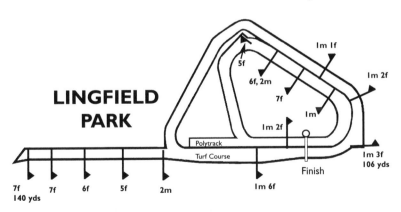

LOCATION: 27 miles south of London.

COURSE DESCRIPTION: Lingfield Park was the first racetrack in England with an artificial surface, called Equitrack. It now has two flat tracks, one Polytrack and one turf, as well as a jumps course.

Most of the best Lingfield races are run on the turf course, a 1½-mile left-handed track with a four-furlong stretch. There is a seven-furlong, 140-yard straight course that connects with the stretch of the left-handed course.

The left-handed course is not dissimilar to Epsom, and so the Lingfield Derby Trial is considered a good test for the even more grueling examination demanded by the Derby.

The Lingfield mile and a half (actually, 1⅜ miles, 106 yards) begins in front of the stands and after less than a furlong swings left. There follows a stiffly uphill three-furlong straight into a second left-hand turn to the highest point of the course, after which it is all downhill to the final turn. The four-furlong stretch is slightly downhill to the finish.

The straight course is slightly downhill until just before joining the stretch, at which point there is a mild incline of half a furlong.

The straight course yields unusually fast times for races in England because of its downhill nature. This must be taken into consideration when judging a horse's overall ability.

Horses that do well at Lingfield tend to be well-balanced, athletic types, like those who show a preference for Epsom.

The Polytrack course lies inside the turf course and is 1¼ miles around with a 380-yard stretch. It follows the turf course until departing from it at the high point of the hill, from where it cuts towards the grandstand. Its gradients are virtually the same as those of the turf course.

HISTORY: Like nearby Kempton and Sandown, Lingfield was one of the early "park" tracks that became increasingly popular toward the end of the 19th century. The first day of racing at Lingfield was a National Hunt, or jump-racing affair held in November 1890. Flat racing followed soon after and became a regular fixture when the Prince of Wales attended on May 16, 1894.

The racing, however, wasn't worth much until Fred Wilmot, the clerk of the course, inaugurated the Lingfield Derby Trial in 1932. It proved an immediate success as its winner, April the Fifth, proceeded to land the Epsom Derby itself, thus creating the theory that Lingfield is the perfect place to prep for the Derby—and the Oaks—because of the similarity of the two courses.

By American standards, such theories on the differences, or

Polytrack racing at Lingfield Park, the first racecourse in the world to have installed a synthetic surface.

similarities, between any two tracks must be taken with a grain of salt. In reality, the difference between the two most similar tracks in Britain is greater than the two most different tracks in the United States.

All told, eight Derby Trial winners have repeated in the Derby. After April the Fifth they were Mid-day Sun (1937), Tulyar (1952), Parthia (1959), the mud-loving Teenoso (1983), who was lucky enough to catch heavy ground in both races, Slip Anchor (1985), Kahyasi (1988), and High-Rise (1998).

But perhaps the most memorable Derby Trial winner was Queen Elizabeth's Aureole. After winning in his owner's coronation year of 1953, Aureole was the great Derby hope of a British nation that needed some patriotic excitement in the midst of the country's postwar doldrums. Aureole tried his best but came home second to Pinza, who gave Britain's great champion jockey Gordon Richards his only Derby triumph.

A year later, Aureole would strengthen the Lingfield-Epsom connection by winning the Coronation Cup at Epsom over the Derby course and distance. While the Derby Trial's success rate of eight Derby winners since 1932 tops any other Derby prep in that time period, this speaks less to the Lingfield-Epsom tie than to the class and talent of the horses who have prepared for the Derby at Lingfield.

The listed Lingfield Oaks Trial has been a less successful pointer to the English Oaks, with just four such dual winners: Sleeping Partner (1969), Ginevra (1972), Juliette Marny (1975), and Aliysa (ultimately disqualified from the 1989 Oaks for a drug positive).

Lingfield has earned its reputation as "leafy Lingfield" because of its lovely surroundings in the Surrey countryside, but the track made real racing history on October 30, 1989, with the first day of racing on a synthetic-dirt surface called Equitrack. The winner of the first race that day, Wizzard Magic, might have felt at home on Keeneland's Polytrack if he were racing there today, as he came from last to first for the victory—and in fact, Lingfield switched to Polytrack in 2001.

The idea behind the first artificial surface was to provide winter-time flat racing in Britain, and, perhaps more importantly, additional revenue for the bookies and the government, but the British term for artificial surfaces, "all-weather" tracks, has proven to be a misnomer—not only in America, where several tracks that switched to synthetic surfaces have encountered problems with extremes of heat, cold, and wet weather, but in Britain as well, where some meetings have been canceled due to flooding, snow, or frozen surfaces.

ANALYSIS: Two factors stand out in attempting to assess Lingfield form transposed to North America. The first is to take care in adapting the relatively fast times recorded on the straight turf course. More ger-mane to the American game is the fact that they are run at a strong pace on the straight track, so a horse that can close well on it is likely to have some success in America regardless of the final time.

The second, of course, revolves around the Polytrack surface. As noted in the section on Kempton Park, more than half of all the British horses imported to the United States since 2006 have run on one of Britain's synthetic surfaces. Most of those have run at the two more prominent tracks (in terms of quality), Lingfield and Kempton. As the more estab-lished of those two, Lingfield probably conducts a slightly higher class of "all-weather" racing, although the difference is minimal.

A more important question is: Where do Polytrack races fit into the American picture? As handicappers around America have been dis-covering, deciphering synthetic-surface form has become something of a bugbear. Most have come to the conclusion that synthetic-surface racing is much more like turf racing than dirt racing. Taking that as step one in deciphering British all-weather form, it can be stated that, while neither Lingfield nor Kempton will ever be mistaken for Ascot or Newmarket, good synthetic form at Lingfield can be transposed onto American turf. But beware, because a turf allowance at Santa Anita, Hollywood, Del Mar, Keeneland, Gulfstream, Belmont, or Saratoga is almost always better than a similar event or a handicap at Lingfield or Kempton.

If a horse has been running consistently well on the Lingfield/Kempton all-weather circuit and is relatively lightly raced, he may still be capable of improvement when switched to American synthetics or turf. Do not be fooled, however, that British synthetic form can be equated to American dirt form. Keep in mind that the United States is the world's only major racing nation that conducts an overwhelming number of its best races on traditional dirt. It is rare that any horse can duplicate his European form—be it on synthetics or turf—on American dirt tracks.

TRACK RECORDS (Turf)

DISTANCE	RECORD TIME	HORSE	DATE	MEDIAN TIME
5f	56.20	Eveningperformance	July 25, 1994	58.20
6f	1:08.20	Al Amead	July 2, 1986	1:11.20
7f	1:20.10	Zelah	May 13, 1998	1:23.20
7f, 140y	1:26.70	Hiaam	July 11, 1987	1:32.30
1⅛m	1:52.40	Quandary	July 15, 1995	1:56.60
1¼m	2:04.60	Usran	July 15, 1989	2:10.50
1⁷⁄₁₆m	2:23.90	Night-Shirt	July 14, 1990	2:31.50
1¾m	2:59.10	Ibn Bey	July 1, 1989	3:10.00
2m	3:23.70	Lauries Crusador	Aug. 13, 1998	3:25.70

TRACK RECORDS (Polytrack)

DISTANCE	RECORD TIME	HORSE	DATE	MEDIAN TIME
5f	57.26	Magic Glade	Feb. 27, 2007	58.80
6f	1:10.06	Maltese Falcon	Nov. 11, 2006	1:11.90
7f	1:22.70	Vortex	April 9, 2005	1:24.80
1m	1:34.77	Baharah	Oct. 30, 2008	1:38.20
1¼m	2:01.79	Cusoon	Feb. 24, 2007	2:06.60
1½m	2:28.22	Descartes	Oct. 5, 2006	2:33.00
1⅝m	2:42.47	Raffaas	July 3, 2007	2:46.00
2m	3:20.00	Yenoora	Aug. 8, 1992	3:25.70

MAJOR RACES (Chronological Order)

RACE	CONDITIONS
POLYTRACK	
Winter Derby Trial (Listed)	1¼m (Polytrack) 4yo+
Cleves Stakes (Listed)	6f (Polytrack) 4yo+
Winter Park Derby-G3	1¼m (Polytrack) 4yo+
Sprint Stakes (Listed)	5f (Polytrack) 4yo+
Spring Cup (Listed)	7f (Polytrack) 3yo

RACE	CONDITIONS
International Trial Stks (Lstd)	1m (Polytrack) 3yo
Lingfield Derby Trial-G3	1⁷⁄₁₆m (turf) 3yo c&g
Chartwell Stakes-G3	7f (turf) 3yo+ f&m
Lingfield Oaks Trial (Listed)	1⁷⁄₁₆m (turf) 3yo f
Fleur de Lys Stakes (Listed)	1m (Polytrack) 3yo+ f&m
Eden Stakes (Listed)	1⅜m (Polytrack) 3yo+ f&m

DAYS OF RACING: Lingfield Park conducts 80 days of flat racing annually—59 on Polytrack spread throughout the year, 20 on turf in late spring, summer, and early autumn, and one on both Polytrack and turf. It also holds eight days of jump racing per year.

HOW TO GET THERE: By train from London via either Victoria Station or London Bridge Station to Lingfield Station, a half-mile from the racetrack.

SURROUNDING AREA: History buffs might want to make a pilgrimage to Chartwell, the home of Winston Churchill during much of his adult life. The house, seven miles from Lingfield in Westerham, Kent, is much as it was during the great man's tenure as wartime prime minister and is filled with mementos from a career that began with mustering mounted cavalry officers and ended with inspecting nuclear weapons. The estate also encompasses a garden and a studio containing many of Churchill's own paintings.

There is a connection between Churchill and racing. As prime minister, he introduced the first betting tax to Britain in 1926. Three years later he founded the Tote, the parimutuel company set up to give British punters an alternative to bookmakers.

Churchill was also a Thoroughbred owner. His first horse, Colonist II, won the Jockey Club Cup, but his best horse was probably Vienna. A son of the queen's excellent racehorse Aureole, Vienna won the Blue Riband Trial and might have started favorite for the 1960 Epsom Derby, but stepped on a nail the morning of the race and was so badly hurt he was withdrawn.

The French champion 3-year-old, Vienna would win the Prix d'Harcourt, now a Group 2, and finish second in the Prix Ganay and Coronation Cup and third in the Champion Stakes, all three of which are now Group 1 events. He was Britain's leading sire in 1972 and 1973 and leading broodmare sire in 1982. His legacy lives on through the achievements of his best son, Vaguely Noble.

Newbury Racecourse
Newbury, Berkshire RG14 7NZ
England
Phone: 011-44-1635-40015
Internet: www.newbury-racecourse.co.uk

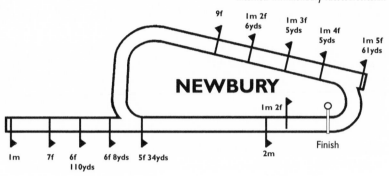

LOCATION: 67 miles west of London, 28 miles south of Oxford.

COURSE DESCRIPTION: Newbury is a left-handed oval with relatively tight turns, especially the first, what Americans would call the clubhouse turn. It measures 1⅞ miles around with a stretch of 4½ furlongs. There is a one-mile straight course that joins the left-handed course at the head of the stretch. Until recently there was a chute beyond the far turn from which races could be run at one mile as well as seven furlongs, 64 yards, but that was discontinued in 2005. All races up to a mile are now run on the straight course.

Newbury is a virtually level track with only very slight undulations on the last half of the straight course. Two-mile races start in front of the stands and make a very tight left-hand turn onto a five-furlong backstretch. A left turn, slightly sharper than 90 degrees, is followed by a two-furlong straight, which in turn is followed by a 90-degree turn into the stretch.

Races of 1⅝ miles, 61 yards (the Geoffrey Freer Stakes) start from a small chute at the head of the backstretch. Mile-and-a-half races begin near the head of the backstretch; mile-and-a-quarter races midway down the backstretch.

One of the fairest courses in England, Newbury, with its long straights, is a track very comfortable for long-striding gallopers.

As a dual-purpose track, it also conducts jump racing in the autumn and winter. The hurdle and steeplechase courses lie inside the flat track.

HISTORY: Thanks largely to the patronage of John Porter, Newbury Racecourse opened its doors for the first time on September 26, 1905. Porter was, at the time, the trainer occupying Kingsclere, from where he trained 23 classic winners. Among them were seven Derby winners, including Shotover and the great, undefeated Ormonde.

The racecourse was, in fact, just waiting to happen, as the property it occupies is surrounded by dozens of training centers, most of them at Lambourn, the English town that rates second only to Newmarket for the number of Thoroughbred trainers who call it home.

But Porter needed the influence of the king himself to get a license to run Newbury. The Jockey Club had refused his request for racing dates in 1903, claiming that there were already too many racetracks in Britain. There were 73 at the time, compared with 60 today, so maybe the Club had a point.

After being turned down at Jockey Club headquarters in Newmarket, a disconsolate Porter bumped into that inveterate race-goer, Edward VII, who was out taking his morning walk.

Porter, who had trained 17 winners for the king when he was the Prince of Wales, made his plea, and the royal ear proved sympathetic.

Even in 1905, British monarchs had been largely stripped of political power. Edward, however, was so popular—and influential—that some historians believe he could have prevented World War I had he not died in 1911, so highly regarded was he by his royal cousins, who sat upon virtually all of Europe's thrones.

Apparently he had plenty of sway at the Jockey Club as well. A few days later, Porter was granted his license.

The first Greenham Stakes was run in 1906. Three years later it earned its place as a key 2000 Guineas prep when it was won by the king's Minoru, who would then win the Guineas and, a few weeks after that, the Derby.

While only two other Greenham winners have gone on to Guineas success—Orwell in 1932 and Wollow in 1976—the seven-furlong Group 3 has been won by good ones such as Epsom Derby winner

Mill Reef, Kris, Lion Cavern, Inchinor, French Derby winner Celtic Swing, and Danehill Dancer. This suggests that the Greenham may be a more accurate guide to success in one Derby or another, or as a stallion.

The Greenham's filly equivalent, the Fred Darling Stakes, first run in 1949, is a 1000 Guineas trial. In 1973, Mysterious became its first winner to take the Guineas, but the race became a seedbed for 1000 Guineas winners in the 1990s when Salsabil, Shadayid, Bosra Sham, and Wince all did the double. Moreover, Sleepytime and Lahan, fourth in the Fred Darlings of 1997 and 2000, respectively, improved enough to land 1000 Guineas of their own.

Founding father Porter was memorialized in 1928 with the initial running of the John Porter Stakes. The race was rather nondescript until the 1953 renewal was won by Wilwyn, who a year earlier had become the first winner of Laurel's now sadly defunct Washington, D.C., International. Niniski, the Ian Balding-Paul Mellon pair of Glint Of Gold and Diamond Shoal, future Japan Cup winner Jupiter Island, and the influential stallion Unfuwain have all won it since, but the race was deservedly downgraded to Group 3 status in 1984.

The one-mile Lockinge Stakes, however, was upgraded to a Group 1 in 1995, victories by Most Welcome and Polar Falcon having helped it achieve that status. Cape Cross in 1998, Keltos in 2002, Hawk Wing, whose outstanding 11-length romp in 2003 earned him European mile championship honors, Rakti in 2005, and the fine fillies Russian Rhythm and Peeress have established the Lockinge as Europe's best early-season mile race.

First run in 1949, the Geoffrey Freer Stakes is something of a dual-purpose race. At 1⅝ miles, 61 yards, it attracts stayers looking to cut back to 1½ miles for the Arc, as well as mile-and-a-half types testing the waters for even longer staying races. As such, it was won for the second time in a row by Ardross on his way to a narrow Arc loss to Akiyda in 1982. Ibn Bey won it in 1989, a year before his Breeders' Cup Classic second to Unbridled, and Mubtaker took it three times from 2002 through 2004, but those results mark the Geoffrey Freer as merely an intriguing Group 2 contest.

Newbury was closed for longer than usual during World War II as it became a major supply depot for the American army in 1942 in preparation for the D-Day invasion of Normandy. Under the guidance of Geoffrey Freer himself, the immense job of clearing the racecourse of its war debris was finally completed in 1949, and the track reopened.

Nowadays, Newbury has the honor of running the last two group races on the British racing calendar, the Horris Hill Stakes and the St Simon Stakes.

ANALYSIS: At first glance of the form of any horse arriving in America that has run at Newbury, one would imagine that as a level, left-handed track, it would be an ideal place for anticipating American success. As a galloping track with long straights, however, that is not necessarily the case, since quite a few American tracks tend—often very strongly—to favor close-coupled types who can sprint to the front, cut corners, and hold off the closers through short homestretches.

While Newbury does have something of the feel of Belmont Park, and while Newbury form may be more adaptable to Belmont because of its relatively wide turns and long—by American standards— straights, there is really no comparison between the two. More important is an understanding of the overall quality of racing at Newbury, which probably ranks just behind Ascot and Newmarket, although tracks like York, Goodwood, Sandown, and even Doncaster rank just as high and sometimes higher on their big race days.

In fact, Newbury's group-race winners rarely succeed in America, but that may have more to do with the time of year many of them are run—April and May, well before the older-horse selling season. The long distances of the stakes races run in the latter part of the flat season do not lend themselves as springboards to American invasions. But with more cost-conscious American buyers disdaining group-race winners, and even group-race-placed horses, Newbury makes a good breeding ground for horses coming out of its many listed contests.

Newbury runs many competitive affairs filled with well-bred horses not owned by the Magniers or any of the big Arab outfits, and these become very eligible for sale to American owners.

TRACK RECORDS

DISTANCE	RECORD TIME	HORSE	DATE	MEDIAN TIME
5f, 34y	59.10	Superstar Leo	July 22, 2000	1:01.40
6f	1:09.42	Nota Bene	May 13, 2005	1:13.00
7f	1:21.50	Three Points	July 21, 2000	1:25.70
1m	1:33.59	Rakti	May 14, 2005	1:39.70
1⅛m	1:49.60	Holtye	May 21, 1995	1:55.50
1¼m	2:01.20	Wall Street	July 20, 1996	2:08.80
1⅜m	2:16.50	Grandera	Sept. 22, 2001	2:21.20
1½m	2:28.26	Azamour	July 23, 2005	2:35.50

DISTANCE	RECORD TIME	HORSE	DATE	MEDIAN TIME
1⅝m, 61y	2:44.90	Mystic Hill	July 20, 1996	2:52.00
2m	3:25.40	Moonlight Quest	July 19, 1996	3:36.90

MAJOR RACES (Chronological Order)

RACE	CONDITIONS
Greenham Stakes-G3	7f 3yo c&g
Fred Darling Stakes-G3	7f 3yo f
John Porter Stakes-G3	1½m 4yo+
Swettenham Stud Fillies Trial (Listed)	1¼m 3yo f
Lockinge Stakes-G1	1m 4yo+
Aston Park Stakes (Listed)	1⅝m, 61y 4yo+
Ballymacoll Stud Stakes (Listed)	1¼m 3yo f
Hackwood Stakes-G3	6f 3yo+
Steventon Stakes (Listed)	1¼m 3yo+
Rose Bowl Stakes (Listed)	6f 2yo
St Hugh's Stakes (Listed)	5f, 34y 2yo f
Washington Singer Stakes (Listed)	7f 2yo
Mill Reef Stakes-G2	6f 2yo
Geoffrey Freer Stakes-G2	1⅝m, 61y 3yo+
Arc Trial-G3	1⅜m 3yo+
World Trophy-G3	5f, 34y 3yo+
Dubai Duty Free Cup (Listed)	7f 3yo+
Hungerford Stakes-G3	7f 3yo+
St Simon Stakes-G3	1½m 3yo+
Horris Hill Stakes-G3	7f 2yo c&g

DAYS OF RACING: There are 28 days of racing annually—16 on the flat, 12 over jumps. The first major dates of the spring include the third Saturday in April, when the Greenham Stakes, Fred Darling Stakes, and the John Porter Stakes are run. Newbury's only Group 1 flat race, the Lockinge Stakes, is run on the third Saturday in May. The track's two Group 2 contests, the Mill Reef Stakes and the Geoffrey Freer Stakes, are run on the second or third Saturday in August. The last flat meeting of the Newbury season, featuring the St Simon Stakes, is held on the final Saturday in October. The highlight of the jump-racing season is the Hennessy Gold Cup Chase, run on the third Saturday in November.

HOW TO GET THERE: By train from London Paddington to Newbury

Racecourse Station, which lets you off directly in front of the track entrance.

SURROUNDING AREA: If Cambridge students are fond of Newmarket, Oxford students are in love with Newbury. The world's most famous university town lies just 28 miles north of Newbury Racecourse and makes a great day trip either way—for the cultural historian determined to see his intelligence transformed into racetrack winnings, or for the degenerate horseplayer keen to improve himself culturally.

Of greater interest to racegoers are the numerous training centers in the immediate area. At least 65 trainers operate within 25 miles of Newbury. Chief among the local training centers is Lambourn. Residing there are British training luminaries Barry Hills, his son John Hills, Jamie Osborne, Marcus Tregoning, and leading jumps conditioner Nicky Henderson.

Brian Meehan of Red Rocks fame is the current master of Manton, the training center once owned by Robert Sangster and where Michael Dickinson, Peter Chapple-Hyam, and John Gosden all once plied their trades. Manton is located in Marlborough, as is Richard Hannon's yard. Mick Channon works out of West Ilsley, and Henrietta Knight, trainer of three-time Cheltenham Gold Cup winner Best Mate, is situated in nearby Wantage.

Ian Balding trained Mill Reef from his Kingsclere yard in Newbury itself. The Balding racing tradition continues as his daughter Clare is one of the BBC's leading racing and sports commentators, while son Andrew has 120 horses at Kingsclere, from where the family proudly sends out its own horses carrying the late Paul Mellon's distinctive Crusader-like black-and-gold European colors.

NEWMARKET

Newmarket Racecourses Trust
Westfield House
The Links
Newmarket
Suffolk CB8 0TG
England
Phone: 011-44-1638-663-482 (Main Office)
011-44-1638-663-762 (Rowley Mile Course)
011-44-1638-662-752 (July Course)
Internet: www.newmarketracecourse.co.uk

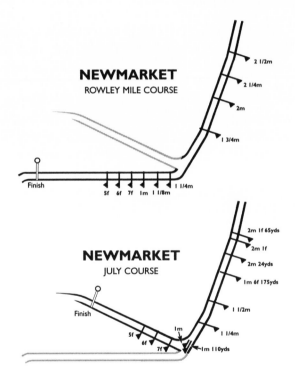

LOCATION: 64 miles northeast of London, 13 miles east of Cambridge.

COURSE DESCRIPTION: Newmarket actually consists of two racecourses that share some common ground but have separate grandstands. The Rowley Mile Course, in actuality 2¼ miles long (known at its full length as the Cesarewitch Course), is used in the spring and fall, while the July Course is used during the summer.

The 2¼ miles of the Cesarewitch Course begin out of sight of the Rowley Mile grandstand. It begins with a one-mile straight followed by a right-hand bend that leads into the 1¼-mile stretch, the scene every October of the Champion Stakes. The last mile of the stretch is technically the Rowley Mile, on which are run both of Britain's classic miles, the 2000 Guineas for colts and the 1000 Guineas for fillies.

The Rowley Mile is undulating, with the famous "Dip" coming a furlong from the finish, from which point it is all uphill.

The July Course, which is two miles, 24 yards in length, shares its first mile with the beginning of the Cesarewitch Course, after which there is a 90-degree right-hand turn into a one-mile stretch. The final mile of the July Course is also undulating, perhaps a bit more severely than the Rowley Mile. The start of races that are 1¼ miles or longer on the July Course cannot be seen from the grandstand. In fact, nothing can be seen of races on the July Course until the horses turn into the mile-long stretch, unless, of course, you are watching on television.

HISTORY: You would not be reading this book today if it were not for Newmarket, for if it had not been for Newmarket, it is likely that horse racing as we have known it for nearly four centuries might never have come into being.

Newmarket is also the place where the phrase *Sport of Kings* was coined. In the 17th century, whatever the king did became the thing to do, and all of that period's rulers were mad about the game, which even at that early date was centered in Newmarket.

The first Stuart king, imported from Scotland as James VI but given the English title James I, first visited Newmarket in 1605 and soon built a palace on Newmarket Heath to be near the fields teeming with game. Racing of an informal sort began on the heath as early as 1622, but started to flourish under the watch of James's son, Charles I. That keen horseman's reign was cut off, however, along with his royal head, in 1649 after the politically intractable man and his Royalist followers lost the second of the Civil Wars fought by Parliament to dethrone him.

From that year until 1660, Oliver Cromwell's Protectorate shielded Britain from the evils of horse racing, banning the sport entirely. An owner of racehorses himself, Cromwell knew that if he allowed race meetings to be held, they would become hotbeds of Royalist activity that might lead to his own downfall.

But after Cromwell died in 1657, the puritanical Protectorate

Newmarket Rowley Mile Course

unraveled and in 1660, Charles I's son, Charles II, was recalled by Parliament from exile in Holland.

Restored to the throne, "the Merry Monarch" loved racing almost as much as he loved women. He was forever driving up to Newmarket to be closer to his horses as well as to his actress mistress, Nell Gwyn; his aristocratic mistress, Barbara Villiers; his Catholic mistress, the French spy Louise de Querouaille; and his kissing cousin, Frances Teresa Stuart.

Charles had a hack named Old Rowley upon which he would chase after the more serious horses training and racing on the Heath. Court followers took to calling the king himself Old Rowley, from which was derived the name of the course on which the Guineas are run.

Charles rode in races himself and in 1664 he founded a race called the Town Plate, declaring that it should be run "on the second Thursday of October forever." Won three times by horses with Charles on board, it was the centerpiece of what would eventually become Newmarket's mid-October Champions Meeting. Considered the first race ever run under rules as we now recognize them, the Town Plate is currently held in late August on the July Course. In 2008 it had its 339th running. Not quite forever, but getting there.

Charles II died in 1685 and was succeeded by his younger brother James II, who was shortly run out of the country for attempting to reinstate Catholicism as the state religion. James was succeeded by his niece, Mary, and her husband, the Dutchman William, Prince of Orange, the royal couple better known as William and Mary.

The early days of Thoroughbred racing at Newmarket were

dominated by the colorful personality of Tregonwell Frampton, who trained all the royal horses belonging to Charles II, James II, William and Mary, and Anne, the last of the Stuart monarchs, whose death in 1714 ushered in a long period of decline in English racing in general and Newmarket in particular.

To rectify matters, the Jockey Club was founded by a group of London owners in 1750 or thereabouts. In those days, the riders of most horses in the four-to-six-mile heats were the owners of the steeds themselves, and the word *jockey* referred as much to the owner as it did to the rider, thus the rather odd name for an organization that, in every racing country in the world, is made up of owners, not riders. The Jockey Club has had its headquarters in Newmarket since 1752.

As the rules of racing were formalized throughout the second half of the 18th century, professional riders of diminutive stature took over more and more riding assignments.

The late 18th and early 19th centuries introduced the first classic races. Under the good and powerful offices of Sir Charles Bunbury, chief steward of the Jockey Club from 1768 to 1820, were run the first St. Leger, the first Oaks, the first Derby, the first 1000 Guineas, and the first 2000 Guineas, the last two at Newmarket itself. The first races for 2-year-olds were also run at Newmarket during this period.

But at the same time, scandal reared its ugly head. It got so bad that in 1791 the Prince of Wales, the future George IV, was virtually ruled

The Freddy Head-trained French invader Marchand d'Or (far left) wins the 2008 July Cup on Newmarket's July Course.

GLOBAL RACING

off for the erratic form of a horse he owned, named Escape. Shamed into defeat, the prince never again set foot on a racecourse.

The inaugural 2000 Guineas in 1809 revolutionized the sport in ways that reverberate to the present day. Races run at a mile were extremely rare in those days, but the idea of testing 3-year-old colts for speed in early May, followed by the middle-distance challenge of the 1½-mile Epsom Derby a month later, concluding with the daunting stayers' classic, the St. Leger Stakes in September, quickly took hold. The English Triple Crown laid the foundation for the idea of a progression, or pattern, that has been followed in every Thoroughbred division in every racing nation since then.

Four years after the first running of the 2000 Guineas (so named because first prize was, simply, a winner-take-all 2000 guineas—that is, 2000 pounds sterling plus 5 percent), it was followed by its filly equivalent, the 1000 Guineas. The first running of each race was won by the same owner/trainer/jockey combination of Christopher Willson, Tom Perren, and Bill Clift, with Wizard in the 2000 and Charlotte in the 1000.

No less an authority than Gordon Richards, Britain's champion rider 26 times between 1925 and 1954, declared that Newmaket is "the fairest course in the world," as it does not confer an advantage on any type of horse or style of running. Moreover, each of its two courses is so wide that any trouble a horse gets into can be blamed almost entirely upon the jockey. If given a clean run at Newmarket, no horse ever has an excuse there.

That fairness has resulted in some of the top names in racing history having competed, and won, at Newmarket. Every Triple Crown winner, among them greats such as West Australian, Gladiateur, Ormonde, Isinglass, Diamond Jubilee, Gainsborough, Bahram, and Nijinsky, started on the path to glory in the 2000 Guineas.

The 1834 winner, Glencoe, would become the most influential foundation sire of the American Thoroughbred. The victories of the great filly Sceptre in the 1000 Guineas, the 2000 Guineas, the Oaks, and the St. Leger constitute a Quadruple Crown of her own curious invention.

The postwar 2000 Guineas winners Tudor Minstrel and My Babu both wound up standing at stud in Kentucky, a transatlantic trend that gained fullest expression when the 1943 Guineas third-place finisher, Nasrullah, was exported from Ireland to Kentucky. He would provide the spark for the best of American racing in the 1950s and 1960s as the sire of Nashua, Jaipur, Bald Eagle, and Bold Ruler, the eight-time American champion sire whose final crop in 1970 included the incomparable Secretariat.

Between 1965 and 1990, 2000 Guineas winners included Sir Ivor, Brigadier Gerard, El Gran Senor, Dancing Brave, and Nashwan, all horses who could carry their speed as far as 10 or 12 furlongs at the top level, but nowadays the Guineas has become a specialist's race, for milers only. Few of its winners since 1989 have excelled at longer distances, with only Golan, Rodrigo de Triano, and Haafhd succeeding beyond a mile, the last two winning, not too surprisingly, the 1¼-mile Champion Stakes on the full length of the straight Rowley Course.

That said, the 2008 runner-up, New Approach, distinguished himself five weeks later by winning the Epsom Derby.

Two years after Sceptre took her 1000 Guineas in 1902, an equally talented filly, Pretty Polly, won hers. In addition, 1000 winners such as Rockfel, Sun Chariot, Imprudence, Musidora, Meld, and Sweet Solera have been memorialized with stakes races named for them. The 1980s produced a plethora of great 1000 Guineas winners in Ma Biche, Pebbles, and Miesque, while the 90s gave us Salsabil, Hatoof, and Bosra Sham. Of those modern-era winners, it is notable that Pebbles, Miesque, and Hatoof would all later win Grade 1 races in the United States, as would Godolphin's 2002 winner, Kazzia, making the 1000 Guineas a key signpost to success in America.

Newmarket's popular three-day July Meeting, held in the middle of the second week of the month, includes among its features the Princess of Wales's Stakes, a 1½-mile race for 3-year-olds and up. Named for Alexandra, the wife of the future King Edward VII, it was long one of Europe's better Group 2 events. The first running in 1894 was won by the previous year's Triple Crown winner, Isinglass. Subsequent winners included Triple Crown champion Rock Sand, the broodmare sire of Man o' War; the influential stallions Swynford, Blandford, Fairway, and Alycidon and, more recently, Lomond; the queen's filly Height of Fashion; Arc winner Carroll House; and Unfuwain and Rock Hopper. Its relative decline of late may be due to the lower quality of the mile-and-a-half Thoroughbred, even in Europe.

The Falmouth Stakes, on the other hand, has gone from strength to strength since its 2004 upgrading to Group 1 status, along with the Prix d'Astarte, the Matron Stakes, and the Sun Chariot Stakes. Those four races give Europe a distaff Group 1 mile series comparable to the open quartet of the Sussex Stakes, the Prix Jacques le Marois, the Prix du Moulin de Longchamp, and Queen Elizabeth II Stakes.

The Falmouth victories of Soviet Song in 2004 and 2005 recalled one of the race's best Group 2 winners, Ryafan, whose 1997 victory kicked off a five-race winning streak that concluded in America with the Queen Elizabeth II Challenge Cup, the Yellow Ribbon, the Matriarch, and an Eclipse Award as best turf filly or mare.

The six-furlong July Cup has long rated as one of Europe's best sprints, keeping in mind that sprinting in Europe is middle-distance racing's poor cousin. Rarely do European sprinters approach the quality of their longer-winded European relations.

That said, the July Cup is a sprint whose winners frequently carry their speed to win over longer distances, among them Soviet Star, Cadeaux Genereux, and Royal Academy, all later winners of Group 1 miles, with Royal Academy taking his in the Breeders' Cup. More recent winners such as Stravinsky, Mozart, and Oasis Dream have proved more one-dimensional, but 1996 winner Anabaa has developed into a sire of 10-to-12-furlong stakes performers.

If the Rowley Mile's springtime Guineas Meeting makes history, its October Champions meeting produces, as might be expected, champions.

The testing, straight 10-furlong Champion Stakes is scheduled in mid-October as a coronation for Europe's best at 1¼ miles. Since 1985 it has been won by Pebbles, In the Groove, Hatoof, Pilsudski, and Kalanisi, all of them subsequent big-race winners in North America.

Add to that illustrious group the names of Ormonde, Sceptre, Pretty Polly, Nasrullah, Migoli (the sire of 1957 Belmont Stakes winner Gallant Man), Sir Ivor, Brigadier Gerard (twice), Time Charter, Triptych (twice), Spectrum, Rakti, and Pride, and you see why they call it the Champion Stakes.

Sharing the Champions Day dais is the Dewhurst Stakes, a race that defines the British, if not the European, juvenile champion. First run in 1875, two years before the first Champion Stakes, the Dewhurst is a seven-furlong affair renowned for producing future classic winners.

It has been taken by three future Triple Crown winners in Ormonde, Rock Sand, and Nijinsky. Its 14 Epsom Derby winners include Hyperion, Mill Reef, The Minstrel, and Generous. Numbered among its 15 2000 Guineas winners are Zafonic, Pennekamp, and Rock of Gibraltar. All told, Dewhurst winners have combined to win 38 British classics. In recent years, 1988 Dewhurst winner El Gran Senor would capture the Irish Derby while its 2004 winner, Shamardal, would take the following year's French Derby, the first run at 1$\frac{5}{16}$ miles. To top it off, the Dewhurst has also been won by Storm Bird, Diesis, Alhaarth, Teofilo, and New Approach, lending credence to the idea that it is the best 2-year-old race in the world.

ANALYSIS: The high quality of racing at Newmarket is, of course, a function of the proximity of some of the best training yards in England. Among the leading men who train in town are, in alphabetical order:

- **MICHAEL BELL (FITZROY HOUSE):** Trainer of 2005 Epsom Derby winner Motivator and the overachieving filly Red Evie, he is one of Newmarket's leading young conditioners.
- **CLIVE BRITTAIN (CARLSBURG STABLES):** The ever-optimistic veteran best known in America for the gallant victory of Pebbles in the 1985 Breeders' Cup Turf at Aqueduct, but who has also tutored such good ones as filly classic winners User Friendly and Sayyedati, as well as Luso, Crimplene, and Warrsan.
- **HENRY CECIL (WARREN PLACE):** Ten times Britain's champion trainer, he has trained Epsom Derby winners Slip Anchor, Reference Point, Commander In Chief, and Oath; Oaks winners Oh So Sharp, Diminuendo, Snow Bride, Lady Carla, Reams of Verse, Ramruma, Love Divine, and Light Shift; 2000 Guineas victors Bolkonski and Wollow; 1000 Guineas laureates One in a Million, Fairy Footsteps, Oh So Sharp, Bosra Sham, Sleepytime, and Wince; and St. Leger winners Light Cavalry, Oh So Sharp, Reference Point, and Michelozzo. All told, Cecil has won 34 classic races worldwide. Add to that list the great stayers Buckskin, Le Moss, and Ardross, plus King George winners Reference Point, Belmez, and King's Theatre, and it is clear why Cecil is considered a living legend.
- **PETER CHAPPLE-HYAM (ST. GATIEN STABLES):** Made an early mark on the British scene at Manton in Lambourn near Newbury with 2000 Guineas and Champion Stakes winner Rodrigo de Triano. After a fallow period in Hong Kong he returned to England to set up shop in Newmarket, where he has been responsible for Epsom Derby and Juddmonte International winner Authorized.
- **LUCA CUMANI (BEDFORD HOUSE STABLES):** A former assistant to Henry Cecil, the cosmopolitan Italian began training at Newmarket in 1976. He trained Kahyasi to victory in the Epsom Derby in 1988 and, 10 years later, High-Rise in the same classic. He created an international sensation when his Tolomeo upset John Henry in the 1983 Arlington Million. He also engineered the victory of his Irish 2000 Guineas winner Barathea in the Breeders' Cup Mile, and won the 2005 Japan Cup with Alkaased.

Always keeping a keen eye turned toward his native Italy, Cumani trained the Italian import Falbrav to victories in five Group

1 races, as well as giving another Italian import, Frankie Dettori, a start to his glorious riding career in England.

- **ED DUNLOP (GAINSBOROUGH STABLES):** The son of the great Arundel-based trainer, John Dunlop, Ed was the trainer of Ouija Board, Lord Derby's two-time winner of the Breeders' Cup Filly and Mare Turf who also accounted for the Nassau Stakes, the Prince of Wales's Stakes, the English Oaks, and the Irish Oaks.
- **DAVID ELSWORTH (EGERTON HOUSE STABLES):** Best known as the trainer of England's most popular steeplechaser, Desert Orchid, as well as the five-time Jockey Club Cup winner Persian Punch, Elsworth took over at Egerton House when David Loder retired in 2004.
- **JOHN GOSDEN (CLAREHAVEN STABLES):** Remembered in California as the trainer of inaugural Breeders' Cup Mile winner Royal Heroine, he keeps a stable of nearly 150 horses, and his main owners include Khalid Abdullah and Sheikh Mohammed. Among his big-race winners since returning to England are champion European sprinter Oasis Dream, Epsom Derby winner Benny the Dip, 1000 Guineas winner Lahan, and St. Leger winners Shantou and Lucarno. His Observatory ended the five-race Group 1 winning streak of Giant's Causeway in the 2000 Queen Elizabeth II Stakes. He also trained 1997 Eclipse Award winner Ryafan to four of her five Group or Grade 1 victories. In 2008 he gave England its first Breeders' Cup Classic winner with Raven's Pass.
- **MICHAEL JARVIS (KREMLIN HOUSE STABLES):** He won with the first horse he ever saddled in 1968, Knotty Pine. In 1989 he landed the Prix de l'Arc de Triomphe with Carroll House, and has also trained good ones such as Bob Back, sprint champion Petong, English Oaks winner Eswarah, and six-time Group 1 winner Rakti.
- **JEREMY NOSEDA (SHALFLEET STABLES):** Having once trained in California, like Gosden, Noseda is regarded as one of the most astute young conditioners in England. He trained Balmont to win the Middle Park Stakes at 2, Carry On Katie to win the filly equivalent, the Cheveley Park Stakes, and Proclamation to win the Sussex Stakes—all Group 1 events. He is best known internationally, however, for engineering Wilko's 28–1 upset of the 2004 Breeders' Cup Juvenile.
- **MICHAEL STOUTE (FREEMASON LODGE):** One of the world's best trainers, Sir Michael has trained four Epsom Derby winners—Shahrastani, Kris Kin, North Light, and the mighty Shergar—four 2000 Guineas winners, and two English Oaks winners. Zilzal, Sonic Lady,

Pilsudski, Singspiel, Islington, Russian Rhythm, and Notnowcato are only some of the other horses he has produced. Most recently he trained his St. Leger winner Conduit to cut back in distance and take the 2008 Breeders' Cup Turf. If a British import sports the line "Previously trained by Michael Stoute" above his past performances, you can be sure he has a solid underpinning.

◾ **SAEED BIN SUROOR (GODOLPHIN STABLES):** The trainer of Sheikh Mohammed's powerful Godolphin outfit since 1995, he has been responsible for Dubai Millennium, Daylami, Fantastic Light, Swain, Lammtarra, Almutawakel, Sulamani, Moon Ballad, Moonshell, Kazzia, Sakhee, Marienbard, Discreet Cat, and Music Note. The list goes on and on but there will always be a lingering doubt as to how much actual input Suroor has in the Godophin operation, in which Sheikh Mohammed himself, Frankie Dettori, racing manager Simon Crisford, and assistants in both England and America probably have as much to say about things as does the nominal trainer.

When interpreting Newmarket form, it must be remembered that most—but not all—Newmarket maiden races are competitive affairs, as good or better than any that are run in England. As on the Parisian circuit, if a horse has won a Newmarket maiden the first time out, he possesses a goodly amount of talent. Such horses usually graduate directly into stakes company, into listed races at least, if not Group 2's or sometimes even Group 1's. If an early Newmarket maiden winner moves on to an allowance race or into handicap company, that is a sign that he is probably not first-class material, although still quite capable of winning allowance races in America.

It isn't just Newmarket trainers who run at Newmarket. As the headquarters of British racing, the prestige of its two tracks attracts horses from all over England, as well as from France and especially from Ireland. Suffice it to say that most races at Newmarket rank near the top of their divisions.

TRACK RECORDS (Rowley Mile)

DISTANCE	RECORD TIME	HORSE	DATE	MEDIAN TIME
5f	56.80	Lochsong	April 30, 1994	59.10
6f	1:09.61	Oasis Dream*	Oct. 3, 2002	1:12.20
7f	1:22.20	Perfolia	Oct. 17, 1991	1:25.40
1m	1:34.54	Desert Deer	Oct. 3, 2002	1:38.60

DISTANCE	RECORD TIME	HORSE	DATE	MEDIAN TIME
1⅛ m	1:47.26	Manduro	April 13, 2007	1:50.60
1¼ m	2:01.00	Palace Music	Oct. 20, 1984	2:05.80
1½ m	2:27.10	Eastern Breeze	Oct. 3, 2003	2:33.50
1¾ m	2:51.59	Art Eyes	Sept. 29, 2005	2:58.50
2m	3:19.50	Grey Shot	Oct. 4, 1997	3:30.80
2¼ m	3:47.50	Whiteway	Oct. 15, 1947	3:54.80

* As a 2-year-old

TRACK RECORDS (July Course)

DISTANCE	RECORD TIME	HORSE	DATE	MEDIAN TIME
5f	56.09	Borderlescott	Aug. 22, 2008	59.10
6f	1:09.51	Stravinsky	July 8, 1999	1:12.50
7f	1:22.59	Ho Leng	July 9, 1998	1:25.70
1m	1:35.53	Lovers Knot	July 8, 1998	1:40.00
1¼ m	2:00.97	Elhayq	May 1, 1999	2:05.50
1½ m	2:25.29	Craigsteel	July 6, 1999	2:32.90
1¾ m, 175y	3:04.20	Arrive	July 11, 2001	3:11.30
2m, 24y	3:20.20	Yorkshire	July 11, 2001	3:27.00

MAJOR RACES (Chronological Order)

RACE		CONDITIONS
CRAVEN MEETING		
Rowley Mile	Nell Gwyn Stakes-G3	7f 3yo f
Rowley Mile	Feilden Stakes (Listed)	1⅛ m 3yo
Rowley Mile	European Free Hcp (Listed)	7f 3yo
Rowley Mile	Craven Stakes-G3	1m 3yo c&g
Rowley Mile	Earl of Sefton Stakes-G3	1⅛ m 4yo+
Rowley Mile	Abernant Stakes (Listed)	6f 3yo+ c&g
GUINEAS MEETING		
Rowley Mile	2000 Guineas Stakes-G1	1m 3yo c&f
Rowley Mile	Dahlia Stakes-G3	1⅛ m 4yo+ f&m
Rowley Mile	Newmarket Stakes (Listed)	1¼ m 3yo
Rowley Mile	1000 Guineas Stakes-G1	1m 3yo f
Rowley Mile	Jockey Club Stakes-G2	1½ m 4yo+
Rowley Mile	Palace House Stakes-G3	5f 3yo+
Rowley Mile	Pretty Polly Stakes (Listed)	1¼ m 3yo f

RACE		CONDITIONS
Rowley Mile	Fairway Stakes (Listed)	1¼m 3yo
Rowley Mile	King Charles II Stks (Listed)	7f 3yo
July Course	Criterium Stakes-G3	7f 3yo+
July Course	Fred Archer Stakes (Listed)	1½m 4yo+
July Course	Empress Stakes (Listed)	6f 2yo f

JULY MEETING

July Course	Falmouth Stakes-G1	1m 3yo+ f&m
July Course	Cherry Hinton Stakes-G2	6f 2yo f
July Course	Princess of Wales's Stks-G2	1½m 3yo+
July Course	July Stakes-G2	6f 2yo c&g
July Course	Bahrain Trophy (Listed)	1⅝m 3yo
July Course	July Cup-G1	6f 3yo+
July Course	Superlative Stakes-G2	7f 2yo
July Course	Aphrodite Stakes (Listed)	1½m 3yo+ f&m
July Course	Sweet Solera Stakes-G3	7f 2yo f
July Course	Hopeful Stakes (Listed)	6f 3yo+

CAMBRIDGESHIRE MEETING

Rowley Mile	Rous Stakes (Listed)	5f 3yo+
Rowley Mile	Noel Murless Stakes (Listed)	1¾m 3yo
Rowley Mile	Middle Park Stakes-G1	6f 2yo c
Rowley Mile	Cheveley Park Stakes-G1	6f 2yo f
Rowley Mile	Somerville Tattersall Stks-G3	7f 2yo c&g
Rowley Mile	Godolphin Stakes (Listed)	1½m 3yo+
Rowley Mile	Sun Chariot Stakes-G1	1m 3yo+ f&m
Rowley Mile	Joel Stakes-G3	1m 3yo+
Rowley Mile	Oh So Sharp Stakes-G3	7f 2yo f
Rowley Mile	Cambridgeshire Handicap	1⅛m 3yo+
Rowley Mile	Darley Stakes-G3	1⅛m 3yo+
Rowley Mile	Boadicea Stakes (Listed)	6f 3yo+ f&m
Rowley Mile	Severals Stakes (Listed)	1¼m 3yo+ f&m

CHAMPIONS DAY

Rowley Mile	Champion Stakes-G1	1¼m 3yo+
Rowley Mile	Dewhurst Stakes-G1	7f 2yo c&f
Rowley Mile	Rockfel Stakes-G2	7f 2yo f
Rowley Mile	Challenge Stakes-G2	7f 3yo+
Rowley Mile	Jockey Club Cup-G3	2m 3yo+

RACE		CONDITIONS
Rowley Mile	Bentinck Stakes-G3	6f 3yo+
Rowley Mile	Cesarewitch Handicap	2¼m 4yo+
Rowley Mile	Bosra Sham Stakes (Listed)	6f 2yo f
Rowley Mile	James Seymour Stks (Listed)	1¼m 3yo+
Rowley Mile	Ben Marshall Stakes (Listed)	1m 3yo+
Rowley Mile	Montrose Stakes (Listed)	1m 2yo f
Rowley Mile	Zetland Stakes (Listed)	1¼m 2yo

DAYS OF RACING: In 2007 there were 18 days of racing on the Rowley Mile course, nine during the spring meeting and nine at the autumn meeting.

The spring season traditionally kicks off with the Craven Meeting, or the Guineas-prep meeting. Formerly a three-day affair held during the third week of April, it was condensed into a two-day, Thursday-Friday meeting in 2007 with the 1000 Guineas prep, the Nell Gwyn Stakes, on Thursday and the Craven Stakes, or 2000 Guineas prep, on Friday.

The Guineas Meeting itself is generally run on the first weekend in May. The 2000 Guineas is almost always run on the same day as the Kentucky Derby, the exception being in those odd years when that day falls on May 7, in which case the meeting is moved forward one week, when the 2000 Guineas is run on April 30. The 1000 Guineas, run for decades on the Thursday before the 2000, has been run on Sunday, the day after the 2000, since 1995.

Two weekend meetings in late May conclude the Rowley spring season, after which the July Course opens its 19-day summer session. Friday and Saturday meetings are held the last two weekends in June prior to the July Course's major three-day July Meeting, now held during the second Wednesday, Thursday, and Friday of the month. Six more Friday-Saturday meetings through July and August, including any number of evening fixtures, conclude the summer season.

The Rowley Mile reopens for business on the third Friday of September with the two-day Cambridgeshire Meeting, which includes two key six-furlong juvenile Group 1 races, the Middle Park Stakes for colts and the Cheveley Park Stakes for fillies. These are run in late September or early October, the Saturday coinciding with the first day of Longchamp's Arc Weekend.

Champions Day, featuring the Champion Stakes and the Dewhurst Stakes, is the second day of a mid-October fixture. The Newmarket season concludes with a pair of Friday-Saturday meetings in late October and early November notable for their large fields as local trainers try and squeeze one last win out of their charges before the arrival of the October and December horses-in-training sales at nearby Tattersalls.

HOW TO GET THERE: Despite being the headquarters of British racing, Newmarket is a difficult place to get to by train. From London's Liverpool Street Station, fast trains take about an hour to get to Cambridge. Infrequent shuttle trains from Cambridge make the 20-minute journey to Newmarket Station. A cab ride from Cambridge to either the Rowley Mile Course or the July Course will set you back about $80. A bus from the Cambridge station to either course is much less expensive, but the driver always manages to take the scenic route.

SURROUNDING AREA: Racing fans owe it to themselves to visit Newmarket at least once in their lives. In addition to its first-class sport, the town has a number of horsey attractions.

Foremost, and most accessible, is the National Horse Racing Museum. Located on the High Street in the center of town, it includes thousands of historical artifacts, silks, trophies, photographs, paintings, and lithographs. Featured in the permanent exhibit is a special section on the life of Fred Archer, the greatest of all 19th-century jockeys. It includes the revolver with which he killed himself shortly after the untimely death of his wife, after having suffered too long himself from the effects of trying to make weight.

An excellent selection of racing films dating back to the early 20th century brings the history of the sport to life. Most extraordinary is a film of the gray flyer Mahmoud sprinting to victory in the 1936 Epsom Derby, in which he set a track record for 1½ miles that stood until 1995.

For students of conformation, the skeleton of the great stallion Hyperion and the head of Edward VII's Derby winner, Persimmon, are also on display. Legendary equestrian artists such as Alfred Munnings are given temporary exhibits on a regular basis, as are contemporary artists.

Tours of the National Stud—which is owned and operated by the British government—as well as Sheikh Mohammed's Dalham Hall Stud are available, as are tours of morning workouts on the gallops. All can be arranged through the museum.

Note, however, that the museum is open only during the flat-racing season, daily from early April through early November.

The Jockey Club has its subsidiary offices in Newmarket, outside of which stands a statue of a fully fleshed Hyperion. Tattersalls, the famous sales company, is headquartered in Newmarket, as is the British

Racing School for prospective young jockeys and the International Racing Bureau, the company largely responsible for recruiting European horses for stakes races in America, Canada, Japan, Hong Kong, Turkey, and Australia.

SANDOWN PARK ☰

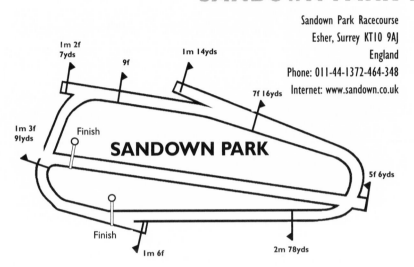

Sandown Park Racecourse
Esher, Surrey KT10 9AJ
England
Phone: 011-44-1372-464-348
Internet: www.sandown.co.uk

LOCATION: 20 miles southwest of London.

COURSE DESCRIPTION: Sandown is a somewhat irregular right-handed oval, 1⅛ miles, 33 yards around. Races of 1¼ miles and two miles, 78 yards start in front of the grandstand, beginning sharply uphill before making a 90-degree turn onto a steep, one-furlong downhill straight. At the bottom of the hill, races of 1¼ miles get their start, among them the Group 1 Eclipse Stakes. From this point the backstretch is a level, easy galloping affair, five furlongs in length and virtually straight. There follows a sharp right-hand turn into the half-mile stretch, which is stiffly uphill all the way.

A five-furlong straight course, entirely uphill, splits the main course in half lengthwise.

Stamina reigns supreme at Sandown because of the stiff uphill finishes. While horses have an easy time of it on the backstretch, they must be prepared for the long haul through the stretch. Thus times are unusually slow by American standards, even on good-to-firm ground. The median time on the five-furlong straight course is just 1:01.60; for seven furlongs, 1:29.50; for a mile, 1:43.30; for 1¼ miles, 2:10.50.

Sandown is also one of British racing's most important jumps courses. The steeplechase course shares part of its 1⅝ miles with the flat course, but the stretch runs outside that of the flat course. The hurdle course shares the stretch with the flat course.

HISTORY: Sandown Park holds an important place in the history of racing if only because of its origins, as it was the first racecourse in Europe to be entirely enclosed. Before it opened in 1875, racetracks were merely laid out on public grounds, and admission was free to all, except those who wanted a place under cover in the grandstand, which was usually reserved for the elites.

The whole plant was bordered by a 10-foot fence at a cost of 2,000 pounds (about $8,000 at the time). That, along with the new practice of charging admission (which cost half a crown on opening day in April 1875), enabled the growing number of female racing fans to attend the races in somewhat more genteel surroundings.

Sandown's founder, Hwfa (pronounced HOO-fa) Williams, built an up-to-date French-style grandstand. In 1886 he inaugurated the Eclipse Stakes. Now one of the most important weight-for-age contests in Europe, the Eclipse was designed from the start as the first test of the season—in early July—between 3-year-olds and their elders.

Named for the great 18th-century racehorse from which virtually all contemporary Thoroughbreds are descended, the Eclipse has always been run at 1¼ miles for 3-year-olds and up. The first running went to Bendigo, who would win the Champion Stakes a year later. Ayrshire, winner of the 1888 Epsom Derby, won it in 1889. Diamond Jubilee won it in his Triple Crown season of 1900, but if there were any doubts about the young race's importance, they were eased three years later when Ard Patrick defeated the great filly Sceptre and the 1903 Triple Crown winner, Rock Sand. Those three horses had won seven classic races between them. It was clear that the Eclipse Stakes was living up to the legacy of its renowned namesake.

Since the great generations of the 1970s, when it was won by Mill Reef and Brigadier Gerard, the Eclipse has gone to Sadler's Wells, Pebbles, Dancing Brave, Nashwan, Kooyonga, Pilsudski, Daylami, Giant's Causeway, Falbrav, and Oratorio, making it one of the highest-ranking races in the world.

In an age when American 3-year-olds rarely dare to challenge older horses until October, it is interesting to note that the Eclipse, run annually on the first or second Saturday in July, has been won by 3-year-olds nine times in the last 26 years through 2008.

The expansive Sandown infield was used as farmland during World War I when there was no racing there from 1915 through 1918. Racing at the track fell victim to war again between 1940 and 1945, but the picture brightened considerably in 1947 when the BBC made the Eclipse Stakes the first race ever to be televised. The horse who had his photo taken was Migoli, the future sire of 1957 Belmont Stakes winner Gallant Man.

Sandown runs a full schedule of jump-race meetings throughout the winter and is home to the last remaining important mixed meeting—that is, a meeting at which both flat and jump races are run. That occurs in late April when the 1¼-mile Sandown Classic Trial shares billing with the 3⅝-mile Sandown Gold Cup Handicap Chase.

In 1962 Sandown Park was threatened by developers, but the racing community combined forces with local residents and saved the track. Always known for its modern facilities, the current grandstand only dates from 1974, but that has not prevented Sandown from being named Britain's Racecourse of the Year many times since then. While American visitors in England may feel cramped in most British grandstands, that is not the case with Sandown Park.

ANALYSIS: The quality of the racing at Sandown can vary. On Eclipse Day, Classic Trial Day, Brigadier Gerard Day, and Sandown Mile Day, it is as good as racing gets in England, but some of the lesser days through the summer are average affairs with a nice listed race or Group 3 juvenile event thrown in along with one or two good maiden races.

As a result, care must be taken when interpreting the form of British imports that have run there. One factor that should never be neglected in attempting to evaluate a Sandown victory is the distance of the race. Because of its uphill finish, Sandown is a track on which a seven-furlong winner can be expected to stay at least a mile, and probably 1⅛ miles, in America. In fact, you can generally grant up to two American furlongs to any Sandown winner who has maintained his form since that win.

The Sandown Classic Trial Stakes, the first group-race prep for the Epsom Derby, rarely yields a winner of the great classic these days, but two other springtime events—the 1¼-mile Gordon Richards Stakes and the 1¼-mile Brigadier Gerard Stakes, both Group 3's—are always competitive affairs.

Since 1991, the Brigadier Gerard has been won by future Group 1 winners Opera House, Pilsudski, Bosra Sham, and Notnowcato. Red Bishop, who won it in 1993, would later finish second in the Grade 2 Red Smith Handicap at Aqueduct, while 1999 winner Chester House would go on to win the 2000 Arlington Million.

The Gordon Richards Stakes, named for the man who was champion rider in Britain 26 times between 1925 and 1954, has gone to future Group 1 winners Indian Skimmer and Singspiel. It was won in 1992 by subsequent Arlington Million winner Dear Doctor and in 2007 by the previous year's Breeders' Cup Turf winner, Red Rocks, who would defeat Curlin in the 2008 Man o' War Stakes.

The Sandown Mile is a serviceable Group 2 event these days but no longer produces winners like its 1985 laureate, Pebbles; its thunder has been stolen by the upgrading to Group 1 status of the Lockinge Stakes, run one month later in May at Newbury. As a result, the Sandown Mile is now the key prep for the Lockinge.

TRACK RECORDS

DISTANCE	RECORD TIME	HORSE	DATE	MEDIAN TIME
5f	58.80	Palacegate Touch	Sept. 17, 1996	1:01.60
7f	1:26.30	Mawsuff	June 14, 1983	1:29.50
1m	1:39.00	Linda's Fantasy	Aug. 19, 1983	1:43.30
1⅛m	1:52.40	Bourgainville	Aug. 11, 2005	1:56.30
1¼m	2:02.10	Kalaglow	May 31, 1982	2:10.50
1⅜m, 9ly	2:21.60	Aylsfield	July 7, 1984	—
1¾m	2:56.90	Lady Rosanna	July 19, 1989	3:06.60
2m, 78y	3:29.90	Sadeem	May 29, 1989	3:39.50

MAJOR RACES (Chronological Order)

RACE	CONDITIONS
Sandown Mile-G2	1m 4yo+
Gordon Richards Stakes-G3	1¼m 4yo+
Sandown Classic Trial-G3	1¼m 3yo
Henry II Stakes-G2	2m, 78y 4yo+
Brigadier Gerard Stakes-G3	1¼m 4yo+
National Stakes (Listed)	5f 2yo
Scurry Stakes (Listed)	5f 3yo+
Gala Stakes (Listed)	1¼m 3yo+
Dragon Stakes (Listed)	5f 2yo

RACE	CONDITIONS
Eclipse Stakes-G1	1¼m 3yo+
Sprint Stakes-G3	5f 3yo+
Distaff Stakes (Listed)	1m 3yo f
Esher Stakes (Listed)	2m, 78y 4yo+
Star Stakes (Listed)	7f 2yo f
Solario Stakes-G3	7f 2yo
Atalanta Stakes (Listed)	1m 3yo+ f&m
Fortune Stakes (Listed)	7f 3yo+
Tingle Creek Hcp Hurdle-G3	2m 5yo+
Triumph Hurdle-G3	2m 5yo+
Sandown Gold Cup Handicap Chase-G3	3⅜m 5yo+

DAYS OF RACING: Sandown Park conducts 16 days of flat racing between late April and mid-September, and nine days of jump racing between early November and late April. The two-day late-April meeting is a mixed meeting with both flat and jump racing and attracts crowds at least as large as those drawn to the Eclipse Stakes, which is run on the first or second Saturday of July.

HOW TO GET THERE: Trains leave London Waterloo frequently for the 25-minute ride to Esher (pronounced EE-shur) Station, which lies adjacent to the Sandown Park backstretch. Follow a tree-covered footpath about 100 yards beyond the station and you will find a quaint 19th-century blockhouse turnstile building through which you will gain entry to the backstretch itself. From there you can walk across the infield, the five-furlong straight course, and the homestretch into the grandstand.

SURROUNDING AREA: Esher is a bedroom community inhabited largely by people who work in London. There are four golf courses in the town of 8,300, but the main attraction always has been and always will be the racetrack.

YORK

York Racecourse
York YO23 IEX
England
Phone: 011-44-1904-620-911
Internet: www.yorkracecourse.co.uk

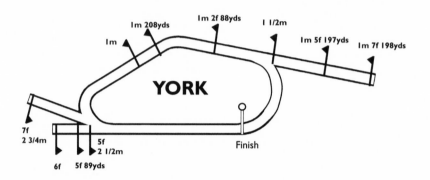

LOCATION: 203 miles north of London.

COURSE DESCRIPTION: York is a left-handed triangular track about 1¾ miles in circumference with a chute on the backstretch for two-mile races and a seven-furlong chute that connects with the stretch 4½ furlongs from the finish. There is a six-furlong straight course that leads directly into the homestretch.

The track is wider than normal and virtually level throughout. As such it is considered one of the fairest courses in England, not least because of its long 4½-furlong stretch.

Until 2005, when York hosted the Royal Meeting while Ascot was building a new grandstand, the configuration of the track did not form an enclosed triangle. The run-out past the finish line had been a mild left-hand bend that emptied onto the infield, but since the Royal Meeting requires races to be run at up to 2¾ miles, York officials extended the run-out to the backstretch. The new configuration has been kept in place since then.

Races of 1¼ miles, 88 yards (the distance of the Juddmonte International) and longer start on the far leg of the backstretch, then make a 45-degree left-hand turn about 1 3⁄16 miles from home onto a three-furlong straight, after which there is a winding turn into the stretch.

The chute for seven-furlong races is 2½ furlongs in length and concludes with a mild left-hand bend into the stretch.

HISTORY: York's long and colorful history pre-dates the first recorded races run in 1731 at the present location of the racecourse. Roman emperor Lucius Septimus Severus organized chariot races on the site in the early third century while at the same time leading his legions against the occasional Scottish invasion.

In medieval times, the aptly named River Ouse (pronounced "ooze") was forever spilling its banks into the valley. Criminals attempting to escape the sheriff of York would invariably head south toward London but were frequently apprehended floundering in the muck. Thus the region became known as the Knavesmire, a name that has stuck to the present day.

The bad guys who were caught would often meet their fate on a contraption the locals christened the three-legged mare. This was a triangular hanging stage set up smack in the middle of the muddy swamp. Long before Yorkshiremen and women learned of the pleasures of the turf on the Knavesmire, they flocked there to enjoy a morning of executions. The custom continued until long after York Racecourse opened for business. On August 20, 1739, the notorious criminal Dick Turpin met his end on the three-legged mare just a few hours before the four-legged mares and their brothers took to the course for a day of more civilized sport.

The state of the ground has always been a problem at York, heavy going being the rule whenever there was any amount of rain. Whoever was the clerk of the course would always have a headache with the going, and while many improvements to drainage have been made through the years, York embarked on yet another renovation during the winter of 2007–08.

Some of the most famous match races in history have been run at York. The first, in 1804, produced what was perhaps the first sporting battle of the sexes.

Alicia Thornton was a society beauty fond of riding. One day she challenged her amorously inclined brother-in-law, one Captain Flint of the Sixth Light Dragoons, to a match race while riding in her jealous husband's park, Thornville. Mrs. Thornton prevailed, and was promptly asked for a rematch, this time in public on the Knavesmire.

Before an estimated crowd of 100,000 (sex really does pack them in), Mrs. Thornton appeared on her husband's horse Vinagrillio, Captain

Assertive nips War Artist in front of York's Ebor Stand in the 2008 Duke of York Stakes.

Flint on Brown Thornville. Sadly, Vinagrillio broke down and was distanced in the four-mile heat. The lady's husband refused to meet his financial obligations, and much bad behavior ensued, Flint allegedly horsewhipping Thornton at York's August Meeting in 1805, and eventually committing suicide.

A year later, Mrs. Thornton challenged the leading rider of the day, Frank Buckle, to a match at York, and the lady gracefully recouped her sporting pride by beating him in a two-mile race, albeit in receipt of 56 pounds.

But the most famous match race in British racing history was surely the great duel between Voltigeur and The Flying Dutchman on May 13, 1851.

The Flying Dutchman had won the Derby and St. Leger in 1849, while Voltigeur had won the 1850 Derby. Three months later Voltigeur won the St. Leger in a run-off after having dead-heated with Russborough. Two days after that, he beat The Flying Dutchman in what turned out to be a match race in the 2 ¼-mile Doncaster Cup.

On match-race day, carrying eight pounds more than his 4-year-old opponent on what was then the scale, The Flying Dutchman won the two-mile test by a length. York has since rewarded the loser by naming its mid-August St. Leger Stakes prep after him, the not too hyperbolic Great Voltigeur Stakes.

But the greatest race run at York these days is without question the Juddmonte International Stakes. First run in 1972, 22 years after the inaugural Great Voltigeur, it was originally the Benson & Hedges Gold Cup, one of the races that helped put corporate race sponsorship on the map in Britain.

It was an immediate success, and an international coup to boot. Only five ran, but they included that year's Epsom Derby winner, Roberto; the Derby runner-up, Rheingold; and the 1–3 favorite, England's favorite racehorse, Brigadier Gerard.

Trained by Vincent O'Brien, Roberto was owned by American tycoon John Galbreath, who had the audacity to ship his regular Darby Dan rider Braulio Baeza across the Atlantic expressly for the assignment. In one of the greatest race-riding performances of all time, Baeza put the 12–1 Roberto on the lead from the start and proceeded to give his British colleagues a lesson in the art of pacemaking. Every time Brigadier Gerard made a move, Baeza would let out a little more on Roberto, a horse who usually did his running from behind. When he crossed the line, Roberto was three lengths in front, both he and Brigadier Gerard having broken the track record for 1¼ miles, 88 yards.

Roberto's mark would withstand subsequent victories by Dahlia (twice), Troy, Assert, Caerleon, and Triptych until 1988, by which time Benson & Hedges had dropped sponsorship. In 1989 the race became known as the Juddmonte International as Khalid Abdullah's powerful racing and breeding operation took up the sponsorship reins. In 2007 it became the first race run at York to top the $1 million mark, weighing in at $1,040,812.

While the Juddmonte is the centerpiece of York's all-important Ebor Meeting in August (Ebor being the name the ancient Romans had given the place), the three-day spring meeting in May is highlighted by Britain's major Epsom Derby trial, the Dante Stakes. Named for just one of two north-of-England-trained Derby winners, the Dante was first run in 1958 when it was won by future American champion Bald Eagle. It has since fallen to nine subsequent Derby winners in St Paddy, Shirley Heights, Shahrastani, Reference Point, Erhaab, Benny the Dip, North Light, Motivator, and Authorized. Other good ones, such as Arc winners Rheingold and Sakhee, and Dubai World Cup winner Moon Ballad, have added luster to the Dante's roll of honor.

ANALYSIS: Just because York, like every single racetrack in North America, is a level, left-handed track, it does not necessarily mean that good York form will translate to good American or Canadian form. York actually bears little or no resemblance to any American track, so British-trained horses arriving in the United States must be evaluated on their inherent ability. Even Woodbine, with its rather long 2½-furlong stretch—which, by the way, is considered on the short side by many British racing professionals—bears little comparison with York.

The nature of racing in Europe—and in particular, racing in Britain, where there are so many different kinds of tracks (right-handed, left-handed, and straight; uphill and downhill; undulating and level), where the ground can be anything from firm to very heavy, and where they have been running on synthetic surfaces for nearly 20 years—means that the European Thoroughbred is a more adaptable animal than its American counterpart.

The British Thoroughbred who arrives in America merely has to learn one more lesson in what has been a career of lesson learning. Since racing in England isn't as far-flung as racing in America, the British racehorse has probably faced more competitive opponents on a regular basis than have his new American rivals, who have many more opportunities to dodge the best competition in their respective divisions.

As far as York is concerned, it is wise to use the same rule of thumb that should apply for all foreign imports. Weigh a horse's chances based on his quality of competition, not on his form at any given racetrack that might or might not resemble the American track at which he is running.

Much is written about the perceived differences between one American racetrack and another, especially now that the British have imported so-called all-weather racing to the Americas. The fact is, the difference between the two major American tracks that are most different from each other, let us say Belmont and Del Mar, is no greater than that of the two British tracks that are most similar to each other, let us say Redcar and Yarmouth.

At York, one should be aware of horses that have done well in any of its group or listed races, or of runners that have done well against those horses. This is the basic rule of handicapping for all foreign imports. Sad to say, there is no magic formula for translating foreign form into American form, although some handicappers who rely on numbers to do most of their work for them might wish there were.

As far as York is concerned, there are some easy lessons to be learned using the quality-of-competition system, albeit at the highest level only, with the Juddmonte International and the Yorkshire Oaks being cases in point.

Since 1999 the Juddmonte has been won by Royal Anthem (subsequently second in the Breeders' Cup Turf and first in the Gulfstream Park Breeders' Cup Handicap), Giant's Causeway (subsequently the winner of the Irish Champion Stakes and second in the Breeders' Cup Classic), Sakhee (subsequently the winner of the Prix de l'Arc de Triomphe and second in the Breeders' Cup Classic), Falbrav (subsequently a neck second in the Irish Champion Stakes, the winner of the Queen Elizabeth II Stakes, and a head third in the Breeders' Cup Turf), Sulamani (subsequently the winner of the Canadian International), and Electrocutionist (the winner the following March of the Dubai World Cup).

Any horse who ever beat or finished close up to any of these horses at almost any point in their careers would be deserving of consideration in his American debut, as long as his form upon arrival in America was still reputable.

Ditto the Yorkshire Oaks, a 1½-mile Group 1 for fillies and mares. Its winners since 2000 include Petrushka, subsequently the winner of the Prix de l'Opera and fifth as the favorite in the Breeders' Cup Filly and Mare Turf, and Islington, subsequently the winner of the Breeders' Cup Filly and Mare Turf.

The lessons are clear. Follow British racing at the highest level on a daily basis, and you will be rewarded with what appears to be inside information in the shape of form lines that remain invisible to anyone who handicaps foreigners on the basis of the bare form or the bare rating.

TRACK RECORDS

DISTANCE	RECORD TIME	HORSE	DATE	MEDIAN TIME
5f	56.20	Oasis Dream	Aug. 21, 2003	59.30
6f	1:08.58	Cape of Good Hope	June 16, 2005	1:11.90
7f	1:21.98	Iffraaj	Sept. 9, 2006	1:25.30
1m	1:36.00	Faithful Warrior	July 11, 2003	1:38.80
1⅛m	1:46.76	Echo of Light	Sept. 5, 2007	1:52.00
1¼m, 88y	2:06.09	Imperial Stride	June 17, 2005	2:12.50
1½m	2:27.40	Islington	Aug. 20, 2003	2:33.20
1¾m	2:52.50	Mamool	May 15, 2003	3.00.20
2m, 78y	3:18.40	Dam Busters	Aug. 16, 1998	3:23.50

RACE	CONDITIONS
MAY MEETING	
Duke of York Stakes-G2	6f 3yo+
Musidora Stakes-G3	1¼m, 88y 3yo f
Dante Stakes-G2	1¼m, 88y 3yo c&g
Middleton Stakes-G3	1¼m, 88y 4yo+ f&m
Hambleton Stakes (Listed)	1m 4yo+
Yorkshire Cup-G2	1¾m 4yo+
Michael Seely Meml Stk (Listed)	1m 3yo f
Marygate Stakes (Listed)	5f 2yo f
Summer Stakes-G3	6f 3yo+ f&m
York Stakes-G2	1¼m, 88y 3yo+
EBOR MEETING	
Juddmonte Intl Stakes-G1	1¼m, 88y 3yo+
Great Voltigeur Stakes-G2	1½m 3yo c&g
Lonsdale Cup-G2	2m, 78y 4yo+
Acomb Stakes-G3	7f 2yo
Ebor Handicap	1¾m 3yo+
Yorkshire Stakes-G1	1½m 3yo+ f&m
Gimcrack Stakes-G2	6f 2yo c&g
Roses Stakes (Listed)	5f 2yo
Nunthorpe Stakes-G1	5f 2yo+
Lowther Stakes-G2	6f 2yo f
City of York Stakes (Listed)	7f 3yo+
Galtres Stakes (Listed)	1½m 3yo+ f&m
Strensall Stakes-G3	1⅛m 3yo+

DAYS OF RACING: York conducts 15 days of racing annually. From 2008, these will include an expanded four-day Ebor Meeting during the third week of August, when the Juddmonte International will be run on Tuesday, the Ebor Handicap on Wednesday, the Yorkshire Oaks on Thursday, and the Nunthorpe Stakes, the only Group 1 five-furlong contest run in Britain, on Friday.

York opens each spring with its three-day Tuesday-through-Thursday meeting in mid-May with the Dante Stakes on Tuesday, the English Oaks prep the Musidora Stakes on Wednesday, and the Yorkshire Cup, an early-season prep for the Ascot Gold Cup, on Thursday.

Two-day meetings in late May, mid-June, mid-July, and late July form the run-up to the Ebor Meeting, which in future will conclude the York season, as the fourth day of the Ebor Meeting will replace the now defunct early September meeting.

HOW TO GET THERE: Express trains—and slower local trains—leave London's Kings Cross Station. The express trains, which include smart dining cars, take two hours to get to York Station, from which it is a short cab ride to the racecourse. It is inadvisable to make a daily day trip to York from London, however. With its myriad attractions and numerous charming bed-and-breakfasts, York is an excellent place to visit during its three-day May Meeting or its four-day Ebor Meeting in August.

SURROUNDING AREA: York is a medieval city in the true sense of the word. The city walls date from the time of the Crusades, for which Richard the Lion-Hearted departed from under the Micklegate, or Great Gate, the south entrance to the city, one sight of which will leave you dreaming of knights in shining armor and their fair ladies in castle keeps. The easily accessible walls still surround three-quarters of the old city and are free to all.

The 800-year-old York Minster is the largest Gothic cathedral north of the Alps and contains some of the most beautiful stained glass in the world. Beware, however. In doing its best contemporary imitation of an amusement park, the Church of England now charges admission to most of its cathedrals. It will cost you at least $11 to get in to York Minster, even if your purpose is to offer a prayer of thanksgiving for that big winner at the track.

Clifford's Tower was originally built by William the Conqueror in the 11th century, the current edifice dating from the era of Henry II in the 13th century. Built on a large man-made mound, it is reputedly the oldest single-turret castle in the world.

The city itself is crisscrossed with narrow, ancient lanes, charming wood-beamed houses dating from the late Middle Ages, and stone churches, some of which are now arts centers.

For history of a more recent sort, there is the National Railway Museum. Situated just outside the city walls, it is the largest museum of its sort in the world, containing original cars from every period of railroad history. Among its attractions are the mythic Flying Scotsman locomotive; Queen Victoria's private car; an early London Underground subway car; and a Chinese locomotive built, of course, by the British, who are largely responsible for building the first railroads in almost every country in the world save the United States. The city's many Japanese visitors delight in climbing aboard the Shinkansen, or Japanese Bullet Train, the fastest train in the world.

A fantasyland for any boy or girl who ever engineered a set of Lionel trains under the Christmas tree, the National Railway Museum does not charge admission.

Other Racecourses in Britain

AYR ☰

Ayr, Scotland
Phone: 011-44-870-850-5666
Internet: www.ayr-racecourse.co.uk

LOCATION: 35 miles southwest of Glasgow, 81 miles southwest of Edinburgh, 380 miles north of London. Trains from Glasgow Central or from London Euston.

A left-handed 1½-mile oval not dissimilar to Belmont Park but with a longer stretch, Ayr is a level course with a four-furlong stretch and a six-furlong straight course that meets the left-handed course a half-mile from the finish. There is also a chute on the backstretch from which races at 1¼ miles and 1⅜ miles are started.

Of the five racetracks in Scotland, Ayr is considered the most important. The current course opened in 1777 and is the home of Scotland's most popular flat fixture. The three-day Western Meeting, held the third weekend (Thursday through Saturday) of September, features one of Britain's most valuable sprint handicaps, the six-furlong Ayr Gold Cup. Originally restricted to Scottish-breds, it was first run in 1804 and was won in 1992 by champion sprinter Lochsong, whose victory completed a handicap sprinting triple crown of sorts as he had previously won the Stewards Cup at Goodwood and the Portland Handicap at Doncaster.

But Ayr, which pinch-hit for Doncaster by running the St. Leger Stakes in 1989 when a hole in the Doncaster stretch forced the rescheduling of the 1¾-mile classic, suffered a setback in 2007 when its most prestigious flat race, the 1¼-mile Group 2 Scottish Derby for 3-year-olds and up, was canceled.

As most British imports to America are trained in the south of England, we see few horses that have run at Ayr, where the best racing is competitive on a level that might be compared to a typical midweek day at Arlington or Monmouth.

The jump racing at Ayr is a cut above the flat sport. The Scottish Grand National in late April makes a nice consolation prize for horses who trailed in or missed Aintree's Grand National two weeks earlier.

Golfers should take note that two courses that are part of the British Open circuit are not far from Ayr. Royal Troon is 10 miles to the north, Turnberry 15 miles to the south.

TRACK RECORDS

DISTANCE	RECORD TIME	MEDIAN TIME
5f	56.90	1:00.10
6f	1:08.90	1:13.60
7f, 50y	1:28.20	1:33.40
1m	1:36.00	1:43.80
1¼m	2:04.00	2:12.00
1⅜m	2:13.30	—

BATH

Bath, Somerset
England
Phone: 011-44-1225-424-609
Internet: www.bath-racecourse.co.uk

LOCATION: 119 miles west of London. Trains from London Paddington Station to Bath Station, from which the track is a two-mile bus ride.

Bath is a kidney-shaped, largely left-handed track about 1½ miles around. Races of 1⅜ miles, 144 yards start from a chute on the backstretch. There is a mild right-hand bend at the mile pole, followed by a 2½-furlong straight leading away from the grandstand. A long sweeping turn leads into a quarter-mile stretch. An even longer, sweeping left-handed chute beyond the turn for home provides a start for races of five furlongs and for races of five furlongs, 161 yards, as well as for races of two miles and longer. This five-furlong course is cambered in toward the rail and is mildly uphill all the way, but the rest of the track is virtually level.

Built at 780 feet above sea level, Bath is the most highly elevated racecourse in Britain, as least geographically. The first races were run there in 1728, shortly after two towering literary figures, Jane Austen (*Pride and Prejudice, Sense and Sensibility*) and Richard Brinsley Sheridan (*The Rivals*), had helped to popularize the town, whose natural springs had been attracting wealthy Britons for decades.

The racing, however, rates near the bottom of the British scale. Its 17 meetings, spread from mid-April to late October, include just two listed races, the five-furlong Lansdown Stakes and the one-mile Dick Hern Stakes, both for fillies and mares. One angle to look for in horses that have run at Bath is that of firm-ground lovers. As a spa town built on limestone, drainage at Bath is excellent and races are frequently run on ground no less than good. Firm ground crops up at Bath more often than most tracks in England.

Bath is a historic city, renowned for its Georgian architecture, particularly the Royal Crescent. It is also the site of the Sulla Minerva Roman Baths, hence the name of the city.

TRACK RECORDS

DISTANCE	RECORD TIME	MEDIAN TIME
5f	58.75	1:02.50
5f, 16ly	1:08.10	1:11.20
1m	1:37.20	1:40.80
1¼m, 46y	2:05.60	2:11.00
1⅜m, 144y	2:25.74	2:30.60

BEVERLEY ≡

Beverley Race Co. Ltd.
Beverley, East Yorkshire
England
Phone: 011-44-1482-867-488
Internet: www.beverley-racecourse.co.uk

LOCATION: 188 miles north of London. Trains from London Kings Cross to Beverley Station. The racetrack is about one mile from the town center.

A right-handed, irregularly shaped oval, Beverley measures just over 1⅜ miles around. Races at 1½ miles start from a chute on the backstretch, which is a level six furlongs followed by a 90-degree turn onto a very mild right-handed downhill bend, nearly two furlongs in length. This leads to a sharpish turn into the 3½-furlong stretch, which is uphill all the way to the line. Straight five-furlong races are run from a chute that joins the homestretch.

The first known races at Beverley were held in 1690, but there was no grandstand until 1767. Beverley's 20 days of racing are held from mid-April through late September. Modest maidens and handicaps make up most of the cards. The only black-type race on the Beverley schedule is the listed five-furlong Beverley Bullet Stakes for 3-year-olds and up, run in late August.

TRACK RECORDS

DISTANCE	RECORD TIME	MEDIAN TIME
5f	1:00.10	1:03.50
7½f	1:29.50	1:33.80
1⁄₁₆m	1:42.20	1:47.60
1¼m	2:01.80	2:07.00
1½m	2:30.80	2:40.90

BRIGHTON ≡

Brighton Racecourse
Brighton, East Sussex
England
Phone: 011-44-1273-603-580
Internet: www.brighton-racecourse.co.uk

LOCATION: 53 miles south of London; a one-hour train ride from London Victoria or London Bridge to Brighton Station. The racecourse is a bus or taxi ride from the station.

Brighton might be described as a U-shaped course (or C-shaped, depending on one's point of view), one that resembles an open-ended square. It is 1½ miles long and begins high on a hill above the grandstand. A quarter-mile straight is followed by a 45-degree left-hand bend. A one-furlong straight precedes another mild left-hand bend followed by a five-furlong straight with a slight right-hand bend halfway through. A nearly 90-degree left-hand turn empties into the four-furlong stretch.

The first three furlongs at Brighton are very slightly uphill. The first three furlongs of the stretch are sharply downhill.

Because of its largely downhill nature, times are fast at Brighton, but they are not to be compared to any other track, as the quality of competition here is low-end. Horses who prefer firm ground frequently do well, as the track is 400 feet above sea level and the chalky ground drains quickly.

Racing began at Brighton in 1782 with the Duke of Richmond (founder of Goodwood Racecourse), Sir Charles Bunbury (co-founder of the Epsom Derby), and Colonel Dennis O'Kelly (the owner of Eclipse) all in attendance. Those were the days, as the sport has been strictly second-rate since then, the general atmosphere defined by Graham Greene in his novel *Brighton Rock*, famous for its description of an all too frequent 1950s bloodletting in the bookies' ring.

Things are a bit more civilized nowadays—the White Cliffs of Dover are visible from the top rows of the grandstand—but the racing is reserved for cheap maidens and low-end handicappers.

Brighton conducts 19 days of racing per year between late April and late October, mostly during the week, 12 of them between June and early September when the nice weather attracts people to the nearby beaches and seaside amusements.

In fact, there is as much reason to visit Brighton for those amenities as there is for the racing. A city of 250,000 people, it is home to a rocky beach on the English Channel beloved of working-class Londoners. Brighton Pier, with a myriad of rides and games and the burnt-out hulk of what was once the world-famous West Pier, with its Crystal Palace, turn the beach into something of a 19th-century wonderland. The Royal Pavilion, a gaudy, Orientalist pleasure palace built under the direction of the prince regent between 1815 and 1823, before he became King George IV, is an acquired taste for fans of architectural vulgarity.

TRACK RECORDS

DISTANCE	RECORD TIME	MEDIAN TIME
5f, 59y	59.30	1:02.30
6f	1:07.30	1:10.20
7f	1:19.40	1:23.10
1m	1:30.50	1:36.00
1¼m	1:57.20	2:03.60
1½m	2:25.80	2:32.70

CHEPSTOW

Chepstow Racecourse
Chepstow, Monmouthshire NP16 6BE
Wales
Phone: 011-44-1291-622-260
Internet: www.chepstow-racecourse.co.uk

LOCATION: 131 miles west of London, 28 miles east of the Welsh capital, Cardiff. Trains from London Paddington via Gloucester, which is 34 miles northeast of Chepstow. The track is 1½ miles from Chepstow Station.

Chepstow is an undulating left-handed oval two miles around with a one-mile straight course that leads into the five-furlong stretch. The undulations are as pronounced as can be found on any racecourse in the world. When horses hit the bottom of the dip early in the stretch, they disappear from the view of anyone sitting in the grandstand. The turns are tight, but rarely figure into the outcome due to the very long straights. All races up to a mile are run on the straight course.

Chepstow is a dual-purpose track, in that it conducts both flat and jump racing, with the quality of the jumpers considerably higher than that of the flat horses. The Welsh Grand National is a good steeplechase race run during Christmas Week and is a key early-season prep for Aintree's Grand National. The Finale Juvenile Hurdle, run in April, is Chepstow's only Grade 1 race.

The Golden Daffodil Stakes, a 1¼-mile contest for fillies and mares, was first run in 1994 as a listed race. Although upgraded to Group 3 status in 2003 after having been won by good fillies such as Fiji (subsequent winner of the Gamely and Yellow Ribbon), One So Wonderful, and Albanova, it was discontinued after the 2005 running, leaving the picturesque course without a single black-type event on the flat.

The racecourse in its present incarnation only opened in 1926, making it one of the youngest in Britain. As it lies not far from the frequently overflowing Severn River in a particularly rainy corner of Britain, the ground is frequently soft or worse. Given the quality of the racing there, runners at Chepstow rarely come into play in America.

The track runs 29 days of racing annually, flat meetings from April to October, jump meetings the rest of the year. Nearby attractions include the mammoth ruins of Chepstow Castle on the River Wye. Built in 1067, just a year after the Norman invasion, it was originally used as a Norman defense against the Welsh. The melancholy ruins of the 900-year-old Tintern Abbey, immortalized by J. M. W. Turner on canvas and by William Wordsworth in poetry, lie not far away in the Wye Valley.

TRACK RECORDS

DISTANCE	RECORD TIME	MEDIAN TIME
5f	56.80	59.30
6f	1:08.80	1:12.90
7f	1:19.30	1:23.20
1m	1:31.60	1:36.20
1¼m	2:04.10	2:10.60
1½m	2:31.00	2:39.00

FOLKESTONE ≡

Folkestone Racecourse
Westenhanger, Hythe, Kent
England
Phone: 011-44-1303-266-407
Internet: folkestone-racecourse.co.uk

LOCATION: 76 miles southeast of London. Trains from London Charing Cross to Westenhanger Station. The racecourse is a two-furlong walk from the station and five miles from the town of Folkestone.

Folkestone is a 1⅜-mile, pear-shaped, right-handed course with a seven-furlong straight course that joins with the 2½-furlong stretch. Both the right-handed course and the straight course are undulating. The first furlong of the stretch is uphill, the last 1½ furlongs level. The turns are mild.

The only racecourse in County Kent in southeastern England, Folkestone opened in 1898, replacing the recently closed track at nearby Dover. The closest point on the British map to France, it was thought that the French aristocracy would make a beeline to Folkestone, but that proved to be wishful thinking. Folkestone, a bottom-rung British track of no little charm, conducts 20 days of racing per year, 12 on the flat and eight over jumps.

As at Brighton and Chepstow, modest handicaps dominate the fare, although John Dunlop, who trains at nearby Arundel, and some big Newmarket stables will sometimes send a well-regarded maiden there in search of an easy baptism. One such was the now famous stallion Pivotal, who holds the course record for five furlongs, set when breaking his maiden as a 2-year-old.

TRACK RECORDS

DISTANCE	RECORD TIME	MEDIAN TIME
5f	58.23	1:00.00
6f	1:09.38	1:12.77
7f (Straight)	1:23.76	1:27.30
7f (RH)	1:22.00	—
1⅛m, 149y	1:59.70	2:04.90
1½m	2:33.20	2:40.90

Great Leighs Racecourse
Moulsham Hall Lane
Great Leighs, Chelmsford, Essex CM3 1QP
England
Phone: 011-44-1245-362-412
Internet: www.greatleighs.com

LOCATION: 30 miles northeast of London, 30 miles southwest of Newmarket.

Britain's newest racecourse and the first to open there since Taunton in 1929, Great Leighs is the fifth track with a synthetic surface in England. The first day of racing on April 20, 2008, was an invitees-only affair but served to introduce the fourth Polytrack course in the country. A level, one-mile, left-handed course with a backstretch chute for the start of seven-furlong and one-mile races, Great Leighs has a two-furlong stretch.

The track has the opportunity to become a popular one, situated as it is not far from London in upmarket Essex. It is also conveniently close to Newmarket, so horses have a short ride from England's main training center.

Early days at Great Leighs suggest that the fare at the start of operations is a cut below that of England's two most important Polytrack facilities, Lingfield and Kempton. Optimistic Great Leighs officials, however, have big plans for the future, among them a Breeders' Cup prep card for European horses, a meeting that might go down well with the 2009 Breeders' Cup being scheduled for Santa Anita's synthetic surface.

During its first, shortened year in business, Great Leighs conducted 56 meetings, 32 of those under the lights.

LEICESTER ≡

Leicester Racecourse
Oadby, Leicester, Leicestershire
England
Phone: 011-44-116-271-6515
Internet: www.leicester-racecourse.co.uk

LOCATION: 159 miles west-northwest of London, 24 miles northeast of Coventry. Trains from London St. Pancras to Leicester Station, which is two miles from the racecourse.

Leicester is an oval, some might say rectangular, right-handed course, with a five-furlong stretch and a one-mile straight course. Both the straight course and the 1¾-mile right-handed course are undulating. Twelve-furlong races start at the head of the backstretch and proceed for five furlongs before making a 90-degree right-hand turn into a short straight, then another 90 degree right-hand turn into the long stretch. Constituted as such, Leicester does not stand comparison to any track in North America.

While there has been racing at Leicester since 1603, the present track dates from 1884. The great Gordon Richards rode his first winner there in 1921, and three-time Cheltenham Gold Cup winner Golden Miller won his first hurdle race there in 1931.

The central location of Leicester—it lies in the heart of the Midlands—means that the racecourse attracts the attention of trainers from almost every corner of England. Thus, even though it can rightly be labeled a minor track, the quality of the racing there is frequently rather good. Leicester is just 70 miles from British-racing headquarters at Newmarket, not at all far in a country where some trainers do not hesitate to ship a horse three times that distance if there is a prize worth taking. It is also just 80 miles from Lambourn, the training center near Newbury Racecourse. Moreover, it is only 75 miles from York and 55 miles from Doncaster, not far from the leading training centers in Yorkshire.

The 19 days of flat racing held annually (there are also 11 days of jump racing) at Leicester include just a single listed race, the Leicestershire Stakes, a seven-furlong contest for older horses in late April. Maidens, conditions races, and handicaps, while not on a par with Newmarket or Ascot, are competitive affairs. Any horse that wins a race at those levels at Leicester has probably run against one of

England's more prominent horses at one time or another during his career.

TRACK RECORDS

DISTANCE	RECORD TIME	MEDIAN TIME
5f	57.85	1:00.00
6f	1:09.40	1:13.50
7f	1:20.80	1:26.20
1m, 60y	1:42.49	1:45.10
1¼m	2:02.40	2:07.90
1½m	2:27.10	2:33.90

NEWCASTLE ≡

Newcastle Racecourse
High Gosforth Park
Newcastle-Upon-Tyne
England
Phone: 011-44-191-236-2020
Internet: www.newcastle-racecourse.co.uk

LOCATION: 276 miles north of London, 80 miles north of York, 105 miles southeast of Edinburgh. Trains from London Kings Cross to Newcastle Central. The track is four miles from the station and requires both a subway ride and a bus ride.

Newcastle is a left-handed triangular course, 1¾ miles in circumference. The stretch is four furlongs long and extends to create a one-mile straight course. Some one-mile races are, however, run on the left-handed course as well. The first three furlongs of the stretch are uphill, the final furlong level. The turns, uncustomarily for most British tracks, are banked. Races of 1½ miles start on a straight just around a 90-degree turn from the finish line and proceed for two furlongs before a sweeping left-hand turn onto the backstretch, which is five furlongs long and contains two very mild left-hand bends. The sharp turn for home is slightly longer than a furlong.

Racing began on Newcastle's Town Moor in 1721. The Northumberland Plate, a two-mile handicap run in late June, was first held in 1833 when it was known as the Pitmen's Derby, a salute to the coal-mining industry that made Newcastle famous the world over. Won in 2005 by subsequent Group 1 Prix du Cadran winner Sergeant Cecil, its $400,000 purse makes it the richest handicap race in Britain.

Of greater interest to Americans are the two stakes races run on the same day as the Northumberland Plate. The six-furlong Group 3 Chipchase Stakes, first run in 1994 as a listed race, was upgraded to its current status in 2001 but remains a low-end Group 3 with generally listed-race cache. Also on Plate Day is the listed 1¼-mile Hoppings Stakes for fillies and mares, but it is a race that rarely produces Group or Grade 3 performers.

Situated as it is in the northeastern corner of England on the North Sea coast, there are few other flat tracks in the vicinity, so trainers from that part of the country have only to choose between it and Redcar, 43 miles to the south, for the best local races. Outside of its three-day Northumberland Plate Festival in late June, the quality of the racing at Newcastle is only average.

Newcastle runs 28 days of racing annually.

The city of 200,000 is the home of Newcastle United, who play their Premier League home soccer matches in St. James's Park, but you may search in vain for traces of the Animals and Duran Duran, Newcastle's two most famous rock bands.

TRACK RECORDS

DISTANCE	RECORD TIME	MEDIAN TIME
5f	58.00	1:00.70
6f	1:10.60	1:15.20
7f	1:23.30	1:29.00
1m (Str)	1:37.10	1:43.70
1m (LH)	1:38.90	1:41.90
1⅛m	1:58.40	1:58.10
1¼m	2:06.50	2:13.50

NOTTINGHAM ≡

Nottingham Racecourse
Colwick Park, Nottingham
Nottinghamshire
England
Phone: 011-44-115-958-0620
Internet: www.nottinghamracecourse.co.uk

LOCATION: 135 miles north of London. Trains from London St. Pancras to Nottingham Main Station. The track is two miles from the town center.

Nottingham is a level, 1½-mile left-handed oval with a stretch that measures slightly longer than four furlongs, from which extends the six-furlong straight course. The five-furlong backstretch is a long, very mild left-hand bend, by nature a virtual straight.

Just 25 miles up the road from Leicester, Nottingham benefits from its central location in attracting horses from both Newmarket and Lambourn. In 2003, Three Valleys, the 2005 winner of the Grade 2 Del Mar Breeders' Cup Handicap and Monmouth's Grade 3 Oceanport Handicap, broke his maiden here first time out going six furlongs. That same year, Attraction did likewise going five furlongs, kicking off an eight-race winning streak that climaxed with a Group 1 triple in the 1000 Guineas, the Irish 1000 Guineas, and the Coronation Stakes.

Top trainers such as Saeed bin Suroor, Michael Stoute, Mark Johnston, John Dunlop, and Michael Bell do not hesitate to send young prospects to Nottingham, but fully developed class horses are thin on the ground here, Nottingham's only black-type race being the listed six-furlong Kilvington Stakes for fillies and mares in mid-May.

Nottingham lies in the center of Nottinghamshire, site of Nottingham Forest, where Robin Hood famously robbed from the rich and gave to the poor, but his admirable legacy has gone the way of the long-gone forest. Nowadays at Nottingham it is more a case of the racecourse bookies robbing from the poor (the bettors), and giving to the rich (themselves).

TRACK RECORDS

DISTANCE	RECORD TIME	MEDIAN TIME
5f	57.60	1:00.70
6f	1:10.00	1:15.10
1m, 54y	1:39.60	1:45.60
1¼m	2:02.30	2:10.70

PONTEFRACT ☰

Pontefract Park Race Co. Ltd.
Pontefract, West Yorkshire
England
Phone: 011-44-1977-703-224
Internet: www.pontefract-races.co.uk

LOCATION: 190 miles north of London, about midway between York to the north and Doncaster to the south. Trains from London Kings Cross to Leeds Station. Local train service from Leeds to Baghill Station, Pontefract.

Pontefract is a country track in every sense of the word, laid-back and charming. It can only be described as a left-handed course in the shape of a parallelogram. An undulating course two miles, 121 yards around, 2¼-mile races start at the head of a two-furlong stretch, one of the shortest in Britain. They proceed around a sweeping 135-degree turn onto the three-furlong backstretch (better described as a side-straight), followed by a mild left-hand bend onto a two-furlong straight, a second similar bend onto a one-furlong straight, then a 90-degree turn onto a second three-furlong straight before a final 45-degree bend into the homestretch.

Times are unusually slow at Pontefract, a fact that has less to do with the mediocre quality of the racing than with the nature of the course itself. It is undulating throughout before the final three furlongs, which are stiffly uphill. What's more, the ground is not infrequently on the soft side.

Racing at Pontefract dates back to the English Civil Wars of the 1640s. Even World War II couldn't force Pontefract to close, it being so far out in the country that German bombers preferred the easier targets of London and Liverpool. They might have made the effort, as Pontefract, or Pomfret, as it is popularly called, sits in the midst of industrial Yorkshire, surrounded by power stations and coal mines.

The Pipalong Stakes, a one-mile listed race for older fillies and mares run in early June about a week before Royal Ascot, is Pontefract's lone stakes race. It was won in 2007 by Expensive in a time of 1:44.81 on good-to-firm ground, a perfect example of the slow times the track produces. She was a filly trained in Newmarket by Chris Wall, who thought nothing of sending her the 270-mile round trip in an effort to earn black type.

Pontefract runs 13 days of racing a year between late March and mid-October.

TRACK RECORDS

DISTANCE	RECORD TIME	MEDIAN TIME
5f	1:00.80	1:03.30
6f	1:12.60	1:16.90
1m	1:41.30	1:45.90
1¼m	2:08.20	2:13.70
1½m	2:33.72	2:40.80

REDCAR ≡

Redcar Racecourse
Redcar, Cleveland TS10 2BY
England
Phone: 011-44-1642-484-068
Internet: www.redcarracing.co.uk

LOCATION: 250 miles north of London, 43 miles south of Newcastle. Trains from London Kings Cross to Redcar Central, a five-minute walk to the track.

Redcar is a track seemingly designed on the template of the ancient Roman chariot track, the Circus Maximus, with long straights and tight turns. A 1¾-mile, virtually level left-handed oval, the backstretch is 5½ furlongs in length, the homestretch fully five furlongs, and it is also quite similar to Yarmouth. There is a one-mile straight course that joins the left-handed course at the five-eighths pole.

A modest, privately run racecourse well served by a nearby seaside resort, Redcar's two big races are the $100,000 Zetland Gold Cup, a 1¼-mile handicap run in late May, and the Redcar Two-Year-Old Trophy, a six-furlong listed race for 2-year-olds run in early October. The latter produces a few runners each year for America after they are sold at the Tattersalls October Sale.

TRACK RECORDS

DISTANCE	RECORD TIME	MEDIAN TIME
5f	56.01	58.60
6f	1:08.60	1:11.80
7f	1:21.00	1:24.50
1m	1:32.42	1:38.00
1⅛m	1:50.40	1:53.00
1¼m	2:02.60	2:07.10

RIPON

Ripon Racecourse
Ripon, North Yorkshire
England
Phone: 011-44-1765-602-156
Internet: www.ripon-races.co.uk

LOCATION: 222 miles north of London, 22 miles northwest of York. Trains leave from London Kings Cross to York, then change there for Harrogate Station, 11 miles from Ripon.

Similar to Leicester, Ripon is a 1⅝-mile right-handed oval with long straights and relatively tight turns. The stretch is five furlongs in length and extends to form a six-furlong straight course. The straight course is mildly uphill with a slight dip a furlong from the finish.

Racing began at Ripon during the early years of Charles II's Restoration in 1664, and was the site of the first race restricted to female riders in the emancipated year of 1723. One horrified masculine observer complained that the lady jockeys appeared on the track in "drawers and waistcoats, their shapes transparent." Those were the days.

Set in the beautiful Yorkshire Dales, arguably the prettiest country-side in the world, Ripon's grandstand and outbuildings are bedecked with flowers on each of its 14 days of racing through the warm-weather season between mid-April and early September. A single listed race, the six-furlong Ripon Two-Year-Old Trophy, is one of three annual highlights along with the Ripon Rowels Handicap and the Great St. Wilfred Handicap, all run in August, when the track is at its loveliest.

A city of 17,000, Ripon is the site of Ripon Cathedral. Built by St. Wilfred, its oldest parts date from 672, helping to make Ripon the oldest city in England.

TRACK RECORDS

DISTANCE	RECORD TIME	MEDIAN TIME
5f	57.60	1:00.70
6f	1:09.80	1:13.00
1m	1:36.62	1:41.40
1⅛m	1:50.40	1:53.80
1¼m	2:02.60	2:05.40

SALISBURY ≡

Salisbury Racecourse
Salisbury, Wiltshire SP2 8PN
England
Phone: 011-44-1722-326-461
Internet: www.salisburyracecourse.co.uk

LOCATION: 90 miles west of London. Trains from London Waterloo to Salisbury Station. Buses to the racecourse.

Salisbury is a one-mile straight course with a very slight right-hand bend at the halfway point, from which it is stiffly uphill to the finish. Races of 1½ miles and 1¾ miles begin in front of the grandstand and head in the opposite direction, breaking off onto a right-handed loop that rejoins the straight course 6½ furlongs from home. Races of 1¼ miles actually start on the loop. All races between five furlongs and a mile are run on the uphill straight course.

Located just 35 miles from Lambourn training center, Salisbury attracts many of the same horses as Newbury. The racing here is competitive on a level just below Newbury. Like Ripon, racing at Salisbury is largely a summertime affair with 16 meetings between early May and early October, 11 of them between mid-June and early September.

Some very good horses appear at Salisbury. Sun Chariot, Mill Reef, and Brigadier Gerard ran there, as well as subsequent four-time Group 1 winner Dylan Thomas, who finished a neck second to Blitzkrieg as a 2-year-old in the Group 3 one-mile Autumn Stakes in August 2005. The two-day Salisbury Summer Festival in mid-August features the Group 3 one-mile Sovereign Stakes for 3-year-olds and up and the listed 1¼-mile Upavon Stakes for fillies and mares, the latter always seeming to produce one or two eventual runners in America.

But any given maiden or conditions race at Salisbury throughout the year can yield some nice horses that could make useful types in the U.S. The stiff uphill finish of the course almost guarantees that if a horse can win at a given distance at Salisbury, he can win going at least another furlong in the States.

Bettors looking for spiritual guidance prior to racing, or consolation afterward, have two surefire options. One is Salisbury Cathedral, whose steeple is the tallest in Britain. The other is Stonehenge, the 4,200-year-old prehistoric monument located eight miles north of the city.

Racing at Salisbury doesn't go back as far as that, but it does date to the time of Elizabeth I, who was in attendance in May 1588 to see the Golden Ball Stakes. History of a more recent sort was made at Salisbury on April 7, 1979, when Steve Cauthen made his British and European debut, winning aboard Marquee Universal, the future winner of Pimlico's Grade 2 Dixie Handicap and Belmont's Grade 3 Edgemere Handicap.

TRACK RECORDS

DISTANCE	RECORD TIME	MEDIAN TIME
5f	59.30	1:00.80
6f	1:11.30	1:14.80
7f	1:24.90	1:29.00
1m	1:38.29	1:43.50
1¼m	2:04.90	2:09.90
1½m	2:31.60	2:38.00

THIRSK ▤

Thirsk Racecourse
Thirsk, North Yorkshire YO7 1QL
England
Phone: 011-44-1845-522-276
Internet: www.thirskracecourse.net

LOCATION: 227 miles north of London, 24 miles northwest of York. Trains from London Kings Cross to Thirsk Station, a half-mile from the racecourse.

Thirsk is as American a course as tracks can get in Britain. A left-handed oval, it is virtually level, 1¼ miles around with a half-mile stretch that is very slightly uphill. The stretch extends to form a six-furlong straight course.

But do not think that its rough similarity to Woodbine or Belmont means that you should plunge on any British import that has won at Thirsk. The occasional hot maiden here is more than outweighed by the average Yorkshire fare. Trainers based at Newmarket and Lambourn, from where the majority of future American winners hail, send horses to Thirsk only occasionally, and then usually to plunder some modest handicap.

Founded in 1855, Thirsk is one of the most charming racetracks in England. It conducts 15 days of racing per year between late April and mid-September in front of a faux-Tudor-style grandstand that adds an old-fashioned country feel to the proceedings.

Thirsk ran a substitute St. Leger Stakes in 1940 but the best races there nowadays are midlevel handicaps on a par with high-end claimers in New York or southern California.

TRACK RECORDS

DISTANCE	RECORD TIME	MEDIAN TIME
5f	56.10	59.60
6f	1:08.80	1:12.70
7f	1:22.80	1:27.20
1m	1:34.80	1:40.10
1½m	2:29.90	2:36.20

WARWICK

Warwick Racecourse
Warwick, Warwickshire
England
Phone: 011-44-1926-491-553
Internet: www.warwickracecourse.co.uk

LOCATION: 94 miles northwest of London. Trains from London Paddington to Warwick Station.

Warwick (pronounced WAR-ick) is a 1¾-mile left-handed track, vaguely resembling a parallelogram with a relatively short stretch of two furlongs. The five-furlong course makes a left-hand bend into the stretch. One-mile races start from a short chute at a point farthest from the grandstand, proceeding straight for five furlongs before making a rather tight left-hand turn into the stretch.

The track favors close-coupled, speedy types to the disadvantage of long-striding gallopers.

They have been racing in Warwick since the early 18th century. The quality of the flat racing is moderate; the jump racing, which shares equally in the 24 annual days of sport, is slightly better. The main flat fixture is the listed seven-furlong, 26-yard Eternal Stakes for 3-year-old fillies, run generally the day after Royal Ascot closes, when horses not good enough to run at the Royal Meeting are looking for spots.

For a city of just 25,000, Warwick is an awfully smart little place. The track is very close to the 11th-century Warwick Castle and not far from the 14th-century Lord Leycester Hospital, one of the oldest health-care centers in the world still in use.

TRACK RECORDS

DISTANCE	RECORD TIME	MEDIAN TIME
5f (Str)	57.80	59.60
5½f	1:03.60	1:05.90
6f, 21y	1:09.60	1:12.10
7f, 26y	1:21.20	1:24.60
1m	1:37.10	1:41.00
1⅜m	2:16.20	2:21.10

WINDSOR ▤

Royal Windsor Racecourse
Windsor, Berkshire
England
Phone: 011-44-1753-498-400
Internet: www.windsor-racecourse.co.uk

LOCATION: 28 miles west of London, eight miles east of Ascot. Trains go from London Waterloo to Windsor Eton Riverside, from which a pleasant 10-minute boat ride on the Thames brings you to the main gate. Trains also depart London Paddington for Windsor Eton Central and the boat ride.

Windsor is one of only two remaining figure-eight courses in England, the other being the steeplechase course at Fontwell Park. It is one mile, 4½ furlongs around, although the longest races start at the head of the "backstretch" and are just 1⅜ miles, 135 yards—about 1⁷⁄₁₆ miles long. Such races make a mild left-hand bend before crossing the homestretch. They then proceed rather more sharply right-handed before making an even sharper right-handed loop into the stretch, which is 4½ furlongs long. The straight course, used for five- and six-furlong sprints, joins the homestretch.

The largely disused "Royal" in Windsor's moniker persists because of the track's proximity to Windsor Castle. It is from the castle that the Royal Family leaves each morning by horse-drawn carriage for the eight-mile ride to Royal Ascot. Henry VIII, he of the many wives, and Charles II, he of the many mistresses, raced at earlier incarnations of Windsor.

The present course dates from 1866 and is famous for its Monday-evening meetings throughout the spring and summer. Windsor ran 25 days of racing in 2007, 21 of them on Mondays, and 16 of those in the evening, all races run before sundown, which comes as late as 9:45 P.M. in midsummer England.

Because it is just 38 miles from Lambourn training center and even closer to the minor training facility at Epsom, Windsor attracts a good class of horse. While it cannot possibly be compared to Ascot, the quality of the racing at the maiden and condition-race levels is quite good. Moreover, the sharpish nature of the track with its tight turns means that a horse that has adapted itself to Windsor and done well will have no trouble with the tight turns on American turf courses.

The big day at Windsor is the last Saturday in August. An evening meeting, it features the 1¼-mile Group 3 Winter Hill Stakes for 3-year-olds and up. It has been won in 10 of the 13 years through 2007 by either Michael Stoute or Saeed bin Suroor, an indication that it is a better than average Group 3 affair.

Annus Mirabilis won the Winter Hill three years in a row from 1996 through 1998 for Godolphin. In 2005 it fell to the Andrew Reid-trained Eccentric, since then the winner of the Group 3 Fayette Stakes on the Keeneland Polytrack as well as the Group 2 King Edward Breeders' Cup and the Group 3 Connaught Cup on turf at Woodbine.

As most of the race meetings at Windsor are evening affairs starting at about 6:00 P.M., it is worth visiting Windsor Castle before the races. The huge 900-year-old edifice is one of Queen Elizabeth II's four official residences but is open to the public, although parts of the castle and sometimes all of it are closed when she is present, as she is during Royal Ascot.

Eton, the elite prep school famous for its playing fields, borders Windsor across the Thames.

RECORD TIMES

DISTANCE	RECORD TIME	MEDIAN TIME
5f	58.75	1:00.30
6f	1:10.06	1:13.00
1m, 67y	1:40.27	1:44.70
1¼m	2:03.00	2:08.70
1⁷⁄₁₆m	2:21.50	2:29.50

WOLVERHAMPTON ≡

Wolverhampton Racecourse
Dunstall Park
Wolverhampton
England
Phone: 011-44-8702-202-442
Internet: www.wolverhampton-racecourse.co.uk

LOCATION: 132 miles northwest of London, 89 miles southeast of Liverpool. Trains from London Euston to Wolverhampton Station, buses to the racecourse.

Wolverhampton very closely resembles an American racetrack. A one-mile, left-handed Polytrack oval, the stretch is a very Del Mar-like 1½ furlongs. Thirty-seven of Wolverhampton's 90 meetings in 2007 were evening affairs run under the lights. That just 30 of those dates fell between May and September is an indication of the level of the sport, since the quality of flat racing in England during the winter is low. Just as "all-weather" racing is the bottom end in Britain, wintertime "all-weather" racing is the bottom of the bottom.

The best Polytrack racing in England is at Lingfield and Kempton. At Wolverhampton, where the track is considered a bit slower than at those two southern tracks, there is little to recommend vis-à-vis American racing. Racing at Southwell, Britain's only Fibresand track, is cheaper still, the track notoriously slow.

TRACK RECORDS

DISTANCE	RECORD TIME	MEDIAN TIME
5f, 20y	1:00.56	1:02.30
6f	1:12.61	1:15.00
7f, 32y	1:26.86	1:29.60
1m, 141y	1:48.08	1:50.50
1³⁄₁₆m	1:57.34	2:01.70

YARMOUTH ☰

Yarmouth Racecourse
Great Yarmouth, Norfolk
England
Phone: 011-44-1493-842-257
Internet: www.greatyarmouth-racecourse.co.uk

LOCATION: 126 miles northeast of London, 68 miles northeast of Newmarket. Trains from London Liverpool Street to Yarmouth Station, one mile from the racecourse.

Yarmouth is a level 1½-mile, left-handed oval. The straights are 5½ furlongs long, the American-style turns are tight, barely 1½ furlongs each. The straight course is one mile in length and joins the stretch at the five-eighths pole. All races up to a mile are run on the straight course.

Founded in 1715, Yarmouth is a seaside track, the far turn just a stone's throw from the North Sea. The town is officially called Great Yarmouth, but is always referred to simply as Yarmouth.

Because of its proximity to Newmarket, maiden races at Yarmouth frequently feature some very nice young horses. Ouija Board won first time out here in 2003, while Warrshan, subsequently a Group 3 winner and Group 1-placed, still holds the track mark for six furlongs—1:10 flat—set in 1988 in his career debut. While most of the best Yarmouth maiden winners graduate immediately to better things at Newmarket, Ascot, or other top tracks, the lesser among that group do return to Yarmouth for allowance races and nursery handicaps. Yarmouth form at these levels is not to be sneezed at. In fairness, however, it must be pointed out that many of Newmarket's lesser lights are to be found in the Yarmouth starting gate as well, as the competition there is considerably easier than it is at "headquarters," as Newmarket is known to British racing professionals.

Because it lies so close to Yarmouth's sandy beaches, the track is dry by nature and drains quickly, so that good and good-to-firm ground, sometimes even firm ground, is commonplace. There are 20 days of racing per year at Yarmouth from April through October. The main meeting is the three-day Eastern Festival in mid-September, during which the listed 1¼-mile John Musker Stakes for fillies and mares is run.

TRACK RECORDS

DISTANCE	RECORD TIME	MEDIAN TIME
5f, 43y	1:00.20	1:02.20
6f	1:10.00	1:14.40
7f	1:22.12	1:26.60
1m	1:33.90	1:40.60
1¼m	2:02.83	2:10.50
1⁷⁄₁₆m	2:23.31	2:28.70

AINTREE ≡

Aintree Racecourse
Ormskirk Road
Aintree, Liverpool
England
Phone: 011-44-151-523-2600
Internet: www.aintree.co.uk

LOCATION: Three miles north of central Liverpool, 225 miles northwest of London. From London's Euston Station, go to Lyme Street Station in Liverpool. Then take the local train from Liverpool's Central Station to Aintree Station, adjacent to the racecourse entrance.

The home of England's most popular race, the Grand National Steeplechase Handicap, Aintree actually has two courses. The regular steeplechase course and the hurdle course outside of that are 1¼-mile, left-handed affairs. The fences on the chase course are standard, like those at all other British jumps courses.

The National Course, over which the Grand National itself is run, is a 2¼-mile left-handed track featuring many of the most prodigious fences in the world.

Becher's Brook—which, like most National Course obstacles, must be jumped twice during the 4½-mile Grand National—is 5½ feet high but the ground is 21 inches lower on the landing side, which slopes down into a water-filled ditch. The five-foot Canal Turn requires horses to make a quick 90-degree turn immediately after jumping it. Valentine's Brook is "only" five feet high but comes with a 5½-foot-wide brook on the landing side.

At five feet, the next fence is hardly intimidating, but is infamous for the carnage it caused in 1967 when virtually the entire field was brought down or severely hampered, allowing the 100–1 Foinavon to win by 15 lengths. The fence is now called the Foinavon after the luckiest winner in the Grand National's 170-year history.

Perhaps the most daunting fence on the course is the Chair, so called because many horses wind up sitting in it. It is five feet, two inches high, but is by far the widest fence on the course and is fronted by a six-foot open ditch. Situated in front of the stands, it is one of only two fences on the course that is jumped just once, the other being the very next, the 2½-foot-high water jump that is equipped with a 12½-foot swimming pool on the landing side.

Statue of Red Rum at Aintree

Vincent O'Brien won the Grand National three times in a row in the early 1950s with Early Mist, Royal Tan, and Quare Times. Americans have been successful twice, with Mary Stephenson's Jay Trump winning in 1965 and the Redmond Stewart-owned, Charlie Fenwick-trained Ben Nevis landing it in 1980.

A year later Aldiniti scored a famous victory for his courageous rider, Bob Champion, who had battled back from cancer for the ultimate sporting triumph of his career.

But the greatest of all Grand National winners was Red Rum. Trained in Ireland by Ginger McCain, the gallant gelding won it in 1973 and 1974, finished second to Cheltenham Gold Cup winner L'Escargot the next year, and second to Rag Trade the year after that. Surely the most popular victory in the history of the race came in 1977 when Red Rum won it for the third time, the only horse ever to do so.

Catastrophes abound in a race of the Grand National's nature, but the most confounding fiasco of all came in 1993 when the race was declared void after many of its starters got tangled in the starting tape. Most of the horses proceeded to run anyway in the biggest embarrassment to which the race has ever been partner.

The Grand National Meeting, held on the first weekend in April unless Easter falls on the first Sunday of the month, is a three-day, Thursday-Friday-Saturday fixture chock full of championship-caliber hurdle and chase events. They feature a number of horses fresh from Cheltenham's National Hunt Festival two or three weeks earlier.

CHELTENHAM ☰

Cheltenham Racecourse
Prestbury Park
Cheltenham, Gloucestershire
England
Phone: 011-44-1242-513-124
Internet: www.cheltenham.co.uk

LOCATION: In England's west country, nine miles east of Gloucester, 100 miles west of London. From London Paddington Station go to Cheltenham Station, from where it is a cab ride into the town center. From there it is a pleasant 20-minute walk to the racecourse through Cheltenham, which is renowned for its Regency Era (1811–20) architecture.

If there is a more beautiful racecourse in the world than Cheltenham, humans have yet to set eyes upon it. Set in the rolling hills of the Cotswolds, the racecourse gives new meaning to the word *picturesque*. While most of the world's prettiest tracks must content themselves with a backdrop of trees or hedges, Cheltenham was built at the foot of a green swath of hill dotted with ancient stone houses and churches, topped by an outcropping of white rock.

The perfect setting for the world's most important jump-race meeting, the National Hunt Festival, Cheltenham puts the lie to the commonly held but misinformed opinion in America that jump racing is inferior to flat racing.

The jewel in Britain's glittering jump-racing industry, the National Hunt Festival, is a mid-March meeting held under frequently appalling conditions 100 miles from London on four weekday afternoons well removed from any holiday season. Yet it regularly attracts daily crowds of between 50,000 and 60,000 jump-racing fanatics, at least 10,000 of whom are Irish, all of whom pay an average of more than $75 a day just to get through the gates.

It is money well spent, for the National Hunt Festival is simply the most exciting race meeting on the planet. Breeders' Cup, Royal Ascot, and Arc Weekend, eat your hearts out.

The three big races at the festival are the 2¹⁄₁₆-mile Champion Hurdle, the two-mile Queen Mother Champion Chase, and the 3⁵⁄₁₆-mile Cheltenham Gold Cup, Britain's championship steeplechase and arguably the world's most important jump race.

First run in 1924, the Gold Cup has had more than its share of great and glorious winners. Golden Miller put the race on the map, winning it five times in a row from 1932 through 1936. Vincent O'Brien won it three times in succession as a trainer from 1948 through 1950 with Cottage Rake. Mandarin won it in 1962, prior to his remarkable reinless victory in the Grand Steeple-Chase de Paris. The next year Mill House looked set to become the greatest chaser of all time, until he was beaten in 1964 by Arkle, who *did* prove to be the greatest chaser of all time with subsequent victories in 1965 and 1966.

L'Escargot, the only horse to win both the Gold Cup and the Grand National, took Cheltenham honors in both 1970 and 1971. Michael Dickinson made history in his own inimitable way by training the first five across the line in 1983: Bregawn; Captain John; Wayward Lad; his 1982 winner, Silver Buck; and Ashley House.

Desert Orchid was front-page news for weeks throughout Britain after his Gold Cup victory in 1989. The Fellow broke the Gold Cup ice for France in 1994 when the Francois Doumen trainee won it after a pair of second-place finishes. More recently, Best Mate emulated Cottage Rake and Arkle by winning it three times in succession from 2002 through 2004.

Vincent wasn't the only O'Brien to hone his training skills in the jumping world. Aidan O'Brien bid jumping farewell in 2000 with his third straight win with Istabraq in the Champion Hurdle.

But it is a mare who is the only horse to win both the Champion Hurdle and the Gold Cup. The legendary, ill-fated Dawn Run, trained in Ireland by Paddy Mullins and ridden by Jonjo O'Neill, took the Champion in 1984 and the Gold Cup two years later. Sadly, she would die a few months after her Gold Cup victory in a fall at Auteuil while seeking a repeat of her 1984 victory in the Grand Course de Haies d'Auteuil, the French Champion Hurdle.

Her statue stands near the Cheltenham paddock, across from that of Arkle.

Racing history is made at Cheltenham every day at each year's Festival. The flavor of jump racing seeps deeply into the bones of the National Hunt Festival racegoer. Just ask anyone who's ever been there. They will tell you that there is no other place to be in middle March, not even heaven itself.

2

France

CHANTILLY ☰

Hippodrome Chantilly
16 Avenue du General Leclerc
60631 Chantilly, France
Phone: 011-33-44-62-41-00
France-Galop phone: 011-33-1-49-10-20-30
Internet: www.france-galop.com

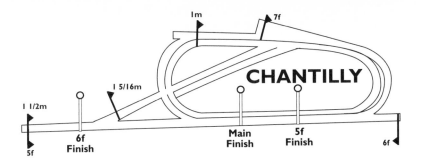

LOCATION: 32 miles north of Paris.

COURSE DESCRIPTION: Chantilly is a right-handed 1¼-mile oval. The Piste du Jockey-Club, over which the Prix du Jockey-Club, or French Derby, was run at 1½ miles until 2005, when it was reduced to 1⁵⁄₁₆ miles, begins at the head of the straight course, but veers left for six furlongs before joining the right-handed course at the six-furlong pole. After a one-furlong straight it makes a right-handed, 1½-furlong turn, the first half of which is downhill, the second half uphill, from which point it enters the three-furlong stretch, which is mildly uphill for a furlong before leveling off.

Since 2005, the Prix du Jockey-Club has been run at 1⁵⁄₁₆ miles, the distance of its fellow classic, the Prix de Diane, or French Oaks. Both races now start 1½ furlongs past the old Jockey-Club start.

One-mile races start on the backstretch, proceeding straight for 3½ furlongs before making the same right-hand turn as longer races. Races of five and six furlongs are run on the straight course in front of the grandstand. This straight also forms part of the right-handed course's homestretch. Sprints at Chantilly are sometimes run left-to-right, finishing in the middle of the homestretch; sometimes right-to-left, finishing well up the track beyond the grandstand.

HISTORY: The racecourse at Chantilly (pronounced Shahn-TEE-ee) first opened its doors on May 15, 1834, six months after the founding of the French Jockey Club, the *societe d'encouragement pour l'amelioration et le perfectionnement des races de chevaux en France* (society for the encouragement of the improvement and perfection of the breed in France), or, in parlance, the Societe d'Encouragement.

Founded under the auspices of the Francophile Englishman Lord Henry Seymour, the Societe d'Encouragement was as much a social club as a racing club. Membership admitted a man into an elite world where business and political deals could be hatched away from the eyes of an interfering public.

Two years later, in 1836, the inaugural Prix du Jockey-Club, patterned precisely on the template set by the Epsom Derby, was run. Worth 5,000 francs, it was won, appropriately enough, by a colt named Frank, but a year later the filly Lydia became the first of seven members of her sex to win it, the most recent being La Morniere, way back in 1900. Lydia was also the first in a long line of elite distaffers to win big French races open to both sexes.

It was Lord Seymour who imported the British stallion Royal Oak to France. Royal Oak would sire three French Derby winners, but the first Epsom Derby winner to sire a French Derby winner was Emilius, the 1823 Epsom laureate whose son Gambetti won the French edition in 1848.

The 1855 winner, Monarque, will go down in history as the sire of Gladiateur, who in 1865 became the first French-bred to win the Epsom Derby. Gladiateur's damsire, Gladiator, was himself the sire of

The field passes the Grandes Ecuries on the Chantilly backstretch.

two French Derby winners while Monarque would sire two others. One of those, the 1869 laureate, Consul, would sire two French Derby winners of his own, an indication that the Societe really was improving the breed.

Some of that improvement can be credited to Omnium II. The winner of the 1895 Prix du Jockey-Club would later win the 2½-mile Prix du Cadran as well as the 3⅞-mile Prix Gladiateur. A great source of stamina, Omnium II was the sire of the filly Kizil Kourgan, the winner of both the Prix de Diane and the Grand Prix de Paris, and was the damsire of the Grand Prix de Paris winner and French foundation stallion Bruleur.

The Prix Omnium II, a listed prep for the French 2000 Guineas run at Saint-Cloud, hit the international headlines in 1991 when Francois Boutin used it as the Kentucky Derby prep for his tearaway Breeders' Cup Juvenile winner, Arazi. The diminutive chestnut breezed to an easy victory on heavy ground but came a cropper at Churchill Downs.

War has frequently interfered with racing at Chantilly. The Prix du Jockey-Club was canceled in 1871 as Prussian forces surrounded the Paris region following their quick victory in the Franco-Prussian War. There was no racing at all at Chantilly between 1915 and 1918 due to World War I. The race was canceled again in 1940, but the uncomfortable truce imposed by the occupying German forces during World War II allowed racing to proceed through the end of hostilities in 1945.

At the conclusion of the First World War, the 1920s ushered in the modern age of French racing with a bang. A good part of the reason was the establishment of the Prix de l'Arc de Triomphe as a late-season championship race at Longchamp. The 1921 Prix du Jockey-Club winner, Ksar, a son of Bruleur, won the Arc that same year and again in 1922. Mon Talisman pulled off the double in 1927 and there has been no turning back. Nine horses have won both races, most recently Peintre Celebre in 1997 and Montjeu in 1999.

The 1931 Jockey-Club winner, Tourbillon, himself a son of Ksar, sired two Jockey-Club winners but is most notable as the sire of Djebel, the winner of both the English and French 2000 Guineas in 1940 and the Prix de l'Arc de Triomphe two years later and five times the leading sire in France.

Tourbillon was the first of 12 Prix du Jockey-Club winners owned by the great owner-breeder Marcel Boussac; the last was Acamas in 1978.

The French Derby scored a moral victory in 1970 when Sassafras upset the seemingly invincible British Triple Crown winner Nijinsky in the Arc, but the Epsom Derby is still generally considered to be a slightly superior race, although French winner Suave Dancer gave favored English winner Generous a sound beating in the 1991 Arc.

The influence of the Prix du Jockey-Club on American racing in recent years has been spotty. The 2002 winner, Sulamani, a son of 1993 winner Hernando, did win the Arlington Million a year later via the disqualification of Storming Home. And 1993 runner-up Dernier Empereur won the Del Mar Handicap three years later. Perhaps the reason for the lack of French Derby winners—or even placed horses—in America has to do with the fact that it is such an important race for French breeders, who tend to keep their stock close to home. That was never more obvious than in 1984, when it was won by the Aga Khan's Darshaan, who defeated Sadler's Wells and Rainbow Quest. All three would go on to become superb European-based stallions.

The Prix de Diane, or French Oaks, was inaugurated seven years after the first running of the Jockey-Club in 1843. Winners through its first century include fillies that have since had stakes races named after them: Finlande (1861), Fille de l'Air (1864), La Jonchere (1877), La Camargo (1901), and Rose de Mai (1903).

In 1973, Allez France ushered the Diane into the modern age of international racing with her brilliant two-length victory over the great Dahlia, a filly who would later win the Irish Oaks, the King George VI and Queen Elizabeth Diamond Stakes, and the Washington, D.C., International. The victory of Pawneese two years later presaged her victory in the Prix de l'Arc de Triomphe. In 1977, runner-up Trillion was the winner of nine Group 1 or Grade 1 races. April Run, who finished third in 1981, would twice win the Turf Classic when it was America's best grass race. And 1982 runner-up Akiyda would win the Arc that same year.

In 1987, runner-up Miesque didn't quite stay 1⁵⁄16 miles, but it might be said that she was the world's best miler over the last 25 years.

French Oaks winners since the great decades of the 1970s and 80s have been good, but perhaps only 2005 winner Divine Proportions and 2008 winner Zarkava could match the best of them. Divine Proportions, however, never got a chance to prove her greatness in the autumn, as she was retired prematurely due to injury.

The Diane, however, has become a very important race vis-à-vis America since the turn of the century. Thirty-five runners in the French fillies' classic from 2000 through 2006 have run at least once in North America. They include nine who have won stakes races here: Latice, Dreams Come True, Asti, Colony Band, Musical Chimes, Arvada, Turtle Bow, Mariensky, Commercante, and Choc Ice, the last two both successful in Woodbine's E. P. Taylor Stakes.

Until the 1990s, Chantilly conducted no more than six days of racing per year, all of them in June, despite the fact that the town serves as France's major training center. Chantilly was used strictly for the Derby and the Oaks, plus a few more days scattered before, between, and after the two big days, which almost always fall on the first Sunday in June (Derby) and the second Sunday of that month (Oaks).

Contemporary economics insist on a more efficient use of properties as large as that of a racecourse. Chantilly now runs approximately 24 days of racing per year, a few less than the other major tracks on the Parisian circuit—Longchamp, Saint-Cloud, Maisons-Laffitte, and Deauville.

ANALYSIS: That French imports do better in America than their British and Irish counterparts there is no doubt. From the top level down, French raiders and French imports have proven again and again that they adapt to American conditions—and outclass the opposition—more frequently than horses from any other country.

Take the Breeders' Cup. Through 2008, horses trained in France or formerly trained in France had won 23 Cup races, while 18 British or ex-British horses had done likewise, and the Irish and the ex-Irish had won just six Cup races.

Long observation and experience lead one to the conclusion that

French imports do as well in lesser races, too. The Turf Classic score is France 9, Britain 2, Ireland 1. In the Arlington Million it is France 8 (after Spirit One's 2008 victory), Britain 5, Ireland 1, Germany 1.

In lesser graded stakes and at the allowance level it is much the same story. The key to understanding this phenomenon lies in understanding the nature of French racing's infrastructure.

In Europe, racetracks do not run meetings for six, 10, or 12 weeks with live racing five or six days per week, then switch to another nearby regional track for another three months of the same.

Meetings in Europe are short. Each track might run for two or three days at a time, then not have another meeting for two weeks. Many tracks in England run just once a week, or twice in one week, then take two or three weeks off before resuming for a one- or two-day meeting.

In France, virtually all the best races are run on what is properly called the Parisian circuit, consisting of five tracks: Longchamp on the western edge of Paris, Chantilly north of Paris, Saint-Cloud in the suburbs just west of Paris, and Maisons-Laffitte further west of Paris, plus Deauville northwest of Paris on the Normandy coast.

While England's main training centers, Newmarket and Lambourn, are 100 miles apart, the main training centers in France, Chantilly and Maisons-Laffitte, are less than half that. More importantly, in England, quality meetings are spread across the country, especially in the south of England, with a certain balance. The top meeting one day may be at Newmarket; the next day, three days at York; the following day at Sandown; the two days after that at Ascot.

In the meantime, there are plenty of decent maidens, allowances, handicaps, and listed races that might be run on any of those days at lesser British tracks. Thus, the British trainer has more opportunities to find a spot for his horses, which is a nice way of saying that he has more chances of dodging the opposition.

In Ireland, the sport is dominated by four trainers: Aidan O'Brien, Dermot Weld, John Oxx, and Jim Bolger. The quality of competition tends to drop off rather markedly wherever there is a race that has not attracted a horse trained by one of those Big Four.

In France, one or another of the five major courses is open at least three or four days a week between April and November. While a top French trainer such as Andre Fabre or Alain de Royer-Dupre might send a horse to Compiegne or Fontainebleau for a maiden or an allowance, most of the time the Chantilly/Maisons-Laffitte conditioners stick to the major Parisian circuit. As trainers there control most of the best horses in France, there will obviously be far fewer chances of dodging the competition than there are in Britain, Ireland, or almost anyplace else in the world, save tiny Hong Kong.

Given the generally high quality of the French-trained Thoroughbred, it follows that a horse trained in France that competes on the Parisian circuit will have more condition under his belt after just three or four races than almost any other Thoroughbred in the world. Whether he is running in maidens, allowances, handicaps, listed races, or group races, whether he is a 2-year-old or a 3-year-old, whether he is a sprinter, a miler, a middle-distance horse, or a stayer, a horse on the Parisian circuit meets a larger number of the better members of his division more frequently than horses trained in any other major racing nation.

Given the far-flung nature of racing in the United States, where the best horses are divided among New York, southern California, and Kentucky, with some nice ones competing in Illinois, New Jersey, Maryland, Louisiana, and Florida, is it any wonder that the battle-tested but relatively lightly raced French racehorse does so well in America?

This is certainly true of Chantilly, whose racetrack lies just a short drive from the town's training facilities. But it is equally true of Longchamp and Deauville, as well as Saint-Cloud and Maisons-Laffitte, two tracks that may not have the group-race cache of Longchamp, Chantilly, or Deauville, but nevertheless conduct races at the maiden, allowance, and handicap levels that are just as good.

Chantilly itself produces maidens and allowance races the equal of Longchamp. This is a rather self-evident statement, given the proximity of so many of France's best trainers. Here is a summary of the best of them.

- **ANDRE FABRE:** Perhaps the best trainer in the world, Fabre has been champion conditioner in France for 20 years dating back to 1988. Napoleonic in stature as well as talent, the diminutive Fabre started his Thoroughbred career, like so many successful trainers, as a jumps jockey, winning France's champion chase race, the Grand Steeple-Chase de Paris on Corps a Corps in 1977 at the age of 31. He began his training career on the jump circuit, winning the French championship six times and the Grand Steeple itself four times in a row from 1980 through 1983.

  His achievements as a flat trainer are unparalleled in French racing history. Through 2007 he had trained the winners of seven

Arcs, nine Grand Prix de Paris, four French 2000 Guineas, two French 1000 Guineas, five Prix Jacques le Marois, five Prix du Moulin de Longchamps, five Grand Prix de Saint-Clouds, six Prix Royal-Oaks, and seven Prix Saint-Alarys, not to mention three French Oaks and a French Derby.

In England his record is better than that of most British trainers. He has taken the Coronation Cup six times, the 2000 Guineas twice, the Champion Stakes twice, plus a King George VI and Queen Elizabeth Diamond Stakes, a St. Leger, and an English Oaks. Two Irish Derby winners and an Irish Oaks winner, plus an Italian Derby and an Italian Oaks, give him a total of 19 European classic triumphs.

In America he has won four Breeders' Cup races—more than any other foreign trainer—plus an Arlington Million.

His best horses include Apple Tree, Arcangues, Banks Hill, Hurricane Run, In the Wings, Intrepidity, Jolypha, Manduro, Peintre Celebre, Pennekamp, Swain, Soviet Star, Xaar, and Zafonic.

As Fabre is the French trainer for Khalid Abdullah's Juddmonte Farms, many Fabre-trained horses are ultimately switched to Juddmonte's American trainer, Bobby Frankel. Frankel's record speaks for itself, as does that of Fabre.

■ **ALAIN DE ROYER-DUPRE:** The Aga Khan's trainer in France since 1981 has saddled the winners of 17 French classics, seven more than Fabre. This may be because the Aga Khan's breeding operation is geared toward winning classics more than any other French outfit. The trainer's big-race triumphs include that of Arc winner Dalakhani as well as the great distaffers Darjina, Kartajana, Mandesha, Pride, and Zarkava. He trained the Aga's foundation sire, Darshaan, to win the Criterium de Saint-Cloud and the Prix du Jockey-Club.

He also trained the Aga's Lashkari to win the first Breeders' Cup Turf. The Aga Khan, however, has tended to avoid American racing in recent years due to the lenient medication rules here, so Royer-Dupre's horses are rarely seen in America anymore.

■ **PASCAL BARY:** Began training in 1981 after serving his apprenticeship under Francois Boutin; since then, he has won the French Derby six times. He won the Breeders' Cup Mile twice in succession with Six Perfections in 2003 and Domedriver in 2004. Like Boutin before him, he is the number one French conditioner for the Niarchos family, for whom he trained Divine Proportions to win the French 1000 Guineas and the French Oaks in 2005. In 2008 he pulled off a British coup when his Natagora won the 1000 Guineas just seven months after her first Group 1 victory in Newmarket's Cheveley Park Stakes. She followed with a game third in the French Derby, the best finish by a filly in that race in more than a hundred years.

■ **ROBERT COLLET:** Best known in America for his 1986 Breeders' Cup Mile win with the five-furlong sprinter Last Tycoon, Collet had, a year earlier, trained River Memories to win the Rothmans (now Canadian) International. In 1987 he achieved the remarkable feat of training Le Glorieux to win Group or Grade 1 races on three different continents: the Grosser Preis von Berlin in Europe, the Washington, D.C., International in North America, and the Japan Cup in Asia. That at a time when it was considerably more difficult to ship horses around the world than it is now. More recently he turned a trick of a different sort with Whipper, saddling him to win Group 1 races in France in three straight years: the Prix Morny as a 2-year-old in 2003, followed by the Prix Jacques le Marois at 3 and the Prix Maurice de Gheest at 4.

While certainly one of the world's most notable trainers, Collet trains a large stable of workaday horses that compete regularly in handicaps at every level.

■ **CHRISTIANE "CRIQUETTE" HEAD-MAAREK:** A member of the originally English Head family, which has played such a prominent role in French racing since the 1920s, Head-Maarek is simply the greatest female trainer in Thoroughbred history. Among her numerous clients is her father, the owner of Haras du Quesnay. Among the many riders she has employed, perhaps the most notable is her brother, Freddy. Her first and only Arc winner came in 1979 with Three Troikas, who was bred by her father, Alec, owned by her mother, Ghislaine, and ridden by her brother. She married her second husband, Gilles Maarek, in 2000.

Illness has forced her to cut back somewhat on her training responsibilities in recent years, during which time she lost the services of the powerful Wertheimer brothers, but she continues to train for Khalid Abdullah.

She has won the French Oaks with Harbour and Egyptband, the French 2000 Guineas with American Post, and the French Derby with Bering. She has always had a particular way with fillies, winning the Prix de l'Opera five times and the French 1000 Guineas six times, among her winners Three Troikas, Baiser Vole, and Ravinella.

■ **FREDDY HEAD:** The winner of four Arcs, four French Derbies, four French Oaks, six French 1000 Guineas, and seven French

2000 Guineas as a jockey, Freddy Head will never be forgotten in America as the rider of the great Miesque, who twice strolled away with the Breeders' Cup Mile.

He retired from the saddle in 1997 and has been training since. Among his owners are Sheikh Hamdan al-Maktoum and the Wertheimer brothers, Alain and Gerard. His best winners to date have been Marchand d'Or, the two-time winner of the 6½-furlong Group 1 Prix Maurice de Gheest as well as Newmarket's Group 1 July Cup; Tamayuz, the 2008 winner of the Group 1 Prix Jean Prat at Chantilly; and Goldikova, the conqueror of Darjina in the Prix Rothschild (ex-Astarte), who with her devastating victory in the 2008 Breeders' Cup Mile made Head the first man to both ride and train the winner of a Breeders' Cup race.

■ **CARLOS LAFFON-PARIAS:** A Spaniard by birth, he is the son-in-law of Criquette Head-Maarek, with a Chantilly stable of more than 125 horses. He served as Head's assistant from 1986 to 1991, and since then he has won the Group 1, 1¼-mile Criterium de Saint-Cloud for 2-year-olds with Spadoun and Goldamix. Among his clients are Wertheimer et Frere, Alec Head, and the increasingly influential Italian outfit Stilvi Compania Financiera.

■ **ELIE LELLOUCHE:** Scored a coup in 1992 when Daniel Wildenstein sent him 42 horses previously trained by Andre Fabre. Since then he has been head trainer for the powerful Wildenstein stable, for which he has sent out Pistolet Bleu and Epervier Bleu and the European staying champion Westerner. His biggest victory, however, came with Enrique Sarasola's Helissio in the 1996 Arc.

■ **JONATHAN PEASE:** An Englishman in France, he trains for the Niarchos family, for whom he won the 2004 Arc with Bago. He combined forces with American-born rider Cash Asmussen to win the 1997 Breeders' Cup Mile with the Niarchos family's Spinning World. Another of his owners is American George Strawbridge, for whom he won the 1994 Breeders' Cup Turf with Tikkanen, as well as the 2007 St. Leger Stakes with Lucarno and the 2006 Group 1 Prix Royal-Oak with Montare.

■ **RICHARD GIBSON:** The third of the four British horsemen in France (the fourth being Richard Pritchard-Gordon), Gibson is best known in America for Doctor Dino, the world-traveling middle-distance horse who won Belmont's Man o' War Stakes and the Hong Kong Vase in 2007 and was third in the Dubai Sheema Classic in 2008.

■ **JOHN HAMMOND:** Another Englishman in Chantilly, he is married to former jockey and current exercise rider Georgina Frost. He is, however, more famous for having trained Suave Dancer, winner of the French Derby and the Prix de l'Arc de Triomphe in 1991, and the excellent young stallion Montjeu, whose victories included the French Derby, the Arc, and the King George VI and Queen Elizabeth Diamond Stakes.

- **JEAN-CLAUDE ROUGET:** If Fabre annually leads French trainers in money won, Rouget leads in races won, heading that category 17 times from 1991 through 2007. Based in Pau in southwestern France, not far from Bordeaux, his breakthrough year came in 1994 when he emerged from the provinces with Millkom, winner of the Prix Jean Prat and the Grand Prix de Paris, two Group 1 events. Millkom was also the easiest winner of a major race this observor has ever seen in the Man o' War Stakes that same year. Rouget now also keeps a small stable in Chantilly to help him prepare his provincial invaders for big races on the Parisian circuit. On March 25, 2007, at Toulouse, he sent out his 4,000th French winner, a remarkable figure considering the relatively short French racing season.
- **AMONG THE OTHER CONDITIONERS** who practice their trade at Chantilly are Nicolas Clement, the older brother of New York-based Christophe, Philippe Demercastel, and David Smaga.

TRACK RECORDS

DISTANCE	RECORD TIME	HORSE	DATE
5f (Left to right)	56.40	Ratio	June 23, 2005
5f (Right to left)	55.20	Kind Music	June 6, 1982
5½f	1:03.20	Gallanta	June 13, 1984
6f	1:06.60	Harifa	June 19, 1984
7f	1:23.40	Coupe de Champe	Sept. 8, 2004
1m	1:36.90	Sacrement	June 4, 1997
1⅛m	1:48.60	Le Triton	June 2, 1996
1¾m	2:05.80	Darsi	June 4, 2006
1½m	2:24.10	Bering	June 8, 1986

MAJOR RACES (Chronological Order)

RACE	CONDITIONS
SPRING-SUMMER SEASON	
Prix de Suresnes (Listed)	1¼m 3yo c&g
Prix Servanne (Listed)	6f 4yo+
Prix Allez France-G3	1¼m 4yo+ f&m

RACE	CONDITIONS
Prix Sigy (Listed)	6f 3yo
Prix de Guiche-G3	1⅛m 3yo c
Prix d'Angerville (Listed)	1m 3yo f
Prix de Royaumont-G3	1½m 3yo f
Prix du Jockey-Club (French Derby)-G1	1 5/16m 3yo c&f
Grand Prix de Chantilly-G2	1½m 4yo+
Prix de Sandringham-G2	1m 3yo f
Prix du Gros-Chene-G2	5f 3yo+
Prix de Diane (French Oaks)-G1	1 5/16m 3yo f
Prix du Chemin de Fer du Nord-G3	1m 4yo+
Prix Paul de Moussac-G3	1m 3yo c&g
Prix Hampton (Listed)	5f 3yo+
Prix Jean Prat-G1	1m 3yo c&f
Prix Pelleas (Listed)	1¼m 3yo c&g
Prix La Moskowa (Listed)	1⅞m 4yo+
FALL SEASON	
Prix de la Cochere (Listed)	1m 3yo f
Prix des Tourelles (Listed)	1½m 3yo+ f&m
Prix de Boulogne (Listed)	1¼m 4yo+
Prix d'Arenberg-G3	5½f 2yo
Prix d'Aumale-G3	1m 2yo f
Prix Charles Laffitte (Listed)	1¼m 3yo f
Prix de Bonneval (Listed)	5½f 3yo+
Prix Eclipse-G3	6f 2yo
Prix Scaramouche (Listed)	1⅞m 3yo+
Prix Le Fabuleux (Listed)	1⅛m 3yo
Prix de Saint-Cyr (Listed)	7f 3yo

DAYS OF RACING: Chantilly runs 24 days of racing between early May and mid-October. The classic meetings of the Prix du Jockey-Club and the Prix de Diane are held on the first two Sundays in June, respectively. Prix de Diane Day is traditionally the one-day French equivalent of Royal Ascot, when Frenchwomen put on their best summer finery. Still, attendance on that most well attended day of the Chantilly racing season never surpasses 18,000.

HOW TO GET THERE: From Paris take the train from Paris-Gare du Nord to Chantilly station. On race days there is a free shuttle-bus service to the track, which is about a 12-minute walk from the station.

SURROUNDING AREA: There is enough to keep one occupied in Chantilly for a full day even on non-racing days. The Grandes Ecuries (Great Stables) were built in 1719 by the eccentric Prince de Conde, who believed he would be reincarnated as a Thoroughbred, and so would require a stable on a palatial scale. The stables stretch almost the entire length of the backstretch, providing the racecourse with the most striking man-made backdrop in the world. Open to the public, they house the Musee Vivant du Cheval (Living Museum of the Horse), featuring dozens of exhibits showing how horses are used in France today, as well as examples of many French breeds.

At what we in America would call the far turn sits the even more fabulous Chateau de Chantilly. Built in the mid-16th century, it was destroyed during the French Revolution and rebuilt in the 1870s. It houses the sumptuous Musee Conde, home of hundreds of French paintings hung ceiling-to-floor in the old-fashioned style. Included in the collection are *Les Tres Riches Heures de Duc de Berry,* perhaps the most beautiful of all medieval illuminated manuscripts, and the definitive portrait of Moliere, France's answer to Shakespeare. Works by virtually all of Europe's old masters from Raphael to Ingres to Watteau to Reynolds cover the walls.

Outside the chateau lies the expansive palace park that was designed by the royal gardener Le Notre, the same man who designed the gardens at the Palace of Versailles.

Both the Grandes Ecuries and the Chateau are open on race days.

There are five training centers in Chantilly. The most important of them is Les Aigles in Gouvieux. The other four are in Lamorlaye, Coye la Foret, Avilly-Saint-Leonard, and La Foret de Chantilly. Guided tours can be obtained through the Chantilly office of tourism.

DEAUVILLE ≡

Hippodrome Deauville-La Touques
45 Avenue Hocquart de Turtot
14800 Deauville, France
Phone: 011-33-2-31-14-20-00
France-Galop phone: 011-33-1-49-10-20-30
Internet: www.france-galop.com
www.hippodromesdedeauville.com

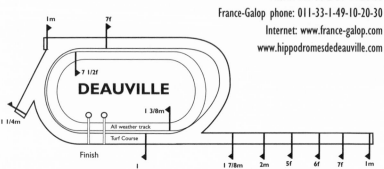

LOCATION: 125 miles west-northwest of Paris.

COURSE DESCRIPTION: Deauville is a level, right-handed 1⅜-mile oval with wide, sweeping turns. A very mildly undulating one-mile straight course joins the right-handed course at the head of the 2½-furlong stretch. On the clubhouse turn there is a chute from which 1¼-mile races are started. All turf races between five and seven furlongs are run on the straight course. One-mile races are run on both the straight course and the right-handed course.

In 2003 a Polytrack course was installed inside the turf course. This is a right-handed 1¼-mile track with a stretch that measures a little shorter than 2½ furlongs.

HISTORY: Deauville is to Paris what Saratoga is to New York and what Del Mar is to Los Angeles. When the Parisian racing community tires of the big city during the dog days of summer, it heads north to Deauville, at virtually the same time the New York Racing Association pulls up stakes for its annual sojourn to Saratoga, or Los Angelenos are heading south to where the turf meets the surf at Del Mar.

The similarities between Deauville and Saratoga are uncanny. Both racetracks opened in August 1864. Both feature their country's most important early-season juvenile stakes races, as well as the unveiling of late blooming 2-year-olds in maiden races. Both towns are the sites of major yearling sales, and both also provide polo as a sidelight

The winner's circle at Deauville in front of the the weighing-room building

attraction—Deauville's polo field is actually on the racecourse infield. Saratoga offers a smattering of jump races throughout the month of August, while the track Clairefontaine, just a few hundred yards up the street from Deauville, provides likewise. And while Saratoga's Canfield Casino went out of business in 1907, Deauville's beachfront casino continues to prosper to this day, attracting gamblers and tourists from around the world.

The racetrack at Deauville is barely a half-mile from the beach, a pleasure with which the August citizens of Del Mar are well familiar.

Deauville, in fact, combines all of what is attractive about Saratoga and Del Mar, making it the best possible racing vacation imaginable.

Founded in 1864 by the Duc de Morny, the racecourse opened on August 15, a national holiday in France. A year later, the Societe des Courses de Deauville (Society of Deauville Races) was founded, but the track wasn't taken over by the Societe d'Encouragement until 1921.

Deauville Racecourse was founded to take advantage of the many well-to-do Frenchmen and women who had begun to migrate to the Normandy coast each summer. The town of Deauville had sprung up a few years earlier as an upmarket response to Trouville, the middle-class resort that lies just east of Deauville.

Trouville had been running occasional strand races—that is, races on the beach—for a number of years. Opening a racetrack at Deauville proved to be a stroke of genius and business boomed, with the lure of sea-bathing in the morning, racing in the afternoon, and casino gambling in the evening proving to be an irresistible combination.

The first Prix Morny, Deauville's preeminent 2-year-old fixture, was run in 1865, but the race was called the Prix des Deux Ans, or Two-Year-Old Stakes, from 1872 to 1911. It was not run from 1914 to 1918, when racing was canceled in Deauville during World War I, as it was just too expensive—and dangerous—to transport horses such a long distance from the training centers of Chantilly and Maisons-Laffitte.

Racing at Deauville was lost again in 1940, but the Prix Morny was run at either Longchamp or Maisons-Laffitte for the duration of World War II.

The history of the Prix Morny is a storied one. Its role of honor includes great names such as Pearl Cap, Brantome, Corrida, Pharamond, Grey Dawn II, Blushing Groom, Irish River, Green Forest, Machiavellian, Hector Protector, Arazi, Coup de Genie, Johannesburg, and Divine Proportions.

When the Societe d'Encouragement, or French Jockey Club, brought Deauville under its wing in 1921, it immediately inaugurated the Prix Jacques le Marois. Run on the straight course, the Jacques le Marois since the 1970s has developed into one of the most important one-mile races in the world. Miesque and Spinning World, both subsequent winners of the Breeders' Cup Mile, each won it twice. Lyphard, Nonoalco, Irish River, Lear Fan, Polish Precedent, Hector Protector, Dubai Millennium, Banks Hill, Six Perfections, and Manduro have all won it as well. Taiki Shuttle became just the second Japanese-trained horse to win a Group 1 race in Europe with his victory in 1998.

A measure of the Jacques le Marois' importance is further reflected by the horses that have placed second or third in it. Since 1988 they include Warning, Linamix, Kingmambo, Daylami, Cape Cross, Banks Hill, Domedriver, Six Perfections, and Manduro. Note that Miesque, Spinning World, Banks Hill, Six Perfections, and Domedriver all vaulted from the Jacques le Marois to win Breeders' Cup races, suggesting that this Group 1 Deauville mile may be Europe's single most important Breeders' Cup prep race.

Deauville's charming Art Nouveau grandstand was refurbished in the early years of the new century. While it seats just 2,000, there is room on the grounds for 10,000 racegoers.

ANALYSIS: An oval course with very wide turns, Deauville might be described as a right-handed Belmont Park. As its base is quite sandy, the turf course drains very well, so the ground is usually no worse than good, although it can become rather choppy in late August.

Beyond the Prix Jacques le Marois, it would be wise for Americans to pay close attention to the juvenile and distaff divisions at Deauville.

Most of the best maiden races in France are restricted to first-time starters, the majority of which are supplemented with monies from the European Breeders' Fund (EBF), the European equivalent of the Breeders' Cup Fund. While this makes French first-time maiden races technically restricted races, it is a restriction of the best kind as, generally speaking, only well-bred horses are enrolled in the EBF program. Many French maiden races that are open to horses that have run are closed to first-time starters. Thus, youngsters that have run in a first-time-starter maiden frequently find themselves competing at the allowance level or higher second time out, another indication of the high quality of French baby races.

Deauville, like Saratoga and Del Mar, is a showcase for juvenile newcomers. The Prix Yacowlef, while atypical even by French standards, provides an idea of the kind of 2-year-old competition one finds at Deauville during the summer.

Run at the start of the August meeting for decades, the Yacowlef was moved forward to the track's four-day early-July meeting a few years ago when its distance was cut from six to five furlongs. Restricted to 2-year-olds that have never run, it is, nevertheless, a listed race. As such it has been dominated in the modern era by fillies, juvenile distaffers coming to hand much earlier than colts in France.

The precociousness of young fillies in France is borne out by the results of Deauville's premier juvenile event, the Prix Morny. The feature race on the third Sunday in August, it was won by a filly five years running from 1984 through 1988, again in 1993 (by Miesque's daughter Coup de Genie) and 1994, and in 2004 by Divine Proportions and 2005 by Silca's Sister. In 2007 the Group 2 Prix Robert Papin's filly winner, Natagora, finished second to Myboycharlie before going on to win the Group 1 Cheveley Park Stakes at Newmarket.

So it pays to make note of a Deauville-raced 2-year-old filly that has competed against colts. Miesque herself could only manage third in her Morny in 1986, finishing behind two others of her sex in Sakuro Reiko and Shy Princess.

Older distaffers with group-race experience at Deauville also belong to a special group whose form translates well in America. The Prix Rothschild, known until 2008 as the Prix d'Astarte, run on the first Sunday of the August meeting, is a one-mile race with at least as much stateside cache as the Prix Jacques le Marois, although in reality it occupies a slightly lower level.

Upgraded to Group 1 status in 2004, this straight mile for fillies and mares has produced six subsequent Grade 1 winners in America in its eight runnings from 2000 through 2007: England's Legend, fourth in 2000, won the Beverly D; No Matter What, 12th in 2000, won the Del Mar Oaks; Six Perfections, the 2003 runner-up, won the Breeders' Cup Mile; 2003 10th-place finisher Musical Chimes won the John C. Mabee; Gorella, third in 2005, won the Beverly D; and 2006 fifth-place finisher Price Tag won the Matriarch.

Other Rothschild/Astarte participants to win graded races in the U.S. since 1998 are Pharatta (Garden City Handicap); Kumba Mela (Noble Damsel); Lovers Knot (De La Rose); Iftiraas (Distaff Turf Mile); Amonita (Suwanee River); and Dedication (Beaugay Handicap). Moreover, Premiere Creation, New Story, Lethals Lady, Turtle Bow, and Campsie Fells have all been Grade 1-placed in the U.S. after having run in the Rothschild/Astarte.

Falling as it does in late July or early August, the Rothschild/Astarte is a perfect fit for horses coming to America for big autumn races. Following the rule that a good European miler can win in the States between a mile and 1¼ miles, the Astarte is one of the key European races for both American bettors and American buyers.

TRACK RECORDS

DISTANCE	RECORD TIME	HORSE	DATE
5f	55.60	Katies First	Aug. 27, 1991
5½f	1:03.90	Ela Merici	July 5, 2003
6f	1:08.20	Gallanta	Aug. 4, 2004
6½f	1:14.70	Seeking the Pearl	Aug. 9, 1998
7f	1:21.10	Proviso	Aug. 18, 2007
7½f (RH)	1:29.30	Guadalupe	Aug. 3, 1974
1m (Str)	1:32.80	Penny's Gold	Aug. 25, 2000
1m (RH)	1:36.50	Ile Flottante	Aug. 10, 1977
1¼m	2:01.10	Rusticaro	Aug. 15, 1979
1⅜m	2:36.60	Campero	Aug. 10, 1977

MAJOR RACES (Chronological Order)

RACE	CONDITIONS

WINTER SEASON (December-January)

Prix Luthier (Listed)*

Prix Petite Etoile (Listed)*	1¾₆m 3yo f
Prix Lyphard (Listed)*	1¾₆m 3yo+
Prix Miss Satamixa (Listed)*	7½f 4yo+ f&m
Prix Montenica (Listed)*	6½f 3yo c&g
Prix Ronde de Nuit (Listed)*	6f 3yo f

JULY SEASON

Prix Yacowlef (Listed-1st-timers)	5f 2yo
Prix de Saint-Patrick (Listed)	1m (RH) 3yo c&g
Prix Amandine (Listed)	7f 3yo f
Prix de Ris-Orangis-G3	6f 3yo+

AUGUST SEASON

Prix Rothschild-G1	1m (Str) 3yo+ f&m
(formerly Prix d'Astarte)	
Prix de Cabourg-G3	6f 2yo
Prix Ridgway (Listed)	1¼m 3yo
Prix Jacques de Bremond (Listed)*	7½f 4yo+
Prix de Psyche-G3	1¼m 3yo f
Prix de Reux (Listed)	1¾₆m 3yo+
Prix du Cercle (Listed)	5f 3yo+
Prix Maurice de Gheest-G1	6½f 3yo+
Prix de Pomone-G2	1¾₆m 3yo+ f&m
Prix de Tourgeville (Listed)	1m (RH) 3yo c&g
Prix Jacques le Marois-G1	1m (Str) 3yo+ c&f
Prix Francois Boutin (Listed)	7f 2yo
Grand Handicap de Deauville (Listed)	1m (Str) 3yo+
Prix Michel Houyvet (Listed)	1⅞m 3yo
Prix Gontaut-Biron-G3	1¼m 4yo+
Prix Vallee d'Auge (Listed)	5f 2yo
Prix Minerve-G3	1¾₆m 3yo f
Prix de Lieurey (Listed)	1m (RH) 3yo f
Prix Guillaume d'Ornano-G2	1¼m 3yo
Prix du Calvados-G3	7f 2yo f
Criterium du EBF (Listed-Restricted)	1m (RH) 2yo
Prix Morny-G1	6f 2yo c&f

RACE	CONDITIONS
Prix Kergorlay-G2	1⅞m 3yo+
Prix Jean Romanet-G2	1¼m 4yo+ f&m
Prix de la Nonette-G3	1¼m 3yo f
Grand Prix de Deauville-G2	1⁹⁄₁₆m 3yo+
Prix Quincey-G3	1m (Str) 3yo+
Prix de Meautry-G3	6f 3yo+
Prix du Haras de la Huderie (Listed)	7f 2yo
Prix Vulcain (Listed)	1⁹⁄₁₆m 3yo
Prix des Reservoirs-G3	1m (RH) 2yo f

* Polytrack

DAYS OF RACING: Deauville conducts about 32 days of racing per year these days. The major August meeting that starts either the last weekend in July or the first weekend in August consists of 16 days. There are three days of racing in early July plus three days in late October. All of those dates are dominated by turf racing, with some races on Polytrack. In recent years Deauville has also been granted days of Polytrack racing between early December and mid-January, plus a short meeting in late March.

In 2008 the August Meeting was expanded to cover all five weekends in the month. Sunday features were, in order, the Prix Rothschild, the Prix Maurice de Gheest, the Prix Jacques le Marois, the Prix Morny, and the Grand Prix de Deauville.

The Deauville August meeting is supplemented by 11 days of racing at Clairefontaine, five on the flat plus six mixed meetings with races on both the flat and over jumps (hurdles and steeplechases). This provides a total of 27 days of seaside racing in Deauville during the month of August.

HOW TO GET THERE: Trains leave Paris-Gare Saint-Lazare for the 2½-hour ride to Deauville station, which is walking distance from the racecourse.

SURROUNDING AREA: Boredom is unknown in Deauville. In the morning and on days when there is no racing at either Deauville or Clairefontaine, there is the lure of the beaches. Lunch at one of the racecourse's two outdoor restaurants, or dinner in town followed by an evening's sport in the Grand Casino, makes the city of 4,500 (swelling to six or seven times that in August) an irresistible racing-holiday attraction.

But Deauville is expensive, so some vacationers may prefer its downmarket neighbor, Trouville. Just east of Deauville across the boat-lined La Touques harbor, Trouville is an older, more charming, and less expensive resort with a casino of its own. Built on the side of a hill that provides perfect nesting places for the flocks of squawking seagulls for which the town is famous, Trouville is notable for the many restaurants that line the harbor on the Rue des Bains. Everything in Deauville, the racetrack included, is within walking distance of Trouville.

A 10-mile drive east along the coast from Trouville to Honfleur provides some stunning views of the English Channel, which the French call Le Manche. Honfleur itself is a most charming fishing port famous for its seafood restaurants and art galleries. The Eugene Boudin Museum specializes in beach scenes of the Normandy coast, paintings that helped cement the reputations of the Impressionists.

The D-Day beaches of Omaha, Utah, Sword, Juno, and Gold are easily reached west of Deauville and make for a memorable day trip.

Upon the conclusion of the August racing season, Deauville hosts the annual American Film Festival for 10 days in early September, when big-name Hollywood stars can be seen strolling along *la planche*, aka the boardwalk.

Deauville is in Normandy, which is the center of France's Thoroughbred breeding industry. Idyllic stud farms dot the countryside. The Head family's Haras du Quesnay, originally founded by William K. Vanderbilt in 1911, is actually headquartered in Deauville, as is the Rothschilds' Haras de Meautry. Nearby farms include the Moussac family's Haras du Mezeray in Ticheville; Haras de Fresnay-le-Buffard, the longtime sponsor of the Prix Jacques le Marois, in Neuvy-au-Houlme; and Haras d'Etreham in Bayeux.

The most important French yearling sales are held in Deauville in August and October, now under the auspices of Arqana, the name of the new company created by the merger of Agence Francaise and Goffs. The sale topper at the 2007 August yearling sale was a Galileo-Clara Bow half-brother to Group 1-winning miler Turtle Bowl, for which Coolmore associate Demi O'Byrne signed the $1.94 million ticket.

LONGCHAMP ≣

Hippodrome Longchamp
Route des Tribunes
Bois de Boulogne
75116 Paris, France
Phone: 011-33-44-30-75-00
France-Galop phone: 011-33-1-49-10-20-30
Internet: www.france-galop.com

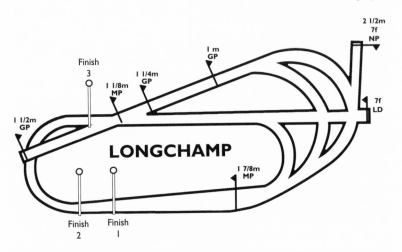

LOCATION: Southwest corner of the Bois de Boulogne, four miles from the center of Paris, one mile west of Auteuil Racecourse, which lies in the southeast corner of the Bois de Boulogne.

COURSE DESCRIPTION: Longchamp is a right-handed track measuring 1¾ miles around its outer perimeter, which is called the Grande Piste, or Main Track. The Moyenne Piste, or Middle Track, is about 1½ miles around. It shares the same ground as the Grande Piste except for a 1½-furlong stretch on the far turn. The rarely used 1⅛-mile Petite Piste (Little Track) joins the Grande Piste at the head of the 2½-furlong homestretch.

The 1½-mile course for the Prix de l'Arc de Triomphe starts from a chute onto the straight, six-furlong backstretch, which is entirely uphill. About halfway up the hill, horses disappear for about 100 yards behind the *petit bois* (little woods), a clump of trees that sits just inside the rail. At the top of the hill—the halfway point of the Arc—begins a sweeping, downhill quarter-mile right-hand turn. A second right-hand bend into the level, one-furlong false straight, so called because it is sometimes mistaken for the home straight by inexperienced jockeys, leads to a mild right-hand bend into the 2½-furlong stretch, finishing at the *premiere poteau* (first post).

The Nouveau Piste, or New Course, begins behind the top of the Grande Piste hill. There is a quick one-furlong straight followed by a one-furlong right-hand turn, all downhill, at which point it joins the Grande Piste at the false straight. All races run on the Nouveau Piste are seven furlongs long and end at the *deuxieme poteau* (second post), after a three-furlong run through the stretch.

The Ligne Droite, or Straight Course, is five furlongs in length. It begins from a chute that cuts through the downhill turns of both the Grande Piste and the Moyenne Piste before joining the backstretch of the Petite Piste. It is perfectly level, but the fact that it is situated out in the middle of the course makes for very difficult grandstand viewing, even when equipped with powerful binoculars.

Most races at Longchamp finish at the *premiere poteau,* but some, including seven-furlong races, the 1⁹⁄₁₆-mile Prix de Royallieu, and the 2½-mile Prix du Cadran, finish at the *deuxieme poteau,* which lies 110 yards farther on. Finishes at the *deuxieme poteau* confuse far more jockeys than does the false straight, much to their embarrassment.

The French 1000 and 2000 Guineas (Poule d'Essai des Pouliches and Poule d'Essai des Poulains) are run at one mile on the Grande Piste, as is the Prix du Moulin de Longchamp. These races start a quarter of a mile before the top of the hill.

On the Longchamp backstretch with the Eiffel Tower in the background

Since the first six furlongs of the Arc and other 1½-mile races at Longchamp, such as the Grand Prix de Paris, are uphill, much jockeying for position takes place during that part of the race. The downhill turn provides a breather during which there is little, if any, change of position as horses stride out and pick up speed, but never approach flat-out top speed, as they must preserve themselves for the final 3½ furlongs comprised of the false straight and the real straight.

And the real running in the Arc generally commences at the top of the stretch, 2½ furlongs from home. Horses tend to fan out at this point in large fields like those in the Arc and the big handicaps. Move too soon, however, and you will flatten out early. Move too late, and the finish comes more quickly than expected.

HISTORY: The first races conducted under the auspices of the Societe d'Encouragement were held in 1833 on the Champs de Mars in what is now a park lying under the eastern shadow of the Eiffel Tower.

At the time, the Champs de Mars (literally, "Fields of War") was the parade ground for the successor to Napoleon's Grande Armee as well as for the cadets of the Ecole Militaire, France's equivalent to West Point. With so much clodhopping going on, the Champs de Mars proved unsuitable for Thoroughbred sport, as the ground was almost always hard.

Came the Duc de Morny to the rescue, engineering the Societe's 1854 lease of a 17-hectare swathe of property in the Bois de Boulogne called the Plaine de Longchamp, or the Longfield Plain.

The paddock at Longchamp

Napoleon Bonaparte's nephew, Emperor Napoleon III, decreed that it should be so on December 17, 1856, and the Hippodrome de Longchamp became a reality.

The site of a monastery until the French Revolution laid waste to every stone on the property save the windmill, Longchamp was, and is, an ideal location for a racecourse, close to the capital but with enough distance between it and the city center to provide a sylvan atmosphere.

Longchamp opened for business on May 23, 1857, the crowd so large that the first race was delayed by half an hour. The emperor and empress themselves were in attendance, but no matter how much cache the presence of the aristocracy might provide, any racecourse still needs a race capable of capturing the public imagination, one that can set the turnstiles spinning.

Napoleon III's half-brother, the Duc de Morny, provided just that with the idea for the Grand Prix de Paris. First run on May 31, 1863, it was an immediate success as it fell to the British invader The Ranger, who beat the outstanding filly La Toucques, the winner that year of both the Prix de Diane and the Prix du Jockey-Club.

A 1⅞-mile contest for 3-year-old colts and fillies, the Grand Prix de Paris was intended as a test of stamina for horses that had previously won middle-distance classics. In 1864 it went to future French foundation sire Bois Roussel, but the next year it secured its seemingly irrevocable place on the international calendar when it was won by the great Gladiateur.

Gladiateur had arrived at Longchamp for his Grand Prix as a national hero, for he was returning to his native land from England after having become the first French-bred, French-owned horse to capture what was then racing's most coveted prize, the Epsom Derby. Known ever since as the Avenger of Waterloo, a reference to Napoleon's final defeat at the hands of the British in 1814, Gladiateur holds an unassailable place in the history of French racing. He is commemorated by a statue that stands just inside Longchamp's Grille d'Honneur, the main gate.

Paris was so captivated by the Grand Prix de Paris that Emile Zola devoted an entire chapter to a fictional late-1860s renewal of the race in his 1880 novel *Nana*. Zola's Grand Prix was won by a filly named, not surprisingly, Nana, after the courtesan who is the book's central character. By the time of its publication and throughout La Belle Epoque, the Grand Prix was attracting *tout le Paris* (all of Paris). If you weren't at Longchamp on Grand Prix Day, the last Sunday in June, you were simply nowhere.

In the early part of the 20th century, when crowds of nearly 100,000 were the rule on Grand Prix Day, horses such as Ajax, Spearmint, and Bruleur, all influential sires-to-be, added their names to the roll of honor, but the race was not run in 1915 and 1916 due to World War I.

When hostilities ceased in 1918, everything in Europe had changed and French racing followed suit. The Societe d'Encouragement decided it needed a new race of championship caliber to end the season. And so was born in 1920 the Prix de l'Arc de Triomphe.

Still, it took more than 50 years from that date for the decline of the Grand Prix de Paris to set in. Great horses such as Mieuxce, Nearco, and Pharis won it during the 1930s, and in 1941, despite war raging on all fronts, it was taken by La Pacha, the first horse to win the Prix du Jockey-Club, the Grand Prix de Paris, and the Prix de l'Arc de Triomphe.

By the 1970s, however, the Grand Prix had begun to stagnate. Since 1953 it had been run at a distance of $1^{15}/_{16}$ miles, a route that was fast becoming anachronistic in the contemporary world of commercial breeding. When Nelson Bunker Hunt's handicapper Swink won it in 1986 before a crowd of no more than 5,000, it was clear that a change was needed.

The Grand Prix was duly reduced to 1¼ miles, but Parisians were staying away in droves as the modern age was now supplying them with myriad other forms of entertainment. Good horses such as subsequent Arc winners Saumarez, Subotica, and Peintre Celebre, who in 1997 became the second and most recent horse to pull off the Jockey-Club/Grand Prix/Arc triple, were victorious. So too was Bago, whose 2004 Grand Prix victory, the last at 1¼ miles, was followed by autumnal success in the Arc.

In 2005, French racing's ruling body, France-Galop, under the auspices of the Baron Edouard de Rothschild, decreed that the Grand Prix de Paris would become a 1½-mile race. At the same time the distance of the Prix du Jockey-Club was cut from 1½ miles to $1^{5}/_{16}$ miles. The controversial move became an immediate success as Scorpion, the first winner of the redesigned Grand Prix—now run on France's national holiday, Bastille Day, July 14—set a track record and went on to win the St. Leger Stakes. The 2006 winner, Rail Link, went one better and doubled up in the Arc.

The Prix de l'Arc de Triomphe has been one of 20th-century racing's biggest success stories. Designed as a championship event, the Arc ushered itself in as just that in its inaugural 1920 running when it was won by Grand Prix de Paris winner Comrade. The first foreign-owned winner came in 1928 when American Ogden Phipps took it with Kantar. Famous Arc doubles were subsequently scored by Ksar (1921–22), Corrida (1936–37), Tantieme (1950–51), and the undefeated Ribot (1955–56).

Sea-Bird, still considered by some to be the best postwar European Thoroughbred, took the 1965 running. The 1970s, recognized on both sides of the Atlantic as racing's most recent golden age, began with Sassafras's upset of Nijinsky and followed with victories by legends Mill Reef, Allez France, and Alleged (twice). The famous filly five-timer from 1979 through 1983 consisted of Three Troikas, Detroit, Gold River, Akiyda, and All Along, who followed her Arc triumph with wins in Canada's Rothmans International, the Turf Classic, and the Washington, D.C., International, becoming the first foreign-based Horse of the Year in the U.S.

When dwindling attendance and handle figures began to take their toll on French racing during the 1980s, the Arc received a shot in the arm in 1988 from the Aga Khan when his international luxury hotel chain, the Ciga Group, began sponsoring what was developing into Arc Weekend. Not only did Ciga pour money into the Arc and its promotion, it sponsored a growing number of races that had previously been run a week before or a week after the Arc. These included the Prix de l'Opera, the Prix de l'Abbaye, the Prix Marcel Boussac, and the Grand Criterium, which has since had its name changed to the Prix Jean Luc-Lagardere in honor of the late owner-breeder. There are now 12 group races run on Arc Weekend—seven Group 1's and five Group 2's. As Ciga fell from fortune and was dissolved by the Aga Khan, the Barriere Hotel Group sponsored the weekend from 2001 to 2006. In 2008, the government of Qatar took over the task, doubling the Arc's purse from 2 million euros to 4 million euros, which made it the world's richest race at $6.2 million.

Lovers of period architecture, as well as the nostalgically minded, decried the razing of Longchamp's old Second Empire grandstand, which was replaced by a new, prefabricated stand in 1966. One-third of the old stand still remains at the head of the stretch, although it is only open nowadays on Arc Weekend.

Still farther up the stretch is the original parimutuel building, which was attacked on October 14, 1906, by bettors furious over the result of a race that was allowed to stand despite the fact that four of the 10 runners, among them the favorite, were left at the start, entangled by a malfunctioning starting tape. The crowd threw chairs onto the track, broke down the rails, and set fire to outbuildings on the infield. Duly chastened, the stewards finally announced that all bets on the race would be refunded.

History, too, has had a way of interjecting itself onto the racing scene at Longchamp.

On June 24, 1936, a group of feminists, more peaceable than those led by Emily Davison at Epsom's Suffragette Derby in 1913, paraded through the stretch shortly before the start of the Grand Prix de Paris, agitating for Frenchwomen's right to vote, which they only received at the conclusion of World War II in 1945.

War has always been hard on Longchamp, with Paris being so close to the center of European hostilities throughout the 19th and 20th centuries. The Franco-Prussian War, during which German troops encircled Paris in late 1870 and early 1871, forced Longchamp to close for nearly a year. There was no racing at all at Longchamp between 1915 and the autumn of 1918 due to World War I. And while an uneasy accord between the Societe d'Encouragement and France's Nazi occupiers saw racing only briefly interrupted at Longchamp during 1940, the Second World War produced one of the most disastrous racing days in history.

During the occupation, the German army used the huge Longchamp infield as a base for anti-aircraft batteries, even as racing was allowed to proceed. On Sunday, April 4, 1943, with a crowd of some 20,000 gathered throughout the course grounds, a jittery-fingered American bomber pilot, part of an Allied reconnaissance mission, dropped his bombs on the infield. Nine civilians died, but panic was averted. Racing was temporarily halted for a while but began again on July 13, 1944, shortly after the liberation of Paris.

Lying so close to the French capital was a dangerous drawback for Longchamp during the war, but in peacetime the closer a racecourse is to the center of a city, the more civilized a day at the races becomes. A short ride from the center of Paris, Longchamp shares with Saratoga, York, Chester, Happy Valley, and Deauville the pleasant distinction of being a city track.

Moreover, Longchamp's wide-open spaces, the line of trees provided by the Bois de Boulogne on the backstretch, the historic medieval *moulin* (windmill)—the sole relic left from the track's days as a monastery—the sunlit arcade behind the grandstand with its outdoor bars, and the historic tree-lined paddock all make a day at Longchamp an experience never to be forgotten—on Arc Day or any other.

ANALYSIS: While Longchamp bears no relation whatsoever in terms of layout to any track in the United States, its effect on American racing is at least as profound as that of any track in the world. As explained in the section on Chantilly, French-trained horses that race on the

Parisian circuit are in a more advanced state of condition after just a few races than their counterparts anywhere else. That Longchamp conducts a higher quality of sport than Chantilly or Deauville—generally speaking—makes any horse that has won there, or placed there in a good conditions or listed race, worth noting upon his arrival in America.

Longchamp compares to Ascot in England, the Curragh in Ireland, and Saratoga in America as the site of the best racing in those countries. The following chart reveals some interesting data concerning the quality of racing at each of those 2008 venues, which are listed in alphabetical order.

TRACK	DATES	RACES*	GI's	G2's	G3's	% Graded Stakes
Ascot (GB)	15	100	10	8	9	27.0
Curragh (Ire)	16	107	10	6	18	31.7
Longchamp (Fr)	30	225	16	11	21	21.3
Saratoga (USA)	36	350	15	13	5	9.4

* Approximate

If five points are awarded for a Grade 1, three for a Grade 2, and one for a Grade 3, Longchamp totals 134 points, Saratoga 106, Ascot 83, and the Curragh 81. On a points-per-date basis, the ratings are: Ascot 5.53, the Curragh 5.06, Longchamp 4.67, and Saratoga 2.94.

Make of this what you will, keeping in mind that Saratoga runs on an almost daily basis and must accommodate many claimers and New York-breds as well as graded-stakes types. Moreover, I strongly believe that European racing in general places a greater emphasis on quality and the improvement of the breed than its American counterpart, which is the underlying reason that so many ex-Europeans—ranging from those sold at public auction to horses from prestigious barns such as Darley, Shadwell, or Wertheimer et Frere—perform so well in America. In addition, the dispersal of so much of the best U.S. bloodstock throughout Europe during the 1980s strengthened the European sport at the expense of the American game.

But the old saw that "there are lies, damn lies, and statistics" is not without some measure of truth. There is thus reason to believe that the overall quality of racing at Longchamp is superior to that at Ascot.

The quality of the allowance races run at Longchamp rates quite a bit higher than at Ascot, and a great deal higher than at the Curragh, where most maidens and stakes races are dominated by the fearsome foursome of O'Brien, Bolger, Oxx, and Weld, after which there is a sharp drop in the overall quality of the stables.

At Longchamp, a typical card—aside from the outstanding programs run on Arc Weekend—usually includes either a pair of maiden first-timer events for both colts and fillies, or a similar pair of allowance races, plus a first-class handicap and a listed race. On Sundays and Bastille Day (Grand Prix de Paris Day) add one, two, or three group races.

Allowances on the Parisian circuit are channels for horses that must quickly make their way into stakes company or drop down into the handicap ranks. Many French horses that come to America are graduates of the Parisian circuit's allowance ranks. Sharp bloodstock agents snatch some of them at that early stage out of the barns of lesser French owners who are frequently willing to strike a deal. Their untapped potential is not infrequently fulfilled in America.

But whether a French horse is still relatively inexperienced or a veteran of stakes competition, it is becoming increasingly difficult to find bargains in France. As prize money increases throughout Europe, as the number of black-type opportunities for French fillies and European fillies in general increases, and as the dollar continues to depreciate, American owners and trainers are having an increasingly difficult time finding value in France.

Not so long ago, in the late 1990s, winners of French Group 2 and Group 3 races, French listed-race winners, and French Group 1-placed horses abounded in southern California.

Now we see more and more listed-placed horses and allowance or maiden winners. Still, they win with a certain frequency in graded company and with a certain regularity in allowance company.

Much has been made of the inability of an Arc winner to double up in the Breeders' Cup Turf. Dancing Brave, Saumarez, Subotica, Carnegie, Bago, Hurricane Run, and Dylan Thomas have all failed, but it must be remembered that the Arc is a championship event of greater value in terms of purse, prestige, and breeding significance than the Turf. Horses that win the Arc are being pointed to that race throughout the summer and are almost always over the top come the Breeders' Cup.

On the other hand, Arc runners that have done well in that race without winning have sometimes run very well in the Turf, for the simple reason that they have not yet peaked on the first Sunday in October. Pilsudski, one of the truly great racehorses of the last 20 years, won the 1996 Turf at Woodbine after having finished second to

Helissio in the Arc. And High Chaparral won the Turf in both 2002 and 2003 after third-place finishes in the Arc.

That 2006 Arc runner-up Pride followed up with victories in both the Champion Stakes and the Hong Kong Cup lends credence to this idea.

The Prix de l'Opera rates as one of the premier races in the world for fillies and mares. It is the best race on the Arc undercard, but we rarely see the winner in America, or the second or third. To finish in the first three in the Opera, which was only upgraded to Group 1 status in 2000, secures a filly's cache as a broodmare, so a trip to America at that point may not be in the cards. Three winners of the Opera when it was still a Group 2—Hatoof, Timarida, and Insight—would later win Woodbine's E. P. Taylor, and one, Donna Viola, would vault to victory in the Yellow Ribbon.

In 2004, Opera third Ouija Board did win the Breeders' Cup Filly and Mare Turf in her next start, and 2003 Opera runner-up Yesterday finished third in that year's F&M Turf, but we have not seen the Opera winner in the F&M Turf since Petrushka in 2000, when she finished fifth at Churchill Downs. In theory, the Prix de l'Opera should be the perfect prep for the Filly and Mare Turf, especially when it is run on good ground.

With more and more sprint races being run on turf in America, the five-furlong Prix de l'Abbaye de Longchamp should attract American turf sprinters looking to add a prestigious prize to their resume. North American horses used to give this race a try but none has tried in the last 10 years.

The 1990 Abbaye winner, Dayjur, narrowly missed in the Breeders' Cup Sprint a few weeks later, a victim of his own shadow-jumping, but the 1991 Abbaye winner, Sheikh Albadou, went one better by winning his BC Sprint. Switching from turf to dirt, however, is a rarity, and with the emergence of the Hong Kong Sprint since the mid-1990s, Abbaye runners are now more likely to travel to Sha Tin in December.

The Prix du Moulin de Longchamp, while not quite the Breeders' Cup Mile pointer that is Deauville's Prix Jacques le Marois, is still a first-class mile and should only be ignored at one's peril. Jacques le Marois winner Spinning World won it in 1997 on his way to Breeders' Cup Mile glory at Woodbine, while 2002 Moulin winner Rock of Gibraltar would have won his Mile but for an errant start.

The Poule d'Essai des Poulains (French 2000 Guineas) and Poule d'Essai des Pouliches (French 1000 Guineas) have never rated quite as highly as their English counterparts at Newmarket. That said, the

Poulains had a great run in the latter part of the last century when it was won by Soviet Star, Blushing John (later a Grade 1 winner on dirt in the U.S.), Linamix, Hector Protector, and Daylami.

Its most recent winner of note was Shamardal, who would next land the French Derby before cutting back to a mile to take the St. James's Palace Stakes. In 2007, Poulains fourth Excellent Art improved to be second in the Breeders' Cup Mile at Monmouth on soft ground that was all wrong for him.

Miesque, Divine Proportions, Darjina, and Zarkava are the best winners of the Pouliches since 1987, but the French 1000 Guineas is a race that should be studied from top to bottom. Like the French Oaks, it almost always produces a number of future American runners.

TRACK RECORDS

DISTANCE	RECORD TIME	HORSE	DATE
5f	54.30	Habibti	Oct. 2, 1983
7f	1:17.90	Russian Revival	May 27, 1999
1m (GP)	1:34.10	Ever Fair	May 27, 1999
1m (MP)	1:34.90	Green Forest	Sept. 5, 1982
1¹⁄₁₆m	1:43.30	Xerco	May 30, 1993
1⅛m	1:48.10	Acago	June 24, 2003
1⅛m, 55y	1:50.10	Royal Heroine	Oct. 2, 1983
1⅛m, 155y	1:55.20	Greek Fire	Sept. 6, 1987
1¼m (GP)	2:00.90	Mandesha	Oct. 1, 2006
1¼m (MP)	2:01.40	Manduro	April 9, 2006
1⁵⁄₁₆m	2:07.40	Pink Cloud	July 14, 2005
		Soldier of Fortune	April 8, 2007
1⅜m	2:14.50	Helissio	April 7, 1996
1½m	2:24.30	Scorpion	July 14, 2005
1¾m	2:58.10	Bussoni	July 14, 2007
1⅞m	3:06.60	Double Eclipse	April 25, 1996
1¹⁵⁄₁₆m	3:15.00	Varevees	Sept. 16, 2007
2½m	4:14.10	San Sebastian	Oct. 1, 2000

GP -Grande Piste
MP-Moyenne Piste

MAJOR RACES (Chronological Order)

RACE	CONDITIONS
SPRING-SUMMER SEASON	
Prix de la Pepiniere (Listed)	1 5/16m 4yo+ f&m
Prix Noailles-G2	1 5/16m 3yo c&f
Prix d'Harcourt-G2	1 1/4m 4yo+
Prix Finlande (Listed)	1 1/8m, 55y 3yo f
Prix de Fontainebleau-G3	1m 3yo c
Prix de la Grotte-G3	1m 3yo f
Prix La Force-G3	1 1/4m 3yo
Prix Lord Seymour (Listed)	1 1/2m 4yo+
Prix Ganay-G1	1 5/16m 4yo+
Prix de Barbeville-G3	1 15/16m 4yo+
Prix Vanteaux-G3	1 1/8m, 55y 3yo f
Prix Hocquart-G2	1 3/8m 3yo c&f
Prix d'Hedouville-G3	1 1/2m 4yo+
Prix de Montretout (Listed)	7f 4yo+
Poule d'Essai des Poulains (French 2000 Guineas)-G1	1m 3yo c
Poule d'Essai des Pouliches (French 1000 Guineas)-G1	1m 3yo f
Prix de Saint-Georges-G3	5f 3yo+
Prix de la Seine (Listed)	1 3/8m 3yo f
Prix d'Ispahan-G1	1 1/8m, 55y 4yo+
Prix Saint-Alary-G1	1 1/4m 3yo f
Prix Vicomtesse Vigier-G3	1 15/16m 4yo+
Prix du Pont-Neuf (Listed)	7f 3yo
Prix du Palais-Royal-G3	7f 3yo+
Prix de l'Avre (Listed)	1 1/2m 3yo c&g
La Coupe-G3	1 1/4m 4yo+
Prix La Fleche (Listed)	5f 2yo
Prix du Lys-G3	1 1/2m 3yo c&g
Prix de la Porte Maillot-G3	7f 3yo+
Prix Daphnis-G3	1 1/8m 3yo c&g
Grand Prix de Paris-G1	1 1/2m 3yo c&f
Prix Maurice de Nieuil-G2	1 3/4m 4yo+
Prix Roland de Chambure (Listed)	7f 2yo
Prix de Thiberville (Listed)	1 1/2m 3yo f

RACE	CONDITIONS
FALL SEASON	
Prix de Liancourt (Listed)	1 15/16m 3yo f
Prix de Lutece-G3	1 7/8m 3yo
Prix du Moulin de Longchamp-G1	1m 3yo+ c&f
Prix La Rochette-G3	7f 2yo
Prix du Pin-G3	7f 3yo+
Prix Vermeille-G1	1½m 3yo+ f&m
Prix Niel-G2	1½m 3yo c&f
Prix Foy-G2	1½m 4yo+ c&f
Prix Gladiateur-G3	1 15/16m 4yo+
Prix du Petit Couvert-G3	5f 3yo+
Prix du Prince d'Orange-G3	1¼m 3yo
Prix des Chenes-G3	1m 2yo c&g
Prix de la Foret-G1	7f 3yo+
Prix du Cadran-G1	2½m 4yo+
Prix Daniel Wildenstein-G2	1m 3yo+
Prix Dollar-G2	1⅛m, 155y 3yo+
Prix de Royallieu-G2	1 9/16m 3yo+ f&m
Prix Chaudenay-G2	1⅞m 3yo
Prix de l'Arc de Triomphe-G1	1½m 3yo+ c&f
Prix de l'Abbaye de Longchamp-G1	5f 2yo+
Prix de l'Opera-G1	1¼m 3yo+ f&m
Prix Marcel Boussac-G1	1m 2yo f
Prix Jean-Luc Lagardere-G1	7f 2yo c&f
Prix du Conseil de Paris-G2	1½m 3yo+
Prix de Conde-G3	1⅛m 2yo
Prix Herod (Listed)	7f 2yo
Prix Royal-Oak-G1	1 15/16m 3yo+
Prix Casimir Delamarre (Lst)	1⅛m 3yo f
Criterium de Vitesse (Listed)	5f 2yo

DAYS OF RACING: Longchamp conducts 28 days of racing annually between early April and late October. The season is divided into halves, the first the 17-day spring-summer season, with French Guineas Day held on the second Sunday in May. The first half of the year climaxes with the Grand Prix de Paris on July 14. The 11-day autumn season begins in early September and is highlighted by Arc Weekend on the first weekend in October. Of Longchamp's 28 annual dates, nine are on Sunday, four on Saturday.

HOW TO GET THERE: Take the No. 10 Metro Line to Porte d'Auteuil, where you will emerge onto the street across from the backstretch entrance to Auteuil Racecourse, Paris's jumps track. At the southern end of the square there are buses that will take you to the main gate at Longchamp. The 15-minute ride through the Bois de Boulogne to the track is free on Sundays, holidays, and on Arc Weekend.

SURROUNDING AREA: Longchamp is virtually a stone's throw from what most people would call the most beautiful city in the world. The attractions offered by Paris are so numerous, so varied, and so delightful that even enthusiastic racegoers will discover that the racing is merely icing on the cake when visiting the City of Light.

Start with the Arc de Triomphe, at which begins the famous shopping street, the Champs Elysees, or Elysian Fields, so-called because it was once a leafy park with a broad riding path well known as an amorous trysting place. The incomparable Gothic cathedral, Notre de Dame de Paris, is the home of Victor Hugo's fictional hunchback Quasimodo and stands literally in the center of Paris and all of France, as it is the point from which all distances in the country are measured.

The Louvre was the palace of French kings and queens until the mid-17th century and is now the site of one of the world's great art museums. The Eiffel Tower can be seen from any point in Paris and is clearly visible from the Longchamp grandstand. The great owner-breeder Marcel Boussac is buried in Montmartre Cemetery near the heart of Montmartre, the now rather touristy bohemian quarter that includes the Moulin Rouge and other less reputable houses of entertainment. The winding River Seine cuts through the heart of the city, runs past Longchamp's main gate, and provides one of the best nightime walking tours known to man, especially when he is with a woman.

And then there are the cafés, where a cup of coffee buys you the right to sit at your table for as long as you please. Linger while watching the world go by, chat up your neighbors, or study the form in the French racing paper, *Paris-Turf,* which, by the way, is a lovely double entendre meaning both "turf betting" and, literally, "Paris turf."

PMU (Pari Mutuel Urbaine): This is the state-run French off-track betting system, closely linked with the state-run PMH, or Pari Mutuel Hippodrome, the system through which on-track bets are placed.

Bets can be made at PMU locations throughout Paris and France at tobacco shops (*tabacs*) until noon each day. Many of the players at this time of day are getting down on the daily *quinte,* a wager on the big handicap of the day in which one must select the first five finishers in any order. It is used as a virtual national lottery as students, housewives, the unemployed, and many others with no interest in racing will risk a euro or two in the hope of winning a big prize.

Most of the serious off-track bettors in Paris converge on the many PMU cafés shortly before the first race each afternoon. These are free of charge to enter and are frequently located on the second floor of a regular café.

PMU cafés can be identified by their green awnings with the letters *PMU* accompanied by the PMU logo, the silhouette of a galloping horse.

One of the nice things about the PMU/PMH system is that the payoffs are the same both on-track and off-track. Moreover, a winning ticket purchased on-track with the PMH can be cashed off-track at a PMU café, or vice versa. Best of all, there is no tax on winnings, no matter at what odds your bet is placed or however much your ticket is worth.

MAISONS-LAFFITTE

Hippodrome Maisons-Laffitte
1 Avenue de la Pelouse
78600 Maisons-Laffitte
France
Phone: 011-33-1-39-12-81-70
France-Galop phone: 011-33-1-49-10-20-30
Internet: www.france-galop.com

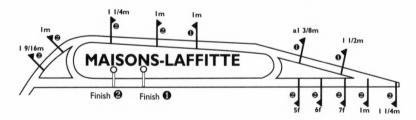

LOCATION: The Hippodrome Maisons-Laffitte is located in the town of Maisons-Laffitte, 12 miles west of Paris on the left bank of the Seine, the same river that runs through Paris.

COURSE DESCRIPTION: Maisons-Laffitte is a 1½-mile oval with very tight turns and long straights. Races are run right-handed on some days and left-handed on others, but there is also a 1¼-mile straight course that joins the right-handed course at the head of the stretch, three furlongs from the line. All races between five and seven furlongs are run on the straight course. One-mile races may be run on any of the three courses, right-handed, left-handed, or straight.

On the right-handed course, races run at 1⁹⁄₁₆ miles start from a chute that makes a right-hand turn onto the backstretch, which is five furlongs long. A tight, right-handed turn leads into the three-furlong stretch. One-mile races on the right-handed course start midway down the backstretch.

On the left-handed course, races of 1⁵⁄₁₆ miles and 1½ miles start from a chute. There is a mild left-hand bend that leads to the five-furlong backstretch, followed by a left-hand turn for home that is not quite as tight as the turn for home when going right-handed. The homestretch on the left-handed course is 2½ furlongs in length.

The turning courses and the straight course are all level. The straight course bears the distinction of being the co-longest in the world along with that on Newmarket's Rowley Mile Course.

HISTORY: Maisons-Laffitte was founded in 1878 by Joseph Oller, the man who invented the parimutuel system of wagering to counteract what was seen as the underhanded ways of the bookmaking confraternity.

The town itself had been founded in 1812 by the Parisian banker Jacques Laffitte, who had bought the 17th-century chateau and built the houses in the nearby park that had formerly comprised the chateau estates. The town, whose name means "Laffitte Houses," was named for those same dwellings.

Oller, a part-time bookmaker himself, had invented parimutuel wagering (the word *parimutuel* means "betting amongst ourselves") in 1864, but his new system had difficulty making headway at Longchamp and Chantilly, so he started his own racecourse at Maisons-Laffitte, which was originally intended as a fashionable gathering place for well-to-do Parisian suburbanites.

By the early 1890s, Oller was in financial difficulty, so in 1892 he sold the track to the Societe Sportiv, which was already in charge of the racecourse at Saint-Cloud.

A century later, the French government decided that two racetracks on the Parisian circuit would have to close in return for the remaining Parisian tracks to continue receiving state aid. A battle began beween

Maisons-Laffitte and Evry, the track 25 miles southeast of Paris. A compromise was reached with the government, which allowed just one track to be closed, and it was decided that Maisons-Laffitte would be that one.

Despite howls of protests from the French training community, Maisons-Laffitte was shuttered from 1993 to 1995 while racing continued at Evry, which had only been opened in 1972 and featured the newest grandstand in France.

But the trainers at Maisons-Laffitte, aided by their confreres in Chantilly and in Newmarket as well, never gave up the fight. When France-Galop took over the administration of all the major tracks on the Parisian circuit on May 3, 1995, it was decided to reopen Maisons-Laffitte in mid-1995.

Evry closed its doors at the end of 1996. In 1999 it was leased by Sheikh Mohammed al-Maktoum for use as a training center for Godolphin 2-year-olds under the care of trainer David Loder. After just two years, Godolphin deemed the Evry operation unfeasible, in part because the limited program for 2-year-olds in France is geared almost exclusively to maidens and stakes-quality horses. Evry has lain fallow since November 2000. It was briefly considered as an auto-racing facility, but those plans never amounted to anything.

In 2000 France-Galop brought up the spectre of closing Maisons-Laffitte again, but the track weathered the storm. With business at France-Galop tracks having improved markedly since 2005, Maisons-Laffitte appears safe and sound for the time being.

ANALYSIS: Along with Saint-Cloud, Maisons-Laffitte might be considered the Parisian racing circuit's meat-and-potatoes track, but meat and potatoes on the scale of haute cuisine.

Good maidens and allowances abound at Maisons-Laffitte. In fact, they are run here almost as frequently as they are at Longchamp or Chantilly.

Many of France's best juvenile races take place here in the month of July. The five-furlong Prix du Bois and the 5½-furlong Prix Robert Papin are steppingstones to Deauville's six-furlong Prix Morny. Their value was never more evident than in 2007, when the filly Natagora set track records in winning them both prior to her second-place finish in the Morny.

Natagora would go on to win the Group 1 Cheveley Park Stakes at Newmarket later that fall and the 1000 Guineas the following spring. While this is a best-case scenario for the Bois and the Robert Papin, it

GLOBAL RACING

is evidence of the standing of a pair of seemingly modest French group races.

As a 3-year-old, Natagora won Maisons-Laffitte's seven-furlong Prix Imprudence as a prep for the 1000 Guineas. A listed race for fillies, it was designed as a trial for the Newmarket Guineas, since both races are run on straight courses, although it can certainly be used as a prep for Longchamp's French 1000 Guineas as well. The colts' equivalent to the Imprudence, the Prix Djebel, is the ideal prep for Newmarket's 2000 Guineas. One of the intriguing things about both the Djebel and the Imprudence is that previous group-race winners don't have to carry a penalty.

With the increase in the prices of French horses in recent years, coupled with the decline in the dollar, we are seeing fewer horses of real quality arrive in America from France. Certain big yards such as Juddmonte Farms, whose French trainer is Andre Fabre, will continue to send some of their better older horses to Bobby Frankel, but except for the few big American spenders with an eye for European talent, owners on this side of the pond are increasingly reticent to shell out the $500,000 or so it takes to buy a ready-made French group-race performer.

Thus we are seeing in America a higher percentage of French maiden winners who may be placed in listed races but are still eligible for "nonwinners of one other than . . ." Yet some of these horses manage to do quite well in graded-stakes company. Astute buyers should be looking at maidens and allowances at Maisons-Laffitte and throughout the Parisian circuit for possible purchases.

That said, form at Maisons-Laffitte can be tricky. The backstretch runs parallel and very close to the Seine, and while numerous efforts have been made to keep the riverbed's waters from seeping into the racecourse base, races at Maisons-Laffitte are often run on soft, very soft, holding, heavy, or very heavy ground, especially after rain.

And interpreting heavy-ground form is not as straightforward as it might seem. At the deep end of European course conditions, heavy ground is peculiar in that horses that act on it are not infrequently able to act on firm or good-to-firm ground as well. This may be because on heavy ground, horses' hooves cut right to the base of the track, where it is firm.

Holding, or sticky, as it is sometimes referred to (*collant,* in French), is another story. This is a track in which the mud is sticky, requiring horses to make an effort to pull their hooves out of the muck. Suffice it to say that races in America are never run on courses the French would label very soft, holding, or heavy.

THE PENETROMETER

In addition to parimutuel wagering, the French have also given racing the penetrometer, a stick by which the going is measured on turf courses. Each morning before racing, the penetrometer is inserted into the ground at specific points to determine the state of the ground. Penetrometer readings and their equivalent course conditions follow.

2.5 or less:	Hard
2.6 to 2.7:	Firm
2.8 to 2.9:	Good to firm
3.0 to 3.2:	Good
3.3 to 3.4:	Good to soft
3.5 to 3.7:	Soft
3.8 to 4.0:	Very soft
4.1 to 4.4:	Holding (sticky)
4.5 to 4.7:	Heavy
4.8 to 5.0:	Very heavy

While this system would appear to be the height of technological measuring capabilities, it is undercut by the fact that French officials only take a single reading of the going, that about three hours before the first race. If the sun is shining brightly with a breeze blowing, the course could well be drying out and firming up. If it begins to rain, the course could be getting softer and softer by the hour.

The ground in France is very rarely better than good. This is because there is a good deal more rain there than there is in the comparatively desertlike conditions in most of the United States. Racecourse officials in France and the rest of Europe also employ a judicious watering of the course whenever firm or even good-to-firm ground threatens.

The term good, or *bon,* in French, means exactly the same thing as it does in Britain and Ireland. Good is the type of ground preferred by most horses. *Firm* is a dirty word in the vocabularies of many European trainers, who feel that running on such ground will jar their horses.

By contrast, in America, it seems that little effort goes into labeling turf conditions accurately whenever there is the slightest bit of rain. Many times turf courses in America that are rated good are really good to firm. Courses labeled yielding are, on many occasions, really soft, as occurred at the 2007 Breeders' Cup at Monmouth Park.

Moreover, many so-called firm courses in America are actually hard. As trainer Phil Johnson once said of Belmont's turf course during the month of July, "It's like a dirt course painted green."

It would be a good idea at this stage in the development of international racing for all parties concerned to sit down and decide on a set of parameters for deciding upon turf-course conditions.

The same holds true for determining dirt-track and synthetic-track conditions. In these cases, it is America that comes closest to providing accurate assessments. Calling a Polytrack surface standard, as is done in England and Ireland, or a dirt track standard, as is done in Japan, just doesn't make it anymore.

TRACK RECORDS

DISTANCE	RECORD TIME	HORSE	DATE
5f	57.20	Natagora	July 1, 2007
5½f	1:03.20	Natagora	July 22, 2007
6f	1:08.60	Zinziberine	Oct. 2, 2002
6½f	1:16.20	Right Place	July 22, 2007
7f	1:23.20	Langostino	May 27, 2000
1m (Str)	1:33.70	Ranelagh	July 22, 2007
1m (RH)	1:35.50	Sequestro	Sept. 16, 2003
1m (LH)	1:37.60	Janjan	June 17, 2005
1⅛m (Str)	1:47.10	Utrecht	July 1, 2007
1⅛m (RH)	1:52.80	Lourinha	Sept. 17, 2002
1¼m (Str)	1:59.40	Fair Mix	Sept. 21, 2004
1¼m (RH)	2:02.38	Look Honey	July 14, 2003
1$\frac{5}{16}$m (LH)	2:08.80	Zanakara	June 17, 2005
1⅜m (RH)	2:16.94	Lost Bay	April 15, 2003
1⅜m (LH)	2:21.00	Winter Silence	July 16, 2005
1½m (LH)	2:30.40	Mr Academy	May 9, 2000
1$\frac{9}{16}$m (RH)	2:34.40	Raintrap	June 22, 1993
1¾m (RH)	2:55.01	Martaline	July 19, 2003
1¾m (LH)	2:57.40	Ostankino	July 10, 2005
1⅞m (RH)	3:08.80	Irik Star	Sept. 29, 2004
1⅞m (LH)	3:12.10	Coralhasi	June 22, 2005
2m (RH)	3:22.10	Karate	June 13, 2002

MAJOR RACES (Chronological Order)

RACE	CONDITIONS
SPRING-SUMMER SEASON	
Prix Jacques Laffitte (Listed)	1⅛m (Str) 4yo+
Prix Right Royal (Listed)	1$\frac{15}{16}$m 4yo+

RACE	CONDITIONS
Prix Djebel (Listed)	7f 3yo c&g
Prix Imprudence (Listed)	7f 3yo f
Prix de Pontarme (Listed)	1m 3yo
Prix Matchem (Listed)	1¼m 3yo c&g
Prix du Carrousel (Listed)	1⅞m 4yo+
Prix du Bois-G3	5f 2yo
Prix Chloe-G3	1⅛m (Str) 3yo f
Prix Messidor-G3	1m (Str) 3yo+
Prix Robert Papin-G2	5½f 2yo c&f
Prix Eugene Adam-G2	1¼m (Str) 3yo
Prix de Bagatelle (Listed)	1m (Str) 3yo f
FALL SEASON	
La Coupe	
de Maisons-Laffitte-G3	1¼m (Str) 3yo+
Prix Saraca (Listed)	6½f 2yo
Prix Le Fabuleux (Listed)	1⅛m 3yo
Criterium de	6f 2yo
Maisons-Laffitte-G2	
Prix Miesque-G3	7f 2yo f
Prix de Seine-et-Oise-G3	6f 3yo+

DAYS OF RACING: Maisons-Laffitte generally conducts 25 days of racing a year, 16 between early April and late July, after which racing shifts to Deauville/Clairefontaine, and 11 between late September and mid-November. The big day is the fourth Sunday in July, when two of the track's three Group 2 contests, the Prix Robert Papin and the Prix Eugene Adam, now subtitled the Grand Prix de Maisons-Laffitte, are run.

HOW TO GET THERE: Take the RER Ligne A (Line A, direction Cergy), the commuter train line that runs through central Paris along the Champs-Elysees, past La Defense and straight to Maisons-Laffitte. The racetrack is a two-mile walk from the station through the town center and the Parc de Maisons-Laffitte, a gated parklike community that runs adjacent to the 1¼-mile straight course. Special shuttle buses run regularly between the Place de la Liberation in the town center and the main gate of the racecourse before and after racing.

SURROUNDING AREA: The town of Maisons-Laffitte is a generally upscale commune of 22,000. Notable among its attractions are the 17th-century Chateau de Maisons-Laffitte, which includes bedrooms used by Louis XVI and Marie Antoinette, and the small Museum of the Racehorse, which houses rotating exhibits. The chateau is located on the left bank of the Seine across from the start of the 1¼-mile straight course and is worth visiting on your way to the track. For those who prefer food to history, La Vieille Fontaine, on the way to the track in the Parc de Maisons-Laffitte at 8 Avenue Gretry, is an excellent place for a Group 1-style lunch.

The town is also a major training center, second only in national prestige to Chantilly. A majority of the 1,200 horses trained in Maisons-Laffitte are jumpers, which might strike some people as odd, since Maisons-Laffitte is strictly a flat track.

Jean Cocteau, poet, novelist, artist, and director of films such as *Orpheus* and *Beauty and the Beast*, was born and raised in Maisons-Laffitte, which might account for the starry-eyed horse that always accompanied his signature. Cocteau would have been brought up watching horses parade by his house from an early age. His house is available for viewing on an appointment-only basis.

SAINT-CLOUD

Hippodrome Saint-Cloud
1 Rue du Camp Canadien
92210 Saint-Cloud, France
Phone: 011-33-1-47-71-69-26
France-Galop phone: 011-33-1-49-10-20-30
Internet: www.france-galop.com

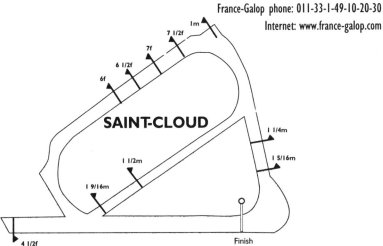

LOCATION: Saint-Cloud Racecourse is located six miles west of central Paris in the town of Saint-Cloud, which lies just across the Seine, not far from Longchamp.

COURSE DESCRIPTION: Saint-Cloud (pronounced San-CLOO), is a left-handed, triangular course, 1⁷⁄₁₆ miles around. Races of 1⁵⁄₁₆ miles start on a side straight and proceed for two furlongs before turning left onto the three-furlong backstretch. There is a wide, sweeping, nearly three-furlong left-hand turn into the stretch, which measures a little longer than a quarter of a mile. One-mile races start at the head of the backstretch at the point farthest from the grandstand. A 4½-furlong straight course that leads into the stretch is used exclusively for early-season juvenile races.

The Grand Prix de Saint-Cloud and other 1½-mile contests begin on an inner chute near the head of the stretch and proceed for 2½ furlongs before turning left to join the main track nine furlongs from the finish.

The track is virtually level except for a mild rise and fall on the inner chute.

HISTORY: The Hippodrome Saint-Cloud will forever be connected with the name of Edmond Blanc, one of France's leading owner-breeders during La Belle Epoque, that happy 25-year period of French history from about 1890 to the start of World War I in 1914.

The magnate of Monaco's grand casino, Blanc had inherited $40 million from his father, who had built up the casino in Monte Carlo into the chicest of all world-class money-spinners. Young Blanc used some of the money to found the racecourse in 1901.

He won the Prix du Jockey-Club four times, most notably with Ajax in 1904, and the Prix de Diane five times, including three times in a row from 1908 through 1910, in the second of those years with Ajax's daughter Union. Ajax was also one of his two Grand Prix de Paris winners.

Upon his death in 1920 at the age of 59, he was honored with a race at Saint-Cloud, the Prix Edmond Blanc, now an early-season Group 3 mile that serves as a prep for the Group 2 Prix du Muguet five weeks later.

The best race on the Saint-Cloud program has always been the Grand Prix de Saint-Cloud. Blanc himself scored his first and last victory in that event when his Poule d'Essai des Poulains winner Gouvernant took the inaugural running in 1904. Since then the race has proven to be not only an informative early-season Arc prep, but also one of the world's most important 12-furlong contests, in Europe rating only below the Arc and the King George VI and Queen Elizabeth Diamond Stakes and equally with the Coronation Cup.

Corrida's 1936 victory was followed by Arc triumphs later that year and in 1937 as well. Important stallions such as Vatellor, Mon Talisman, and Djebel, who followed his 1942 Grand Prix victory with a win in the Arc, are amongst its more notable winners. Eight Grand Prix de Saint-Cloud winners have gone on to win nine Arcs, among them the great Sea-Bird in 1965. Montjeu would follow his 1999 Arc victory with a Grand Prix score a year later. Among the other famous Grand Prix winners are Exceller; the Paul Mellon-owned pair of Glint of Gold and Diamond Shoal in 1982 and 1983; the great German stallion Acatenango; and Daniel Wildenstein's duo of Epervier Bleu in 1991 and Pistolet Bleu in 1992. Apple Tree, later the winner of the Turf Classic, along with Hellissio, Japanese invader El Condor Pasa, and the gallant mare Pride, have also won it.

Saint-Cloud's functional grandstand is made even less attractive by sparse crowds, especially on the track's many weekday meetings, but it does have an attractive, tree-lined paddock. The track has room for 15,000 customers and places—if not seats—in the grandstand for 10,000.

ANALYSIS: In terms of black-type racing, Saint-Cloud ranks a close fourth on the Parisian circuit, behind Longchamp, Chantilly, and Deauville, but ahead of Maisons-Laffitte. It bears repeating, however, that good maidens and allowances pop up at Saint-Cloud almost as frequently as they do at Longchamp, Chantilly, and Deauville.

Not too much should be made of the fact that Saint-Cloud is the only one of five tracks on the Parisian circuit that runs left-handed on a regular basis. The European-trained Thoroughbred is well used to going left-handed and right-handed, both on the gallops and on the racecourse. There might be some legitimate concern in the minds of American handicappers if they came across a horse, particularly a sprinter, that had run all of his races on straight tracks. Such a horse might have some difficulty negotiating tight left-handed turns in America. Normally, however, European horses are athletic enough— and experienced enough—to handle whatever wrinkles American racing might present.

Except, that is, getting out of the gate properly. European trainers, and the French especially, seem to take little interest in schooling their horses on how to get into the starting gate, much less in teaching them how to get out of it.

Races in France are run at a notoriously slow pace. It is not at all unusual for the first quarter-mile of a one-mile race run on good ground to go in 29 or 30 seconds. Even in five-furlong sprints, the first quarter rarely goes more quickly than 24 seconds, and then only in stakes races run on good ground or better.

This makes for very exciting finishes in France, as horses bunch up approaching the quarter pole for a mad dash to the line. The finishes of French races are much closer than they are in American turf races, even closer than their British and Irish counterparts, so it is a wise handicapper who gives extra credit to French winners who win consistently by at least two lengths.

A general if not universal rule says that the winning margin of a race in France might nearly be doubled to find its American equivalent.

Yet French horses do remarkably well in America despite the dawdling pace at which most of their races are run. There are two reasons for this. One is that horses are pack animals. Therefore, a well-trained Thoroughbred possessed of a certain class will have the ability to stay close, even when races are run at an uncustomarily fast pace. There are exceptions to this rule, however, especially in sprint races. European sprinters, and especially French sprinters, stand little chance in American sprints, in no small part because they are apt to lose so much ground at the start.

The second reason is that French horses are trained to produce a big finish. Even if they are going faster than usual early on in America, they are still frequently able to finish well. And if they find themselves in an American race run at a slow pace, one with an opening quarter of 25 and change or so, they will be forgiven for thinking they are back home in France, where fast finishes are the product of slow early fractions.

A glance at the major races run at Saint-Cloud provides a key to the orderliness of the French racing season. The Prix Altipan and the Prix Exbury are course and distance preps for May Day's Group 2 Prix du Muguet, which, in turn, is a steppingstone for horses considering better Group 1 miles such as Royal Ascot's Queen Anne Stakes or the Prix Jacques le Marois and the Prix du Moulin de Longchamp later in the summer.

In the 1990s, the Muguet produced winners such as Exit to Nowhere, subsequent Eclipse Award winner Hatoof, and Breeders' Cup Mile winner Spinning World. The 2000 winner, Dansili, is a full brother to Banks Hill, Intercontinental, and Cacique, but since then the Muguet winner has been nothing more than a solid Group 2 type.

There is a very nice pattern at Saint-Cloud for 3-year-old fillies pointing toward the French Oaks. The Prix Penelope in mid-April and the Prix Cleopatre on May 1, both at the Oaks distance of 1⁵⁄₁₆ miles, always produce a few American-bound fillies. If horses emerging from these two races are found to be incapable of the French Oaks, they can be rerouted to the 1½-mile Prix de Malleret on Grand Prix de Saint-Cloud Day, usually the last Sunday in June.

While Saint-Cloud usually has the honor of both opening and closing the Parisian flat season, it is especially honored with two key first-class juvenile races in November.

The Criterium International came into being in 2001 when one of French racing's periodic reshufflings saw the demise of Longchamp's seven-furlong Prix de la Salamandre and the reduction in distance of the Grand Criterium (subsequently renamed the Prix Jean-Luc Lagardere) from a mile to seven furlongs.

France thus found itself in need of a late-season race for 2-year-olds at a mile, and so the Criterium International was born. It has been a resounding success from the outset. Its first running went to the appropriately named Act One, who extended his unbeaten record to five in the now-defunct Group 1 Prix Lupin, only to be narrowly beaten by Sulamani in the French Derby, which would be the last race of his abbreviated career.

Dalakhani and Bago, the Criterium International winners in 2002 and 2003, would both win the Prix de l'Arc de Triomphe at 3. In 2007, it was won by Thewayyouare, a half-brother to three-time Group 1 winner Peeping Fawn.

First run in 1946, the 1¼-mile Criterium de Saint-Cloud is a stern test of stamina for 2-year-olds. It was won by the Aga Khan's foundation sire Darshaan in 1983. While it has since been won by nice ones such as Pistolet Bleu and Sunshack, most of its winners seem to peak in the race itself, failing to reach classic standards at 3, although its 2007 winner, Full of Gold, got his 3-year-old season off to a good start at Longchamp when winning the Group 2 Prix Noailles, a key French Derby prep.

TRACK RECORDS

DISTANCE	RECORD TIME	HORSE	DATE
4f	44.30	Last Bac	Oct. 4, 2000
4½f	49.40	Ziria	May 31, 2001
6f	1:11.40	Hewitt	June 25, 2003
7f	1:24.20	Shamaniya	July 3, 1994
1m	1:35.90	Redhead	May 1, 1984
1¼m	2:00.70	Audacious Choice	June 25, 2003
1⁵⁄₁₆m	2:07.40	Mystery Rays	June 18, 1988
1½m	2:26.15	Moon Madness	July 5, 1997
1¾m	2:59.30	Epaphos	May 31, 1993
1⅞m	3:17.10	Caprice Meill	Sept. 19, 2006

MAJOR RACES (Chronological Order)

RACE	CONDITIONS
SPRING-SUMMER SEASON	
Prix Altipan (Listed)	1m 4yo+
Prix Exbury-G3	1¼m 4yo+
Prix Maurice de Caillault (Listed)	1⁵⁄₁₆m 3yo c&g
Prix Rose de Mai (Listed)	1⁵⁄₁₆m 3yo f
Prix Omnium II (Listed)	1m 3yo c&g
Prix La Camargo (Listed)	1m 3yo f
Prix de la Porte de Madrid (Listed)	1½m 4yo+
Prix Francois Mathet (Listed)	1¼m 3yo c&g
Prix Edmond Blanc-G3	1m 4yo+
Prix Penelope-G3	1⁵⁄₁₆m 3yo f
Prix du Muguet-G2	1m 4yo+
Prix Cleopatre-G3	1⁵⁄₁₆m 3yo f
Prix Greffulhe-G2	1¼m 3yo c&f
Prix Corrida-G2	1⁵⁄₁₆m 4yo+ f&m
Prix des Lilas (Listed)	1m 3yo f
Grand Prix de Saint-Cloud-G1	1½m 4yo+
Prix de Malleret-G2	1½m 3yo f
FALL SEASON	
Prix Coronation (Listed)	1m 3yo f
Prix Joubert (Listed)	1½m 3yo f
Prix Turenne (Listed)	1½m 3yo c&g
Prix Thomas Bryon-G3	1m 2yo

RACE	CONDITIONS
Prix du Ranelagh (Listed)	1m 3yo+
Prix de Flore-G3	1⅜m 3yo+ f&m
Criterium International-G1	1m 2yo c&f
Prix Perth-G3	1m 3yo+
Prix Isola Bella (Listed)	1m 3yo
Criterium de Saint-Cloud-G1	1¼m 2yo c&f
Prix Denisy (Listed)	1¹⁵⁄₁₆mm 3yo+
Prix Ceres (Listed)	7f 3yo f
Prix Isonomy (Listed)	1m 2yo
Prix Belle de Nuit (Listed)	1½m 3yo+ f&m

DAYS OF RACING: Saint-Cloud has 28 days of racing annually between early March and mid-November. It has long held the distinction of being the first of the Paris-region flat tracks to open each year, as well as being the site of not only the first French group race of the season but also the first group race of the year in Europe, the Group 3 Prix Exbury, generally run in mid-March.

The first 15 days of the Saint-Cloud season conclude at the end of June. The fall season begins in late September and ends in late November or early December.

The better early-season races at Saint-Cloud are mostly in the one-mile and 10-furlong divisions. At the tail end of the year, Saint-Cloud hosts two of Europe's most important races for 2-year-olds, the one-mile Criterium International and the Criterium de Saint-Cloud, which, at 1¼ miles, is the world's most severe juvenile test of stamina, especially as it is frequently run on soft or heavy ground, rain being more frequent in spring and autumn in northern France than it is in England.

HOW TO GET THERE: Trains leave the Gare Saint-Lazare in Paris every half-hour for the 20-to-25-minute ride to Saint-Cloud, which is about a 15-minute walk to the track. It is a bit quicker to get off a station earlier at Le Val d'Or for a somewhat shorter and more scenic walk that will take you past the side straight of the racecourse.

SURROUNDING AREA: Saint-Cloud is town of 29,000 with no little history of its own. The now-ruined Chateau de Saint-Cloud was the headquarters of the coup d'etat by which Napoleon overthrew the Directory, leading to his coronation as emperor. The chateau was destroyed by fire in 1870 during the Franco-Prussian War.

The town's rather odd name is derived from Clodoald, the son of Clovis who was canonized as Sanctus Clodoaldus, and who was buried on the site of what was then just a village. The city of Saint Cloud, Minnesota, was named after Saint-Cloud by its French settlers.

The ruined 16th-century chateau is one of the highlights of a visit to the Parc de Saint-Cloud, as is the *cascade*, or waterfall, the centerpiece of the gardens designed by the great landscaper Le Notre, who also designed the gardens at Louis XIV's Palace of Versailles and the Prince de Conde's chateau in Chantilly.

Other Racecourses in France

CAGNES-SUR-MER ≡

Boulevard John F. Kennedy
06800 Cagnes-sur-Mer, France
Phone: 011-33-4-92-02-44-44
Internet: www.hippodrome-cotedazur.com

LOCATION: 570 miles southeast of Paris, a 5½-hour train ride from Paris-Gare de Lyon. Cagnes-sur-Mer is nine miles west of Nice on the Riviera or, as it is known in France, the Cote d'Azur. The town is not to be confused with Cannes, site of the famous film festival, which is 13 miles northeast of Cagnes-sur-Mer.

Cagnes-sur-Mer (pronounced can-soor-mare) opened in 1951. A virtually level, left-handed track, the turf course is a ¹⁵⁄₁₆-mile oval with a three-furlong stretch. The inner course is 1³⁄₁₆ miles around and has a two-furlong stretch. Races between one mile and 1¼ miles are one-turn affairs starting on the backstretch. There is a five-furlong straight course that joins the homestretch at the three-eighths pole.

A Polytrack course was installed outside the turf course in 2004. It can be compared to the main track at Belmont as it is a level, left-handed track, 1½ miles long, but with a three-furlong stretch.

The backstretch runs parallel to the Mediterranean Sea (Cagnes-sur-Mer means "Cagnes by the sea"), providing some extraordinary views from the grandstand, which seats 6,000; the grounds are capable of holding 12,000.

Cagnes-sur-Mer is French flat racing's winter quarters. The

Parisian turf season shuts down in late November or early December, and while Deauville runs nine meetings on its Polytrack between then and mid-February, Cagnes-sur-Mer conducts as many as 15 meetings between late January and late February, with races on both turf and Polytrack. Some of those days are mixed, with jump races included. There are 30 days and/or nights of trotting on the 6½-furlong trotting track in July and August.

The quality of the flat racing is not quite on a par with that at Paris's secondary tracks, Compiegne, or Fontainebleau, as few of the big Chantilly stables have runners at Cagnes-sur-Mer. Even the smaller provincial stables will usually send only their second-stringers. In short, the fare at Cagnes-sur-Mer is strictly wintertime stuff, albeit in charming surroundings.

The track does conduct a handful of competitive listed races. These are the 7½-furlong Prix de Californie on turf, the 1¼-mile Grand Prix de la Riviera Cote d'Azur on Polytrack, the 1¼-mile, 165-yard Prix Policeman on turf, and the 1½-mile Grand Prix du Conseil General des Alpes-Maritimes on turf. Most of the winners of these races would be hard pressed to win a listed race on the Parisian circuit.

With the Alps on one side of the track and the Mediterranean on the other, Cagnes-sur-Mer is an ideal tourist destination, although the weather during the February flat-racing season is too cold for sea-bathing. The Impressionist painter Pierre Auguste Renoir made the small Cagnes-sur-Mer estate of Les Collettes his final home. He died there on December 3, 1919.

CLAIREFONTAINE ≡

Route de Clairefontaine
14800 Tourgeville, France
Phone: 011-33-2-31-14-69-00
Internet: www.hippodrome-deauville-clairefontaine.com

LOCATION: 120 miles northwest of Paris, two miles west of Deauville.

One of the most charming racecourses on the face of the earth, Clairefontaine might be called Deauville's sister track, both because of its proximity and because its 10 or 11 August flat meetings help to make Deauville-Clairefontaine the August place to be in France.

Outdoor dining area at Clairefontaine

Founded in 1928, Clairefontaine is a 1¼-mile, right-handed oval. Races of 1½ miles (the distance of the track's climactic Grand Prix de Clairefontaine, run on the last day of the August meeting) begin 110 yards in from the start of the 2½-furlong stretch. Shortly past the finish there is a wide, right-handed 90-degree turn onto the backstretch, at the head of which one-mile races are started. The backstretch is 2½ furlongs long and empties into an even wider 90-degree right-hand turn that is more than two furlongs long. The shortest races run at Clairefontaine are seven-furlong affairs.

Inside the flat track there is a hurdle course and a steeplechase course, the latter of which makes use of both a diagonal and a figure-eight course that cut through the infield.

The top trainers who dominate Deauville use Clairefontaine for their lesser lights, which are not infrequently trumped by horses from the smaller stables. The racing at Clairefontaine is very competitive but doesn't really figure into the American scheme of things. Sometimes, however, a trainer will use Clairefontaine as a debut for a seemingly modest runner who may blossom afterward. Winning or placing at Clairefontaine is nothing to be sneezed at. The form there is really rather good, frequently better than that at Compiegne or Fontainebleau.

The listed 1½-mile Grand Prix de Clairefontaine always concludes Clairefontaine's August meeting. Alain de Royer-Dupre sent out the Aga Khan's 2006 winner, Daramsar, a Rainbow Quest colt who would later win Longchamp's Arc consolation prize, the Group 2 Prix du Conseil de Paris. The following year, when the race became restricted to 3-year-olds, it went to the Andre Fabre-trained Not Just Swing.

A day at Clairefontaine is very likely to be a memorable one. The grounds are exquisite. Bathed in summer flowers, as are many of the track's outbuildings, the grandstand is a timbered masterpiece with faux medieval chandeliers hanging in the main betting hall. Access to the paddock is open to the public. And the terrace restaurant (La Terrasse) offers one of the world's great trackside dining experiences.

COMPIEGNE ≡

Avenue du Baron Roger de Soultrait
60200 Compiegne, France
Phone: 011-33-3-44-20-24-43
Internet: www.hippodromes.fr

LOCATION: Known locally as the Hippodrome du Putois, Compiegne Racecourse lies 45 miles north of Paris. Trains leave Paris-Gare du Nord for a 50-to-70-minute journey. The racecourse is a 10-minute walk north from the station.

Compiegne (pronounced cahm-PYAN) is a virtually level, 1⅛-mile left-handed oval with a three-furlong stretch. Mile-and-a-half races start midway through the stretch. Races of 1¼ miles start from a chute beyond the finish line. Races of 1⅛ miles, a mile, and seven furlongs start on the backstretch. The turns are mild and sweeping, the course favoring long-striding gallopers. Rarely run races of six furlongs are run on a straight course that starts on the top of a hill and is steeply downhill through the first two furlongs.

The racing at Compiegne is a cut below that found on the major Parisian circuit, although the track is patronized by all the major trainers from nearby Chantilly. Those trainers, however, rarely send their better horses to Compiegne, although the maidens and allowance races at the track are competitive affairs.

The listed 1¼-mile Grand Prix de Compiegne for 4-year-olds and up, run in late June or early July, is the best race run at the track. Won in 2006 by Advice and in 2007 by Elasos, a measure of its value can be found in Musketier, who finished fourth in both those renewals.

Trained by Pascal Bary for Gary Tanaka, Musketier would subsequently finish third in the Grade 2, 1⅜-mile Red Smith Handicap at Aqueduct in 2007.

Compiegne has recently been awarded two other listed races formerly run at Chantilly and Maisons-Laffitte. These are the 1¼-mile Prix Pelleas for 3-year-old colts and geldings in early July and the one-mile Prix Tantieme for 3-year-olds and up in late October.

The track conducts 13 days of flat racing per year, plus one mixed meeting (flat and jumps), and three meetings consisting of a combination of flat, jumps, and trotting. Two jumps-only dates bring the annual total to 21 days.

Compiegne is a historic town of 41,000. On the morning of the day she was arrested, Joan of Arc prayed at Saint-Jacques, a little church just north of the town on the way to the racecourse. Her visit is commemorated in a small side chapel. In the Compiegne Forest, a taxi ride from the town center, is a replica of the railway car in which the armistice ending World War I was signed in 1918. In 1940, with Hitler in attendance, the Germans forced the French to surrender in the same car at the start of World War II. That original car was blown up by the French Resistance in 1944 as the Germans fled France.

FONTAINEBLEAU ☰

Hippodrome de la Solle
77300 Fontainebleau, France
Phone: 011-33-1-64-22-29-37
Internet: www.fontainebleau-tourisme.com

LOCATION: 35 miles southeast of Paris. Trains leave Paris from the Gare de Lyon; travel time 45 minutes. It is a four-mile taxi ride from Fontainebleau Station to the racecourse.

Fontainebleau is a country track in the best sense. Carved out of a section of the Forest of Fontainebleau, the racecourse is thickly surrounded by trees. The track is a left-handed affair, the main course being 1½ miles around and a virtual oval, the "clubhouse turn" slightly tighter than the turn for home. Races of 1⅜ miles start at the head of the backstretch and make a slight left-hand bend onto the backstretch proper. Races between seven furlongs and 1¼ miles all start on the backstretch. Races between five and six furlongs are run on the straight course, which meets the left-handed course at the start of the half-mile stretch. The course is sometimes used for cross-country races that take a byzantine route through the infield.

When Evry Racecourse 20 miles southeast of Paris closed its gates in 1996, Fontainebleau gained in importance on the Parisian scene, but the racing here will never be as good as it was at Evry, nor as good as it currently is at Maisons-Laffitte. The quality at Fontainebleau can be compared with that of Compiegne, north of Paris.

Fontainebleau generally holds 19 or 20 days of racing per year between mid-March and late November. As France-Galop is trying to spread the wealth of its black-type races around France, Fontainebleau has recently been awarded five listed races, among them the 5 ½-furlong Prix Cor de Chasse in late March and the 1¼-mile Prix Melisande for 3-year-old fillies in early June. These are in addition to three listed races on the track's big day in late November: the 1⅛-mile Prix Solitude for 3-year-old fillies, the six-furlong Prix Contessina for 3-year-olds and up, and the six-furlong Prix Zeddaan for 2-year-olds.

The first races were run at Fontainebleau in 1776 by Louis XVI. The first official races were held there on June 22, 1862, with Emperor Napoleon III and Empress Eugenie in attendance. The Chateau de Fontainebleau, still open to the public, had always been something of a weekend getaway for the king and his courtiers, especially during the autumn hunting season when the surrounding forest was filled with stags and boars.

LYON-PARILLY

Hippodrome Lyon-Parilly
4-6 Avenue Pierre Mendes-France
69500 Lyon, France

LOCATION: 260 miles southeast of Paris. Trains leave Paris-Gare de Lyon for the two-hour journey via fast train, the Tres Grande Vitesse (TGV). The racecourse is about five miles from the city center and is best reached by taxi.

Lyon-Parilly is a level, left-handed oval, 1⅛ miles around. Races of 1½ miles start at the head of the 2½-furlong stretch. One-mile races start from a chute off the "clubhouse turn" and make a mild left-hand bend onto the 3½-furlong backstretch, making it quite similar to Belmont Park's Widener Course mile. A five-furlong straight course joins the stretch.

Lyon-Parilly is one of France's better provincial tracks, as it draws runners not only from Bordeaux, Marseille, and Toulouse, but from the Paris region as well, especially for the big *quinte* handicaps. Top provincial trainers such as Jean-Claude Rouget and Henri-Alex Pantall do not hesitate to send horses here, raising the overall quality up to the standards at Compiegne and Fontainebleau, and sometimes beyond.

There are 15 days of racing per year at Lyon-Parilly from mid-April to early December. The Criterium de Lyon, a one-mile listed event for 2-year-olds run in late September, was used in 2007 by the Andre Fabre-trained Thewayyouare as a winning prep for his victory five weeks later in Saint-Cloud's Group 1 Criterium International. A year earlier the same race went to Literato, who as a 3-year-old would win Newmarket's Group 1 Champion Stakes, suggesting that the Criterium de Lyon is ripe for an upgrade to Group 3 status. Lyon's second listed race is the 1½-mile Prix du Grand Camp in late November.

The 1¼-mile Group 3 Prix Andre Baboin, formerly known as the Grand Prix des Provinces, rotates between Lyon-Parilly, Bordeaux-Le Bouscat, and Marseille-Borely.

As France's second city, Lyon is a historic and architectural treasure trove. It is home to numerous beautiful cathedrals and chapels. It is also the culinary center of France, the seed ground for many of France's best chefs, so there is no dearth of fine dining in this city of 470,000 hungry souls.

When leaving for Lyon from Paris, start your culinary adventures with lunch at the fabulous Gare de Lyon restaurant, Le Train Bleu, in which diners are transported back to La Belle Epoque by means of décor as well as cuisine.

The Lumiere brothers, Auguste and Louis, pioneers of the early film industry, were raised and educated in Lyon, living there for most of their lives. The house in which they lived and worked is now a museum devoted to their many cinematographic inventions as well as hundreds of their films and photographs. They are credited with having presented the first public film screening in history on December 28, 1895, in Paris, a program that included the incomparable *Arrival of a Train at La Ciotat,* a film so realistic it had viewers jumping out of their seats and running for cover.

VICHY

Hippodrome de Vichy-Bellerive
03200 Bellerive-sur-Allier, France
Phone: 011-33-4-70-32-47-00
Internet: www.courses-de-vichy.fr

LOCATION: 216 miles southeast of Paris, a three-hour journey by train from Paris-Gare de Lyon.

Founded in 1875, Vichy Racecourse is a level, 1⅜-mile, right-handed oval with a quarter-mile stretch. Races of 1½ miles start in front of the grandstand and make a complete loop around the two 90-degree turns. Races of 1¼ miles start from a chute and travel two furlongs before making a 45-degree right-handed turn onto the backstretch. One-mile races and seven-furlong races are one-turn affairs starting on the backstretch. There is a five-furlong straight course that meets the homestretch two furlongs from the line. The backstretch extends to form a 2¹⁄₁₆-mile jumps course. There is also a 6 ¼-furlong dirt trotting track inside the turf course.

Vichy runs 18 days of flat racing per year, beginning in late May and concluding in mid-September. La Grande Semaine ("the Great Week") consists of seven consecutive days of racing between the third Sunday and fourth Saturday of July, one or two of those dates at night, the rest daytime affairs. This meeting, the longest consecutive-day flat-race meeting on turf in Europe, serves as something of a table setter for the more important doings to follow at Deauville. It attracts more than the usual number of runners from Chantilly and Maisons-Laffitte, especially those that have no plans of traveling up to Deauville.

First run in 1900, the 1¼-mile, Group 3 Grand Prix de Vichy is run on the Wednesday night of the Grande Semaine meeting. In recent years it has become a prep for the Arlington Million. Its winner in 2005 and 2006, Touch of Land, would finish fifth and eighth in his respective Millions. The 2003 winner, Vangelis, would next finish seventh in Sulamani's Million before going on to multiple graded-race placings in America. Cheshire, the 2002 winner, would finish seventh in Beat Hollow's Million.

This indicates that the Grand Prix de Vichy winner in any normal year will be an Arlington Million also-ran, although some of them have gone on to become decent Group 2 types.

Vichy is a spa town famous for its mineral water, but it is no longer the fashionable resort it once was, its reputation tarnished in no small part by its role as the seat of Marshal Petain's collaborationist government during the Nazi occupation of France between 1940 and 1944.

Its population is aging and the town only seems to perk up—at least a little bit—for the big week of racing in late July.

AUTEUIL

Route d'Auteuil aux Lacs
75016 Paris, France
Phone: 011-33-1-49-10-20-30
Internet: www.france-galop.com

LOCATION: In the southeast corner of the Bois de Boulogne, adjacent to Paris's 16th arrondissement.

Auteuil is not only France's major jumps course, it is also one of the most beautiful racecourses in the world. As a city course that abuts the cosmopolitan Parisian neighborhoods of Auteuil and Passy, it provides nearby residents the luxury of walking to the track for the high-class jump racing that takes place there.

Opened in 1873, Auteuil is the site of France's two championship jump races, the 3⅝-mile Grand Steeple-Chase de Paris, run on the last Sunday in May, and the 3³⁄₁₆-mile Grande Course de Haies d'Auteuil (French Champion Hurdle), run on the fourth Sunday in June.

The first weekend of November is Le Grand Week-End de l'Obstacle, a cornucopia of six hurdle and chase races of championship caliber.

In 1962, Auteuil was the scene of what was surely the greatest ride in the history of horse racing. For that year's Grand Steeple-Chase de Paris, Fred Winter traveled across the English Channel to ride Mandarin in the race, which in those days was 3⅞ miles long. A few jumps into the race, Mandarin's bit broke, effectively leaving Winter without brakes or steering.

Somehow, Winter kept Mandarin jumping with the others, but when he had to throw his body weight to one side to keep his mount on course at the next-to-last fence, Mandarin lost his action and appeared to break down. Incredibly, horse and rider carried on, winning by a short head. Winter even won the next race, but Mandarin had suffered a bowed tendon and was retired as a riding horse.

The Grand Steeple, as Parisians call it, has been won by many great chasers, among them the country's most popular jumper, Katko, who took it three times from 1988 through 1990. In 1991 it went to The Fellow, who, three years later, would become the first and only French-trained horse to win the Cheltenham Gold Cup, making this brave "AQPS" the only horse to win the champion steeplechase races of both France and England.

AQPS sounds as if it belongs on a Roman banner. It is, in fact, the acronym for Autre Quand Pur-Sang, or horses other than Thoroughbred. A mix of Thoroughbred stock with traditional French mares of a stout-hearted breed, AQPS's are slightly larger and heavier than Thoroughbreds, with big feet and rather large, ugly heads. They are almost completely devoid of acceleration but can gallop all day long at a high rate of speed. They are a source of great stamina and are always prominent among the leading French long-distance chasers and hurdlers.

The Fellow's full brother, Al Capone II, won the Grand Steeple in 1997 to add to his seven straight victories in Auteuil's three-mile, 3½-furlong Prix La Haye Jousselin from 1993 through 1999. In 2000 he nearly won it an eighth time, finishing second to First Gold. In flat-racing terms, his is a feat comparable to winning the Jockey Club Gold Cup seven times in a row. Al Capone II's statue stands near the Auteuil paddock in memoriam.

Like any great racecourse, Auteuil has had its share of tragedy. In 1995, Ubu III, already a two-time winner of the Grande Course de Haies, landed the Grand-Steeple on a steaming-hot, airless, muggy Sunday in late June. A hundred yards past the finish, as winning rider Philippe Chevalier reached out to shake the hand of a rival rider, Ubu's legs turned to jelly. As Chevalier leaped off, Ubu collapsed, dead from an aneurism. The incident prompted France-Galop officials to reschedule the Grand-Steeple to May, when the weather is considerably cooler and less humid.

But Auteuil was the scene of an even sadder event in 1986 when Dawn Run fell while seeking a second victory in the Grand Course de Haies. She broke her neck and died instantly. Hailed as the greatest jump-racing mare in history, she had also won both the Champion Hurdle and the Cheltenham Gold Cup.

Auteuil Racecourse is neat as a pin, its hedges and jumps always kept in a pristine state. And it is those jumps that set the track apart from its British counterparts. Fences with names such as bullfinch, double barriere, oxer, rail-ditch et fence, and gros open-ditch need no translation. The different tests they provide the French jumper have led to an admission by many leading British trainers that French jump-ers are the best-schooled in the world.

With three large 1920s-era grandstands that were renovated in 1967, plus the exclusive president's stand, Auteuil still presents a Belle Epoque aura. The track holds 41 days of racing per year, 21 between late February and late June, 20 between early September and early December. An American racing fan in Paris could not enjoy himself more than by spending a day at Auteuil, preceded by lunch at Le Congres in the Porte d'Auteuil on the Boulevard Exelmans, one of the best brasseries in Paris.

To get to Auteuil, which is a stone's throw from Roland Garros Stadium, site of tennis's French Open, and across the Bois de Boulogne about two miles from Longchamp, take the Metro Ligne 10 to Porte d'Auteuil. The rear entrance to the track is visible from the Metro exit, after which you walk across the infield to the grandstand.

THE SOUTH OF FRANCE ▤

The southern provinces of France produce a good deal of competitive racing that has begun to make an impact in America of late, probably because horses trained there are less expensive than those trained near Paris. There are three centers of racing in the south of France: Bordeaux, Toulouse, and Marseille.

The names of two French-provincial trainers must be kept in mind when interpreting French form. In terms of total winners Jean-Claude Rouget, based in Pau, not far from Bordeaux, and Henri-Alex Pantall, who trains near Toulouse, are the only conditioners in France with numbers that compare to those of Andre Fabre, who has been the lead-ing trainer in France every year since 1987.

LEADING TRAINERS IN FRANCE 1998–2007

Name	Starts	Wins	Pct.	Earnings*
Fabre	4,426	1,415	.320	42,927,890
Rouget	6,625	1,544	.233	28,705,191
Pantall	7,948	1,538	.194	20,127,577

* In euros

There are two tracks in Bordeaux, Bordeaux-Le Bouscat and Bordeaux-La Teste, also known as La Teste de Buch or the Hippodrome Bequet.

Bordeaux-Le Bouscat is a 1¼-mile, right-handed oval with a stretch that is slightly longer than two furlongs. This is Rouget country as much as it is wine country. He dominates there, frequently sending his more prominent horses up to Paris to hunt bigger game.

Bordeaux-Le Bouscat is the site of four listed races, starting with the 1³⁄₁₆-mile Grand Prix de Bordeaux for older horses and the 1½-mile Derby du Midi for 3-year-olds, both run in late May. The 1³⁄₁₆-mile Prix Occitanie for 3-year-old fillies is held in early September. The one-mile Grand Criterium de Bordeaux for 2-year-olds goes in early October, and was run in 2008 on the same card as the 1¼-mile Group 3 Prix Andre Baboin, or Grand Prix des Provinces.

Bordeaux-La Teste is a 1¼-mile oval with a 4½-furlong stretch. Races of 1⅛ miles and 1¼ miles start out of a chute on the backstretch. La Teste runs 16 meetings per year.

The listed Prix La Sorellina at one mile for 3-year-old fillies in late June attracts a number of future American runners. Cicerole, who ran in the 2008 Beverly D, finished second in the 2007 edition in which future Calder allowance winner Tanguista finished third. The listed Criterium du Bequet is an early-August six-furlong juvenile contest. Its 2006 winner, Iron Lips, went on to win a subpar renewal of the six-furlong Prix Eclipse for trainer Carlos Laffon-Parias and owners the Wertheimer brothers, but later failed when ninth for Todd Pletcher in Golden Gate's Bienville Stakes, a perfect example of a precocious 2-year-old that fails to train on at 3.

Rouget will frequently send horses to run in Toulouse, which is 130 miles southeast of Bordeaux. But when he does so he is trespassing in Pantall territory. The track in Toulouse is a 1³⁄₁₆-mile right-handed oval with a two-furlong stretch. Toulouse is the only racecourse in the south of France to have a Group 3 all its own. That is the 1⁵⁄₁₆-mile Prix Fille de l'Air for fillies and mares. Run late in the season during the second week of November, it is frequently targeted by big outfits from Paris. Toulouse also runs the 1½-mile Derby du Languedoc in mid-June, the 1½-mile Prix Panacee for fillies and mares in mid-October, as well as the one-mile Criterium du Languedoc for 2-year-olds in early November.

There are two racetracks in Marseille, the hardscrabble Mediterranean port that lies about 100 miles east of Toulouse. Marseille-Borely is the more prominent. A left-handed mile, it very much resembles American tracks and hosts five listed races per year. In early May there is the 1¼-mile Prix Georges Trabaud for 3-year-old fillies, a race won in 2007 by All Is Vanity, subsequent winner of the Group 2 Prix de Sandringham at Chantilly and also the winner of a very hot Gulfstream allowance with Grade 2 cache in her U.S. debut.

In late September Borely is the site of the 1¼-mile La Coupe de Marseille, in which Pantall and Rouget finished one-two in 2007 with Criticism and Becher. In the 2007 Grand Prix de Marseille at 1¼ miles, Pantall took the first two places with Arlington Million veteran Touch of Land and Criticism. That those two were owned, respectively, by Gary Tanaka and Sheikh Mohammed gives you an idea of the kind of owners Pantall attracts.

The last two listed races on the Marseille-Borely program are the 1⅛-mile Prix Delahante for 2-year-olds and the 1½-mile Prix Max Sicard, which went in 2007 to the Rouget-trained Cristobal, an Aptitude colt owned by American Edmund Gann.

The other track frequented by les Marseillaise is Marseille-Vivaux. A bandbox by any definition, Vivaux is a left-handed six-furlong turf oval reminiscent of Timonium.

3

Ireland

THE CURRAGH ≣

The Curragh Racecourse
County Kildare
Ireland
Phone: 011-353-45-441-205
Internet: www.curragh.ie

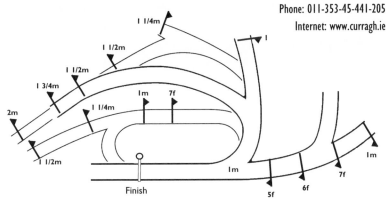

THE CURRAGH

LOCATION: 30 miles west of Dublin

COURSE DESCRIPTION: The Curragh is a two-mile, horseshoe-shaped, right-handed course. There are mild rises and descents on the turning course. The 1½-mile Irish Derby starts halfway through the half-mile back straight followed by a mild right-hand bend, a one-furlong straight, then another right-hand bend, a two-furlong straight, and the turn into the three-furlong stretch, which is mildly uphill most of the way.

The Irish 1000 and 2000 Guineas are run on a one-mile course that is virtually straight, consisting of a two-furlong straight before a very mild right-hand bend onto the five-furlong stretch, which joins the right-handed course's stretch three furlongs from home.

All races between five and seven furlongs are run on the straight course, as are all but a very few one-mile races.

The Curragh is a galloping track on which short-striding, close-coupled types are at something of a disadvantage. Stamina is paramount, the ability to see out a trip up the stretch essential. Horses that can't stay are inevitably found out, no matter what the distance.

HISTORY: The name Curragh is derived from the Gaelic word *currech,* meaning "racecourse." There has been racing on the site and elsewhere in Ireland for as long as the Irish and their Celtic and Gaelic ancestors have known how to ride horses, and that is a very long time, indeed.

Races were held in pre-Christian Ireland dating back to the time of Christ. When the Normans conquered Ireland in the 12th century, they declared the Curragh to be a royal common, but it wasn't until the Restoration of Charles II in England in 1660 that a more formal representation of the sport began to develop.

For better or worse, the histories of England and Ireland are forever intertwined, both in the general and racing senses. Lord Protector Oliver Cromwell, to this day still the most reviled Englishman in Ireland, banned racing there in 1649 as he had in England. Charles

The 2003 Irish 2000 Guineas on the broad swathe of the Curragh straight. Eventual winner Indian Haven is on the far right.

II encouraged it and by the mid-18th century, regular if infrequent meetings were being held on the Curragh.

These were, however, legally restricted to the English hierarchy that ruled Ireland. The infamous penal laws that made it illegal for a Catholic to own a horse worth more than five pounds made it all but impossible for the native population to participate in racing as owners.

But where there is a will there is a way, and Irish ingenuity found one. Some of the better horses in Ireland during this period were in fact owned by Catholics, who had the temerity to register them in the names of English Protestant friends.

A Jockey Club came into existence in 1757. In 1790 this became known as the Irish Turf Club or, as it is called in Ireland, simply the Turf Club. Before the end of 1800, leading Irish owners and trainers had built training centers around the Curragh. Many of these exist to this day in much the same form as they did more than 200 years ago.

Competition between the Irish and the English has always been keen in racing. The first Irish-trained horse to be genuinely competitive in top-class English company was Bran. A two-time winner at York in 1834, he finished second in that year's classic St. Leger at Doncaster.

Harkaway won 8 of 15 starts in England, among them the Goodwood Cup in 1838 and 1839, but it was Birdcatcher, or Irish Birdcatcher, as he is sometimes called, who signaled the start of a peculiarly Irish touch for Thoroughbred breeding that has persisted to this day.

A very good racehorse in his own right, Birdcatcher was foaled at Brownstown Stud in County Kildare in 1833. He won 7 of 15 career starts, all of them at the Curragh, before retiring to stud duty in 1838 at his place of birth. He spent 10 seasons in Ireland and 11 in England, where he was champion sire twice. He was the first Irish-bred stallion to sire an English classic winner, The Baron in the 1845 St. Leger. All told he sired three St. Leger winners, two 1000 Guineas winners, an Oaks winner, and a Derby winner, Daniel O'Rourke, in 1852. Birdcatcher is commemorated at the Curragh with an important nursery handicap run every September.

But those horses were all trained in England. It wasn't until 1907, nine years before the Easter Rising, that an Irish-trained horse, Orby, would win the Epsom Derby. Orby was trained by F. F. McCabe at Glencairn for his owner, Richard "Boss" Croker, an Irish-born, American-raised personage who had fought his way to the top of New York City's infamous Tammany Hall. Croker left his adopted country under a cloud of scandal in 1903, soon to become an Irish horseman with a legendary reputation.

The Curragh has long billed itself as the Home of the Irish Classics. Patterned after the English classics, the first Irish Derby was run there in 1866, the Irish Oaks had its start in 1895, the Irish St. Leger was first run in 1915, and both the Irish 2000 Guineas and Irish 1000 Guineas were inaugurated in 1921.

The 1866 Irish Derby, run at a distance of 1¾ miles, went to the English-owned-and-trained Selim. His Yorkshire owner, James Cockin, won again with Golden Plover in 1867. Only two horses ran for a mere 115 pounds in the 1868 renewal when the race appeared to be on the brink of extinction.

The Derby distance was finally reduced to the Epsom distance of 1½ miles in 1872 when it was won for the second year in a row by a filly, Trickstress. Eight fillies have won the Irish Derby, the most recent being Salsabil in 1990 and, four years later, Balanchine. Named, by mistake, for the great choreographer and founder of the New York City Ballet, George Balanchine, Balanchine the racehorse joined Nijinsky and Nureyev as the last of three great racehorses from the Northern Dancer line named for Russian dancers.

The 1895 Irish Derby went to Portmarnock, a son of the Isonomy stallion Gallinule, who is considered the first major Irish stallion in racing history. Gallinule sired six Irish Derby winners but was immortalized by the exploits of his great filly Pretty Polly, whose victories in the English versions of the 1000 Guineas, the Oaks, and the St. Leger, as well as the Coronation Stakes, the Nassau Stakes, and two Coronation Cups, stamped her as one of the great distaff Thoroughbreds of all time.

Ireland was officially neutral in World War II, the conflagration referred to on the Emerald Isle as "the emergency." Racing proceeded apace at the Curragh from 1940 through 1945, albeit without British participation. Four of the six wartime Irish Derbies were won by three of Irish racing's most noteworthy owners: the Aga Khan with his Bahram colt Turkhan in 1940; Joe McGrath with Windsor Slipper in 1942; and Major Dermot McCalmont's Slide On in 1944 and Piccadilly a year later.

Ballymoss can be credited with having introduced the modern age of Irish racing, courtesy of his trainer, Vincent O'Brien. Owned by American builder John McShain, Ballymoss would make up for his neck defeat to Crepello in the Epsom Derby by winning the St. Leger at Doncaster.

That the Irish Derby was being won by very good—and very well-bred—horses was evident in the victories of Ribocco in 1967 and Ribero in 1968. Both were sons of the undefeated two-time Arc winner Ribot, Ribero winning his Irish classic at the expense of the O'Brien-trained Epsom Derby winner Sir Ivor.

Ribocco and Ribero were both owned by American metals magnate Charles Engelhard. Stung, perhaps, by the defeat of Sir Ivor at the hands of the man who was reputedly the template for Ian Fleming's most famous villain, Goldfinger, O'Brien managed to convince Engelhard to send him a strapping 2-year-old Northern Dancer colt in 1969.

That was Nijinsky, who gave the superb Irish trainer, considered by many to be the best who has ever plied the trade, his third Irish Derby triumph in 1970. Already the winner of the 2000 Guineas and the Epsom Derby, Nijinsky was a handy three-length winner of the Curragh's mile-and-a-half classic at pinched odds of 4–11.

O'Brien would win two more Irish Derbies with The Minstrel in 1977 and El Gran Senor in 1984, bringing his total to five, one less than his six Epsom Derbies.

But perhaps the greatest of all Irish Derby performances came in 1983. With Lester Piggott deputizing for a suspended Walter Swinburn, the great Shergar recorded the handiest of four-length victories in following up on his astounding 10-length triumph in the Epsom Derby.

In an ideal world, the Irish Derby should serve as a kind of final between the winners of the English and French Derbies, which are always run three or four weeks earlier than the Curragh classic. This has happened less than one would hope, although the 1991 Irish Derby produced a memorable clash between Epsom winner Generous and Chantilly winner Suave Dancer, Generous giving his French rival a sound beating. Two years later Epsom Derby winner Commander In Chief beat French Derby winner Hernando. In 2000, Epsom Derby winner Sinndar beat French Derby winner Holding Court into sixth place at the Curragh.

In recent years the Irish Derby has proved to be an early-season pointer to the Breeders' Cup Turf. High Chaparral, the 2002 winner, would take that year's Turf as well as the 2003 edition, but Hurricane Run and Dylan Thomas would fail in their respective BC Turf tries, while Galileo would finish unplaced in the Breeders' Cup Classic.

The Irish Oaks has always played second fiddle to the English Oaks. In fact, it is really only the third-best Oaks after the Prix de Diane (French Oaks) and the English version. Nelson Bunker Hunt and his French trainer, Maurice Zilber, gave the race a shot in the arm in 1973 when they sent over Dahlia to win it after she had finished second to Allez France in the Diane.

User Friendly (1992) and Wemyss Bight (1993) were above-average winners, but Ramruma's 1999 score started a string of victories that has enabled the Irish Oaks to challenge its French and English counterparts for the title of the world's best Oaks.

Ramruma was followed in the winner's circle by Petrushka, later the winner of the Yorkshire Oaks and the Prix de l'Opera. English Oaks winner Ouija Board's 2004 Irish victory presaged triumphs in five more Group or Grade 1 races, among them two Breeders' Cup Filly and Mare Turfs. Aidan O'Brien, better known for his acumen with colts, landed the 2006 renewal with Alexandrova, then followed up with Peeping Fawn in 2007 and Moonstone in 2008. Alexandrova would win a total of three Group 1 races, Peeping Fawn four, but neither raced beyond her 3-year-old season.

American trainers are traditionally loath to test Europe's classic waters, but that was not the case in 1991 when Leo O'Brien returned to the Old Sod with Richard Bomze's homebred Fourstars Allstar to win the Irish 2000 Guineas. Although that was hardly a vintage renewal of the Irish Guineas, it produced the kind of excitement rarely seen in American racing circles outside of our annual plundering missions to Dubai. A product of astute breeding, outstanding training, great sportsmanship, and a superb ride from Mike Smith, Fourstars Allstar's victory in the Irish 2000 Guineas remains the only time an American-trained horse has ever won a European race on the flat.

ANALYSIS: The "Home of the Irish Classics" is really much more than that. Not only are 10 of Ireland's 12 Group 1 races run at the Curragh—and 34 of the country's total of 55 group races—the venerable County Kildare track is the site of the majority of Ireland's most competitive maidens and handicaps.

Only Leopardstown has anything approaching the quality of the sport produced at the Curragh, and the reasons for this are plain. The Curragh has always been the home of most of Ireland's best trainers. As the oldest track in the country, it stands to reason it should have a near-monopoly on the best prizes at almost every level in a country as small as Ireland, geographically speaking.

But even at the Curragh, there are four trainers who rule the roost, winning most of the best races, be they maidens or Group 1's. This may sound as if Irish racing is rather elitist, but it must be remembered that Ireland has a population of just 4.1 million, about half that of New York City.

The trainers that dominate at the Curragh are household names even in American racing circles. Three of them are connected to a trio of the world's leading owner-breeders, and two of them train not very far from the Curragh itself.

■ **AIDAN O'BRIEN:** The latest "Master of Ballydoyle," in Cashel, County Tipperary, is the private trainer for John Magnier and his Coolmore Stud associates, the most prominent of whom are Michael Tabor, Derrick Smith, and James Nagle.

Ireland's champion amateur rider in 1993 and 1994, O'Brien started out training both on the flat and over jumps, just like his predecessor at Ballydoyle, Vincent O'Brien, to whom he is not related.

Aidan's biggest achievement over jumps came with Istabraq, whose three consecutive victories from 1998 through 2000 in Cheltenham's Champion Hurdle recalled Vincent's three-timer in the same race with Hatton's Grace (1949–51).

Since taking out a license in 1993, Aidan O'Brien has won the four Irish classics 18 times. Among his winners were Galileo, High Chaparral, and Dylan Thomas in the Derby; Alexandrova and Peeping Fawn in the Oaks; Rock of Gibraltar and Henrythenavigator in the 2000 Guineas; and Imagine, Yesterday, and Halfway to Heaven in the 1000 Guineas.

His 12 British classic winners include Galileo and High Chaparral in the Derby; Imagine and Alexandrova in the Oaks; Rock of Gibraltar, George Washington, and Henrythenavigator in the 1000 Guineas; and Milan and Scorpion in the St. Leger.

He has also won the French 2000 Guineas three times and the French 1000 once. Altogether, O'Brien landed 33 European classics from 1997 through 2008, an average of 2.75 per year.

Add a pair of King George VI and Queen Elizabeth Diamond Stakes winners, Galileo and Dylan Thomas, along with the latter's Prix de l'Arc de Triomphe score, plus two Breeders' Cup Turf victories with High Chaparral and a Juvenile victory with Johannesburg, and you get the picture.

Yet that list does not include his five-time Group 1 winner Giant's Causeway, champion stayers Yeats and Septimus, dual classic winner Desert King, Arlington Million winner Powerscourt, and assorted champions such as Oratorio, Rumplestiltskin, Hawk Wing, Fasliyev, and Holy Roman Emperor.

Backed by Magnier, whom some people consider the most powerful man in Ireland, O'Brien probably gets even more out of the horses he trains than could be expected. Even though he was still a year shy of his fortieth birthday as this was published, it is not too early to state that he is one of the greatest trainers in the history of racing.

- **DERMOT WELD:** Trains just around the corner from the Curragh's main gate at Roswell House, where Moyglare Stud is his number one owner. Three times the Irish champion amateur jumps rider, he began his training career in 1972. He has won five Irish classics and one in England, that with Refuse To Bend in the 2000 Guineas of 2003. His international reputation, however, stretches at least as far as that of O'Brien.

  Weld is the only trainer based in the Northern Hemisphere to have won the Melbourne Cup, doing it twice, with Vintage Crop in 1993 and Media Puzzle in 2002, then finishing second in 2004 behind the great Makybe Diva with his four-time Irish St. Leger winner, Vinnie Roe. He is also the only foreign trainer to win an American classic, taking the 1990 Belmont Stakes with Go and Go. In 2003 Weld added to his American haul when he engineered Dimitrova's victory in the American Oaks at Hollywood Park and the Flower Bowl Handicap at Belmont Park. He dominated Arlington Park's American Derby from 2000 through 2004, winning it three times with Pine Dance, Evolving Tactics, and Simple Exchange. In 2008 he went one better at Arlington when he trained Bert Firestone's Winchester to a 7¼-length trouncing of the Grade 1 Secretariat Stakes.

- **JOHN OXX:** The Aga Khan's Irish conditioner began his training career in 1979 and works out of Killabeg Stables at the Curragh. His first classic winner, Ridgewood Pearl in the 1995 Irish 1000 Guineas, doubled up in the Breeders' Cup Mile. Since then he has won the Irish Derby twice, the Irish Oaks twice, the Epsom Derby once, the King George twice, and the Arc once, his best horses being Sinndar (Epsom Derby, Irish Derby, Arc) and Alamshar (Irish Derby, King George). He was also responsible for the filly Timarida, winner not only of the Beverly D and the E. P. Taylor in North America, but also the Irish Champion Stakes against colts at Leopardstown.

- **JIM BOLGER:** Born on Christmas Day in 1941, he is based at Glebe House in Coolcullen, County Carlow, some 40 miles south of the Curragh, closer to Kilkenny and Gowran Park. He has been long renowned in Ireland, but his international reputation has only fully blossomed in the last two decades. Not attached to any of the world's great owner-breeders, Bolger has always had a knack with juveniles, especially those on the distaff side.

  Among his big-race winners are Give Thanks (Irish Oaks), two-time Group 1 winners Flame of Tara and Park Appeal, Irish

Champion winner Park Express, and Jet Ski Lady, the 12-length winner in 1991 of the English Oaks. A year later, he scored a 12-length victory with St. Jovite in the Irish Derby, which he followed with a six-length score in the King George for American owner Virginia Kraft Payson.

The excellent racemare Alexander Goldrun provided him with five Group 1 tallies in four countries: Ireland, England, France, and Hong Kong. Bolger, however, has surpassed himself in recent seasons, training Teofilo to an undefeated juvenile championship season in 2006, the same year he guided Finsceal Beo to the European 2-year-old filly title.

Finsceal Beo would go on to capture both the English 1000 Guineas and the Irish version, missing by just a head in what would have been an unprecedented Guineas triple in the Poule d'Essai des Pouliches. In 2007, Bolger literally duplicated his 2006 achievement with Teofilo, taking the European juvenile championship with New Approach, who won the same five races as had Teofilo. New Approach would train on to win the 2008 Epsom Derby.

Bolger rarely, if ever, sends horses to run in America, primarily because he objects to this country's policy of allowing race-day medication, and that is our loss.

These are the four men who command the greatest attention at the Curragh and the other major Irish tracks. It is really quite rare to see another Irish trainer winning an Irish Group 1, although English and French trainers do pick up their share of top Irish prizes. It is even rarer to see another Irish trainer win a Group 1 or even a Group 2 outside of Ireland.

That the Irish horseman has a special way with Thoroughbreds cannot be denied. Until it began capitalizing on its membership in the European Union, Ireland was a relatively poor country, yet it had begun to build up a powerful breeding industry in the early 20th century. Under the guidance of Englishman Robert Sangster's Swettenham Stud, Irish breeding boomed in the 1980s. But it was one of Sangster's partners, John Magnier, who led the revolution that has made Ireland, pound-for-pound, the world's leading Thoroughbred-breeding nation.

This is due in no small part to Magnier's influence in high Irish places.

By maintaining a close relationship with Irish lawmakers, Irish racing has pulled its prize money out of the doldrums. A typical maiden at the Curragh goes for $23,000, Group 3's for at least $120,000. More important, the Irish bloodstock industry benefits from a sweetheart law that enables owners of stallions to elude taxation on stud fees.

No one has capitalized more on this situation than John Magnier and his Coolmore Stud, where the presence of established stallions such as Sadler's Wells, Montjeu, Galileo, Rock of Gibraltar, Danehill Dancer, Peintre Celebre, and Night Shift has been supplemented in recent years by the likes of Dylan Thomas, High Chaparral, Hurricane Run, and Holy Roman Emperor.

Even in Kentucky, where the tax breaks are hardly as generous, Coolmore stands Fusaichi Pegasus, Giant's Causeway, Johannesburg, Grand Slam, Scat Daddy, Tale of the Cat, and Thunder Gulch. Moreover, selected Coolmore stallions will commute to Australia for the Southern Hemisphere breeding season.

International in outlook, with classic and major Group 1 victories the objective, Coolmore is the template for the modern bloodstock operation. If it is true that whoever controls the means of production controls the future, then Coolmore Stud is writing the most important chapters on horse racing's future.

TRACK RECORDS (unofficial)

DISTANCE	RECORD TIME	HORSE	DATE
5f	57.17	Bali Royal	July 16, 2005
6f	1:08.10	Invincible Spirit	Sept. 15, 2001
6f, 63y	1:12.40	Bold Tack*	June 11, 1975
7f	1:20.90	Hawk Wing	Sept. 16, 2001
1m (Str)	1:35.00	Arctic Storm	May 16, 1962
1m (RH)	1:34.30	Llyn Gwynant	July 19, 1989
1⅛m	1:50.40	Adaala	July 17, 2005
1¼m	2:00.60	Market Booster	June 27, 1992
1⅜m	2:18.60	Lisieux Rose	Aug. 15, 1998
1½m	2:25.60**	St. Jovite	June 28, 1992
	2:27.10	Galileo	July 1, 2001
1¾m	2:55.40	Thetford Forest	July 15, 1990
	2:55.40	Arrikala	June 28, 1992
2m	3:21.80	King Carew	Sept. 14, 2003

* Disqualified

** Under dispute. Considered by many clockers to be at least 1.5 seconds too fast.

MAJOR RACES (Chronological Order)

RACE	CONDITIONS
Park Express Stakes-G3	1m 3yo+ f&m
Gladness Stakes-G3	7f 4yo+
Alleged Stakes (Listed)	1¼m 4yo+
Loughbrown Stakes (Listed)	7f 3yo
Tetrarch Stakes-G3	7f 3yo c&f
Athasi Stakes-G3	7f 3yo+ f&m
Mooresbridge Stakes-G3	1¼m 4yo+
Irish 2000 Guineas-G1	1m 3yo c&f
Greenlands Stakes-G3	6f 3yo+
Ridgewood Pearl Stakes-G3	1m 4yo+ f&m
Marble Hill Stakes (Listed)	5f 2yo
Irish 1000 Guineas-G1	1m 3yo f
Tattersalls Gold Cup-G1	1 5/16m 4yo+
Gallinule Stakes-G3	1¼m 3yo
Silver Stakes (Listed)	1¼m 3yo+
Balanchine Stakes (Listed)	1¼m 3yo f
Pretty Polly Stakes-G1	1¼m 3yo+ f&m
Curragh Cup-G3	1¾m 4yo+
Sapphire Stakes-G3	5f 3yo+
Irish Derby-G1	1½m 3yo c&f
Railway Stakes-G2	6f 2yo
Celebration Stakes (Listed)	1m 3yo+
Irish Oaks-G1	1½m 3yo f
Anglesey Stakes-G3	6f, 63y 2yo
Minstrel Stakes-G3	7f 3yo+
Kilboy Estate Stakes (Listed)	1⅛m 3yo+ f&m
Phoenix Stakes-G1	6f 2yo c&f
Coolmore Stakes (Listed)	5f 2yo
Sweet Mimosa Stakes (Listed)	6f 3yo+ f&m
Debutante Stakes-G2	7f 2yo f
Royal Whip Stakes-G2	1¼m 3yo+
Phoenix Sprint Stakes-G3	6f 3yo+
Futurity Stakes-G2	7f 2yo
Ballycullen Stakes (Listed)	1m 3yo+
Moyglare Stud Stakes-G1	7f 2yo f
Flying Five-G3	5f 3yo+
Round Tower Stakes-G3	6f 2yo
Dance Design Stakes (Listed)	1⅛m 3yo+

RACE	CONDITIONS
Goffs Million (Restricted)	6f 2yo c&g
Goffs Fillies Million (Restricted)	6f 2yo f
Irish St. Leger-G1	1¾m 3yo+
Blandford Stakes-G2	1¼m 3yo+ f&m
Renaissance Stakes-G3	6f 3yo+
Flame of Tara Stakes (Listed)	6f 2yo f
National Stakes-G1	7f 2yo c&f
Solonaway Stakes-G3	1m 3yo+
Blenheim Stakes (Listed)	6f 2yo
Beresford Stakes-G2	1m 2yo
Park Stakes-G3	7f 2yo f
Testimonial Stakes (Listed)	6f 3yo+

DAYS OF RACING: The Curragh holds 18 days of racing per year between late March and late September. The Guineas meeting is run on the last weekend of May. The three-day Derby meeting is generally run on the last weekend of June, sometimes the first weekend of July. The Oaks is run on the second Sunday after the Derby. The St. Leger meeting is run on the second weekend of September.

HOW TO GET THERE: Trains for the Curragh leave Dublin's Heuston Station direct to the racecourse on classic and Group 1 days only. On all other days, trains stop a few miles away in Kildare, but there is a shuttle bus at Kildare Station to take you to the racecourse.

SURROUNDING AREA: Unlike London and Paris, Dublin is a one-horse town. Its pubs are convivial and there is a lively, if rather small, theater scene. Fans of Irish literature can visit the Dublin Writers Museum, the James Joyce Museum, and the Shaw Birthplace while asking themselves why so many of Ireland's greatest writers—Joyce, Shaw, Swift, Sheridan, Beckett, and Trevor—left Ireland to spend the larger part of their careers in England or France.

Phoenix Park, the largest urban public park in Europe, lies just two miles west of the city center. It is the site of the Dublin Zoo, but may be of greater interest to racing fans as it is also the site of the now sadly defunct Phoenix Park Racecourse.

But if you want to visit what remains of the ghostly grandstand and the outline of the track, you must hurry, as the land on which the racecourse lies has been marked for a housing development.

Phoenix Park Racecourse opened in 1902. Built on a site originally used for "flapping races"—races run without the sanction of the local Jockey Club—it was modeled on England's enclosed "park courses." It proved to be very popular with Dubliners until the 1980s, when attendance tailed off. Facing a threat of closure, the track was rescued by Robert Sangster and company, but finally closed its doors for good in 1995.

Phoenix Park was the home of the Phoenix Stakes, a six-furlong Group 1 sprint for 2-year-olds that was sponsored for years by Heinz and known as the Heinz 57 Phoenix Stakes. The 1¼-mile Irish Champion Stakes, which has become one of the highest-rated races in the world over the last decade, was born as the Phoenix Champion Stakes, its first winner in 1984 the great future stallion Sadler's Wells.

Closer to the Curragh itself is the Irish National Stud in Tully, County Kildare. Owned by the Irish government and open to the public, it includes a racing museum in which stands the skeleton of Arkle, widely regarded as the greatest jumper in history. Among the stallions standing at the stud is four-time Irish St. Leger winner and Melbourne Cup runner-up Vinnie Roe.

LEOPARDSTOWN

Leopardstown Racecourse
Foxrock
Dublin 18, Ireland
Phone: 011-353-1-289-0500
Internet: www.leopardstown.com

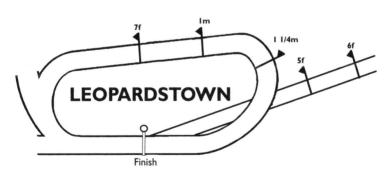

LOCATION: Six miles south of the center of Dublin.

COURSE DESCRIPTION: A left-handed, virtually level, somewhat irregularly shaped oval 1¾ miles around, the clubhouse turn being slightly milder and wider than the far turn, which is mild by American standards. Races of 1¼ miles, like the Irish Champion Stakes, start midway on the first turn, then proceed for a furlong on the bend before reaching the three-furlong backstretch. The homestretch is slightly longer than two furlongs.

There is a five-furlong straight course, recently reduced from six furlongs, that cuts diagonally through the clubhouse turn, resembling somewhat the old Widener chute at Belmont Park.

HISTORY: The site of the racecourse was from medieval times until the 17th century a leper colony called Leperstown, a name that ultimately morphed into Leopardstown. The racecourse opened in 1888 and was an immediate success, the crowd on opening day, August 27, so large that many people got no closer to the track than the Foxrock train station, from where a young Samuel Beckett, future author of *Waiting for Godot,* watched the races from the platform.

Leopardstown is a park racecourse and was modeled on the most successful of those tracks in England, Sandown Park. The track proved very popular with fans in its early days, but has always played second fiddle to the Curragh as far as horses are concerned, primarily because many of Ireland's best Thoroughbreds are trained at or near the Curragh. Few are trained near Leopardstown or Dublin.

This caused problems in 1910 when railroad strikes severely impeded the transport of horses to Leopardstown. In 1911 there was no racing at the track for just that reason.

In 1969 Leopardstown was taken over by the Irish Racing Board, which upgraded the entire facility, making it, in 1971, Ireland's first truly modern racetrack. The problem of shipping horses from the Curragh's training centers was no longer a problem, what with the advent of auto transport.

Leopardstown continues to be a popular destination for Dublin racing fans, although its proximity to the capital had a great deal to do with the demise of Phoenix Park in 1995.

ANALYSIS: While the general fare at Leopardstown is not quite in the same league as that at the Curragh, any given maiden, conditions race, or handicap here is comparable and, occasionally, superior. And while the Curragh overwhelms Leopardstown in terms of sheer class (it runs 10 Group 1's and six Group 2's to Leopardstown's two Group 1's), L'town's Group 3 races are every bit as good as those at the Curragh.

What's more, Leopardstown is the site of the best race run in Ireland, the 1¼-mile Irish Champion Stakes.

Since its inception at the now defunct Phoenix Park in 1984, when it was won by Sadler's Wells, the horse who would become Europe's leading stallion through the late 20th and early 21st centuries, this race has commanded the attention of handicappers and breeders alike. Its winners since then have been a veritable who's who of Thoroughbred royalty.

Kostroma, Stagecraft, Alhaarth, Xaar, Islington, Powerscourt, Alexander Goldrun? They could only manage third in the Irish Champion.

Seattle Song, St. Jovite, Opera House, Desert King, Galileo, Hawk Wing, Falbrav, Ouija Board? They were merely runners-up.

Besides Sadler's Wells, its winners include Triptych, Suave Dancer, Dr Devious, Timarida, High Chaparral, Azamour, and Dylan Thomas (twice). But it was the five-year stretch from 1997 through 2001 during which the Irish Champion Stakes was without question the best race in the world.

Its winners those years were Pilsudski, subsequent winner of the Breeders' Cup Turf and the Japan Cup; Swain, previous winner of two King Georges and subsequently an unlucky third in the Breeders' Cup Classic; Daylami, who came to Leopardstown off victories in the

Fantastic Light (right) and Frankie Dettori outgame Galileo and Michael Kinane in Leopardstown's memorable 2001 Irish Champion Stakes.

Coronation Cup and the Prince of Wales's Stakes and who would win the Breeders' Cup Turf two starts later; five-time Group 1 winner Giant's Causeway, second by a whisker in the Breeders' Cup Classic; and Fantastic Light (in an epic duel with Galileo), a seven-time Group/Grade 1 winner in five countries who would win the Breeders' Cup Turf later the same year.

Not even the Prix de l'Arc de Triomphe has had a roll call of winners at that caliber during any five-year period since the early 1990s.

The Irish Champion Stakes makes a perfect prep for the Breeders' Cup Turf and the Filly and Mare Turf, as well as the Breeders' Cup Classic, as long as the horse can handle dirt, as could Swain and Giant's Causeway. All told, its winners since 1997 have won five Breeders' Cup races, its runners-up one (Ouija Board in the 2006 Filly and Mare Turf), and its third-place finishers one (Islington in the 2003 Filly and Mare Turf).

Leopardstown's other Group 1 contest, the one-mile Matron Stakes, has had a dizzying ascent to the heights since it moved to the Dublin track from the Curragh in 2002 when it was still a Group 3. A year later it was upgraded to Group 2 status, and a year after that to Group 1, but this rise has been due as much to European racing's effort to upgrade their filly-and-mare program in general, a policy engendered in no small part as an effort to dissuade owners from selling their better fillies to America, where there has always been a strong graded-race program for older females.

The 1991 Matron winner, Kooyonga, would beat colts in the Group 1 Eclipse Stakes a year later. Timarida followed her 1995 Matron win with an Irish Champion score the next year. Two starts after her Matron tally in 1996, Donna Viola won the Yellow Ribbon as she embarked on an American career that would net her two Grade 1 victories and a Grade 2.

Since it became a Group 1 race in 2004, the Matron has lived up to its exalted billing with victories by seven-time Group 1 winner Soviet Song, dual 1000 Guineas winner Attraction, and the overachieving Red Evie, but it is not quite the race that is Deauville's Prix Rothschild (ex-Astarte) or Goodwood's Nassau Stakes, both of which are annually contested by some of the very best European distaffers.

Among Leopardstown's 15 Group 3 contests are a number of important springtime classic preps. Galileo pulled off the Ballysax Stakes-Derby Trial double in 2001 before landing the more prestigious Epsom Derby-Irish Derby double. High Chaparral engineered the same four-timer a year later. Sinndar had been second in the Ballysax and first in the Derby Trial before pulling off his Epsom-Irish Derby double in 2000.

In 2003 Alamshar won the Derby Trial before finishing third at Epsom and then winning the Irish Derby. In 2004, Grey Swallow used victory in the 2000 Guineas Trial as an early steppingstone to his Irish Derby victory. And Dylan Thomas won the Derby Trial prior to his head third in the Epsom Derby, which he followed with victory in the Irish Derby.

From all this, it can be argued that Leopardstown's Derby Trial is the most informative classic trial in Europe, if not the world.

MAJOR RACES (Chronological Order)

RACE	CONDITIONS
Leopardstown 2000 Guineas Trial-G3	1m 3yo c&g
Leopardstown 1000 Guineas Trial-G3	7f 3yo f
Ballysax Stakes-G3	1¼m 3yo
Heritage Stakes (Listed)	1m 4yo + c&g
Derrinstown Stud 1000 Guineas Trial-G3	1m 3yo f
Derby Trial-G3	1¼m 3yo
Amethyst Stakes (Listed)	1m 3yo+
Saval Beg Stakes (Listed)	1¾m 4yo+
Ballyogan Stakes-G3	6f 3yo+ f&m
Glencairn Stakes (Listed)	1m 4yo+
Ballycorus Stakes-G3	7f 3yo+
Rochestown Stakes (Listed)	6f 2yo
Nijinsky Stakes (Listed)	1⅛m 3yo+
Brownstown Stakes-G3	7f 3yo+ f&m
Golden Fleece Stakes (Listed)	7f 2yo
Silver Flash Stakes-G3	7f 2yo
Challenge Stakes (Listed)	1¾m 3yo+
Meld Stakes-G3	1¼m 3yo+
Tyros Stakes-G3	7f 2yo
Ballyroan Stakes-G3	1½m 3yo+
Desmond Stakes-G3	1m 3yo+
Hurry Harriet Stakes (Listed)	1¼m 3yo+ f&m
Irish Champion Stakes-G1	1¼m 3yo+
Matron Stakes-G1	1m 3yo+ f&m
Kilternan Stakes-G3	1¼m 3yo+
Killavullan Stakes-G3	7f 2yo
Trigo Stakes (Listed)	1¼m 3yo+
Eyrefield Stakes (Listed)	1⅛m 2yo
Knockaire Stakes (Listed)	7f 3yo+

DAYS OF RACING: Leopardstown runs 15 days of flat racing annually between early April and early November, including most Wednesday evenings from late May through late July. The big day is the first Saturday in September when both of the track's Group 1 races, the Irish Champion Stakes and the Matron Stakes, are run, along with the Group 3 Kilternan Stakes.

Leopardstown also conducts seven days of jump racing per year over both hurdles and steeplechase fences between late December and early March. The highlight is the four-day Christmas Meeting that begins on Boxing Day, December 26. This meeting features three important Grade 1 events—a chase, a novice chase, and a hurdle.

HOW TO GET THERE: From Dublin use the DART commuter line to Blackrock Station.

Other Racecourses in Ireland

CORK ≡

Cork Racecourse (Mallow) Limited
Killarney Road
Mallow, County Cork
Ireland
Phone: 011-353-225-0213
Internet: www.corkracecourse.ie

LOCATION: 120 miles southwest of Dublin, 18 miles north of the city of Cork, and one mile from the town of Mallow. Trains from Dublin's Heuston Station to Cork change for Mallow, from where there is a free shuttle bus to the racecourse.

The area around Mallow is hallowed ground for lovers of Irish racing, for it was just five miles north of what is now Cork Racecourse that the first steeplechase race gave birth to jump racing.

It was in 1752 when Edmund Blake challenged a certain Mr. O'Callaghan to race their steeds from Buttevant Church to St. Leger Church in Doneraile, 4½ miles away. The race was contested over natural terrain, which meant that they would be jumping stone walls, hedges, streams, and ditches, as well as traversing lengthy sections on the flat.

This was the first steeplechase race. Posterity does not record the winner, but is it merely a coincidence that the world's most famous steeplechase, Aintree's Grand National, is run at the same 4½-mile distance?

Mallow Racecourse opened in 1924. In 1996 the track underwent a complete overhaul, reopening in 1997 with its name changed to Cork. The flat track is a 1½-mile, right-handed oval, its first turn sharper than its second. The stretch is more than a half-mile long, extending to form a straight six-furlong course.

There are 19 days of racing a year at Cork, 10 days on the flat from late March to late August, seven days over jumps, plus two mixed meetings in mid-October.

Six black-type races are run on the flat, chief among them a pair of Group 3's, the Noblesse Stakes in mid-June and the Give Thanks Stakes in early August, both at 1½ miles for fillies and mares. It is a measure of Cork's value that the first two in the 2007 Give Thanks were owned by Mrs. John Magnier (Downtown, who sported a fancy Danehill-User Friendly pedigree) and the Aga Khan (his Kalanisi filly Hasanka).

Cork's four listed races are the six-furlong Cork Stakes in early May, the juvenile six-furlong Rochestown Stakes on Noblesse Stakes day, the one-mile Platinum Stakes on Give Thanks day, and the 1¹⁄₁₆-mile Navigation Stakes in mid-October.

The 2007 Give Thanks winner, Downtown, was trained by David Wachman, one of southern Ireland's leading conditioners. Married to John Magnier's daughter Katie, Wachman trains in Fethard in County Tipperary, less than 50 miles from Cork Racecourse, where he has a number of his father-in-law's horses under his care.

The 34-year-old Wachman has had a number of black-type winners in the last few years, among them Castledale, who went on to win Hollywood's Generous Stakes in his American debut and the Santa Anita Derby as a 3-year-old. His Damson won the juvenile Group 1 Phoenix Stakes in 2004. A year later he sent Luas Line to Hollywood Park, where she finished fourth behind Cesario in the American Oaks. Back in Ireland, Luas Line beat older colts in the Platinum Stakes, won a listed race at Gowran Park, then returned to America to win the Grade 1 Garden City at Belmont Park.

An Englishman in Ireland, Wachman (pronounced "Watchman") is clearly a trainer to watch.

GOWRAN PARK ≣

Gowran Park Racecourse
Gowran, County Kilkenny
Ireland
Phone: 011-353-56-772-6225
Internet: www.gowranpark.ie

LOCATION: 60 miles south-southwest of Dublin.

Perhaps Ireland's most picturesque racecourse, Gowran (pronounced GO-ran) Park became the sixth Irish track to receive a Group 3 race when the 1³⁄₁₆-mile Denny Cordell Lavarack Stakes for fillies and mares was upgraded from listed status in 2006. In its 2007 running, Timarwa won it as a prelude to her sixth-place finish in the Breeders' Cup Filly and Mare Turf. Generally speaking, however, the race does not produce runners as talented as Timarwa, who was a daughter of the immensely talented mare Timarida.

An undulating, 1½-mile right-handed track with a three-furlong stretch, Gowran has 16 days of racing per year. Six of these are flat meetings, eight are over jumps, and two are mixed.

While Newmarket's 2000 Guineas winner Refuse To Bend, Belmont Park's Garden City winner Luas Line, and Ascot's Royal Lodge Stakes winner Admiralofthefleet all won earlier races at Gowran Park, the day-in, day-out fare here is average, albeit of a competitive nature. As is the case with most of Ireland's midlevel tracks, the quality of the jump racing is markedly better than that on the flat. Hedgehunter was the eight-length winner of a three-mile handicap chase here a year prior to his Grand National triumph in 2005.

LAYTOWN ≣

Laytown Racecourse
Laytown, County Meath
Ireland
Phone: 011-353-41-984-2111
Internet: www.air.ie

LOCATION: 29 miles north of Dublin on the coast of the Irish Sea.

Racing at Laytown

While Laytown is not a major racing venue by any stretch of the imagination, it holds a special place on the racing calendar as the only remaining strand, or beach, meeting officially sanctioned by the Jockey Club of a major racing nation.

In fact, Laytown is not a racecourse at all; it is a small seaside resort. The townsfolk began conducting race meetings on the beach in 1876 under the auspices of the local parish priest, with officially sanctioned meetings starting in 1901.

The current once-a-year meeting is held on the last Tuesday in May or the first Tuesday in June. At midmorning of the big day, stewards clad in hip-boots wade into the receding sea to mark out the course, inserting rails into the sand. Shortly after noon the tide rolls out and the beach is cleared to prepare for the first race.

The course used to be a right-handed affair with a single, very tight turn that horses frequently had difficulty maneuvering. When, in 1995, four horses died in a horrific accident caused by two that had blown the turn, it was decided that future meetings at Laytown would be run on a straight course.

The quality of the racing is low-end. Longtime maidens, weak handi-cappers, and jumpers looking for a little exercise make up the majority of the fields. In 18 years of preparing foreign form for *The Racing Times* and the *Daily Racing Form,* this observor can remember only one horse with Laytown form who ever made it to the United States.

But excellence is not the point of Laytown. It is a country-fair meeting, an excuse for the locals to have a special day out on the beach. In 1950, they were joined by the Aga Khan and his wife, the Begum Khan. Some of the horses that will be running later in the afternoon might be ridden out into the sea for a late-morning bath. The paddock is on a lawn overlooking the beach. Nearby are tents for dining and drinking. The bookies set up their stalls and even the Irish Tote is present for those who prefer parimutuel wagering.

Dermot Weld always sends a few runners to Laytown, and if the sun is shining, so much the better, for if the bookies have taken you for a bath during the races, you can refresh yourself later with a real bath in the soothingly cool waters of the Irish Sea.

NAAS ☰

Naas Racecourse
Tipper Road
Naas, County Kildare
Ireland
Phone: 011-353-45-897-391
Internet: www.naasracecourse.com

LOCATION: 18 miles southwest of Dublin, 10 miles east of the Curragh. Trains depart Dublin's Heuston Station for Sallins Station just outside Naas, from where there is a shuttle-bus service to the track.

The first races were run at Naas (pronounced "Nayce") on June 19, 1924. It is a somewhat triangular, left-handed course about 1¾ miles around. Races at 1½ miles start from a chute just beyond the finish line, one-mile races from a chute at the farthest point from the grandstand. These go straight for three furlongs before making a 95-degree turn into the half-mile stretch, which extends to form a six-furlong straight course.

Naas is known for its large fields, especially in maidens, due to the fact that it is so close to the many training facilities at the Curragh, but the quality of those maidens and Naas's handicaps is generally a cut below those run at the Curragh. One race that always manages to draw a good, competitive field is the six-furlong Birdcatcher Nursery Handicap for 2-year-olds, run on the second Sunday in October, when it shares top billing with the Garnet Stakes, a one-mile listed race for fillies and mares.

Like Cork, Naas plays host to a pair of Group 3 races each year. The 1¼-mile Blue Wind Stakes for fillies and mares in mid-May is a prep for the Curragh's prestigious Group 1 Pretty Polly Stakes in late June.

The early June meeting features the six-furlong Swordlestown Stud Sprint Stakes for juvenile fillies, an event that attracts precocious young ladies from many of Ireland's best barns, as it makes a perfect prep for the 2-year-old filly races at Royal Ascot. In 2007 the Aidan O'Brien-trained You'resothrilling, a full sister to Giant's Causeway, won it as a prelude to her victory in Newmarket's Group 2 Cherry Hinton Stakes, defeating the Jim Bolger-trained Saoirse Abu, who would later beat colts in the Group 1 Phoenix Stakes before defeating members of her own sex in the Group 1 Moyglare Stud Stakes.

A year later, Cuis Ghair won the Swordlestown as a prelude to her victory in Royal Ascot's Group 3 Albany Stakes.

On the same day as the Swordlestown, the track runs the listed five-furlong Naas Sprint Stakes, which serves as a prep for the two Group 1 Royal Ascot sprints, the King's Stand Stakes and the Golden Jubilee Stakes.

Naas conducts 15 days of racing per year. Six of these are on the flat, seven over jumps, and two are mixed meetings. The quality of the jump racing is considerably better than that on the flat. Two of the greatest jumpers in history, Arkle and Mill House, were both winners here back in the 1960s.

TIPPERARY

Tipperary Racecourse
Limerick Junction
County Tipperary
Ireland
Phone: 011-353-625-1357
Internet: www.tipperaryraces.ie

LOCATION: 114 miles southwest of Dublin, 54 miles north of Cork.

Racing in Tipperary dates back to 1848. The current course, which was called Limerick Junction until 1986, opened in 1916. It is a left-handed, rectangular track measuring 1½ miles with a three-furlong stretch and a five-furlong straight course. Like all Irish tracks save the Curragh and the strand course at Laytown, it is used for both flat racing and jump racing.

Because there is so much rain around Tipperary in the winter, racing is confined to 12 meetings between mid-April and early October.

Tipperary is the only Irish track other than the Curragh, Leopardstown, Cork, Naas, and Gowran Park that has the honor of running a group race on the flat. That is the seven-furlong Group 3 Concorde Stakes, a race inevitably lost in the shuffle of much bigger doings in France, as it is always run on Arc Day, the first Sunday in October. The Concorde might be seen as a prep for the Group 2 Challenge Stakes at Newmarket two weeks later, but as it is a bottom-rung Group 3 contest, it is more frequently an end in itself for horses with few ambitions.

Three listed races, the El Gran Senor Stakes at 7½ furlongs for 2-year-olds in early August, the 7½-furlong Fairy Bridge Stakes for fillies and mares, and the five-furlong Tipperary Stakes for 2-year-olds complete Tipperary's black-type program.

FESTIVAL MEETINGS, NORTHERN IRELAND, AND DUNDALK

Racing in Ireland is as much about sociability, or *craique* (pronounced "crack"), as they call it in old Irish, as it is about horses and betting. Festival meetings—where people are expected to enjoy themselves despite the winning or the losing—last between three and seven days. The most notable of these is the fabulously popular Galway Festival.

A seven-day extravaganza beginning on the last Monday of July, it is a mixed meeting with some very good hurdles and chases supplemented by some nice maidens and handicaps on the flat. More important, it is a racing fan's delight in which deep pockets and the ability to consume large quantities of alcoholic beverages while remaining upright are of equal importance. The track is located three miles outside of Galway (pronounced "GAUL-way") city on Ireland's west coast on Galway Bay. Convivial crowds of up to 40,000 are the rule.

A similar, if less chic, festival meeting is held at Tralee, a five-day Tuesday-to-Saturday affair during the third week of August at the cozy, old-fashioned track in County Kerry. Punchestown's five-day, Tuesday-to-Saturday festival is a cornucopia of high-class jump racing in late April. Many horses, both Irish and English, that were seen at the Cheltenham Festival or Aintree's Grand National Meeting turn out for Punchestown, which is located 20 miles southwest of Dublin.

While Northern Ireland is politically a part of the United Kingdom, racing there falls under the jurisdiction of the Irish Turf Club. There are two racecourses in the northern counties. Down Royal, 15 miles southeast of Belfast, is the site of the Ulster Derby on the third Saturday in June. At Downpatrick, 25 miles southeast of Belfast, they have been racing since 1685, and at the present site for 200 years.

Ireland was a late entry onto the synthetic-track scene, not installing its first Polytrack course until August 2006 at Dundalk. Located 50 miles north of Dublin and 45 miles south of Belfast in County Louth, just south of the border separating the northern counties from the Republic, Dundalk is a 1¼-mile left-handed track that conducts 18 days of racing per year, most of them in early spring and late autumn. The quality is well toward the bottom end of things, although we are already beginning to see some horses with Dundalk form arrive in America, given the recent increase in synthetic tracks here.

4

Germany

BADEN-BADEN ≡

Baden-Baden Racecourse
Rennbahnstrasse 16
76463 Iffezheim, Germany
Phone: 011-49-7229-1870
Internet: www.baden-galopp.com

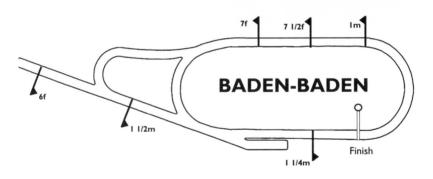

LOCATION: Baden-Baden Racecourse is actually located in Iffezheim, a small town about eight miles west of the city of Baden-Baden, which itself is nestled away in the foothills of the Black Forest in southwestern Germany, 105 miles south of Frankfurt and 30 miles east of Strasbourg, France.

COURSE DESCRIPTION: Baden-Baden is a 1¼-mile, left-handed oval with a 2½-furlong stretch. The nearly straight six-furlong course includes a mild left-hand dogleg into the stretch. Virtually level throughout, the track includes a New Course consisting of a loop extending off the backstretch that meets the six-furlong course just prior to the dogleg.

HISTORY: The racecourse at Baden-Baden is a by-product of the casino, the casino having opened in the early 19th century to give the wealthy patrons of the town baths the opportunity to do something with their excess cash in the evenings. This has been the progression in many spa towns. Deauville, Vichy, Bath, and Saratoga all followed the same pattern: baths to casinos to racetracks.

The racecourse opened in 1858 and was run by France's Societe Sportive d'Encouragement, the same club that was then in charge of Saint-Cloud and Maisons-Laffitte. At the time, the German Jockey Club, located in faraway Berlin, didn't take the new course seriously.

Baden-Baden is situated in an area of Germany that, like France's Alsace and Lorraine, is frequently under dispute between Europe's two most populous countries. The Baden-Baden Casino was owned by a Frenchman, Edouard Benazet, for whom the springtime sprint the Benazet-Rennen is named. The Franco-Prussian War of 1870–71, which was handily won by the Prussians and their assorted German allies, reclaimed Alsace and Lorraine for Germany, but closed Baden-Baden for the duration. It was reopened under the aegis of the new Internationaler Club, which has run the track to this day.

As a spa track, Baden-Baden serves German racing in precisely the same way that Deauville serves France, Saratoga serves New York,

The grandstand at Baden-Baden

GLOBAL RACING

and Del Mar serves southern California. The difference is the brevity of the Grosse Woche, or "Great Week," meeting, a six-day affair spread over nine days in late August and early September.

The climax of the Grosse Woche is the Grosser Preis von Baden. Perhaps its most famous winner was Kincsem, the great Hungarian racemare who won 54 races without a single defeat, among them three Grosser Preis von Badens from 1877 through 1879.

The race was not run in 1940 because of World War II. It was canceled again between 1945 and 1947 as the occupying powers put a stop to frivolities like horse racing during the postwar period.

As international racing experienced a marked upswing in the 1980s, the Grosser Preis became something more than Germany's championship event. Paul Mellon and his British trainer, Ian Balding, won it with three of Mellon's best horses outside of Mill Reef: Glint of Gold in 1982, Diamond Shoal in 1983, and Gold and Ivory in 1985. The 1984 running went to 1983 Australian Horse of the Year Strawberry Road. His effort earned him German Horse of the Year honors and he would go on the next season to win the Grand Prix de Saint-Cloud in France and finish a neck second to Pebbles in the Breeders' Cup Turf.

The German foundation sire Acatenango took the Grosser Preis in both 1987 and 1988, while Carroll House was the winner in 1988, one year before his victory in the Prix de l'Arc de Triomphe.

Pilsudski added to his many international Group 1 victories when winning the 1996 Grosser Preis. Two starts later he would win the Breeders' Cup Turf at Woodbine. In 2002, the Godolphin runner Marienbard used his Grosser Preis victory as a steppingstone to victory in the Prix de l'Arc de Triomphe four weeks later.

ANALYSIS: The impact of German racing in America, while considerably less than that of Britain, France, and Ireland, is notable nonetheless. Besides the aforementioned Strawberry Road and Pilsudski, any number of German winners have made their mark in the United States and Canada.

In 1999, the highlight of Baden-Baden's May Spring Meeting, the Grosser Preis der Badischen Wirtschaft, went to the Andreas Wohler-trained Silvano. Two starts later Silvano bid Germany good-bye forever as he embarked on a year-long, nine-race tour of the world that brought him to five different countries and resulted in Group or Grade 1 victories in the 2000 Arlington Million as well as Hong Kong's Queen Elizabeth II Cup.

That kind of form suggests that a good Group 2 winner at Baden-

Baden will be competitive in North American Grade 1 events. This is borne out by Paolini, whose 2001 Grosser Preis fourth was followed by a half-length second in the Canadian International. Three years later history repeated itself when the Wohler-trained Simonas followed his Grosser Preis fourth with a second-place finish to Sulamani at Woodbine.

Two starts after her 1997 Grosser Preis victory, Borgia ran Chief Bearhart to three-quarters of a length in the Breeders' Cup Turf. Switched to Andre Fabre, the gallant daughter of Acatenango would cap her career two years later by ending a 12-race losing streak endured in France, America, Dubai, England, and Japan by winning the Hong Kong Vase.

With few exceptions, most of the best horses coming out of Baden-Baden, or anywhere in Germany, for that matter, are 12-furlong types. The Germans are refreshingly traditional in their attitude toward breeding, as they still believe that stamina is more important than speed. Sires such as Sternkonig, Acatenango, Surumu, Lando, and most recently, Monsun, are renowned for their ability to produce what in Europe are called middle-distance horses—that is, those that can stay between 1¼ and 1½ miles.

But there is another reason why the German breeding industry hits above its weight. Not only is race-day medication banned in Germany, but also, no stallion can stand in Germany if he has ever run *anywhere* on race-day medication. Nor can a mare be bred in Germany if she has ever run on race-day medication. The results, despite the relatively limited funds available to German breeders and owners, are healthy Thoroughbreds that run to their potential, thanks in large part to some astute pairings being made by German matchmakers.

A German-bred daughter of Monsun, Royal Highness was never trained in Germany, having started her career in France under the tutelage of Pascal Bary, for whom she won the 1½-mile Group 2 Prix de Malleret. Switched to Christophe Clement in the U.S., she won Gulfstream's 1⅜-mile The Very One Handicap and Arlington's 1³⁄₁₆-mile Beverly D.

In 2007, Manduro became the first German-bred in history to be crowned European champion. Trained at 2 and 3 in his homeland by Peter Schiergen, the son of Monsun was sent by his owner, Baron Georg von Ullmann, to France to be trained by Andre Fabre. At 4, Manduro won the 1¼-mile Prix d'Harcourt before suffering narrow losses in the 1⅛-mile Group 1 Prix d'Ispahan, the one-mile Group 1

Prix Jacques le Marois, and the 1¼-mile Group 2 Prix Dollar, the last to the Schiergen-trained, British-bred Soldier Hollow.

At 5, Manduro fulfilled his promise with Group 1 scores at a mile, 1⅛ miles, and 1¼ miles, as well as a Group 2 tally at 1½ miles. He was the favorite for the Prix de l'Arc de Triomphe when injury forced his retirement.

TRACK RECORDS

DISTANCE	RECORD TIME	HORSE	DATE
5f	57.80	El Maimoun	June 1, 1997
6f	1:07.00	Starkey	May 17, 1998
7f	1:22.50	Garzer	May 16, 1974
7½f	1:27.80	Restitution	Aug. 30, 1998
1m	1:35.98	Zabar	Aug. 31, 1993
1⅛m	1:50.10	Leopoldo	May 29, 1991
1¼m	2:00.83	Wiesenpfad	Aug. 25, 2007
1⅜m	2:12.90	Oxalagu	June 1, 1997
1½m	2:26.30	Pacajas	May 27, 1997
2m	3:20.00	Sought Out	May 23, 1992

MAJOR RACES (Chronological Order)

RACE	CONDITIONS
FRUHJAHRS-MEETING (Spring Meeting)	
Benazet-Rennen-G3	6f 3yo+
Badener-Meile-G3	1m 3yo+
Lanson-Cup (Listed)	6f 3yo
Betty Barclay-Rennen-G3	2m 4yo+
Festa-Rennen (Listed)	1⅛m 3yo f
Preis der Hotellerie Baden-Baden	1⅜m 4yo+ f&m
Grosser Preis der Badischen Wirtschaft-G2	1⅜m 4yo+
GROSSE WOCHE (Great Week)	
Spreti-Rennen-G3	1¼m 4yo+
Goldene Peitsche-G2	6f 3yo+
Preis des Casino Baden-Baden (Lstd)	1m 3yo
Oettingen-Rennen-G2	1m 3yo+
Kronimus-Rennen (Listed)	6f 2yo
Furstenberg-Rennen-G3	1¼m 3yo

RACE	CONDITIONS
Badener Steher-Cup (Listed)	1¾m 3yo+
Maurice Lacroix-Trophy-G3	7f 2yo
Baden-Baden Cup (Listed)	1¼m 3yo+
Grosser Preis von Baden-G1	1½m 3yo+
Preis von Schlenderhan (Listed)	1m 3yo+
Gontard-Rennen (Listed)	1⅜m 3yo f
SALES AND RACING FESTIVAL	
Flieger-Preis (Listed)	5f 3yo+
Baden-Wurtemberg-Trophy-G3	1⅜m 3yo+
Preis der Winterkonigin-G3	1m 2yo f
Badener Sprint Cup-G3	7f 3yo+

DAYS OF RACING: Baden-Baden has 15 days of racing per year. The six-day Spring Meeting lasts from the third Saturday in May to the last Sunday of that month. The big week from the last Saturday in August through the first Sunday in September is also a six-day affair. The Sales and Racing Festival is a three-day meeting held over the last weekend of October.

HOW TO GET THERE: Trains on the Hamburg-Frankfurt line run directly to Baden-Baden. Travel time is five hours from Hamburg, about 1½ hours from Frankfurt. Baden-Baden Station is a short cab ride to the city center. The racetrack is located in Iffezheim, eight miles west of Baden-Baden. On race days there is a bus service between Baden-Baden and the racecourse.

SURROUNDING AREA: The town so lovely they named it twice actually got its name in much the same way New York City came to be called New York, New York. Baden, the city, is located in a state that was also named Baden (now Baden-Wurttemberg). Until 1931 the town's name was written as Baden, Baden, but it was hyphenated to become Baden-Baden, and that name stuck. The word *baden* itself means "baths."

Perhaps the most romantic spa town in Europe, Baden-Baden was, during the 19th century, one of the chief watering holes of the European aristocracy. Especially popular with the Russians, it is the place where Fyodor Dostoevsky wrote his autobiographical novella *The Gambler* while dropping a small fortune at the casino.

Baden-Baden has always been known for its reserved elegance.

Marlene Dietrich called the casino "the most beautiful in the world," and who would argue with Marlene Dietrich? Open 24 hours a day and located just off the town center, it specializes in French roulette and baccarat in the most elegant rooms imaginable, but also serves players who prefer American roulette, blackjack, and poker.

The Kurhaus, or bathhouse, is where your aching bones are given the treatment, and you can partake of the healing waters at the Trinkehalle (Drinks Hall). Music lovers may want to visit the house in the southern end of town where Johannes Brahms spent 10 summers composing. A few blocks away is the childhood home of his friend Clara Schumann, the future wife of composer Robert Schumann.

The beautiful Russian church with its golden onion dome is where Dostoevsky might have better spent some of his time. Like Dostoevsky, Ivan Turgenev was a frequent summer visitor. He based his early novel *Smoke* on some of his romantic Baden-Baden adventures.

The Lichtentaler Allee is a lush and lovely park famed as a riding venue and trysting place. Just beyond it lies the entrance to the foothills of the Black Forest. Baden-Baden has any number of outdoor cafes where one can appreciate the sun glinting off a tall, golden glass of beer as only the Germans can serve it.

COLOGNE

Cologne Racecourse (Kolner Renn-Verein)
Rennbahnstrasse 152
50737 Cologne
Germany
Phone: 011-49-221-974-5050
Internet: www.koeln-galopp.de

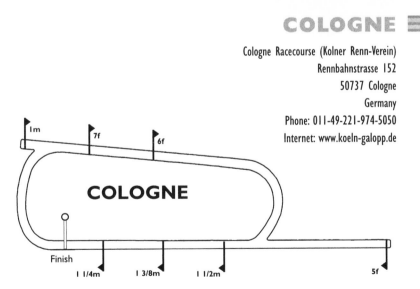

LOCATION: The racecourse is actually situated in Weidenpesch, which, like Cologne itself, lies on the Rhine River. Cologne is in west-central Germany, 220 miles southwest of Hamburg, 140 miles northwest of Frankfurt, and 15 miles north of Bonn, the German capitol during the Cold War. The track is three miles north of the Cologne city center.

COURSE DESCRIPTION: Cologne (or Koln, as it is spelled in German) is a level, right-handed oval, 1⅜ miles in circumference with a three-furlong stretch. Races of 1½ miles start near the head of the stretch and make a wide, sweeping turn onto a 3½-furlong backstretch. The turn for home is slightly tighter than the first turn. One-mile races start from a chute on the backstretch. The homestretch extends to form a five-furlong straight course.

HISTORY: Cologne Racecourse opened in 1897. A year later, the first Preis des Winterfavoriten was run. A one-mile race for 2-year-olds, since World War II it has been Germany's championship juvenile race. The first Gerling-Preis was run in 1934 in an effort to create a top-class middle-distance race in opposition to the better races being run at Hoppegarten in Berlin. World War II obviously had a devastating impact on German racing, especially on Hoppegarten, which found itself in Communist East Germany after the dust had settled.

It was Cologne that took up the slack. The surrounding area became Germany's leading training center. The headquarters of the Direktorium fur Vollblutzucht und Rennen, or the Directory for Thoroughbreds and Racing, aka the German Jockey Club and called, in parlance, the Direktorium, is in Cologne.

The first Preis von Europa, a 1½-mile test for older horses run in late September, took place in 1963. It became something of a political cause celebre when the best horse ever produced in the Soviet Union, Anilin, won it three times in a row from 1965 through 1967. The Soviet standard-bearer would finish second to the French-trained Behistoun in Laurel's Washington, D.C., International in 1966, just failing to take them all the way on the front end.

The Preis von Europa has a rich history, having been being won by Paul Mellon's international travelers Glint of Gold in 1982 and Gold and Ivory three years later. Ibn Bey won it in 1989, a year before his second-place finish to Unbridled in the Breeders' Cup Classic, and the Andre Fabre-trained Apple Tree won it in 1992, a year before his Turf Classic triumph at Belmont. Monsun, now Germany's leading stallion and the sire of 2007 European champion Manduro, won it in 1993 and 1994.

In recent years, the race has declined a bit. Godolphin won it with Group 2 types Kutub (2001) and Mamool (2003). The fine filly Albanova won it in 2004, while 2007 Arc runner-up Youmzain landed the prize in 2006.

Platini, now one of Germany's leading sires, was a Cologne course specialist. In addition to his Preis von Europa second to Apple Tree, he won the German 2000 Guineas here as well as the Preis des Winterfavoriten. The great Monsun also took the Gerling-Preis twice.

ANALYSIS: Really good German horses rarely make it to the United States unless it is for a single race like the Arlington Million or the Breeders' Cup. A good filly or mare is very likely to remain in Germany, or at least be kept out of America (avoiding the temptation to use race-day medication), and thus remain eligible to be bred in Germany.

But any horse that has finished first or second in any of Cologne's Group 1 or Group 2 races would probably be competitive in a similar American race. Beware of the distances at which such horses have been running. There is a tendency among some American handicappers to consider all races run beyond a mile as "route races," as if a race at 1⅛ miles is the same as a race run at 1¼ or 1⅜ miles simply because it is run around two turns. This is simplistic thinking. A horse that has been winning at 1½ miles, especially one coming from Europe, is not necessarily going to run well going 1⅛ miles, or vice-versa.

As for horses emerging from Cologne whose best form appears in allowance races or handicaps, they are probably no better than midlevel allowance types in America, perhaps even claimers. Suffice it to say that German group-race form outside of its Group 1's and the best Group 2's is at least a notch below the American equivalent, although races at Cologne, Baden-Baden, and Hamburg during its German Derby meeting are better than those run anywhere else in the country.

As far as Cologne is concerned, this is due primarily to the proximity of so many key training centers. Peter Schiergen, perennially the champion jockey in Germany during the 1990s, runs a powerful stable that includes many of Baron Georg von Ullmann's best horses. Schiergen was lucky enough to join the ranks of German trainers the same year the legendary Heinz Jentsch retired. As Jentsch had been von Ullmann's number one trainer, Schiergen inherited all of his horses at the baron's Gestut Schlenderhan.

Ralf Suerland, Peter Remmert, Andreas Lowe, Andreas Trybuhl, and Waldemar Hickst also train in and around Cologne.

TRACK RECORDS

DISTANCE	RECORD TIME	HORSE	DATE
6f	1:10.00	Polish Magic	Aug. 1, 2006
1m	1:33.00	Miss Tobacco	Aug. 1, 1999
1⅜m	2:13.00	Kornado	June 1, 1993
1½m	2:26.40	Oriental Tiger	April 1, 2008

MAJOR RACES (Chronological Order)

RACE	CONDITIONS
Grand Prix Aufgalopp-G3	1¼m 4yo+
Gerling-Preis-G2	1½m 4yo+
Ernst-Meile (Listed)	1m 4yo+
Jean Harzheim Sprint-Rennen (Lstd)	6f 4yo+
Mehl-Mulhens-Rennen (German 2000 Guineas)-G2	1m 3yo c&f
Schwarzgold-Rennen-G3	1⅜m 3yo f
Oppenheim-Union-Rennen-G2	1⅜m 3yo
Diana-Trial-G3	1⅜m 3yo f
Silberne-Peitsche-G3	6½f 3yo+
Oppenheim-Rennen (Listed)	6½f 2yo
Sommer-Trophy (Listed)	1⅞m 3yo+
Rheinland-Pokal-G1	1½m 3yo+
Preis von Europa-G1	1½m 3yo+
Grosse Europa-Meile-G2	1m 3yo+
IVG-Euroselect-Preis (Listed)	1½m 3yo+ f&m
Europa-Sprint (Listed)	6½f 3yo+
Junioren-Preis (Listed)	7f 2yo
Preis des Winterfavoriten-G3	1m 2yo
Weidenpescher Stutenmeile (Listed)	1m 3yo+ f&m
Herbst-Stuten-Meile (Listed)	1m 3yo+ f&m

DAYS OF RACING: Cologne conducts 14 days of racing per year between late March and mid-November. The Mehl-Mulhens-Rennen (German 2000 Guineas) is run on the second Sunday in May, a bank holiday. The Rheinland-Pokal is run on the third Sunday of August. The Preis von Europa on the last Sunday of September is a kind of consolation prize for German horses not quite good enough for the Prix de l'Arc de Triomphe a week later.

HOW TO GET THERE: From the Cologne city center, take the No. 18 U-Bahn, or subway, for the 12-minute ride to the Scheibenstrasse station near the racecourse.

SURROUNDING AREA: Cologne is the oldest city in Germany and has a rich cultural tradition. There are at least 30 museums in the city proper, which maintains a population of just under one million. During World War II it was one of the most heavily bombed of all German cities. Its center was completely destroyed but managed to build itself back up rather quickly as part of the postwar German economic miracle.

Cologne Cathedral suffered 14 hits during the war but never fell, remaining upright in the midst of the devastation, probably because Allied bombers needed it as a guidepost. Between 1880 and 1884 it ranked as the tallest building in the world until the Washington Monument was built. Today it is the symbol of Cologne, a prosperous modern city renowned as an international media center.

HAMBURG ☰

Hamburg Racecourse
Rennbahnstrasse 96
Hamburg 22111
Germany
Phone: 011-49-40-651-3682
Internet: www.galopp-hamburg.de
www.deutsches-derby.de

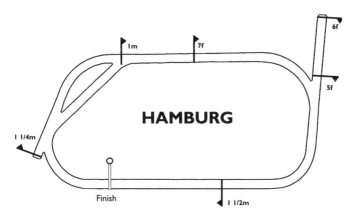

LOCATION: Hamburg Racecourse is located five miles outside of the northern German port city of Hamburg.

COURSE DESCRIPTION: Hamburg is a 1⅝₆-mile right-handed track, virtually level with a 2½-furlong homestretch. Races of five and six furlongs start from a chute beyond the turn for home. Ten-furlong races start from a chute just beyond the finish line. The 1½-mile German Derby starts in midstretch and makes one complete circuit of the track.

HISTORY: Like the city from which it takes its name, Hamburg Racecourse is a peculiar place. Racing has been conducted there since 1869 and the track has somehow managed to retain its hold on the German Derby, the country's most popular race. This, despite being in a region where there are no training centers.

The track drains poorly, making for heavy ground whenever there is substantial rain, as in 2007, when many races went off with a flag start because the turf course was so soggy it could not have withstood wheeling the starting gate on and off it.

The Deutsches Derby, or German Derby, was first run in 1869, the year the track opened. Surprisingly, racing was interrupted at Hamburg only once by World War II, for a few weeks after the German surrender in May 1945.

Until 1993, the mile-and-a-half classic was restricted to German-breds. It was opened to all comers in part because the astute if rather impecunious German breeding industry had managed to prove its caliber with winners such as Surumu in 1977, Konigsstuhl in 1979, and, in 1985, the outstanding Acatenango, a son of Surumu who reigned as Germany's most prominent stallion until his death in 2005.

Lando, a son of Acatenango, won the first running of the open Derby in 1993 and has since gone on to become a prominent sire, which, after all, is what a Derby is supposed to be all about. A daughter of Acatenango, Borgia, won it in 1997, four months prior to her second-place finish in the Breeders' Cup Turf. Shirocco's 2004 Derby triumph came 16 months before his victory in the BC Turf. Acatenango would also sire 2004 French Derby winner Blue Canari and 2002 E. P. Taylor winner Fraulein.

From this, we can see that the German Derby winner is generally a horse that can be expected to compete on the Group 1 level anywhere in the world.

An influx of sponsorship money from Hamburg-based automobile manufacturer BMW increased the Deutsches Derby purse to $865,000 from $510,000 in 2006, when the race was won by Schiaparelli, a son of Monsun who in 2007 won three Group 1 races: Dusseldorf's Deutschlandpreis, Cologne's Preis von Europa, and Milan's Gran Premio del Jockey Club.

ANALYSIS: Hamburg holds much the same place in German racing that Epsom has in British racing. Its six-day German Derby meeting in late June-early July is the only racing held there each year, making it somewhat similar to Epsom's two-day Derby meeting, the only time of the year when Epsom attracts top-class horses.

While the stakes racing at Hamburg is as good as that at Baden-Baden and Cologne, the balance of the cards are no great shakes. They may be better than at tracks like Hoppegarten or Dresden in the former East Germany, but are not as good as Bremen, Dortmund, Dusseldorf, or Frankfurt, four tracks on the regular western German circuit within fairly easy traveling distance from the main German training centers around Cologne.

The Grosser Hansa Preis, called now for many years the Idee Hansa Preis, as it is sponsored by coffee manufacturer Idee, is a good Group 2 contest for 3-year-olds and up at 1⅜ miles. The talented Schiaparelli, trained near Cologne by Peter Schiergen, won it in 2007, a year after his German Derby victory. The 2006 Hansa Preis winner was Egerton, who would win the Group 2 Gerling-Preis at Cologne a year later.

TRACK RECORDS

DISTANCE	RECORD TIME	HORSE	DATE
6f	1:07.90	Dream Talk	1992
1m	1:32.00	Up and Away	2003
1⅜m	2:14.00	Caitano	1999
1½m	2:25.80	Belenus	1999

MAJOR RACES (Chronological Order)

RACE	CONDITIONS
DERBY WOCHE (Derby Week)	
Hamburger Meile-G3	1m 3yo+
Idee Hansa-Preis-G2	1⅜m 3yo+
Sierstorpff-Rennen (Listed)	6f 2yo
Hamburg-Dresden Pokal (Listed)	2m 4yo+
Hamburger Stutenpreis-G3	1m 3yo+ f&m

RACE	CONDITIONS
Fahrhofer Stutenpreis-G3	1⅜m 3yo f
Hamburg Trophy-G3	6f 3yo+
Hanshin Cup (Listed)	1⅜m 4yo+ f&m
Deutsches Derby	
(German Derby)-G1	1½m 3yo c&f

HOW TO GET THERE: From the center of Hamburg, racegoers should use the U-Bahn, or subway, for the 25-minute ride to the track.

DAYS OF RACING: Hamburg runs just six days of racing over the nine-day period of its Derby Week Meeting from the last Thursday in June through German Derby Day itself on the first Sunday in July.

SURROUNDING AREA: As any American might have guessed, Hamburg is responsible for one of America's great culinary innovations, the hamburger. A meat patty devised by late 19th-century German-American immigrants from Hamburg, it bears a brotherly association with that contribution of immigrants from a bit farther south in Germany, the frankfurter, later nicknamed the hot dog because of its resemblance to a dachshund.

Hamburg was one of the world's most important ports until the end of World War I, when Germany lost all its colonies. A spirited city that was all but destroyed during World War II, it made its mark on modern pop culture as the place where the Beatles honed their art from 1960 to 1962 in the Reeperbahn, the main drag in Hamburg's notorious St. Pauli red-light district. The lads from Liverpool could be heard regularly at either the Kaiserkeller or the Top Ten Club. They never forgot their German roots, later re-recording "I Want to Hold Your Hand" as "Komm, Gib Mir Deine Hand" and "She Loves You" as "Sie Liebt Dich." Both the Kaiserkeller and the Top Ten Club are still in existence.

Other Racecourses in Germany

Most of the best racing in Germany takes place in or near the cities that make up the country's industrial west. From north to south these are Hamburg, Bremen, Dortmund, Dusseldorf, Cologne—around which lie many of Germany's most important training centers—and

Frankfurt. The other leading German tracks are Baden-Baden in the southwest, Munich in the southeast, and Hoppegarten near Berlin in the northeast.

BREMEN ≡

Bremen is a right-handed oval with wide turns and a three-furlong stretch. It conducts 18 days of racing scheduled throughout the year, as there is also a dirt track inside the turf course. Racing at Bremen is typical German fare, rating somewhere in the middle of the general scheme of things. The listed Derby-Trial is run in late June, about three weeks before the German Derby at Hamburg. The track's lone Group 3 is the 1⅜-mile Walter Jacobs-Stutenpreis for fillies and mares.

DORTMUND ≡

Dortmund is a 1⅝-mile right-handed oval with a three-furlong stretch and a five-furlong straight course. Its 18 days of racing include the Group 3 Grosser Preis der Wirtschaft, a one-mile, 165-yard test for 3-year-olds and up. It was won by solid Group 2 types Lord of England and Soldier Hollow in 2006 and 2007. Dortmund also hosts the Deutsches St. Leger, a 1¾-mile race recently upgraded to Group 3 status.

DUSSELDORF ≡

Right-handed Dusseldorf ranks as the best of Germany's tracks outside of Baden-Baden, Cologne, and Hamburg as it is the site of the Group 2 German 1000 Guineas in late May or early June, the 1½-mile Group 1 Deutschlandpreis in late July, and the 1⅜-mile Group 1 Preis der Diana, or German Oaks, in early August.

Frankfurt ranks just behind Dusseldorf in quality. A left-handed course with 10 days of racing annually, it runs five Group 3 races, some of which resemble French or British Group 3's in quality. The 1¼-mile Fruhjahrpreis (Spring Stakes) was won in 2006 by Prince Flori on his way to victory in Germany's best race, the Grosser Preis von Baden. The Grosse Hessen-Meile is a modest mile for 3-year-olds and up in mid-July. The 1¼-mile Euro-Cup is the mid-September version of the Fruhjahrpreis. The Frankfurter Stutenpreis is a 1⁵⁄₁₆-mile event of little import for fillies and mares. Closing out the German season is the last of Frankfurt's 1¼-mile Group 3's, the Hessen Pokal.

Munich is a left-handed track that has 16 single-day meetings per year. One of two group races on its calendar, the 1¼-mile Bavarian Classic, is an early-June Group 3 prep for the German Derby a month later.

Munich steps onto the international stage for one day each year in late July with the Bayerisches Zuchtrennen, or, as it is known nowadays in an age of corporate sponsorship that threatens to obliterate registered race names from memory, the Grosser Dalmyr-Preis. This is a 1¼-mile contest that in theory makes a perfect prep for either the Arlington Million or the Juddmonte International at York. Since attaining Group 1 status in 1990 it has been won by a number of good horses.

The 1991 victory of the French-trained Kartajana preceded her neck third in the Million. In 1992 the Irish-trained Kooyonga could only manage 12th in the Juddmonte International next time. The Irish-trained Market Booster followed her 1993 victory with a fourth-place finish in the Irish Champion Stakes but later scored at Belmont in the New York Handicap and at Aqueduct in the Long Island Handicap. Germany, the Kentucky-bred son of Trempolino, won the Grosser Preis von Baden after his Bayerisches score in 1995 and would end his career with a game second to subsequent Breeders' Cup Turf winner Pilsudski in the 1996 Grosser Preis.

In 1996 the Irish-trained Timarida, the previous year's E. P. Taylor winner, vaulted from her Bayerisches victory to land Arlington's Beverly D. In 1998 the outstanding Andreas Schutz-trained filly Elle

Danzig added to her victories in the German 1000 Guineas, German Oaks, and Idee-Hansa-Preis with a hard-fought triumph at Munich. A year later Tiger Hill, now a prominent Darley stallion, used victory in the Bayerisches as a prep for victory in the Grosser Preis von Baden.

Since then, however, the quality of Munich's top race has slipped a bit. The best foreign horses have turned their interests elsewhere, although good German horses such as Soldier Hollow (2005 and 2007) and Lord of England (2006) have kept the race up to a well-deserved Group 1 status.

HOPPEGARTEN ≡

The recent history of Berlin's racecourse, Hoppegarten, parallels the rise and fall of the fortunes of the great city that lies 20 miles to its west. Hoppegarten was Germany's leading track before World War II, when most of the country's best trainers worked nearby. A Sunday at Hoppegarten before the war was for Berliners what a Sunday at Longchamp has always been for Parisians.

After the war, Hoppegarten found itself in Communist East Germany where racing was frowned upon. While the track took its annual turn with Prague, Warsaw, Budapest, and Moscow as part of the Soviet bloc's rotating Socialist Festival of Racing, the sport in Berlin was moribund from 1945 until German reunification in 1990—at which stage the Direktorium had great plans for Hoppegarten. After 15 years, however, most of them have gone up in smoke. The legacy of Communism, coupled with the misguided policies of the German government, has left the region impoverished. People without extra spending cash cannot support a racetrack, and so Hoppegarten has failed to prosper.

Hoppegarten is now reduced to just seven days of racing per annum. A lovely track set in the midst of a lush forest, it is a right-handed, irregular oval whose turn for home is markedly tighter than its "clubhouse turn." Slightly more than 1½ miles around, it has a 2½-furlong stretch that extends to form a seven-furlong straight course that emerges from the dense forest with trees overhanging the rails on both sides.

Hoppegarten has a country feel to it. Dogs are allowed onto the premises and even into the paddock viewing area, a charming if rather dangerous custom that hearkens back to the more leisurely prewar era.

But these are hard times for racing in eastern Germany. Hoppegarten has lost the Grosser Preis von Berlin and the Berlin-Brandenburg-Trophy to western tracks while its 1½-mile Europachampionat has been lost to history.

That leaves Hoppegarten with just a single Group 3 race on its schedule. Run at 1¼ miles on Germany's National Day, October 3, that is the Grosser Preis der Deutschen Einheit, which can be translated as the Grand Prize of German Unification, a race that might be better named the Leftovers of German Unification. Still, it is a better than average Group 3 race by German standards.

5

Italy

CAPANNELLE ☰

Ippodromo delle Capannelle
Via Appia Nuova 1245
Rome, Italy
Phone: 011-39-6-716-771
Internet: www.hid.it
www.capannelleippodromo.it

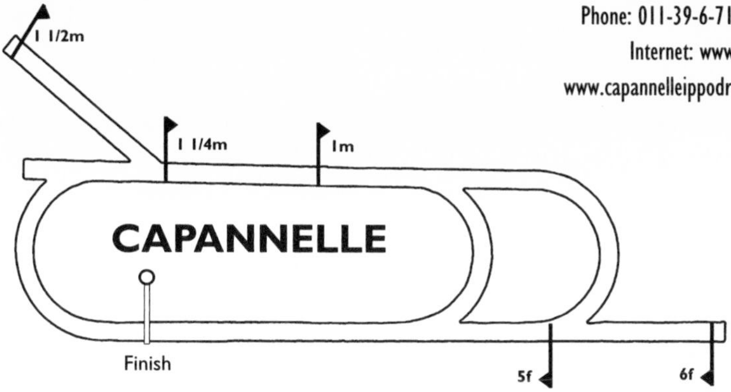

LOCATION: Six miles southwest of central Rome.

COURSE DESCRIPTION: The Capannelle's *grande corse* (main track) is a 1⅝-mile right-handed oval with a five-furlong stretch that extends to form a six-furlong straight course. The 1½-mile Derby Italiano starts from a quarter-mile spur that joins the backstretch at the 1¼-mile mark after making a mild left-hand turn.

The 1⅜-mile *piccola corse* (small course) departs the backstretch a furlong before the far turn on the main track, joining the stretch three furlongs from the finish.

Inside the small course is a 1¼-mile Polytrack with a 2½-furlong stretch. All three courses are level.

HISTORY: The Capannelle, or Rome, as it is generally referred to outside of Italy, opened in 1881. The first Derby Italiano, or Italian Derby, was run three years later. Its official name at that time was the Derby Reale, or King's Derby, as the race was instituted in part to celebrate the rise of the Italian monarchy, which had returned the Italian capital to Rome.

The Derby was restricted to horses trained in Italy until 1981, when it was opened to all comers. That didn't prevent the great French conditioner Francois Boutin from training the last three Derby winners under the old restricted system by using an Italian-based assistant to keep watch for their Italian owners.

The first winner of an open Italian Derby was Glint of Gold for the magnetic Anglo-American team of Ian Balding and Paul Mellon. British trainers dominated affairs from 1981 through 2001, saddling 14 of the 21 Derby winners during that period. The best of them were Peter Chapple-Hyam's White Muzzle in 1993 and Clive Brittain's Luso in 1995. With Alain de Royer-Dupre chiming in with Houmayoun in 1990 and Dermot Weld with In a Tiff two years later, Italian trainers found themselves winning their most important classic just five times in those 21 years.

In 2002, Bruno Grizzetti produced one of the race's very best winners in the last 30 years with Rakti, a British-bred son of Polish Precedent who would go on to record six more Group 1 triumphs, five of them after being switched to Newmarket with Michael Jarvis, who had earlier trained two Italian Derby winners himself in Prorutori and Morshdi.

Italian racing was embodied throughout the 20th century by Federico Tesio. If not the greatest breeder in history, he was certainly the most scholarly, his contributions to the sport incalculable. In 1898, he and his wife, Lydia, founded the Razza Dormello Olgiata (Dormello Stud) in Lombardy near Lake Maggiore, from where they would breed and own the winners of 22 Italian Derbies, 18 Premio Regina Elenas (Italian 1000 Guineas), and 13 Premio Pariolis (Italian 2000 Guineas), all three of which are run at the Capannelle.

Tesio is best known as the breeder of Ribot, the undefeated two-time winner of the Prix de l'Arc de Triomphe, but the great man had died the year before his horse's first Arc triumph in 1955. Ribot was owned in partnership by Tesio's widow, Lydia, and the Marchese Incisa della Rochetta and trained by Ugo Penco. He is regarded as one of the 20th century's very best Thoroughbreds.

Ribot stood at John Galbreath's Darby Dan Farm, beginning a trend that continues to this day as a European stallion standing in Kentucky that produced primarily for the European market. While he did sire Graustark, Tom Rolfe, and Arts and Letters, all big winners in America, his European runners included Arc winners Molvedo and Prince Royal II. The full brothers Ribocco and Ribero both won the Irish Derby and the St. Leger, as did Ragusa, who also won the Eclipse Stakes and the King George VI and Queen Elizabeth Diamond Stakes. Boucher won the St. Leger and Exception took both the Italian and Irish Oaks.

And yet Tesio's greatest contribution to the game may have been Nearco. Like Ribot, he was undefeated on the racecourse, distancing the field in the 1938 Italian Derby and following that triumph with a victory in the Grand Prix de Paris, avenging the loss of Tesio's 1937 Italian Derby winner, Donatello.

Retired to Newmarket after his victory in the Grand Prix, Nearco had a profound effect on the Thoroughbred breed through his two best sons, Nasrullah and Nearctic.

Nasrullah was the sire of eight-time champion America sire Bold Ruler, himself the sire of Secretariat. Nearctic was the sire of Northern Dancer, the most influential stallion of the last half of the 20th century and the sire of Nijinsky. Other truly great horses that descend from the Nearco line include Mr. Prospector, Shergar, Sir Ivor, Invasor, and Arkle.

The death of Tesio and the havoc wrought upon Italy by World War II brought an end to the heyday of Italian racing. The breeding industry there has struggled since the 1950s, most of the best horses from Italy, like Rakti and Falbrav, having been bred elsewhere in Europe.

Italian racing did experience something of a revival in the 1990s. Prize money generally surpassed that of England, but since 2000 the sport has declined in popularity. The Italian classics now only occasionally attract worthwhile challengers from England, Ireland, or France.

ANALYSIS: With the exception of Rakti and Falbrav, few Italian-trained horses have amounted to much in recent years. In Rome, where there is no racing from mid-June until mid-September due to what Italians perceive as unusually hot and humid weather, the day-in, day-out racing is not quite on a par with that at the other major Italian track in northern Italy, Milan's San Siro.

The Italian Derby still attracts the best middle-distance 3-year-olds in the country plus two or three modest foreign invaders—usually a British conditions-race type and a German horse or two of listed-race quality—but in reality, it is difficult to see how the race maintains its Group 1 status. Since the turn of the new century it has rarely been better than a mid-level Group 3.

The Premio Presidente della Repubblica has a checkered history over the last 20 years, sometimes well deserving its Group 1 status but more often resembling a Group 2. It was won by Tony Bin in his Arc-winning year of 1988, by subsequent Pretty Polly Stakes winner and Gamely Handicap runner-up Flagbird in 1995, and by Falbrav in 2002 and Rakti in 2003.

The Premio Roma bears the distinction of being the last European Group 1 race of the season for older horses. As such it is more deserving of its exalted status than either the Derby Italiano or the Presidente della Repubblica. British-trained horses won 11 of its 20 runnings from 1988 through 2007, among them Sikeston (a two-time winner of the Presidente della Repubblica), Misil, Flemensfirth, and Cherry Mix. Perhaps the most notable Roma winners of late have come from Germany. The outstanding filly Elle Danzig won it in 1999 and 2000, and the very good middle-distance performer Soldier Hollow took it in 2004 and 2005.

The Roma would make an ideal prep for the 1¼-mile Hong Kong Cup four or five weeks later at Sha Tin, but soft or heavy ground in Rome in early November sometimes spoils the chances of horses who need the good-to-firm ground they always encounter in Hong Kong.

The Capannelle has never been a seedbed for future American horses. That perception is even more pronounced nowadays. The 2007 Italian 1000 Guineas winner, Lokaloka, came to America a year later and finished fourth in her U.S. debut at Belmont, the ungraded 1¼-mile Sabin Stakes. That result just about sums up Capannelle form, where a Group 3 winner will be unplaced in a so-so ungraded stakes race at Belmont.

MAJOR RACES (Chronological Order)

RACE	CONDITIONS
SPRING SEASON	
Premio Trattato di Roma (Listed)*	7f 4yo+
Premio Daumier (Listed)*	7½f 3yo c
Premio Circo Massimo (Listed)*	1⁵⁄₁₆m 4yo+
Premio Botticelli (Listed)	1⁵⁄₁₆m 3yo c&g
Premio Natale di Roma (Listed)	1m 4yo+
Premio Carlo Chiesa-G3	6f 3yo+ f&m
Premio Torricola (Listed)	7½f 3yo f
Premio Signorino (Listed)	1⅛m 4yo+
Premio Tadolina (Listed)	1m 4yo+ f&m
Derby Italiano-G1	1½m 3yo c&f
Premio Carlo d'Alessio-G3	1½m 4yo+
Premio Tudini-G3	6f 3yo+
Pr Presidente della Repubblica-G1	1¼m 4yo+
Premio Regina Elena	
(Italian 1000 Guineas)-G3	1m 3yo f
Premio Roberto Baldassari (Listed)	7f 4yo+
Premio Tullio Righetti (Listed)	1m 3yo
Premio Allesandro Perrone (Listed)	5½f 2yo f
Premio Alberto Giubilo (Listed)	5½f 2yo c&f
FALL SEASON	
Premio Repubbliche Marinare (Lstd)	7½f 2yo f
Premio Rumon (Listed)	1m 2yo c
Premio Archidamia (Listed)	1¼m 3yo+ f&m
Premio Villa Borghese (Listed)	1¼m 3yo+
Premio Lydia Tesio-G2	1¼m 3yo+ f&m
Premio Guido Berardelli-G3	1⅛m 2yo
Premio Nearco (Listed)	1m 3yo
Premio Ubaldo Pandolfi (Listed)	6f 2yo f
Premio Roma-G1	1¼m 3yo+
Premio Ribot-G2	1m 3yo+
Criterium Femminile (Listed)	7½f 2yo f
Premio Umbria-G3	6f 2yo+
Premio Giuseppe Valiani (Listed)	1¼m 3yo+ f&m

---
* Polytrack

DAYS OF RACING: There are 110 days of racing per year at the Capannelle, but the track is closed from early July until mid-September.

HOW TO GET THERE: The FM4 train leaves the main Roman station, Termini, for the eight-minute ride to the Capannelle station, a five-minute walk to the racecourse. Shuttle-bus service to the track is provided on Sundays and holidays.

Via Rome's Metro commuter line, take the A train to the Cinecitta station and transfer for the 664 bus.

SURROUNDING AREA: Rome, the Eternal City, offers the Vatican and the extraordinary treasures of its museums, St. Peter's Basilica, the ruined Roman Forum, and—best of all—the Coliseum, the prototype for every outdoor sports stadium in the world.

Film fans who use the Metro to get to the Capannelle will pass by Cinecitta, the famous studio where Federico Fellini made almost all of his great classics, including *La Strada, Nights of Cabiria, 8 ½, La Dolce Vita,* and *Fellini Roma.* Big-budget American movies such as *Ben-Hur, Cleopatra,* and *Quo Vadis* were also made there. Cinecitta is sometimes open to the public during the summer when fewer films are in production.

SAN SIRO ☰

Ippodromo di San Siro
Piazzale dello Sport 16-18-20
Milan, Italy
Phone: 011-39-2-482-16345
Internet: www.ippodromimilano.it

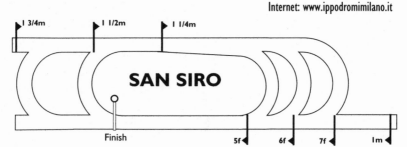

LOCATION: In Milan, 300 miles northwest of Rome, 160 miles northwest of Florence, 140 miles west of Venice, three miles from Milan's city center.

COURSE DESCRIPTION: San Siro is not dissimilar to the Capannelle in that it is a Circus Maximus-like track with long straights and relatively tight turns, at least by European standards. A right-handed track, its outer course is two miles long and entirely level, but its full length is rarely used. The Gran Premio course, on which are run both the Gran Premio di Milano and the Gran Premio del Jockey Club, leaves the straight more than a furlong before the larger course's turn and proceeds down the backstretch before turning back into the half-mile homestretch, which extends to form a one-mile straight course.

HISTORY: Racing at San Siro as officially recognized by the Italian Jockey Club began in 1889 as a counterpoint to the Capannelle in Rome, where most of the Italian classics have always been run. But the development of the major training and breeding centers in northern Italy, led by the founding of Federico Tesio's Dormello Stud, soon made San Siro the bedrock course in Italy. Tesio trained many of his horses on the track at San Siro itself, and in 1920 his influence led to a complete overhaul of the racecourse and its facilities.

The Gran Premio di Milano, originally called the Premio del Commercio and run at a distance of 1⅞ miles, was the first important race run at San Siro and remains the key race for older horses in Italy during the first half of the year. Run at 1½ miles in mid-June since 1972, it vies for runners with the more prestigious Coronation Cup at Epsom a week earlier and the Grand Prix de Saint-Cloud a week or two later, yet it still almost always manages to attract a low-end Group 1-type winner.

The 1988 Arc winner, Tony Bin, won it in both 1987 and 1988. Snurge's 1991 victory preceded by a year his win in the Canadian International. Falbrav won in 2002 and Electrocutionist was the winner in 2005, a year before his victory in the Dubai World Cup. Victories by good German horses such as Platini (1993), Lando (1995), and Paolini (2001) helped to maintain the Gran Premio's stature.

ANALYSIS: The racing at San Siro is a bit better than it is at the Capannelle, primarily because most of Italy's leading trainers are located nearby. While the quality of Italian group races is similar at both tracks, the daily fare in the maidens, allowances, and handicaps is generally a cut above in terms of depth at San Siro.

In recent years, the Gran Premio del Jockey Club has supplanted the Gran Premio di Milano as San Siro's best race, probably because of its position on the calendar. Run in mid-October, it makes an attractive spot for any European middle-distance type not quite good enough for the Prix de l'Arc de Triomphe, which is generally run exactly one week before the Jockey Club.

In 2004 the Jockey Club was won by Shirocco. Trained at the time in Germany by Andreas Schutz, Shirocco was switched to Andre Fabre's yard the next year, when he capped his career with a victory in the Breeders' Cup Turf.

In 2005, Godolphin's Cherry Mix, a Group 2 winner at Deauville in 2004, won the Jockey Club. In 2006 he would win the Group 1 Europa-Preis at Cologne and the Group 1 Premio Roma at the Capannelle, but failed in all his attempts in between in England and France.

The 2006 winner, Laverock, had won the 1⅛-mile Group 1 Prix d'Ispahan at Chantilly a year earlier but, like Cherry Mix, he could never recover that form against the tougher competition he later faced in England and France.

Schiaparelli, the 2006 German Derby winner, took the 2007 Jockey Club, following up on Group 1 victories over the same 1½ miles in the Deutschlandpreis and the Europa-Preis. That about sums up the quality of a Gran Premio del Jockey Club winner—a horse that might be competitive in Group 1 or Group 2 events in France, England, or Ireland, but is best placed in Italy or Germany.

The Gran Criterium, run the same day as the Jockey Club, is a Group 1 only in the Italo-German sense. Italy's juvenile championship race, it is usually won by a foreign invader looking for an easy Group 1 spot.

Aidan O'Brien sent Spartacus to win it in 2002, yet that Danehill colt would finish last the next year in two genuine Group 1 contests. Reduced to the role of a pacesetter, he trailed in both the Grand Prix de Paris and the Sussex Stakes.

The Gran Criterium winners in 2006, Kirklees, and 2007, Scintillo, were both subsequently revealed as low-end Group 3 types when returned to England.

Few horses make it to America with substantial San Siro form. While it is the better of Italy's two major racecourses, most of its Group 3 winners would struggle in top-class American allowance company.

MAJOR RACES (Chronological Order)

RACE	CONDITIONS
SPRING/SUMMER SEASON	
Premio Gardone (Listed)	1m 3yo c&g
Premio Certosa (Listed)	5f 3yo+
Premio Emanuele Filiberto (Listed)	1¼m 3yo c&g
Premio Ambrosiano-G3	1¼m 4yo+
Premio Seregno (Listed)	1m 3yo f
Coppa d'Oro (Listed)	1⅞m 4yo+
Premio Baggio (Listed)	1⅜m 3yo+ f&m
Premio Zanoletti (Listed)	1⅛m 3yo f
Premio Bereguardo (Listed)	1m 4yo+
Premio Mario Incisa-G3	1¼m 3yo f
Premio Paolo Mezzanotte-G3	1¼m 3yo+
Premio Emilio Turati-G2	1m 3yo+
Premio Merano (Listed)	1¼m 3yo
Premio Nogara (Listed)	1m 3yo f
Gran Premio di Milano-G1	1½m 3yo+
Oaks d'Italia-G2	1⅜m 3yo f
Gran Premio d'Italia (Listed)	1¼m 3yo
Premio Bersaglia (Listed)	6f 3yo+
Premio Royal Mares (Listed)	1m 3yo+ f&m
Premio Vittorio Crespi (Listed)	6f 2yo f
Premio Primi Passi-G3	6f 2yo
Premio d'Estate (Listed)	1m 3yo
Premio FIA (EBF) (Listed)	1m 3yo+ f&m
Premio del Giubileo (Lsted)	1m 3yo+
Premio Giuseppe de Montel (Listed)	7½f 2yo c&g
Premio Mantovani (Listed)	7½f 2yo f
FALL SEASON	
Premio del Piazzale (Listed)	1m 3yo+
Premio Cancelli (Listed)	5f 3yo+
Premio Federico Tesio-G3	1⅜m 3yo+
Premio Coolmore (Listed)	7½f 2yo f
Premio Pietro Bessaro (Listed)	1m 3yo+ f&m
Premio Vittorio Riva (Listed)	1m 2yo
Premio Duca d'Aosta (Listed)	1m 3yo f
Premio Eupili (Listed)	6f 2yo
Premio Vittorio di Capua-G1	1m 3yo+

RACE	CONDITIONS
Premio Dormello-G3	1m 2yo f
Premio Sergio Cumani-G3	1m 3yo+ f&m
Gran Premio del Jockey Club-G1	1½m 3yo+
Gran Criterium-G1	1m 2yo c&f
Premio Omenoni-G3	5f 3yo+
St. Leger Italiano (Listed)	1¾m 3yo+
Premio Giovanni Falck (Listed)	1½m 3yo+ f&m
Premio Chiusura-G3	7f 2yo+
Premio Campobello (Listed)	1⅛m 2yo

DAYS OF RACING: San Siro has 81 days of racing per year between mid-March and mid-November. The first half of the season ends in early July; the second half begins in late August. There is racing on virtually every Sunday save during the summer vacation.

HOW TO GET THERE: Take Metro Line A to the Lotto station, from where it is a short walk to the main gate.

SURROUNDING AREA: Milan is Italy's business capital, and aside from that, it is a highly sophisticated city with many attractions. In many ways it is to Rome what Chicago is to New York. The racecourse at San Siro is situated in the same sports complex as the Maezza, better known as the San Siro football stadium where both of Milan's very popular teams, Inter Milan and AC Milan, play.

La Duomo in the city center is one of the world's most beautiful cathedrals, while La Scala is one of the world's most important opera houses.

6

United Arab Emirates

NAD AL SHEBA ☰

Dubai Racing Club
City Tower 1
Office 206
PO Box 9035
Dubai, United Arab Emirates
Phone: 011-971-4-332-2277
Internet: www.emiratesracing.com
www.dubairacingclub.com

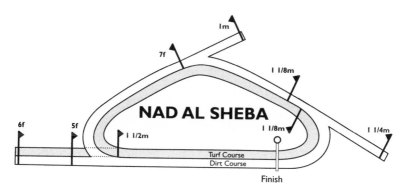

LOCATION: Dubai is located on the eastern tip of the Arabian peninsula on the southeastern shore of the Persian Gulf, 75 miles northeast of Abu Dhabi, 530 miles east of Riyadh, and 850 miles southeast of Baghdad.

Curlin and Robby Albarado storm clear at Nad Al Sheba to win the 2008 Dubai World Cup.

It is 3,452 miles from London, 3,706 miles from Hong Kong, 4,940 miles from Tokyo, 6,833 miles from New York, 7,484 miles from Sydney, and 8,311 miles from Los Angeles.

COURSE DESCRIPTION: The dirt track at Nad Al Sheba is a left-handed, triangular course, 1 ⁷⁄₁₆ miles around. The Dubai World Cup and other 1¼ miles races start from a chute beyond the finish line. One-mile races start from a chute at the top of the triangle. The stretch is just over 2½ furlongs and extends to form a six-furlong straight course.

The turf course lies inside the dirt track. It is 1¼ miles around and its stretch is also just under 2½ furlongs, and extends to form a straight, six-furlong turf course. Both the dirt and turf courses are entirely level.

HISTORY: As its first Thoroughbred races were only held on November 13, 1992, Nad Al Sheba is one of the sports world's modern miracles in that the track should rank as highly as it does today. It attracts horses from every corner of the globe, not just for the $6 million Dubai World Cup, but for its 10-week Dubai Racing Carnival as well.

In 1992, the racing was strictly the province of the four Maktoum brothers—Maktoum, Hamdan, Mohammed, and Ahmed—along with their cousins, in-laws, and business associates. A few of the Maktoums' British trainers were invited to send some of their horses

GLOBAL RACING

for the winter, but the racing was modest, as even the brothers four were not quite ready to try their best European horses on a brand-new track with no history.

Plans for an extravagant, ultra-valuable day of racing at Nad Al Sheba were already in the works when the first race was run there in 1992. In March 1995, the Emirates Racing Association put together an international jockey challenge, inviting the world's racing press, along with representatives of racecourses and Jockey Clubs from around the globe, to watch some of the world's best riders compete, among them Pat Day, Chris McCarron, and Frankie Dettori.

That six-race card served as a dry run for the first Dubai World Cup a year later. Thoroughbred history was made on March 27, 1996, when Cigar extended his winning streak to 14 with a heart-pounding nose victory over Soul of the Matter. Sheikh Mohammed al-Maktoum, whose brainchild the Dubai World Cup is, had attracted the best horse in the world to win a race that even then was the richest on the planet at $4 million. Cigar's connections—owner Allen Paulson, trainer Bill Mott, and rider Jerry Bailey—had pulled off an international coup, but the happiest man in Dubai that night was Sheikh Mohammed.

The co-feature on the inaugural World Cup undercard was the Dubai Duty Free. Run then on dirt at the same 1¼ miles as the World Cup, but worth just $300,000, it was won by Key of Luck, who slammed the European Group 1 winner Cezanne by 20 lengths with Gary Stevens aboard. Conditioned by Kiaran McLaughlin—whose racetrack travels had taken him from his native Kentucky to New York to Dubai, where he trained for the Maktoums—Key of Luck would be sent to Pimlico less than two months later to win the Pimlico Special. The American connection in Dubai had been established, and it remains one of the greatest showcases for American bloodstock.

Now worth $6 million, the Dubai World Cup has been bandied back and forth throughout its history between the Maktoum family and one American owner or another. Sheikh Mohammed won it in 1997 with Singspiel; Almutawakel and Invasor were owned by Hamdan al-Maktoum; and Dubai Millennium, Street Cry, Moon Ballad, and Electrocutionist raced for the brothers' Godolphin operation, giving the Maktoums seven wins, while Americans have won with Silver Charm, Captain Steve, Pleasantly Perfect, Roses in May, and Curlin—in addition to Cigar—for six victories.

In terms of trainers, however, the U.S. has seven World Cup triumphs, as Invasor was trained by McLaughlin (who returned to New

York in 2003 but continued to train for the Maktoums). Saeed bin Suroor has five victories, while Michael Stoute gave Europe its lone tally with Singspiel.

In the meantime, World Cup Night was developing into a big-race card filled with very rich events.

The first World Cup card to include the Dubai Duty Free as a 1⅛-mile turf race, along with the Dubai Sheema Classic, the Dubai Golden Shaheen, the UAE Derby, and the Godolphin Mile, was run in the millennial year 2000. Fittingly enough, Godolphin's Dubai Millennium won the World Cup, setting a track record that still stands today in what was the most impressive of all World Cup victories.

Dubai World Cup Night now holds a place on the international racing calendar that ranks among the biggest of big-race days, including the Breeders' Cup, Arc Weekend, and Hong Kong International Race Day.

ANALYSIS: In the last 10 years, group and listed races at Nad Al Sheba have risen to the point where they are now virtually on a par with those run in England, France, or America. This surmise certainly holds true for Dubai World Cup Night but perhaps is less applicable to such races run at the Dubai Racing Carnival prior to World Cup Preview Night in early March.

Allowance and handicaps are another story. There are any number of good allowances at Nad Al Sheba, but the track also has more than its share of duds. This is because so many of the lesser horses in Dubai are Maktoum retreads, frequently sent to family members for a small fee so that they might enjoy themselves on race night.

That is often the case in November and December, a period when the better barns, such as Godolphin and the stable run by Doug Watson—a former assistant to Kiaran McLaughlin whose clients include Hamdan al-Maktoum and assorted Maktoum relatives and business associates—are waiting in the wings for the wintertime Dubai Racing Carnival.

Since 2006, Nad Al Sheba has become a pre-World Cup magnet for some talented horses from around the world. Mike de Kock, one of the very best trainers on the planet, has established a pipeline from his native South Africa. It supplies him with some very good horses such as Ipi Tombe and Jay Peg, both winners of the Dubai Duty Free. Ipi Tombe went on to win a Grade 3 at Churchill Downs before injury cut her career short. Jay Peg set a course record in the 2008 Duty Free.

Both Sheikh Hamdan and Sheikh Mohammed have begun extending their worldwide grasps to South America in recent years, buying up young horses from Argentina and Brazil, not to mention Uruguay, where Hamdan picked up the undefeated Argentine-bred Invasor, who went on to become America's 2006 Horse of the Year and 2007 Dubai World Cup winner.

Many of these South Americans, such as Asiatic Boy and Honour Devil, are classic winners in their native lands. If they maintain their form in Dubai and manage to make it to America with either Godolphin or McLaughlin, they are always worth considering.

Early each spring we begin to see an influx of horses from Dubai as Godolphin decides which of the runners from the Al Quoz training center will go to America, which to England, and which will remain behind. Most of their best prospects will wind up at Newmarket, which is, after all, Godolphin's headquarters between mid-April and mid-November. McLaughlin always receives a good selection from Sheikh Hamdan, and in 2008 began to train a few for Godolphin as well. Many of these horses are well worth backing, but beware of some of the older horses among them. If their recent form is poor, it is likely they have been sent to the U.S. with little more hope than can be found at the Last Chance Saloon.

But the most important question concerning American handicappers faced with Dubai form is what to do with American-trained horses returning home from Dubai World Cup Night.

Some horseplayers staunchly believe that horses coming back from Dubai are never the same. Don't believe it. Recent history has shown that many horses not only do well upon their return from Dubai, but also actually improve afterward—provided they are given enough time to rest and reacclimate. For example:

- **INVASOR:** Imported to Florida from Uruguay in January 2006, he was trained up to the UAE Derby by Kiaran McLaughlin at the Palm Meadow training center. At Nad Al Sheba he suffered the only defeat of his career when fourth to Discreet Cat, but returned to America and won the Pimlico Special less than two months later on his way to becoming Horse of the Year.
- **THE TIN MAN:** After finishing second in the 2006 Dubai Duty Free for Richard Mandella, he came back to the States and ran off consecutive victories in the American Invitational Handicap, the Arlington Million, the Clement L. Hirsch, and the Shoemaker Mile.

- **HOST:** Eleventh in the 2007 Dubai Sheema Classic over 1½ miles, which was too long for him, the Todd Pletcher trainee ran well eight weeks later, winning the Elkwood Stakes at Monmouth Park.
- **ENGLISH CHANNEL:** Twelfth in the 2007 Dubai Duty Free for Pletcher, he reappeared two months later and finished a head second in the Manhattan Handicap, after which he won the United Nations Handicap.
- **LAVA MAN:** A horse who failed miserably every time he ran without his usual drugs, he was dead last in the 2007 Dubai Duty Free. Back in action 10 weeks later—and back on Bute and Lasix—he finished second in the Charlie Whittingham Handicap. Three weeks after that, he won the Hollywood Gold Cup. Lava Man's poor performance in Dubai had everything to do with his dependence on medication, and nothing to do with the strain of travel.
- **THOR'S ECHO:** Finished second in the 2006 Dubai Golden Shaheen, then returned to the U.S. and won the Breeders' Cup Sprint and the De Francis Dash to be named champion American sprinter.
- **SHAMOAN:** Fifth in the 2006 Godolphin Mile, he ran very much to that same form in his next start 10 weeks later when winning an optional claimer at Hollywood Park.
- **ISLAND FASHION:** Third in the Bayakoa Handicap prior to her seventh in the 2006 Godolphin Mile, she returned to California as good as ever when finishing a neck third in Del Mar's John C. Mabee Handicap four months later.
- **OUR NEW RECRUIT:** The winner of the 2004 Dubai Golden Shaheen was given some time off by John Sadler upon his return after sustaining some cuts on his leg at the start, and won first time back on September 6 in Del Mar's Pirate's Bounty Handicap, getting the six furlongs in 1:08.25.
- **HARD BUCK:** Second in the 2005 Dubai Sheema Classic, the Ken McPeek trainee returned on June 12 to be second in Churchill Downs' Opening Verse Handicap. Two starts later he made his third transoceanic journey of the year, finishing second in the King George VI and Queen Elizabeth Diamond Stakes at Ascot.
- **PLEASANTLY PERFECT:** Having won the 2004 Dubai World Cup for Mandella, he finished second in his American return in the San Diego Handicap, then won the Pacific Classic.
- **BENNY THE BULL:** He returned from his 2008 victory in the Dubai Golden Shaheen to win the True North Stakes at Belmont two months later, then followed up with a victory in a Grade 2 sprint at Calder.
- **WELL ARMED:** Followed his distant third behind Curlin in the 2008

Dubai World Cup with a comparable effort when winning the San Diego Handicap at Del Mar in his American reappearance 3½ months later.

■ **CURLIN:** The 2007 American Horse of the Year slammed his outclassed rivals in the 2008 World Cup, yet showed no ill effects from his seven-week stay in Dubai, or from his long trip back to Kentucky, as he returned with a victory in the Stephen Foster at Churchill Downs.

■ **BARCOLA:** After weakening to finish 12th in the 2008 Godolphin Mile, the Mark Hennig trainee returned just six weeks later to win Delaware's Brandywine Stakes, his best effort since having won the Kelso Stakes at the same track the previous September. Perhaps Dubai's desert air did him some good.

The problems facing American runners returning from Dubai have less to do with the length of the round-trip journey than with the ability of a trainer to select a horse for Dubai that travels well. Knowing how to ship a horse there and back is also a key element in keeping the horse at peak form upon his return.

In the early days of the Dubai World Cup, many American trainers made mistakes on those two counts. With a body of knowledge and a wealth of experience accumulated since 1996, fewer trainers are getting things wrong these days.

TRACK RECORDS

DISTANCE	RECORD TIME	HORSE	DATE
DIRT			
5f	56.60	Conroy	Jan. 10, 2002
5½f	1:02.50	Kabalevsky	Jan. 27, 2000
6f	1:08.10	Big Jag	March 25, 2000
6½f	1:16.11	Festival Of Light	March 11, 2001
7f	1:21.18	Kahal	Feb. 11, 1999
7½f	1:28.70	Fire Thunder	Dec. 23, 1999
1m	1:34.67	Cornish Snow	Feb. 21, 1999
1¹⁄₁₆m	1:42.40	Blue Snake	Jan. 23, 2000
1⅛m	1:46.92	Altibr	Feb. 11, 1999
1¼m	1:59.50	Dubai Millennium	March 25, 2000
1½m	2:28.32	Ambassador	Jan. 28, 1999
1¾m	2:57.90	Rasin	Feb. 8, 2001
2m	3:23.50	Nadeem	March 15, 2001

DISTANCE	RECORD TIME	HORSE	DATE
TURF			
5½f	1:07.15	Mile High	Nov. 21, 1999
6f	1:10.82	Prince Aaron	Jan. 20, 2005
6½f	1:15.78	National Icon	March 10, 2005
7½f	1:29.47	Cat Belling	Feb. 21, 2004
1m	1:36.27	Desert Destiny	March 10, 2005
1 1/16m	1:44.40	Siege	March 5, 2000
@1⅛m	1:46.20	Jay Peg	March 29, 2008
1¼m	2:01.18	Boule d'Or	Jan. 27, 2005
1½m	2:27.40	Razkalla	March 10, 2005
1¾m	2:55.84	Mamool	Feb. 27, 2003
2m	3:22.74	Kayseri	April 10, 2003

MAJOR RACES (Chronological Order)

RACE	CONDITIONS
DUBAI RACING CARNIVAL	
Maktoum Challenge (Round 1)-G3	1m (D) 4yo+
Al Shindagha Sprint-G3	6f (D) 3yo+
Al Rashidiya-G3	@1⅛m (T) 4yo+
Maktoum Challenge (Round 2)-G3	1⅛m (D) 4yo+
Cape Verdi Stakes (Listed)	1m (T) 4yo+ f&m
UAE 1000 Guineas (Listed)	1m (D) 3yo f
UAE 2000 Guineas-G3	1m (D) 3yo
Al Fahidi Fort-G2	1m (T) 4yo+
Balanchine Stakes (Listed)	@1⅛m (T) 4yo+ f&m
UAE Oaks (Listed)	1⅛m (D) 3yo f
Al Quoz Sprint (Listed)	6f (T) 3yo+
Zabeel Mile (Listed)	1m (T) 4yo+
DUBAI WORLD CUP PREVIEW NIGHT	
Maktoum Challenge (Round 3)-G2	1¼m (D) 4yo+
Jebel Hatta-G2	@1 1/16m (T) 4yo+
Dubai City of Gold-G3	1½m (T) 4yo+
Mahab Al Shimaal-G3	6f (D) 3yo+
Burj Nahaar-G3	1m (D) 4yo+
Al Bastikiya (Listed)	1⅛m (D) 3yo

RACE	CONDITIONS
DUBAI WORLD CUP NIGHT	
Dubai World Cup-G1	1¼m (D) 4yo+
Dubai Duty Free-G1	@1⅛m (T) 4yo+
Dubai Sheema Classic-G1	1½m (T) 4yo+
Dubai Golden Shaheen-G1	6f (D) 3yo+
UAE Derby-G2	1⅛m (D) 3yo
Godolphin Mile-G2	1m (D) 4yo+

DAYS OF RACING: Nad Al Sheba conducts 21 days of racing during its November-to-March season, all of them evening meetings. There is racing every Thursday night from the start of the season through the first Thursday in March, which is Dubai World Cup Preview Night, followed by the grand finale, Dubai World Cup Night, on the last Saturday in March. There are also two days of racing on Friday nights in February.

The Dubai Racing Carnival is run on the last 11 nights of the meeting from mid-January through Dubai World Cup Night.

HOW TO GET THERE: If you are in Dubai for the World Cup or any other night of racing, the best way to get to Nad Al Sheba from your hotel is by taxi or car rental.

SURROUNDING AREA: Little more than a desert outpost 25 years ago with a two-story palace occupied by the Maktoum family, Dubai today is a bustling metropolis. But while new state-of-the-art office buildings and hotels are being built annually, the areas in which visitors will be comfortable are limited, outside of extravagant places like the seven-star Burj Al Arab Hotel and other tourist hotels and beach resorts.

The beachfront is charming, if exclusive. For more adventurous types, touring the city has its rewards, but do not expect an old-fashioned Arabic layout like that of the Casbah in Morocco. Dubai has a man-made creek on which can be found one of the few areas where both locals and tourists can meet and mingle in restaurants. The Dubai Museum in the 1799 Al Fahidi Fort provides a brief history of the emirate. The Gold Souk is an open-air marketplace where authentic souvenirs can be found.

Racing fans looking for a different experience might make it to the camel-racing track, which is also called Nad Al Sheba but is a few miles away from the Thoroughbred track. Fields of 40 camels traverse the four-mile dirt track (no Polytrack or Tapeta for these ships of the desert, thank you) as their trainers follow the action in their SUVs, sending instructions to the riders via walkie-talkies embedded in their helmets. The paddock area resembles nothing so much as a medieval Arabian bazaar. Races are held every Thursday and Friday throughout the winter months. For information call 011-971-4-322-277.

Most visitors to the Dubai World Cup find that they will feel most comfortable in their Westernized hotels, where Western food and alcoholic beverages are available, as they are in the areas of Nad Al Sheba reserved for Westerners.

Other Racecourses in the UAE

Suffice it to say that Nad Al Sheba lords it over all other racetracks in the United Arab Emirates. Only a handful of horses that are imported into America even have as many as a single race outside Nad Al Sheba.

ABU DHABI is an all-turf course in the UAE's largest and richest emirate. They have been racing there since 1976 and on turf since 1980. Prior to 1991, all races were restricted to Arabian-breds. A new grandstand was opened in 1994 at the same time that the track's fibreturf grass course was laid. Turf racing is Abu Dhabi's staple because the track is located in an oasis-like area that receives more than its share of desert rain.

Abu Dhabi is a level 1¼-mile right-handed oval with a 2½-furlong stretch. Five-furlong races start from a chute beyond the far turn and are 90-degree, one-turn affairs. All meetings—there were 15 of them from November through March during the 2007–08 season—are run on Sunday evenings.

Because the turf is generally firm, times are on the fast side at Abu Dhabi, where the track record for seven furlongs is 1:20.32; for a mile, 1:32.80; and for 1⅜ miles, 2:10.34.

Opened in 1990, JEBEL ALI is Dubai's second racecourse after Nad Al Sheba. A dirt track, it frequently attracts some fairly decent Nad Al Sheba runners, especially for its handful of listed races.

It is a 1⅜-mile right-handed oval with a steep uphill 4½-furlong stretch. Races between one mile and 1³⁄₁₆ miles start from a chute on the backstretch. Five- and six-furlong races are run on the largely uphill straight course.

Jebel Ali generally has 10 days of racing per year between November and March, all of them on Friday afternoons.

Despite its uphill stretch, Jebel Ali produces decent times. The record for six furlongs is 1:09.88; for seven furlongs, 1:22.76; for a mile, 1:36.48; for 1⅛ miles, 1:48.88.

SHARJAH is to Nad Al Sheba what Mountaineer Park is to Belmont Park. Located in the tiny emirate of Sharjah, it is a left-handed, one-mile dirt oval with a six-furlong straight course that joins the oval at the head of the two-furlong stretch.

Sharjah had just three days of racing in 2007–08, one in December, one in January, and one in February, all of those on Saturday afternoons.

MEYDAN

The racecourse of the future, Meydan will be unveiled in the winter of 2010, in time for that year's Dubai World Cup. Currently under construction within view of Nad Al Sheba, its 60,000-capacity Millennium Grandstand will be a state-of-the-art structure measuring one kilometer (more than five-eighths of a mile) in length, extending from the head of the stretch and curving around the beginning of the first turn.

Meydan will have a 1½-mile turf course outside a dirt track that will measure 1,750 meters, or about one mile, 155 yards. The new Dubai World Cup will start from a short chute at the head of the stretch and make two American-style turns around the level oval. Both tracks will be left-handed. The turf course will have a chute on the backstretch for 1¼-mile races. The dirt track will have two backstretch chutes, one for seven-furlong races, one for races at a mile.

Obviously, Meydan's configuration will differ markedly from that of Nad Al Sheba. That track has been hosting an increasing number of turf races in recent years. Meydan, with its turf course given prominence over its dirt track, looks as if it will be carding a majority of its races on the turf.

At Dubai World Cup Night in 2008, the man behind Meydan and everything else that happens in Dubai, Sheikh Mohammed, hinted at big changes on the World Cup card, especially on the money front. Expect the 2010 World Cup to have its purse doubled to $12 million with the Duty Free and Sheema Classic rising from $5 million to $10 million.

Also expect to see World Cup Night expanded to a two-night meeting with the addition of at least four new races, perhaps a turf sprint, a turf race for fillies and mares, and the incorporation of the UAE Oaks onto the program. Total prize money approaching a fantastic $40 million for 10 Thoroughbred races could become a reality.

7

Japan

TOKYO

Tokyo Racecourse (Fuchu Racecourse)
Hiyoshi-cho
Fuchi-shi
Tokyo 183-0024
Japan
Phone: Japan Racing Association, Stamford, CT: 203-973-0661
Japan Racing Association, Tokyo: 011-81-3-5785-7373
Internet: www.japanracing.jp

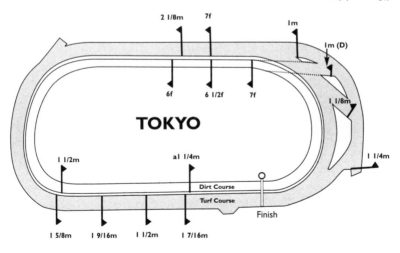

LOCATION: 20 miles west of central Tokyo

COURSE DESCRIPTION: Tokyo is a left-handed, slightly irregular oval. The turf course is 1⁵⁄₁₆ miles around. Just past the finish onto the clubhouse turn there is a mild decline to the 6½-furlong pole, then a rise followed by a mild decline around the far turn. The ground rises again from the half-mile pole to the three-sixteenths pole, from where it is level to the finish. The stretch is 2½ furlongs, 30 yards long. There are chutes on the clubhouse turn for the starts of races at 1⅛ miles and 1¼ miles.

The dirt track lies inside the turf course. It is 1³⁄₁₆ miles around and features the same undulations as the turf course. Its stretch is just a few yards shorter than that of the turf course. A steeplechase course just under 1¹⁄₁₆ miles long lies inside the dirt track.

HISTORY: Horse racing in Japan has a long and colorful history dating back to the samurai period. In fact, it was an incident involving a group of samurai and some English gentlemen that led to the formation of the first racecourse designed on Western lines in Japan.

A park in the southern part of Yokohama, the port city south of Tokyo on Tokyo Bay, was well known to riders of both nationalities as a place conducive to equine exercise. One day in 1861 a group of samurai riders was approached from the opposite direction by a group of English gentlemen. Neither group gave way and blood was ultimately shed. Protests were lodged on both sides. The diplomatic English and the accommodating Japanese decided that the standoff might be eased by a series of races around the park.

That was the beginning of Negishi Racecourse.

The first Tenno Sho, or Emperor's Cup, was run there in 1867. It became an annual event at which the emperor himself, considered a god in those pre-World War II days, was invariably present. A European-style grandstand was built in 1932. Based very much on the stand at Longchamp, its glory was short-lived, as the war ground racing to a halt in Japan.

During the conflict the grandstand was turned into a printing center for propaganda publications. Upon the arrival of the American occupying forces, it was magically transformed into a center for the publication of American propaganda, on orders from General MacArthur himself.

Located as close as it was to Yokohama harbor, Negishi was soon taken over by the U.S. Navy. The naval base created there in 1946 functions to this day. Only the grandstand remains. Immediately in front of the stands, on what had been the track apron and homestretch, lies the naval base. The area behind the grandstand is a playground

Deep Impact, widely regarded as the greatest horse in the history of Japanese racing, cruises to victory in the 2006 Japan Cup with Yutaka Take aboard before a packed grandstand at Tokyo Racecourse.

for local children, many of them the sons and daughters of American naval personnel.

Tokyo Racecourse, or Fuchu, as it is also known, being located in the western Tokyo suburb of Fuchu, also opened in 1932, the year of the first running of the Tokyo Yushun, or Japanese Derby. That winner, Wakataka, was not fully a Thoroughbred; the same was true of Kaiso, the winner in 1944, the last Derby that was run before the war and the occupation stopped all Japanese racing for the next two years.

In 1941, St. Lite became the first Japanese Triple Crown winner, taking the Derby after having won the Satsuko Sho (Japanese 2000 Guineas) and later winning the Kikuka Sho (Japanese St. Leger), a pattern made on the model of the British Triple Crown.

Throughout its history, Japanese racing has progressed slowly—but surely—in its long-term efforts to catch up with the West. This is due in part to the strong and cautious control exerted by the government-associated Japan Racing Association. Established in 1954, it limits owners' and trainers' licenses to Japanese nationals and never seems to be in much of a hurry to open its best races to all comers.

An advance of sorts was made when the 1975 Derby was won by Kaburaya O, a son of the French stallion Pharamond. But it was the

Derby victory of Symboli Rudolf in 1984 that provided Japanese racing with hope that it might someday reach a level of Thoroughbred excellence on a par with that of Europe and America.

The Triple Crown-winning Symboli Rudolf won the Japan Cup and the Arima Kinen in 1985 and was considered good enough to take his chance in America. He was sent to Santa Anita for the San Luis Rey but ran poorly, injuring a tendon and being forced into retirement.

It was the importation of Sunday Silence to Japan in 1991 that produced a quantum leap in the quality of Japanese racing. The 1989 winner of the Kentucky Derby, Preakness, and Breeders' Cup Classic has had an influence on the Japanese Thoroughbred unparalleled in any nation since the sport's earliest days in England when Eclipse laid the foundation of the breed. Bought by Zenya Yoshida to stand at his Shadai Stallion Station in Hokkaido, Japan's northernmost island, which serves as the country's Thoroughbred breeding grounds, Sunday Silence topped the Japanese sire standings every year from 1995 through 2007—five years after his death!

His progeny include Deep Impact, widely regarded as the greatest racehorse in the history of Japan; Heart's Cry, the Dubai Sheema Classic winner who beat Deep Impact in the Arima Kinen; Special Week, a Japanese Derby winner who is a leading sire himself; Stay Gold, who helped put Japanese racing on the international map with victories in the Hong Kong Vase and the Dubai Sheema Classic; Still In Love, winner of the Japanese Fillies Triple Crown; Zenno Rob Roy, whose victory in the Japan Cup boosted his two-year career earnings to $8.9 million; and Agnes Tachyon, the winner of the Japanese St. Leger who emerged as Sunday Silence's best son at stud through 2008.

In 1998, the victory of El Condor Pasa as a 3-year-old in the Japan Cup encouraged his trainer, Yoshitaka Ninomiya, to stage an assault on the 1999 Prix de l'Arc de Triomphe. Japanese horses had been having success in France with Seeking the Pearl winning the Group 1 Prix Maurice de Gheest at Deauville in 1998 and Taiki Shuttle taking the Group 1 Prix Jacques le Marois at the same track a week later.

Ninomiya had the bold idea of sending El Condor Pasa to Chantilly for his entire 4-year-old season. He started off with a sharp second in the Prix d'Ispahan over an inadequate 1⅛ miles, 55 yards. There followed victories in the Group 1 Grand Prix de Saint-Cloud and the Group 2 Prix Foy, both at his preferred distance of 1½ miles.

In the Arc, El Condor Pasa went straight to the front and was three lengths clear at the three-sixteenths pole. It took a horse as good as Montjeu to run him down, which he did, as the gallant Japanese son of Kingmambo battled back to be second by a half-length. It was six lengths back to the third-place finisher, Croco Rouge, the horse that had beaten El Condor Pasa in the Ispahan.

The next serious Japanese assault on the Arc came in the shape of the redoubtable Deep Impact. Lionized by the Japanese press in terms that would make Secretariat seem like a mere mortal, Deep Impact swept undefeated to the 2005 Japanese Triple Crown, only to be defeated on Christmas Day by Heart's Cry in the Arima Kinen. At 4, he ran off three more victories at the highest level before finishing third in the Arc, from which he was disqualified for lingering traces of a banned drug.

Deep Impact bounced back, however, winning both the Japan Cup and the Arima Kinen in 2006 to retire with $12,825,285 in earnings from 12 victories in 14 starts, second only to countrymate T.M. Opera O, the son of Opera House who had bankrolled $16,300,347 with 14 wins in 25 starts, all of them in Japan from 1998 through 2001.

Ever in the forefront of racecourse design, the JRA completed its renovation of Tokyo Racecourse in April 2007. It was a project that saw its perfectly up-to-date grandstand replaced step-by-step by a glittering new stand, and yet the very traditional Japanese have not forgotten their past. On a clear day while contemplating what horse to back in the next $300,000 allowance race, you can take a stroll to the Fuji View Stand for a look at a snowcapped Mount Fuji in the distance beyond the clubhouse turn.

ANALYSIS: Funded by a populace that loves betting on the horses at least as much as it loves sake, sushi, sumo, or baseball, racing in Japan has always been flush with money. Maidens in Tokyo go for between $90,000 and $110,000. No Grade 3 is worth less than $650,000. Grade 2's hover at just above or below the $1 million mark, while Grade 1's are worth between $1.5 million and $4.5 million. The same is true at the three other major Japanese tracks, Nakayama, Kyoto, and Hanshin. This, in spite of a stagnant Japanese economy since the late 1990s.

But the values of Japanese races must be taken with a grain of salt. While the quality of the sport has improved by leaps and bounds since the mid-nineties, and the best Japanese Grade 1 types are the equal of those in any country in the world, the money they race for is merely one of many factors that are helping to create a better Japanese Thoroughbred.

Ultimately, horses will always gravitate to where the money is, but the protective nature of the racing industry in Japan has slowed the process.

That said, it is important to remember that the upper tier in most Japanese Grade 1's is world-class. After that, there is a distinct drop in quality, even in any given Grade 1 contest, in which it is typical to find three or four Grade 1 runners plus a handful of Grade 2 types, just as in any Group or Grade 1 race in Europe or America.

The JRA likes to have full fields of 18 horses and there has always been the suspicion that trainers are exhorted to enter in graded stakes just to make up the numbers. The bottom five or six horses in any Japanese Grade 1 are merely allowance types, sometimes not very good ones at that.

Sadly, few horses that run in Japan ever make it to America. Why should they, when they are already running for the best purses in the world? But what we have seen from the first few editions of Hollywood Park's American Oaks and CashCall Mile, not to mention those races in France and Hong Kong that Japanese trainers have grown adept at winning, confirms the idea that the best Japanese horses can compete anywhere in the world.

They have made great strides since the first running of the Japan Cup in 1981, won by the American filly Mairzy Doates, partnered by Cash Asmussen. Another American, Half Iced, beat the outstanding fillies All Along and April Run in the second running. In fact, Japanese-trained horses won only two of the first 11 runnings of the Japan Cup: Katsuragi Ace in 1984 and Symboli Rudolf a year later.

Charlie Whittingham won America's third and last Japan Cup in 1991 with Golden Pheasant as the Cup balance tipped toward Europe and then Japan. Japanese horses have taken seven of the last 10 runnings. The closest American finisher during that time was the Neil Drysdale-trained Sarafan, who lost a controversial nose decision to Falbrav in 2002, when the race was run at 1⅜ miles at Nakayama.

The reversal of Japan Cup fortunes vis-à-vis America and Japan reflects the overall direction the two countries have been taking of late. As Japanese horses rack up big-race victories in France, England, Hong Kong, Australia, America, and Dubai, American horses have difficulty winning anywhere away from Nad Al Sheba's dirt track.

The one exception to that came in 2003 when the Doug O'Neill-trained Fleetstreetdance caught a sloppy track at Tokyo in nipping the locally trained Admire Don in the Japan Cup Dirt. That result also defined the Japan Cup Dirt as a Grade 2 race despite its official Grade 1 status. The best winner of Japan's most important dirt race remains the Kunihide Matsuda-trained Kurofune, who in 2001 defeated Wing Arrow by seven lengths, setting a track record for 1⁵⁄₁₆ miles of 2:05.90 that stood until the Tokyo dirt track was reconfigured two years later.

A LONG DAY AT THE TRACK

A day at the races at Tokyo or any one of the JRA's other nine tracks is truly a day-long affair. The first race goes off about 10:30 A.M. After the fourth race there is a lunch break, during which racegoers either line up for a sit-down meal at one of the many restaurants in place at all JRA tracks or open a bento box they brought with them to the track. At 1:15 it's back to the races, with the last of 12 events going off about 5:00 P.M.

TRACK RECORDS

DISTANCE	RECORD TIME	HORSE	DATE
TURF			
7f	1:20.00	Eishin Dover	May 12, 2007
1m	1:32.00	Millennium Bio	Oct. 25, 2003
1⅛m	1:44.20	Chosan	Oct. 7, 2007
1¼m	1:58.00	Symboli Kris S.	Nov. 2, 2003
1⁷⁄₁₆m	2:18.50	Tokai Tony	June 8, 2003
1½m	2:22.10	Alkaased	Nov. 27, 2005
1⅝m	2:29.80	Opera City	May 21, 2005
2⅛m	3:30.30	Macky Max	Feb. 12, 2006
DIRT			
6½f	1:16.40	Mighty Spring	Oct. 8, 2005
7f	1:22.30	Tosho Gear	May 26, 2007
1m	1:34.70	Meisho Bowler	Feb. 20, 2005
1⁵⁄₁₆m	2:06.70	Vermilion	Nov. 24, 2007
1½m	2:28.60	Groovin' High	Feb. 18, 2007

MAJOR RACES (Chronological Order)

RACE	CONDITIONS
WINTER SEASON	
Tokyo Shimbun Hai-G3	1m (T) 4yo+
Negishi Stakes-G3	7f (D) 4yo+
Shirafuji Stakes	1¼m (T) 4yo+
Kyodo News Service Hai	1⅛m (T) 3yo
Diamond Stakes	2m (T) 4yo+

RACE	CONDITIONS
Queen Cup	1m (T) 3yo f
February Stakes-G1	1m (D) 4yo+
SPRING SEASON	
Metropolitan Stakes	1½m (T) 4yo+
NHK Mile Cup	1m (T) 3yo c&f
Oasis Stakes	1m (D) 4yo+
Keio Hai Spring Cup-G2	7f (T) 4yo+
Victoria Mile	1m (T) 4yo+ f&m
Yushun Himba (Jpn Oaks)	1½m (T) 3yo f
Keyaki Stakes	7f (D) 3yo+
Tokyo Yushun (Jpn Derby)	1½m (T) 3yo c&f
Meguro Kinen	1⁹⁄₁₆m (T) 3yo+
Yasuda Kinen-G1	1m (T) 3yo+
Brilliant Stakes	1⁵⁄₁₆m (D) 3yo+
Epsom Cup-G3	1⅛m (T) 3yo+
FALL SEASON	
Mainichi Okan-G2	1⅛m (T) 3yo+
Fuchu Himba Stakes-G3	1⅛m (T) 3yo+ f&m
Fuji Stakes-G3	1m (T) 3yo+
Autumn Tenno Sho-G1	1¼m (T) 3yo+
Musashino Stakes-G3	1m (D) 3yo+
Copa Republica Argentina	1⁹⁄₁₆m (T) 3yo+
Japan Cup-G1	1½m (T) 3yo+

DAYS OF RACING: The year at Tokyo Racecourse is divided into three seasons. The brief winter season consists of eight days in February. The spring classic season, which includes the Japanese Oaks and the Japanese Derby, has 16 days of racing. The climactic fall season, highlighted by the Japan Cup, also has 16 days of racing. All 40 days of racing are run in pairs on Saturdays and Sundays.

HOW TO GET THERE: First, get yourself to the gigantic Shinjuku station in the western part of central Tokyo. From there take the Keio line for a 20-to-22-minute ride to Higashi-Fuchu station. Change there for the brief one-stop ride to Fuchu Keiba Seimon Mae, the racecourse station that is a two-minute walk from the main gate.

SURROUNDING AREA: While Tokyo Racecourse does lie within the boundaries of the sprawling city that is Tokyo, Fuchu is really more like a suburb than part of the city proper.

Racegoers are advised to stay in Tokyo and make the commute to and from the track.

In Tokyo you will find a beautiful and cosmopolitan, if sometimes bewildering, metropolis. While English is spoken in hotels and in the business world, there is little English on the streets. Travelers seeking help in train stations or on the street may experience some difficulty.

Advance planning and knowledge of a few key words in Japanese is therefore essential. It is amazing how far the simple word *arrigato* ("thank you") can go, especially if accompanied by a slight bow.

When in Japan, do as the Japanese do. Keep in mind that the Japanese respect anyone that shows a genuine interest in their culture.

And what a culture it is. When in Tokyo be sure to visit Ueno Park in the eastern part of the city. On its grounds are the Tokyo National Museum, the city's major venue for Japanese art; the Tokyo Metropolitan Art Museum, featuring the full range of Western art from medieval times to the present; and the Shitamachi Museum, detailing life in Tokyo before World War I.

Southeast of Ueno is the Ryogoku Kokugikan, the sumo-wrestling arena where the May Grand Sumo Tournament is held every day during the middle two weeks of the month.

The Yomiuri Giants play baseball in the massive indoor Tokyo Dome. Their crosstown rivals, the Yakult Swallows, play outdoors in the intimate confines of the Meiji Jingu Stadium.

The easiest way to get most anywhere in Tokyo is via the Yamanote line. An elevated train, it circles the center of the city in both directions (21.3 miles around), making stops at all the major locales: Tokyo (near Ginza and the Imperial Palace), Ueno, Ikebukuro, Shibuya, and Shinjuku, where you can change for the Keio line to Tokyo Racecourse.

Nakayama Racecourse
1-1-1 Kosaku
Funabashi-chi
Chiba 273-0037
Japan
Phone: Japan Racing Association, Stamford, CT: 203-973-0661
Japan Racing Association: Tokyo: 011-81-3-5785-7373
Internet: www.japanracing.jp

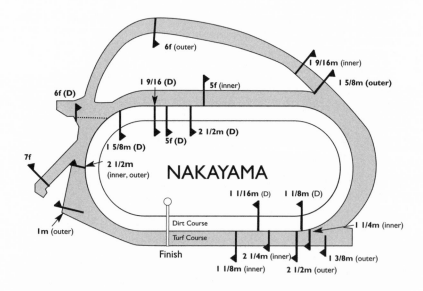

LOCATION: Nakayama is a suburb of Tokyo just north of Tokyo Bay, about 20 miles east-northeast of central Tokyo.

COURSE DESCRIPTION: Nakayama is a right-handed track consisting of two courses that share a common homestretch. The inner course is a 1¹⁄₁₆-mile oval and is used for races at five furlongs, 1⅛ miles, 1¼ miles (Japanese 2000 Guineas), and 2¼ miles. The outer course of 1⅛ miles, 50 yards extends well beyond the backstretch of the inner course and is used for races at six furlongs (Sprinters Stakes), seven furlongs, one mile, 1⅝ miles, and two miles. Races of 1⁹⁄₁₆ miles (Arima Kinen) start on the outer course beyond the far turn and make a complete circuit of the inner course. The stretch is an uncustomarily short 1½ furlongs.

The backstretch on both courses is largely downhill. The final furlong of the homestretch is uphill.

Inside the inner turf course is a 7½-furlong dirt oval with a 1½-furlong stretch. There is also a twisting figure-eight steeplechase course that winds its way around the infield. This is the course used for the Nakayama Grand Jump.

HISTORY: Opened in 1920, Nakayama is the site of three of Japan's most important races: the Satsuki Sho, or Japanese 2000 Guineas; the Sprinters Stakes, the best sprint race in the country; and the Arima Kinen, still the most coveted prize in Japanese racing.

Run on the Sunday either immediately before or after Christmas (and occasionally on Christmas Day itself), the season-ending Arima Kinen is so highly valued by Japanese horsemen that most will tell you that they would rather win it than the more internationally prestigious Japan Cup. Founded by Yoriyasi Arima, it was first run in 1956 as the Nakayama Grand Prix. A few months later Arima died and the race was renamed in his honor as the Arima Kinen, or Arima Memorial. It is still sometimes referred to as the Arima Kinen Grand Prix.

As it is run four or five weeks after the Japan Cup, it is certainly possible to run in both races. Since the inception of the Japan Cup in 1981, four horses have pulled off the Japan Cup-Arima Kinen double: Symboli Rudolf (1985), a horse who had also won the Arima Kinen a year earlier; all-time leading earner T.M. Opera O (2000); Zenno Rob Roy (2004); and Deep Impact (2006). Tokai Teio accomplished the same double but in consecutive years, winning the Japan Cup in 1992 and the Arima Kinen in 1993.

In 2005 the Arima Kinen was the race in which Deep Impact lost his perfect record at the hands of Heart's Cry, the horse that would next win the Dubai Sheema Classic by four lengths, racing on the front end throughout. At the time, Deep Impact's loss was blamed on Nakayama's short 1½-furlong stretch, but the great son of Sunday Silence put the lie to that theory when he came from behind to land the race in completing his Japan Cup-Arima Kinen double a year later.

ANALYSIS: As the site of the Satsuki Sho, or Japanese 2000 Guineas, much of the early-season action for 3-year-old colts in Japan is centered on Nakayama. The 1¼-mile Yayoi Sho and the 1⅛-mile Spring Stakes are the two key preps for the Satsuki Sho, which is not run at a mile, like the European Guineas, but at 1¼ miles, as a nod to the first jewel in the American Triple Crown, the Kentucky Derby.

Winning the Japanese Triple Crown requires more stamina than it does in any other country. The Japanese version (Guineas-Derby-St. Leger) totals 37 furlongs, the British version is a little more than 34½ furlongs, while the American edition is 31½ furlongs.

But the Japanese 2000 Guineas is less of a test of stamina than, say, Newmarket's Champion Stakes over the same distance because of the short dash after entering the stretch. The Japanese Derby, on the other hand, is run over the 12 furlongs of Tokyo Racecourse with a stretch measuring 2½ furlongs, through which there is no place to hide.

Keeping in mind that there is a rather significant drop in class in Japan beneath the top rung of Grade 1 types, Nakayama form at the Grade 1 and Grade 2 level must be respected.

The Sprinters Stakes, now run on the first Sunday in October, aka Arc Day, is a case in point. First run in 1967, this six-furlong dash achieved domestic Grade 1 status in 1990 and became an international Grade 1 in 2006, although foreign-trained horses have been eligible since 1994.

It was won in 1997 by Taiki Shuttle, who would stretch his speed to win the one-mile Prix Jacques le Marois at Deauville a year later. In the 14 runnings since 1994, however, it has been won only twice by foreign invaders, and those two were exceptional sprinters. Silent Witness, one of the very best horses ever trained in Hong Kong, won it in 2005. A year later it went to Takeover Target, Joe Janiak's bargain-basement Australian sprint champion and winner of the King's Stand Stakes at Royal Ascot.

But it is the Arima Kinen that holds pride of place at Nakayama. Unfortunately, no Arima Kinen runner has ever competed in America, although it pays to follow the form of this race, since Heart's Cry followed his 2005 victory over Deep Impact with a score in the Dubai Sheema Classic. Deep Impact himself would finish third in the next year's Prix de l'Arc de Triomphe.

GRADED OR UNGRADED?

In 2006, the Japan Racing Association opened 40 races to foreign-trained horses. This brought to 59 the number of stakes races run in Japan that are open to all comers. All of these races, from the Grade 1 Japan Cup to lesser Grade 3's such as the CBC Sho and the Aichi Hai at Chukyo, are recognized by the International Cataloguing Standards Committee as graded races on the international calendar.

The Japanese classics, however, along with a number of other seriously important races such as the Victoria Mile, the NHK Mile Cup, the Shuka Sho, and the two most important juvenile events in the country, the Hanshin Juvenile Fillies and the Futurity Stakes, remain closed to foreign competitors.

Because these races are restricted to horses trained in Japan, they are not considered graded races. A problem thus arises, because the Japanese horses that contest them are the same that run in recognized Grade 1 races such as the Yasuda Kinen, the Mile Championship, the Takarazuka Kinen, the Queen Elizabeth II Commemorative Cup, the Japan Cup, the Japan Cup Dirt, and the Arima Kinen. With the exception of the Yasuda Kinen, the Japan Cup, and the Japan Cup Dirt, the aforementioned races rarely, if ever, attract foreign runners.

Ungraded races such as the Tokyo Yushun (Japanese Derby), the Yushun Himba (Japanese Oaks), and the Victoria Mile are therefore on a qualitative par with officially sanctioned Grade 1 contests like the Takaruzaka Kinen, which never attract foreign runners.

In this book, we have decided to denote races that are not graded by the International Cataloguing Standards Committee as ungraded races. Keep in mind, however, that the best of these races—the Japanese Derby, Japanese Oaks, Japanese 2000 Guineas, Japanese 1000 Guineas, Japanese St. Leger, Victoria Mile, and NHK Mile—are all, from a handicapping point of view, Grade 1 races of international status, despite what the International Cataloguing Standards Committee thinks.

GLOSSARY OF TERMS

Japanese race names can be confusing to English readers. The following list of words may help to sort things out.

Daishoten: award

Hai: cup

Kinen: memorial

Okan: crown

Sho: prize

TRACK RECORDS

DISTANCE	RECORD TIME	HORSE	DATE
TURF			
6f	1:07.00	Trot Star	Sept. 30, 2001
7f	1:23.20	Linda UFO	April 11, 1987
1m	1:31.50	Zenno El Cid	Sept. 9, 2001

DISTANCE	RECORD TIME	HORSE	DATE
1⅛m	1:44.90	Sakura President	Feb. 29, 2004
1¼m	1:58.50	Kris the Brave	Sept. 11, 1999
1⅜m	2:10.10	Cosmo Bulk	Sept. 19, 2004
1 9/16m	2:29.50	Zenno Rob Roy	Dec. 26, 2004
2m	3:19.30	Kiri Spurt	April 3, 1993
2¼m	3:41.60	Air Dublin	Dec. 10, 1994
DIRT			
5f	58.40	Nishino Green	July 1, 1978
6f	1:09.10	Super Nakayama	Jan. 1, 1998
1 1/16m	1:43.10	Ehre Volk	June 27, 1976
1⅛m	1:48.50	Kiyo Hidaka	Jan. 6, 1993
1½m	2:28.80	Peach Shadai	Jan. 6, 1993

MAJOR RACES (Chronological Order)

RACE	CONDITIONS
WINTER/SPRING SEASON	
Nakayama Kimpai-G3	1¼m (T) 4yo+
Garnet Stakes-G3	6f (D) 4yo+
American Jockey Club Cup	1⅜m (T) 4yo+
Nakayama Kinen-G2	1⅛m (T) 4yo+
Ocean Stakes	6f (T) 4yo+
Yayoi Sho	1¼m (T) 3yo
Nakayama Himba Stakes-G3	1⅛m (T) 4yo+ f&m
Spring Stakes	1⅛m (T) 3yo
Flower Cup	1⅛m (T) 3yo f
Kochi Stakes	1m (T) 4yo+
Nikkei Sho-G2	1 9/16m (T) 4yo+
March Stakes-G3	1⅛m (D) 4yo+
Pegasus Jump Stakes	2m, 165y (S) 4yo+
Syunrai Stakes	6f (T) 4yo+
Nakayama Grand Jump-G1	2⅝m, 55y (S) 4yo+
Satsuki Sho (Jpn 2000 Guineas)	1¼m (T) 3yo c&f
Lord Derby Challenge Trophy-G3	1m (T) 4yo+
FALL SEASON	
Autumn Handicap-G3	1m (T) 3yo+

RACE	CONDITIONS
Sankei Sho All-Comers-G2	1⅜m (T) 3yo+
Sprinters Stakes-G1	6f (T) 3yo+
Stayers Stakes	2¼m (T) 3yo+
Capella Stakes	6f (D) 3yo+
Futurity Stakes	1m (T) 2yo c&f
Arima Kinen-G1	1⅝m (T) 3yo+
Nakayama Daishogai	2⁹⁄₁₆m (S) 3yo+

DAYS OF RACING: Nakayama has 36 days of racing a year. The year is actually divided into thirds with eight days of racing in both December and January. Eight days in March and four in April are followed by a five-month hiatus before resuming with six days in September and two in October. All 36 days are run on Saturdays and Sundays.

HOW TO GET THERE: From Tokyo Station in eastern Tokyo, take the JR Sobu line or the Tozai line to Nishi-Funabashi Station. From there you have the option of a 30-minute walk to the main gate or of transferring to the JR Musashino line to the Funabashi-Hoden Station, from where it is a 10-minute walk via the underpass to the racetrack's Hoden Gate.

SURROUNDING AREA: Nakayama is located in Funabashi, not far from Funabashi Racecourse, one of the National Association of Racing's leading tracks.

Kyoto Racecourse
32 Yoshijima-Watashibajima-cho
Fushimi-ku
Kyoto-shi, Kyoto 612-8265
Japan
Phone: Japan Racing Associaton, Stamford, CT: 203-973-0661
Japan Racing Association, Tokyo: 011-81-3-5785-7373
Website: www.japanracing.jp

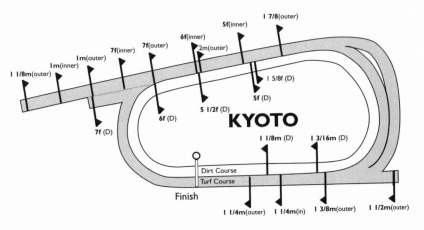

LOCATION: Kyoto is located 82 miles west of Tokyo and 25 miles east of Osaka in Kyoto prefecture, Kansai region.

COURSE DESCRIPTION: Kyoto Racecourse is an irregularly shaped right-handed oval. The outer course measures 1³⁄₁₆ miles around; the inner course, differentiated from the outer only by a shorter loop around the far turn, is 1⅛ miles around. There is a chute on the backstretch for the starts of races between seven furlongs and 1⅛ miles. The course is level except for a rise between the six-furlong and half-mile poles, followed by a rather steep decline from the half-mile pole to the three-eighths pole. Inside the turf course is a one-mile dirt track. Inside the dirt track is a seven-furlong steeplechase course.

HISTORY: Kyoto first opened its doors in 1924, when Japanese racing was still in its formative years. It wasn't until 1936, with the establishment of the quasi-governmental Japan Racing Society, that racing as it is known today began to take shape.

GLOBAL RACING

Like Tokyo, Nakayama, and Hanshin, Kyoto now falls under the jurisdiction of the Japan Racing Association. As the main racecourse in western Japan, Kyoto hosts the Spring Tenno Sho, a race of near hallowed proportions. Tenno Sho means "Emperor's Cup," and in a country in which the emperor was considered a god until 1945, the race brings with it an aura of Japan's august past—especially when the emperor himself is present on the day, which invariably falls in the midst of Kyoto's beautiful cherry-blossom season.

The Spring Tenno Sho is run at a distance of two miles (as opposed to the Autumn Tenno Sho at Tokyo, which is a 1¼-mile affair). In some respects it occupies a place on the Japanese calendar similar to that of the Ascot Gold Cup in England in that, ideally, it is the springtime race for the previous season's classic winners to prove that they can stay a distance of ground. The great Deep Impact did just that in 2005, setting a new course record for two miles the year following his Triple Crown season.

Most of the best action at Kyoto, however, takes place in the fall when the cherry blossoms have given way to a riot of autumn colors. The Kikuka Sho, or Japanese St. Leger, the crowning jewel of the Japanese Triple Crown, is followed by a pair of championship events in the Queen Elizabeth II Commemorative Cup for fillies and mares and the Mile Championship. The QEII Commemorative also serves as the ideal distaff prep for the Japan Cup.

ANALYSIS: Kyoto draws the bulk of its runners from the Japan Racing Association's Ritto Training Center in Shiga Prefecture, 28 miles from the racetrack. Most of the big Japanese outfits, such as Northern Farm and Shadai Farm, have horses in training at Ritto as well as the big training facility at Miho, northeast of Tokyo. However, while the sport is good at Kyoto, it is just a tad better at Tokyo.

In 2007, Meisho Samson followed in Deep Impact's footsteps in becoming the second successive Japanese 2000 Guineas and Japanese Derby winner to land the Spring Tenno Sho as a 4-year-old. The victories of these two horses are an indication of just how exciting racing can be beyond the American parameters of six furlongs to a mile and a sixteenth. Stamina is still more important in Japan than speed, although races in the Land of the Rising Sun are run at an early pace only slightly slower than they are in America.

First run in 1976, the Queen Elizabeth II Commemorative Cup filled a pressing need on the Japanese calendar for a defining filly-and-mare event. In 1996 it fell to Dance Partner, who a year earlier had won the Japanese Oaks. The 2001 winner, To the Victory, had finished a surprising second to Captain Steve in the Dubai World Cup seven months earlier. Admire Groove became the only filly to win it twice in a row in 2003 and 2004, her first victory coming at the expense of that year's Japanese 1000 Guineas and Japanese Oaks winner, Still in Love. In 2007, the very fine filly Daiwa Scarlet would clinch Japanese champion distaff honors five weeks before narrowly missing in the Arima Kinen.

The Mile Championship was first run in 1984, a year that marked the first of two victories for Nihon Pillow Winner. Taiki Shuttle repeated the double in 1997 and 1998, sandwiching his victories around his historic triumph in the Prix Jacques le Marois. Agnes Digital, a son of the incredibly fast Crafty Prospector, won his Mile Championship in 2000, a year before he earned his international stripes in the Hong Kong Mile. A son of Sunday Silence, Hat Trick won the 2005 Mile Championship three weeks before his own Hong Kong Mile victory. A year later, Daiwa Major, second to Hat Trick in 2005, won the first of his two consecutive Mile Championships.

All of which suggests that the Queen Elizabeth II Commemorative Cup and the Mile Championship are absolutely first-class Grade 1 events, not just on the Japanese level, but on the international level as well.

TRACK RECORDS

DISTANCE	RECORD TIME	HORSE	DATE
TURF			
5½f	1:05.00	Yama Pit	Sept. 4, 1996
6f	1:06.90	Eishin Berlin	April 20, 1997
7f (inner)	1:20.60	Iide le Vent	May 12, 2001
7f (outer)	1:19.30	Sugino Hayazake	Oct. 26, 1996
1m (inner)	1:33.40	True Surpass	April 28, 2002
1m (outer)	1:32.10	Behind the Mask	May 13, 2001
1⅛m	1:44.70	Maruka Candy	May 13, 2001
1¼m	1:57.50	Generalist	April 19, 1997
1⅜m	2:10.20	Dantsu Seattle	June 4, 1995
1½m	2:22.60	San M.X.	Oct. 15, 2000
1⅞m	3:02.70	Song of Wind	Oct. 22, 2006
2m	3:13.40	Deep Impact	April 30, 2006
DIRT			
5½f	1:06.50	Long Sovereign	Aug. 29, 1982
6f	1:09.20	Broad Appeal	May 14, 2000

DISTANCE	RECORD TIME	HORSE	DATE
7f	1:21.90	Taiki Python	June 4, 1995
1⅛m	1:48.40	Premium Thunder	Nov. 15, 1997
1 3/16m	1:56.60	Ryu Boy	May 7, 1983
1⅝m	2:43.40	Erimo Roller	Jan. 22, 1984

MAJOR RACES (Chronological Order)

RACE	CONDITIONS
WINTER SEASON	
Kyoto Kimpai-G3	1m (T) 4yo+
Manyo Stakes	1⅞m (T) 4yo+
Yodo Tankyori Stakes	6f (T) 4yo+
Nikkei Shinshun Hai-G2	1½m (T) 4yo+
Heian Stakes-G3	1⅛m (D) 4yo+
Kyoto Himba Stakes-G3	1m (T) 4yo+ f&m
Silk Road Stakes-G3	6f (T) 4yo+
Subaru Stakes	7f (D) 4yo+
Kisaragi Sho	1⅛m (T) 3yo
Kyoto Kinen-G2	1⅜m (T) 4yo+
SPRING SEASON	
Australia Trophy	1⅛m (T) 4yo+
Antares Stakes-G3	1⅛m (D) 4yo+
Spring Tenno Sho-G1	2m (T) 4yo+
Miyakooji Stakes	1m (T) 4yo+
Ritto Stakes	6f (D) 4yo+
Keyaki Stakes	7f (D) 3yo+
Meguro Kinen	1 9/16m (T) 3yo+
FALL SEASON	
Kyoto Daishoten-G2	1½m (T) 3yo+
Shuka Sho	1¼m (T) 3yo f
Kikuka Sho (Jpn St Leger)	1⅞m (T) 3yo c&f
Swan Stakes-G2	7f (T) 3yo+
Queen Elizabeth II Commemorative Cup-G1	1⅜m (T) 3yo+ f&m
Mile Championship-G1	1m (T) 3yo+
Keihan Hai-G3	6f (T) 3yo+

DAYS OF RACING: Kyoto's 38 days of racing per year closely mirror Tokyo's 40 days. Generally speaking, the two tracks are open on the same days—Kyoto (Japanese for "western capital") in the western part of the country; Tokyo (Japanese for "eastern capital") in the eastern part of the country.

Kyoto runs 14 days of racing during January and February, eight days during April and May, and 16 days during October and November. All race days are on Saturday and Sunday.

HOW TO GET THERE: Kyoto is best reached from Tokyo via the bullet train that leaves from Tokyo's Shinjuku Station. From central Kyoto, take the Keihan line to Keihan Dentetsu Yodo Station, from which it is a five-minute walk to the racecourse.

SURROUNDING AREA: A city of 1.5 million people, Kyoto is Japan's historic cultural center. The capital of Japan from 794 to 1868, when the shogunate fell and was replaced by a revivified emperor who moved house to Tokyo, Kyoto retains much of the old-world charm that was destroyed in Tokyo by two 20th-century calamities—the great earthquake of 1923 and the fire-bombings of World War II.

As Kyoto was of no strategic importance, the city was spared American bombs. Its modern-day attractions are many. For the spiritually minded there is the Golden Pavilion, a 1955 replica of the 1397 original that was burned down by a discontented monk in 1950. For those wedded to the physical world there is the Gion, Kyoto's geisha district, where the viewing is at its best during the April cherry-blossom season.

Hanshin Racecourse
1-1 Komano-cho
Takarazuka-shi
Hyogo 665-0053
Japan
Phone: Japan Racing Association, Stamford, CT: 203-973-0661
Japan Racing Association, Tokyo: 011-81-3-5785-7373

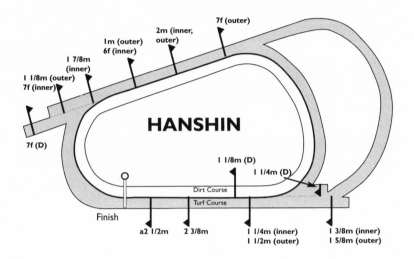

LOCATION: Hanshin Racecourse, located outside Osaka in the suburb of Hyogo, is 25 miles west of Kyoto and 107 miles west of Tokyo.

COURSE DESCRIPTION: Hanshin is a right-handed, irregularly shaped oval whose clubhouse turn is much sharper than its far turn. The outer course measures 1⅚ miles with a stretch of 2¼ furlongs. The inner course is 1¹⁄₁₆ miles with a stretch slightly longer than 1½ furlongs. There is a very mild decline from the five-eighths pole to the eighth pole, followed by a quick rise from the eighth pole to about 50 yards before the finish. Inside the turf course is a 7½-furlong dirt track with a steeplechase course inside of that.

HISTORY: Hanshin Racecourse opened in 1949 and came under the wing of the Japan Racing Association in 1955. Serving both the industrial city of Osaka and the culturally predisposed citizenry of Kyoto, it attracts much the same kind of horse as its neighbor, Kyoto Racecourse.

Hanshin has one of the world's sharpest-looking grandstands. Ultra up-to-date, as are all JRA facilities, it is a handsome, triangular-shaped building that resembles something like a silver manta ray from above.

Track management scored a coup when the JRA announced that the prestigious $2.6 million Japan Cup Dirt would be run there beginning in December 2008. At the same time, the race will be reduced in distance from 1⁵⁄₁₆ miles to 1⅛ miles, ostensibly in an effort to attract more American runners, for whom the old distance was a bit too long.

It remains to be seen, however, how many—if any—connections of top-class American horses will allow themselves to be seduced by the Japan Cup Dirt's new conditions. The fact that it will be run on the race-course's 7½-furlong inner dirt track, one that has a quarter-mile stretch, may appeal to American trainers. That it will be run right-handed may not. That Japanese drug rules remain the stiffest outside of Hong Kong might also dissuade American hopefuls, who have not managed to place in the first three in the race's old incarnation at Tokyo since 2003, when the Doug O'Neill-trained Fleetstreetdancer nosed out Admire Don on a sloppy Tokyo track at most generous odds of 48.30–1.

Which brings to mind the nature of the Japanese betting community. A tight-knit society with a keen sense of its homogeneity, the Japanese racing crowd loves nothing more than to back a winner, as do bettors everywhere else in the world. There is in Japan, however, a great desire to be a part of what can only be called the communal victory. The Japanese play favorites like bettors in no other nation, in many cases because it is the easiest way to enjoy a communal triumph, especially if the immensely popular Yutaka Take, Japan's champion rider 18 times between 1989 and 2007, is aboard.

For this reason, favorites, even in 18-runner races, are frequently bet down to less than 2–1. In international races, respect will be paid to horses like Pilsudski, who won the Japan Cup in 1997 at 4.30–1, but a horse like Fleetstreetdancer, who had been winless for a year in 10 starts prior to his Japan Cup Dirt victory, is always going to be an overlay.

So, aside from the favorite, who is almost always an underlay, there is value to be found in almost every horse running in every Japanese race. Sometimes so much money is bet on the favorite that he is allowed to go off at odds of 0–1 in order to prevent a minus pool. If that horse wins, winning bettors will merely receive their stake back, and yet the Japanese continue to pour it in on such horses.

ANALYSIS: The home of the first Japanese classic of the season, the Oka Sho, or Japanese 1000 Guineas, Hanshin is, naturally enough, also the site of the two key preps for that race, the Tulip Sho and the Hochi Hai Fillies Revue. These races bear watching from an American point of view as they are also early-season pointers to the Japanese Oaks, a race from which there frequently emerges at least one filly for Hollywood Park's American Oaks.

Moreover, any of the first three home in the Japanese 1000 Guineas could eventually be aimed at Hollywood's CashCall Mile a year later.

Cesario was a neck second to Rhein Kraft in the 2005 Oka Sho before winning the Japanese Oaks at Tokyo on her way to taking the American Oaks. Dance in the Mood won the 2004 Oka Sho two starts before finishing second to Ticker Tape in that year's American Oaks.

In 2006 Asahi Rising was only fourth in her Oka Sho, but after a third-place finish in the Japanese Oaks, she traveled to Hollywood to be second to Wait a While in the American Oaks. Kiss to Heaven, who won that Oka Sho, would finish fourth in the CashCall Mile a year later. Robe Decollete, fourth in the 2007 Oka Sho, would finish fifth in the American Oaks after having won the Japanese Oaks.

It is fitting that so much early-season 3-year-old filly action should come at Hanshin, as the track also plays host to the definitive juvenile filly race in Japan, the Hanshin Juvenile Fillies, every December.

But the biggest race run at Hanshin is the Takarazuka Kinen. Held on the last Sunday in June, this 1⅜-mile test for 3-year-olds and up signals the end of the spring season in Japan, after which there is no Grade 1 racing until early October.

First run in 1960 at 1⅛ miles, the Takarazuka Kinen has been won by some of Japan's very best horses since the turn of the new century. All-time leading earner T.M. Opera O took it in 2000. Tap Dance City won it in 2004, and the great Deep Impact landed the prize in 2006. The 2007 renewal went to Admire Moon on his way, like Deep Impact the year before, to Japanese Horse of the Year honors.

TRACK RECORDS

DISTANCE	RECORD TIME	HORSE	DATE
TURF			
6f	1:07.10	Believe	Sept. 8, 2002
7f	1:19.90	Sakura Bakushin O	Oct. 29, 1994
1m	1:32.00	Meiner Polite	June 16, 2007
1⅛m	1:45.30	Perfect Joy	June 17, 2007
1¼m	1:58.10	Tap Dance City	Sept. 9, 2002
1⅜m	2:10.90	Ask Commander	June 16, 2002

DISTANCE	RECORD TIME	HORSE	DATE
1½m	2:24.70	Liverpool	June 23, 2007
1⅞m	3:02.50	Narita Top Road	March 18, 2001

DIRT

6f	1:09.70	Select Green	Sept. 27, 1998
7f	1:21.90	Gold Tiara	June 18, 2000
1⅛m	1:48.50	Saqalat	July 10, 2004
1¼m	2:01.00	Wonder Speed	Dec. 23, 2007

MAJOR RACES (Chronological Order)

RACE	CONDITIONS

SPRING SEASON

Arlington Cup	1m (T) 3yo
Hankyu Hai-G3	7f (T) 4yo+
Tulip Sho	1m (T) 3yo f
Nigawa Stakes	1¼m (D) 4yo+
Osaka Jo Stakes	1⅛m (T) 4yo+
Hochi Hai Fillies Revue	7f (T) 3yo f
Hanshin Daishoten-G2	1⅞m (T) 4yo+
Coral Stakes	7f (D) 4yo+
Osaka Hai-G2	1¼m (T) 4yo+
Oka Sho (Jpn 1000 Guineas)	1m (T) 3yo f
Osaka-Hamburg Cup	1½m (T) 4yo+
Hanshin Himba Stakes-G2	7f (T) 4yo+ f&m
Yomiuri Milers Cup-G2	1m (T) 4yo+

SUMMER SEASON

Mermaid Stakes-G3	1¼m (T) 3yo+ f&m
Takarazuka Kinen-G1	1⅜m (T) 3yo+

FALL SEASON

Procyon Stakes	7f (D) 3yo+
Centaur Stakes-G2	6f (T) 3yo+
Asahi Challenge Cup-G3	1¼m (T) 3yo+
Sirius Stakes-G3	1¼m (D) 3yo+
Naruo Kinen-G3	1⅛m (T) 3yo+
Japan Cup Dirt-G1	1⅛m (D) 3yo+
Hanshin Juvenile Fillies	1m (T) 2yo f
Hanshin Cup	7f (T) 3yo+

DAYS OF RACING: Hanshin runs 38 days of racing per year, 16 in March and April, six in June and July, eight in September and October, and eight in December. All race dates are held on Saturday and Sunday.

HOW TO GET THERE: From Osaka and Kobe take the Hankyo Kobe Line. Transfer at Nishinomiya-Kitaguchi Station to Nigawa Station, from which it is a five-minute walk through an underpass to the main gate.

SURROUNDING AREA: Hanshin Racecourse is located in Hyogo, a suburb east of Osaka proper. A city of 2.6 million, Osaka has been the commercial and industrial hub of Japan for centuries. While it has numerous museums and temples, it lacks the overall charm of Kyoto, in large part because it was virtually leveled during World War II.

The Orix Buffaloes play baseball in the Osaka Dome, but the Hanshin Tigers, who play in Koshien Stadium, not too far from the racecourse, are the city's most popular team. They are notable for their rabid bleacher fans, who maintain a racket of dinlike proportions from start to finish of every home game.

Other JRA Racecourses

In addition to Tokyo, Nakayama, Kyoto, and Hanshin, the Japan Racing Association has six other racecourses under its control. Like the four major tracks, the racing at these six is held on Saturdays and Sundays.

CHUKYO is the most important of the other six. Located about 50 miles east of Kyoto, it is a one-mile oval with tight American-like turns and an American-style stretch measuring about 1¾ furlongs. The dirt track inside the turf course is seven furlongs, 20 yards long. The JRA's only left-handed track other than Tokyo and Niigata, Chukyo is the site of the six-furlong Takamatsunomiya Kinen. Run in late March, it is Japan's only Grade 1 sprint outside of Nakayama's Sprinters Stakes.

The racecourse in the ski-resort town of NIIGATA is on Japan's west-central coastline of the Japan Sea. The outer turf course is a 1⅜-mile, 25-yard left-handed oval with a three-furlong, 60-yard stretch. The one-mile, 30-yard inner turf course shares the first turn with the outer course but breaks away early from the backstretch, joining the stretch about 365 yards from the line. The dirt track is slightly longer than 7½ furlongs in length. The best events at Niigata's 28 days of racing between May and early September are Grade 3 contests, so this track rarely sees the best Japanese horses.

About 70 miles east of Niigata is FUKUSHIMA. An undulating, right-handed one-mile oval with a short stretch of just 300 yards, it has a 7¼-furlong dirt track inside its turf course. As at Niigata, the best races at Fukushima's 24 days of racing are Grade 3 affairs.

Located on the same southern Japanese island (Kyushu) as Nagasaki, KOKURA is a right-handed, one-mile, 20-yard turf oval with a seven-furlong, 50-yard dirt track inside of that. The stretch is 1½ furlongs long. Its 24 days of racing are divided into two meetings, eight days in January and February, and 16 days from late July to early September.

SAPPORO is located in the city of the same name, the largest on Japan's Hokkaido island north of the main island, Honshu. It is to Japanese racing what Saratoga is to New York racing. Come mid-August, Japanese horsemen head north for the cooler weather in Sapporo for the start of the good 2-year-old racing and the annual yearling sales. Hokkaido is also where most of the country's leading stud farms are located, among them Northern Farm and Shadai Farm

Sapporo has 16 days of racing from mid-August to early October. The big race is the 1¼-mile Grade 2 Sapporo Kinen for 3-year-olds and up on the last Sunday in August.

The track itself is a virtually level, right-handed oval with very wide, mild turns. The turf course is one mile, 50 yards long with a very short stretch of just 270 yards. The dirt track inside the turf course is 7½ furlongs and has a 268-yard stretch.

HAKODATE is the only other JRA track on Hokkaido. An undulating, right-handed oval of one mile, 30 yards, it has 16 days of racing on eight weekends between mid-June and mid-August, closing just as Sapporo opens.

National Association of Racing tracks

While the Japan Racing Association runs the 10 major Japanese tracks that operate on weekends and funnels revenue to the national government, the National Association of Racing (NAR) is in charge of 20 tracks that run exclusively during the week for the benefit of local prefectural governments.

Established in 1962, the NAR conducts races for Thoroughbreds and Arabians as well as a number of exotic events called Ban-ei races for Percheron, Breton, and Belgian workhorses pulling cement rollers weighing up to a ton over a one-furlong straight course that includes two humps. Representatives of PETA are never invited to these events.

Most of the NAR fare is for Thoroughbreds, however, and all of it is on dirt. The best NAR events are the equivalent of JRA Grade 2's, but most of the maiden and allowances rate well below their JRA equivalents.

That said, the prize money at NAR tracks is very good, and at their three major courses—Ohi, Kawasaki, and Funabashi, all located in the vicinity of Tokyo—Japanese Grade 1 contests are worth in excess of $1 million, with maidens going for about $80,000.

OHI is the NAR's most popular track. It is famous for its twinkle races, so called because the festive infield with its amusement-park atmosphere is illuminated after nightfall by thousands of spiraling lights between races, helping to attract upward of 25,000 fans in nice weather. Ohi is a perfectly level, right-handed oval measuring 1¹⁄₁₆ miles with a 1½-furlong stretch.

Located in eastern Tokyo well away from the city center, it conducts 30 afternoon meetings between late November and March, and 69 night meetings (which actually begin in late afternoon and continue until 11 P.M.) between April and early November when the lights twinkle. Ohi's meetings, like all NAR meetings, are conducted in consecutive three, four, or five-day clusters.

The Tokyo Derby in early June and the Japan Dirt Derby five weeks later in July, both at 1¼ miles, are Ohi's major races for 3-year-olds. The track's best weight-for-age events are the 1¼-mile Teio Sho in June; the six-furlong JBC Sprint and the 1¼-mile JBC Classic (which was won in 2007 by two-time Dubai World Cup runner Vermilion), both run on the same night in late October; and the late-December Tokyo Daishoten.

KAWASAKI, not to be confused with the motorcycle manufacturer, is a left-handed oval measuring a bandbox-like six furlongs around with an abrupt little stretch of slightly less than 1½ furlongs. Located about 25 miles south of Tokyo, it has 64 days of racing annually, 17 day meetings between December and February, and 47 night meetings between April and November. Its chief wintertime event is the 1$\frac{5}{16}$-mile Kawasaki Kinen in late January, sometimes used as an early prep for the Dubai World Cup. The 1$\frac{5}{16}$-mile Kanto Oaks in June is the NAR's main event for 3-year-old fillies.

East of Tokyo, not too far from the JRA's Nakayama Racecourse, is FUNABASHI. This left-handed oval has a seven-furlong outer dirt track with a 1½-furlong stretch and a six-furlong, 55-yard inner dirt track with a stretch a few yards short of 1½ furlongs.

Funabashi races throughout the year with 54 afternoon meetings consisting of single three-to-five-day meetings each month. The 1½-mile Diolite Kinen in January, the one-mile Marine Cup in February, and the one-mile Kashima Kinen in March are the track's major events.

8

HONG KONG

SHA TIN ☰

Sha Tin Racecourse
Penfold Park
Sha Tin Road
Sha Tin, Hong Kong
Phone: 011-852-2966-8111
Internet: www.hkjc.com

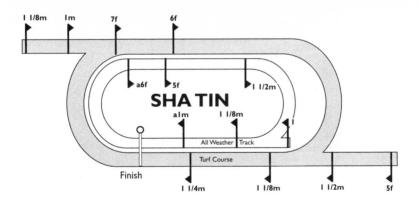

LOCATION: Hong Kong is 1,794 miles southwest of Tokyo; 7,195 west of Los Angeles; 8,054 miles west of New York; 5,982 miles southeast of London; and 4,584 miles north of Sydney.

Sha Tin Racecourse is situated in Sha Tin, 12 miles north of Hong Kong Island, Hong Kong's central district.

COURSE DESCRIPTION: Sha Tin is a perfectly level right-handed oval, 1³⁄₁₆ miles around. The five-furlong straight course meets the two-furlong, 35-yard homestretch just before its halfway point. There is a chute at the head of the backstretch for the start of races at one mile and 1⅛ miles. The turns are relatively mild, similar to those on Belmont's Widener Turf Course. In races of 1¼ miles, like the Hong Kong Cup and the Queen Elizabeth II Cup, there is a short run of just 160 yards to the first turn, leaving horses that have drawn wide at a disadvantage.

An all-weather track (largely traditional dirt but with some wax-coated sand in its makeup) lies inside of the turf course. This is about 30 yards short of a mile and has a stretch that is about 15 yards short of two furlongs. The races run on this track are reserved for Hong Kong's low-end performers.

Generally speaking, Sha Tin is a track that favors long-striding gallopers and closers, while Happy Valley favors close-coupled types and front-runners or trackers.

HISTORY: Founded in 1978, Sha Tin was built expressly to handle the racing boom that had been gaining momentum at nearby Happy Valley across the bay on Hong Kong Island. Hong Kong had been rated the freest market economy in the world year after year by *The Wall Street Journal,* and its wealthiest businessmen were poised to make a big splash on the international racing scene at the time, but they needed a world-class racecourse, as the charming but antiquated confines of Happy Valley were no longer able to fulfill their requirements.

Built on a strip of reclaimed land (Sha Tin means "sand field") in the New Territories north of Hong Kong Island, the new racecourse was state-of-the-art upon its completion and has maintained the highest standards since then, in terms of both amenities and quality of racing. Crowds of 80,000 on Hong Kong International Race Day and Hong Kong Derby Day still leave the racegoer with plenty of breathing room.

It has always been the objective of the Hong Kong Jockey Club (HKJC) to attract as many of the best horses in the world to Sha Tin as it can. The first running of the 1⅛-mile Hong Kong Cup in 1988 was intended to lure an international field, but foreign trainers were slow on the uptake and didn't win the race for the first time until 1995, when Hideyuki Mori brought Fujiyama Kenzan from Japan for the victory. Jimmy Picou and Cash Asmussen combined for the 1997 Cup with Val's Prince.

The Cup had its distance increased by a furlong in 1999, the

French invader Pride (left) holds off Japanese raider Admire Moon in the 2006 Hong Kong Cup at Sha Tin.

inaugural year of the four-race Hong Kong International Race Day. Jim and Tonic, trained in France by Francois Doumen, won it, just as he had won the seven-furlong Hong Kong Bowl a year earlier.

The Cup now rates as one of the world's premier 10-furlong contests, and its winners in recent years include Fantastic Light, Falbrav, the locally trained Vengeance of Rain, Pride, and Ramonti.

In 1991 the Club had introduced the seven-furlong Bowl and invited horses from around the globe to compete. The Dermot Weld-trained Additional Risk took advantage of a group of Hong Kong trainees that were not quite ready for prime time. A year later, Bill Shoemaker engineered the second and most recent victory by an American trainee when Glen Kate won. One of Hong Kong's earliest good horses, Winning Colors, broke the Bowl ice for the home side in 1993.

The Bowl had its distance increased by a furlong and its name changed to the Hong Kong Mile in 1999. Docksider, third in the Breeders' Cup Mile a few weeks earlier at Gulfstream, claimed the prize and the race has been one of the world's chief one-mile events since then. Among its winners have been Sunline from New Zealand, Hat Trick from Japan, and the locally trained Good Ba Ba.

The first 1½-mile Hong Kong Vase in 1994 went to the John Hammond-trained Red Bishop just a month after the French horse had finished second in Belmont's Red Smith Handicap. The fine German mare Borgia took the 1999 running. Phoenix Reach in 2004 and Collier Hill in 2006 both vaulted from victory in the Canadian International to win the Vase. Ouija Board in 2005 and Doctor Dino in 2007 have ensured that the Vase remains a first-class international Group 1.

The new race on the first International Race Day was the five-furlong Hong Kong Sprint. This has been a hit since its first running, when it fell to the outstanding local sprinter Fairy King Prawn. The Australian speedster Falvelon nosed out the Randy Morse-trained Morluc in both 2000 and 2001, becoming the only foreign-trained horse to win the Sprint in its nine-year history.

The great Silent Witness, the leading sprinter of his day anywhere in the world, took the 2003 and 2004 runnings for Tony Cruz, the Macau-born trainer who had been a leading rider in France in the 1990s. The Sprint was upped in distance to six furlongs in 2006, and since then it has been taken by two of the world's best turf sprinters, Absolute Champion and Sacred Kingdom, both trained in Hong Kong.

The Hong Kong Jockey Club has been at the forefront of many technical innovations. Ultrasophisticated fractional timing generated through chips imbedded in jockeys' helmets was introduced in 2003. A year later, Sha Tin opened a new paddock behind the grandstand, one that has a viewing capacity of 5,000, more than the number of people who come racing on a single day at most American tracks.

Racing in Hong Kong—at both Sha Tin and Happy Valley—is thriving, thanks to a populace that is passionate about the game and an administration that responds to all of their needs.

ANALYSIS: With prize money that is second worldwide only to Japan, racing at Sha Tin has improved by leaps and bounds since the turn of the new century to the point where the best Hong Kong horses can compete with the best horses from any country in the world. This, in spite of the twin facts that Hong Kong lacks a breeding industry and has been, since 1998, under the auspices of the mainland Communist government in Beijing.

All of the horses that run in Hong Kong are bought privately either as yearlings or horses in training or at public sales around the world. A majority of these come from Australia, a country that has always had close links to the former British colony, as it was once a British colony itself.

As a result of this system, there is no 2-year-old racing in Hong Kong, as horses arriving from foreign climes are given plenty of time to adapt. There are a relatively small number of maiden races, called griffins, in the Australian manner. Likewise, the starting gate is called the barrier, as it is down under.

The overwhelming majority of races run in Hong Kong are handicaps. In fact, most of the older horses that have already run step right into the handicap division. A small percentage of these ultimately prove good enough to graduate to stakes company.

And that is very good company indeed. With 11 million-dollar races scheduled annually, there are more such races in Hong Kong (all of them run at Sha Tin) per person than in any other country. The cheapest handicaps go for $70,000, the best for $125,000.

As there is no breeding industry in Hong Kong, most of the horses there are gelded—even the best ones, such as Silent Witness, Vengeance of Rain, Viva Pataca, and Sacred Kingdom. In fact, most of the best horses there are males, as Hong Kong horsemen see no point in bothering with fillies or mares since they cannot be bred locally.

While horses from Hong Kong do travel to compete in Japan (Bullish Luck won the 2006 Yasuda Kinen at Tokyo) and Dubai (Vengeance of Rain won the 2007 Dubai Sheema Classic at Nad Al Sheba), we rarely see them in North America. This is due in part to the huge prize money in Hong Kong. If a Hong Kong owner is going to send a horse to run in a foreign country, he is going to send him for a race worth a million dollars. The Breeders' Cup comes at the wrong time of the year for Hong Kong, as its season only begins in September after a 2½-month summer vacation when it is much too hot and humid to race there.

But if the best horses from Hong Kong ever do get around to coming to America, we had better be ready for them, for they have proven at home that they can beat the best that the rest of the world has to offer.

In fact, American-trained horses have all but disappeared from Hong Kong International Race Day in recent years. In 2006 the United States had only one runner, the Rick Dutrow-trained Rebel Rebel, who finished eighth in the Hong Kong Mile. Another American representative, Fast Parade, made the trip that year to run in the Hong Kong Sprint, but ended up bowing out after his trainer, Peter Miller, said the horse was not eating and hadn't shipped well. (HKJC officials also said that Fast Parade's tests showed a "blood irregularity," so he would not have been allowed to run even if Miller had not voluntarily opted out.) In 2007 there wasn't a single American-trained horse at Sha Tin on Hong Kong International Race Day.

Given the rich purses up for grabs, why isn't there a stronger American presence in Hong Kong? One reason may be that Hong Kong International Race Day falls in mid-December, about six weeks after many top U.S. horses have completed their campaigns with a season-ending race in the Breeders' Cup. It may also have something to do with the Hong Kong Jockey Club's drug policy. The strictest in the world, it will generate the removal of a horse from a race no matter what trivial level of a prohibited substance may be detected.

That is exactly what happened to the superb Australian sprinter Takeover Target in 2006. He had arrived at Sha Tin for the Hong Kong Sprint with a trace of an anabolic steroid in his system. All foreign horses that arrive in Hong Kong for the big day in December are tested. Should one come up positive, the owner is given a choice. If the horse is scratched voluntarily, the HKJC will pay for transport and accommodations for the horse, jockey, groom, trainer, and owner; that is, they will receive the same benefits as all of the foreign runners. Or, the owner can attempt to tough it out, hoping that a second test on race-day morning will prove negative.

That was the route taken by Takeover Target's trainer and co-owner, Joe Janiak, who said that Takeover Target had been injected with the steroid several weeks earlier in order to help him cope with the stress of a flight from Japan, where he had won the Grade 1 Sprinters Stakes in October. That victory moved Takeover Target within reach of a $1 million bonus offered for winning a series of races called the Global Sprint Challenge, which he could have wrapped up with a victory in the Hong Kong Sprint.

With so much at stake, Takeover Target was tested seven times while in Hong Kong while Janiak kept hoping for the drug to clear his horse's system in time for the Sprint. When the gelding failed the final test, he was withdrawn by the stewards, and Janiak had to foot the entire bill—and pay a $25,000 fine.

Perhaps this cautionary tale has been a deterrent for owners and trainers of American horses, who are free to race and train on drugs that are met with a zero-tolerance policy in Hong Kong.

TRACK RECORDS

DISTANCE	RECORD TIME	HORSE	DATE
TURF			
5f	54.70	Sacred Kingdom	March 31, 2007
6f	1:07.50	Sacred Kingdom	Nov. 17, 2007
7f	1:20.40	Flying Lamborgini	Jan. 10, 2006
		Pocket Money	April 22, 2007
1m	1:33.10	Down Town	Oct. 21, 2007
1⅛m	1:46.20	Packing Winner	Jan. 10, 2007
1¼m	2:00.10	Jim and Tonic	April 18, 1999
1⅜m	2:13.90	Top Champ	April 17, 1982
1½m	2:24.60	Viva Pataca	June 3, 2007
ALL-WEATHER			
6f	1:07.80	Watch What Happens	May 12, 2007
1m, 55y	1:37.40	Crocker	May 10, 2003
		Packing Angel	May 16, 2004
1⅛m	1:47.60	Rocket Win	March 31, 2007
1¼m	2:01.30	Dynamic Fun	Dec. 12, 2006
1½m	2:29.10	Winning Years	May 12, 1999

MAJOR RACES (Chronological Order, September to June)

RACE	CONDITIONS
Sha Tin Sprint Trophy Hcp-HK G3	5f (T) 3yo+
National Day Cup Hcp-HK G3	7f (T) 3yo+
Premier Bowl Hcp-HK G3	6f (T) 3yo+
Sha Tin Trophy Hcp-HK G3	1m (T) 3yo+
International Cup Trial-HK G2	1¼m (T) 3yo+
International Mile Trial-HK G2	1m (T) 3yo+
International Sprint Trial-HK G2	6f (T) 3yo+
Hong Kong Cup-G1	1¼m (T) 3yo+
Hong Kong Mile-G1	1m (T) 3yo+
Hong Kong Vase-G1	1½m (T) 3yo+
Hong Kong Sprint-G1	6f (T) 4yo+
Chinese Club Challenge Hcp-HK G3	7f (T) 4yo+
Bauhinia Sprint Trophy Hcp-HK G3	5f (T) 3yo+
Stewards Cup-HK G1	1m (T) 3yo+
Hong Kong Classic Mile-HK G1	1m (T) 4yo
Centenary Sprint Cup-HK G1	5f (T) 3yo+

RACE	CONDITIONS
Centenary Vase Hcp-HK G3	1⅛m (T) 3yo+
Chairman's Sprint Prize-HK G1	6f (T) 3yo+
Hong Kong Derby Trial-HK G2	1⅛m (T) 4yo
Hong Kong Gold Cup-HK G1	1¼m (T) 3yo+
Hong Kong Macau Trophy Hcp-HK G3	7f (T) 3yo+
Hong Kong Derby-HK G1	1¼m (T) 4yo
Queen's Silver Jubilee Cup-HK G1	7f (T) 3yo+
Premier Plate Hcp-HK G3	1⅛m (T) 3yo+
Chairman's Trophy-HK G2	1m (T) 3yo+
Queen Elizabeth II Cup-G1	1¼m (T) 3yo+
Champions Mile-G1	1m (T) 3yo+
GOME Sprint-HK G2	6f (T) 3yo+
Queen Mother Memorial Cup Hcp-HK G3	1½m (T) 3yo+
Hong Kong Champions and Chater Cup-HK G1	1½m (T) 3yo+
Sha Tin Vase Hcp-HK G3	6f (T) 3yo+
Premier Cup Hcp-HK G3	7f (T) 3yo+

DAYS OF RACING: During the 2007–08 season that ran from September 9 through July 1, Sha Tin held 47 race meetings. Of those, 45 were day meetings, most of them on Saturday or Sunday. Sha Tin also ran two Wednesday-evening meetings under the lights. Hong Kong International Race Day is always held on the second Sunday in December.

HOW TO GET THERE: If you are staying on Hong Kong Island, like most tourists, the best way to get to Sha Tin is by public transport. Hong Kong's subway system is one of the cleanest and most efficient in the world. Take the Shenzhen line to the Sha Tin Racecourse station that is located across the highway from the track.

SURROUNDING AREA: Sha Tin Racecourse is located near what passes for a suburban section of Hong Kong. The Temple of the 400 Buddhas, statues that line the long and winding staircase up to the temple itself, is located across the highway from the racetrack. Otherwise Sha Tin has little to recommend it save a concert hall in the local shopping mall at which concerts of both Chinese and Western classical music are presented.

Happy Valley Racecourse
2 Sports Road
Happy Valley, Hong Kong
Phone: 011-852-2895-1523
Internet: www.hkjc.com

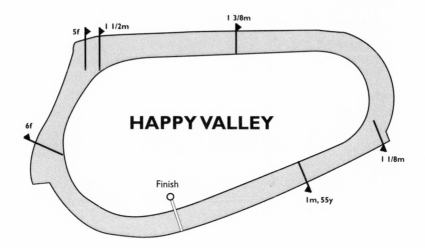

LOCATION: Happy Valley Racecourse is located in the heart of Hong Kong Island, easily accessible from all parts of the island as well as from Kowloon and Sha Tin to the north.

COURSE DESCRIPTION: Happy Valley is a right-handed, 7½-furlong triangular track with a home turn that is much tighter than its far turn. The short, American-like stretch is barely 1½ furlongs. Shortly past the finish line there is a chute for six-furlong races that start with a brief one-furlong straight before turning right onto a backstretch that measures slightly less than 1½ furlongs. There is a 6½-furlong dirt track inside the turf course with a 1½-furlong stretch. The dirt track is used for Hong Kong's lowest handicap divisions.

HISTORY: Like every other place in the world where the British had a colony, Hong Kong has a long and rich history of horse racing. Happy Valley first opened its doors in 1845, only five years after the British had set up camp on the hilly little island just south of the Chinese mainland. The fare was strictly Chinese pony racing, with most of that stock coming from northern China. Imports of stout-hearted little animals from Australia improved the sport considerably during the ensuing years. Thoroughbred racing was never considered during those early days, as Hong Kong was so small it could not possibly support a breeding industry.

The track was built on what had been a virtual swamp. Infested with mosquitoes and suchlike unneighborly insects, the very humid Hong Kong Island was virtually uninhabitable when the British arrived, which makes the existence of the racecourse, and of course the bustling vertical city that surrounds it, something of a miracle.

Happy Valley was the scene of the worst disaster in racing history on February 26, 1918, when the women's grandstand, situated beyond the far turn and restricted to Chinese women and their children, burned to the ground. The fire, which had broken out in the basement kitchen and spread rapidly, claimed the lives of 576 people by the official count, although the actual death toll is believed to have been much higher.

The Royal Hong Kong Jockey Club was founded in 1884, but did not become a fully professional body until 1971, when Thoroughbreds replaced the ponies. The club was renamed the Hong Kong Jockey Club (HKJC) in 1995 in anticipation of the 1997 British handover of Hong Kong to Beijing.

In 1997 the Hong Kong Racing Museum was opened in the Happy Valley grandstand just around the far turn from the Hong Kong Jockey Club headquarters. The museum details the history of racing in Hong Kong at both Happy Valley and Sha Tin, with exhibits and videos available on all of Hong Kong's greatest horses.

A nonprofit organization, the HKJC contributes more than $8 million annually to charities. After the devastating earthquake in Sichuan province in 2008, the Club engineered a special fundraising drive that provided $1.5 million for the relief effort.

ANALYSIS: Horses with Happy Valley form rarely make an appearance in the United States. While there is no question that it plays second fiddle to Sha Tin in terms of quality, Happy Valley more than makes up for that deficiency with an atmosphere that is unparalleled anywhere in the racing world. Arriving at Happy Valley shortly after the sun has set, stepping into the brightly lit amphitheater surrounded by the seven-story grandstand and the high-rise apartment buildings that surround the track, is an exhilarating experience. Even on a typical Wednesday evening when the card consists of seven or eight modest handicaps, there is a buzz at Happy Valley that most racegoers only experience on Kentucky Derby Day or Epsom Derby Day.

Hong Kongers take their betting seriously. The 78 meetings held during the 2007–08 season at Sha Tin and Happy Valley generated $12 billion in handle, an astonishing figure considering that Hong Kong is a city with a population of just seven million. That is an average of $1,714 bet per person per year.

TRACK RECORDS

DISTANCE	RECORD TIME	HORSE	DATE
TURF			
5f	56.40	Fifty Fifty	Oct. 10, 1987
6f	1:08.70	Tiger Prawn	Nov. 6, 2007
1m, 55y	1:38.70	Dordenma	Sept. 27, 2006
		Floral Pegasus	Sept. 27, 2006
1⅛m	1:48.20	Art Trader	Nov. 1, 2005
1⅜m	2:15.90	Magic Hands	Feb. 11, 2004
		Greenessy	May 10, 2006
1½m	2:30.40	Good Fortune	May 27, 1998

MAJOR RACES: Racing at Happy Valley is largely meat-and-potatoes stuff compared to Sha Tin. While there are any number of good handicaps run there, there are no stakes races. All of those are run at Sha Tin.

DAYS OF RACING: Most of the racing at Happy Valley takes place at night. The 2007–08 season began on September 12 and concluded on July 3, during which there were 31 meetings, 28 of them under the lights on Wednesday evenings, two on Sunday afternoons, and one on Tuesday, November 6, an afternoon meeting held to coincide with a simulcast of the Melbourne Cup.

HOW TO GET THERE: The most amusing way to get to Happy Valley from points west, where most of the tourist hotels are located, is by tram. Taking one of these heavy metal antiques is like stepping into Hong Kong's mysterious past. The double-decker cars are the same ones that were in use when the system opened for business in 1904 and provide intimate views into the hustle and bustle of Hong Kong life, especially on race nights, when the city is switching from work mode to play mode.

The No. 1 line runs along Gloucester Road to the main gate of the racetrack at a price of just HK$2 (25 cents in American money). The less adventurous can take a taxi and surely wind up missing the first race because of the dreadful early-evening Hong Kong traffic.

SURROUNDING AREA: One of the world's most vibrant cities, Hong Kong literally throbs with excitement as night falls. The Hollywood Road area is filled with an array of restaurants serving cuisine to suit every taste. At the Temple Street Night Market in Kowloon you can find antiques, souvenirs, and junk to bring back home, have a bowl of noodles, and listen to an impromptu concert of Chinese opera. Serious fans of Cantonese opera should make a beeline to the Sunbeam Theatre in North Point. Served by the tram and the subway, the productions there are explosions of sound and color.

For lovers of Chinese art, the Hong Kong Museum of Art in Tsim Sha Tsui on the south shore of Kowloon is a must. The museum is next door to the three-theatered Hong Kong Cultural Centre, a venue for both Chinese and Western classical music and dance. Taking the funicular train to the Peak, the highest point in Hong Kong, provides breathtaking views of the island city below as well as the bustling traffic in the bay. The island's south shore includes some lovely beaches, Stanley Beach the best of them as it comes well equipped with a number of beachside bars and restaurants.

Other Racecourses in Asia

MACAU

As most of HappyValley's racing takes place on Wednesday nights and most of Sha Tin's on Sunday afternoons, a day trip to Macau on Saturday for the afternoon racing at the track located on Taipa Island, south of and across the bridge from downtown Macau, is the thing to do. Fast ferries from Hong Kong get you to Macau in about an hour. From the docks it is a short cab ride to the racecourse, and a short one back to downtown Macau, where there are dozens of casinos from which to choose, some of them the height of elegance, others down and dirty in a rather dangerous way.

The Macau Jockey Club and a number of Macau casinos are run by Stanley Ho, the owner of Hong Kong's multiple Group 1 winner Viva Pataca. The pataca is Macau's unit of currency, but both the racetrack and the casinos in the former Portuguese colony accept Hong Kong dollars, which are worth about 10 percent more than the pataca.

VELIEFENDI ≡

This racetrack in Istanbul might be the next big thing in Thoroughbred racing. Astute management by the Turkish Jockey Club has led to great improvements at Veliefendi in recent years. In 2007 it held its first million-dollar race, the $1.02 million, 1½-mile Bosphorus Cup. That race, along with the one-mile, $680,000 Topkapi Trophy and two new races added in 2008—the seven-furlong, $425,000 Istanbul Stakes for fillies and mares and the 1¼-mile Anatolia Stakes on the track's new Fibresand surface—are helping Veliefendi make a splash on the international racing front. The four races are run on the first weekend in September under the banner of the Turkish International Racing Festival, ostensibly to serve as preps for Arc Weekend.

Veliefendi has a level, 1¼-mile, 44-yard, right-handed turf oval with the 1¹⁄₁₆-mile, 22-yard Fibresand track inside of that. They sit in front of a modern grandstand that very much resembles Longchamp. While the racing cannot compare with that at the French track, the low-end group-race types attracted from Europe each year for the festival frequently meet their matches in the home-grown Turkish product.

9

Argentina

HIPODROMO ARGENTINO DE PALERMO

Avenida del Libertador 4101
Buenos Aires, Argentina
Phone: 011-5411-4778-2800
Internet: www.palermo.com.ar

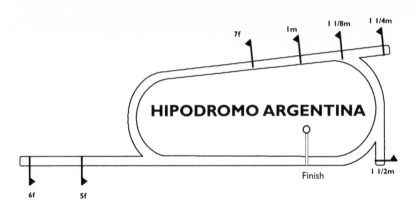

LOCATION: The Hipodromo Argentino, or Palermo, as it is commonly called, lies within the city limits of the Argentine capital of Buenos Aires, which is 5,300 miles south of New York, 6,100 miles southeast of Los Angeles, 3,800 miles south of Miami, and 1,230 miles southwest of Rio de Janeiro.

COURSE DESCRIPTION: Palermo is a perfectly level, left-handed dirt oval measuring 1⅜ miles around. The homestretch is three furlongs. A six-furlong straight course meets the stretch at its halfway point.

It is noteworthy to point out that, rain or shine, the track is not harrowed between races, giving the proceedings a rough-hewn appearance. This may account in part for the general toughness of the Argentine Thoroughbred, who must be able to slog his way through all sorts of tracks in all sorts of weather.

HISTORY: The Hipodromo Argentino opened on May 7, 1876, in a strikingly beautiful Second Empire grandstand designed to please the upwardly mobile Argentines who had followed the elitist lead of Argentine Jockey Club founder Carlos Pellegrini. The Jockey Club is more than a group of men with an interest in horse racing. Indeed, membership in the Jockey Club has long been a pass into the highly exclusive world of Argentine business and politics. Since the late 19th century, virtually all of the members of Argentina's ruling class have been members of the Jockey Club, otherwise it would have been difficult for them to have risen any higher than midlevel management in the nation's hierarchy.

A new grandstand (Tribuna Nueva) for the common people was added in 1908, at which time the original stand was made even grander in the Belle Epoque style. In Buenos Aires, it has always been about style, and nowhere is that more evident than in the racing world.

The pampas region is a perfect place to breed and raise racehorses, as well as the cattle that produce the nation's world-famous steaks, and has provided a platform for the equine-loving Argentines to produce horses that often attain international quality despite the country's relatively limited resources. Horses such as Gentlemen, Bayakoa, Paseana, and Invasor are only a few of the great Argentine-bred Thoroughbreds that have become champions in the United States.

The Gran Premio Nacional, or Argentine Derby, was first run in 1884. In 1991 Argentina emulated the United States with the first running of the Carreras de las Estrellas, or Argentine Breeders' Cup.

Following the American trend, the Hipodromo now has 3,000 slot machines in its basement, catering to players 24 hours a day and helping to prop up a purse structure that was devastated by the 2001–02 collapse of the national currency, the much beleaguered peso.

ANALYSIS: Prior to the Argentine financial crisis of December 2001, the peso had been pegged to the American dollar, so that a maiden race worth 26,000 pesos was worth $26,000, as much or more than many maidens in the United States. In June 2002, six months after being set free from the dollar, the peso was worth just 25 cents, so a maiden with a value of 26,000 pesos was suddenly worth just $6,500.

In struggling to crawl back to respectability, the Argentine peso is now worth about 33 cents, but with inflation taken into account, Argentine races are still worth less than one-third of what they were in 2001.

This has led to a marked increase in the sale of Argentine horses to America, a minor phenomenon that seems even more marked as the decline of the dollar vis-à-vis the British pound and the euro has seen a concomitant rise in the price of European horseflesh, one that has led to a slight decline in the number of European imports to the U.S. and a rather precipitous decline in their quality.

But the increased number of Argentine imports in recent years has not been accompanied by an increase in the quality of Argentine horses running in America. The days of Gentlemen, Bayakoa, and Paseana are beginning to look like the misty golden age of Argentine-American Thoroughbred trading.

One reason for this may be the intervention of the Maktoums. Dubai's ruling family, seeing how tough the Argentine-bred Thoroughbred can be, began buying many of the country's classic winners shortly after the decline of the peso. Asiatic Boy and Honour Devil are just two such high-profile examples. The last two winners of the UAE Derby, they were both purchased by Sheikh Mohammed's brother-in-law, Mohammed bin Khalifa al-Maktoum, who promptly turned them over to South Africa's ace international conditioner, Mike de Kock.

Buying ready-made group-race winners out of foreign countries has always been a risky business. Taking a 4-year-old out of familiar surroundings where he has become used to the regimen that made him a Group 1 or Group 2 winner, and bringing him to the United States for a completely different style of training, not infrequently fouls a horse up.

But in Miss Terrible, we have a case of discovering almost exactly where top-class Argentine form fits into the American picture at this stage. The winner of 8 of her 9 starts for Miguel Garcia and a Group 1 winner on dirt at Palermo and on turf at San Isidro, Miss Terrible wasn't nearly as effective in the U.S., where she won 2 of 9 starts, both of them Grade 3's. Nevertheless, the fact that one of those victories came at six furlongs on turf at Santa Anita and the other at one mile on dirt at Churchill Downs, together with a career-ending second-place finish in the Grade 1 Santa Monica Handicap at seven furlongs on dirt at Santa Anita, stood as a testament to the toughness and versatility of the Argentine-bred Thoroughbred.

Many American importers buy Argentine allowance-race winners that have never been tried in stakes, as they come much more inexpensively. The hope is that they will continue to improve once reaching America, but in most cases they turn out to be little better than claimers.

One recent exception has been Solar Flare. An allowance winner on dirt at both Palermo and San Isidro, this Haras La Quebrada-bred son of Salt Lake finished second in Belmont's Suburban Handicap before failing as the favorite in Saratoga's Whitney Handicap. While no Gentlemen, he more than repaid his American owners at Fox Hill Farms in his first three American outings.

TRACK RECORDS

DISTANCE	RECORD TIME	HORSE	DATE
4f	42.40	Trinchette	Nov. 23, 2002
5f	53.60	Mesmo	Aug. 18, 1981
		Rufus	June 19, 2006
6f	1:07.84	Blues For Sale	April 27, 2007
6½f	1:15.14	El Ejecutor	Aug. 16, 1996
7f	1:20.30	Medal Play	April 19, 2002
7½f	1:26.27	Southern Spring	May 18, 1996
1m	1:32.22	Rincon Americano	July 26, 1996
1⅛m	1:45.89	Le Pont Neuf	April 16, 2000
1¼m	1:59.13	Akiro	March 22, 1998
1⅜m	2:30.99	Dorian Gray	June 19, 1995

MAJOR RACES (Alphabetical Order by Group)

RACE	CONDITIONS
CARRERAS DE LAS ESTRELLAS (Even-numbered years)	
Estrellas Classic	1¼m 3yo+
Estrellas Distaff	1¼m 3yo+ f&m
Estrellas Junior Sprint	5f 2yo
Estrellas Juvenile	1m 2yo c
Estrellas Juvenile Fillies	1m 2yo f
Estrellas Sprint	5f 3yo+

RACE	CONDITIONS
GROUP 1	
Gran Premio Ciudad de Buenos Aires	5f 3yo+
Gran Premio Criadores	1 9/16m 3yo+ f&m
Gran Premio de las Americas	1m 3yo+
Gran Premio General San Martin	1 1/8m 4yo+
Gran Premio Gilberto Lerena	1m 3yo+ f&m
Gran Premio Jorge de Atucha	7 1/2f 2yo f
Gran Premio Julio e Carlos Menditeguy	1 1/4m 3yo+
Gran Premio Maipu	5f 3yo+
Gran Premio Montevideo	7 1/2f 2yo c
Gran Premio Nacional (Argentine Derby)*	1 9/16m 3yo c
Gran Premio Palermo	1m 3yo+
Polla de Potrancas (Argentine 1000 Guineas)	1m 3yo f
Polla de Potrillos (Argentine 2000 Guineas)*	1m 3yo c
Gran Premio Republica Argentina	1 1/4m 3yo+
Gran Premio Santiago Luro	6f 2yo c
Gran Premio Saturnino J Unzue	6f 2yo f
Gran Premio Seleccion (Argentine Oaks)	1 1/4m 3yo f

* Argentine Triple Crown race, along with San Isidro's Gran Premio Jockey Club. The fillies' classics are the Polla de Potrancas and the Gran Premio Seleccion.

RACE	CONDITIONS
GROUP 2	
Clasico Arturo R. Bullrich	1 1/4m 3yo+ f&m
Clasico Benito Villanueva	1m 3yo+
Clasico Carlos Casares	5f 2yo f
Clasico Carlos Tomkinson	1m 3yo+ f&m
Clasico Chacabuco	1 9/16m 4yo+
Clasico Chile	1 3/8m 4yo+ f&m
Clasico Comparacion	1 9/16m 4yo+
Clasico Coronel Miguel Martinez	1 1/8m 3yo c
Clasico Eduardo Casey	1 3/8m 3yo c
Clasico Francisco J. Beazley	1 1/8m 3yo f
Clasico General Belgrano	1 9/16m 3yo+
Clasico General Luis Maria Campos	1m 3yo f
Clasico Ignacio e Ignacio F. Correas	1 9/16m 4yo+ f&m
Clasico Miguel Angel e Tomas Juarez Celman	1m 3yo+ f&m
Clasico Miguel Cane	1m 3yo c

Clasico Otono	1¼m 3yo+
Clasico Peru	1⅛m 4yo+
Clasico Ramon Biaus	1⅜m 3yo+ f&m
Clasico Venezuela	5f 3yo+ f&m

GROUP 3

Clasico Apertura	1¼m 3yo+ f&m
Clasico Asociacion de Propietarios de Caballos de Carrera	7f 3yo+ f&m
Clasico Ayacucho	1⁹⁄₁₆m 4yo+
Handicap Bolivia	7f 3yo+ f&m
Clasico Buenos Aires	1m 3yo+
Clasico Circulo de Propietarios de Caballerizas Sangre Pura de Carrera	1m 3yo+ f&m
Clasico Coronel Pringles	5f 3yo+
Clasico Estados Unidos de America	5f 3yo+
Clasico General Arenales	5f 3yo+ f&m
Clasico General Lavalle	5½f 2yo f
Clasico Guillermo Paats	5f 3yo+
Clasico Hipodromo Argentino	5½f 2yo
Clasico Ines Victorica Roca	1m 3yo+ f&m
Clasico Irlanda	5f 3yo+
Clasico Italia	1¼m 4yo+
Clasico Loteria Nacional	5f 3yo+ f&m
Clasico Manuel J. Guiraldes	7f 3yo f
Clasico Mexico	5f 3yo+ f&m
Clasico Old Man	7f 3yo c
Clasico Paraguay	5f 3yo+
Clasico Republica de Panama	5f 3yo+ f&m
Clasico Republica Federativa del Brasil	1m 4yo+
Clasico Republica Oriental del Uruguay	1m 3yo+ f&m
Clasico Ricardo P. L. Sauze	1m 3yo+ f&m
Clasico Vicente L. Casares	1⁹⁄₁₆m 3yo+

As Argentina is in the Southern Hemisphere, their spring comes during the North American autumn. Thus, the schedule for their classics has the Polla de Potrillos and Polla de Potrancas being run in September, while the Gran Premio Nacional and the Gran Premio Seleccion take place in November.

The Carreras de las Estrellas (Races of the Stars), the Argentine equivalent of the Breeders' Cup, are run on the last Sunday in June as the weather begins to cool at the end of the Southern Hemisphere racing season. The Estrellas are run in even-numbered years at Palermo on dirt, and in odd-numbered years at San Isidro on turf. This may seem strange, but in Argentina many horses are switched back and forth between dirt and turf with a certain regularity.

Argentina's major dirt race for older horses, outside of the Estrellas Clasico (when it is run at Palermo), is the Gran Premio Republica Argentina in May. When the Estrellas are run at Palermo, the Gran Premio Republica Argentina serves as the Estrellas Clasico's major prep in much the same way that the Jockey Club Gold Cup serves as a key trial for the Breeders' Cup Classic.

DAYS OF RACING: The Hipodromo Argentino generally runs two or three meetings per week, 52 weeks of the year, with between 12 and 16 races per day. There are a total of 10 meetings per month, or 120 per year. The track shares the Buenos Aires-area calendar with San Isidro and La Plata, both of which also run two or three meetings per week.

HOW TO GET THERE: The racecourse is located in Buenos Aires just north of the fashionable Palermo district and just south of the Aeroparque Jorge Newbery, the city's domestic airport. Take the D line on the Subte (subway) to the Palermo station, from which it is a 10-minute walk to the main gate. From the main-line Retiro station, take a regular train to Tres de Febrero station, across the street from the main gate.

If you prefer to take a taxi, telephone from your hotel for a *remise*, or private car, and do so again on your way back from the racetrack, as it is dangerous to hail a cab in Buenos Aires, the taxi drivers there not particularly known for their honesty or their friendliness.

SURROUNDING AREA: Buenos Aires is the most European of South American cities, with numerous attractions, although it is wise to keep a closer than usual watch on your belongings, as the city is a little rough around the edges, especially since the collapse of the peso in 2002. The tranquil area surrounding Recoleta Cemetery resembles Paris, and the street across from the cemetery's main entrance has a row of restaurants where you will be served the best steaks this side of paradise.

In fact, any racing fan that loves steak owes it to himself to visit

Buenos Aires at least once in his life. The quality of Argentine beef is unparalleled. Most restaurants prepare their steaks as simply as possible on an open grill and serve them even more simply on plain white plates without garnish, yet they make American steakhouses seem like burger joints in comparison. Even a trip to a cheap steakhouse in a dodgy neighborhood will be rewarded with a better than average steak. At a first-class restaurant, the red meat will send you to seventh heaven.

In bohemian San Telmo there is an open market every Sunday in a square that is surrounded by charming old-fashioned bars and restaurants. A late-night visit to Bar Sud is de rigueur if you want to see real tango performers.

A trip to Boca, south of downtown, is also well worth the effort. Its colorfully painted buildings house cafes offering tango, opera, and the national drink, *mate*. Boca is also the home of the city's most popular soccer team, the working-class Boca Juniors, blood foes of their hated crosstown rivals at upmarket River Plate.

SAN ISIDRO

Hipodromo San Isidro
Avenido Marquez 504
San Isidro
Provincia de Buenos Aires, Argentina
Phone: 011-54-11-4743-4010
Internet: www.hipodromosanisidro.com

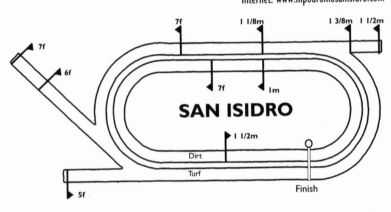

LOCATION: The Hipodromo San Isidro is located 13 miles northwest of Buenos Aires.

COURSE DESCRIPTION: San Isidro is a perfectly level left-handed turf oval 1¾ miles around with a 2½-furlong stretch. The turns are very wide and mild. There is a chute at the head of the backstretch from which 1½-mile races, like the Gran Premio Carlos Pellegrini, are started. There is a five-furlong straight course and a six-furlong course that makes a slight left-handed bend into the stretch. Inside the turf course is a 1⅜-mile dirt track with a stretch slightly longer than three furlongs. San Isidro holds the distinction of being the largest racecourse in the Americas.

HISTORY: San Isidro opened on December 8, 1935, as a turf-only racecourse. Due to the demands of both horsemen and bettors, a dirt track was opened on December 1, 1994.

The turf track is the site of the Gran Premio Carlos Pellegrini, the 1½-mile race that is generally regarded as the South American equivalent of the Prix de l'Arc de Triomphe. First run in 1887 at the Hipodromo Argentino, it was transferred to San Isidro in 1940.

A record crowd of 102,600 jammed the stands for the 1952 running at the height of the Peron regime. Between 1971 and 1979 it was back to Palermo again when San Isidro was victimized by a horsemen's embargo, during which time the Argentine Jockey Club took the opportunity to rebuild the grandstand.

The track reopened on December 8, 1979, the 44th anniversary of its original opening. The Carlos Pellegrini returned to San Isidro in 1980.

As might be expected, the Carlos Pellegrini was dominated in its early years by horses bred in Britain and France. The first Argentine-bred winner in 1889 was named, fittingly enough, Bolivar, after the famous South American liberator. The second Argentine-bred winner in 1893 was named Buenos Aires.

Many of the race's best winners have been immortalized with stakes races named for them: Porteno (1896), Pippermint (1902), Old Man (1904 and 1905, the first two-time winner), Ocurrencia (1915), and Congreve (1928).

The Carlos Pellegrini has traditionally been dominated by Argentine-trained horses, but the race took on an international flavor in 1938 when the Uruguayan-trained Romantico landed the first of two consecutive victories. Brazilians Escorial (1959), Immensity (1983), and Much Better (1994), along with the Peruvian Laredo (1993), added to the mix, and in 1996, the Peruvian-trained Fregy's became the first and only American-bred to win it.

The 1990 winner, Algenib, would later race in the United States for Wally Dollase, but it was Ron McAnally who saddled him for his biggest North American victory in the Golden Gate Handicap.

Much Better became an international traveler, preceding his big Argentine triumph with a 14th-place finish in Carnegie's 1994 Prix de l'Arc de Triomphe. Fregy's, a Kentucky-bred son of the Storm Bird stallion Combsway, was trained by Jorge Salas in Peru, where he was Horse of the Year in 1996 before being sent to Eduardo Inda, for whom he finished second in the 1997 Ack Ack at Santa Anita.

Great as the Carlos Pellegrini may be, its winners have had little success outside of South America. The 1999 winner, Asidero, followed with a victory first time out at Santa Anita in a one-mile allowance the following July, but never won again in six American starts, his best try a close third in the Clement Hirsch. The 2002 winner, Freddy, was subsequently 0 for 5 in California, after which he was 0 for 9 in the handicap ranks in England. Latency, the 2007 winner, was sent to Dubai, where he finished eighth in the 1¼-mile Maktoum Challenge on dirt before coming home 11th in the 1½-mile Dubai Sheema Classic on turf.

ANALYSIS: While racing and training customs differ in every country, Argentine racing incorporates a number of peculiarities that distinguish it as the land of the gaucho. Horses are regularly galloped bareback on days when they are doing a serious piece of work. Jockeys are not given a leg up by the trainer before a race; they must, instead, jump aboard themselves. More tellingly, the amount of time a horse spends in the saddling enclosure, the paddock, and out on the track before a race can sometimes reach nearly two hours.

First, horses are brought into the pre-paddock nearly two hours before their race. After leaving the paddock they are sometimes out on the track very shortly after the previous race has been run.

Starting gates in Argentina are generally much farther behind the official starting point of a race, sometimes as much as 100 yards, accounting in part for the fast times recorded at both San Isidro and Palermo. Another reason for the fast times at San Isidro is the shortness of the grass on the turf course, which makes the Hollywood turf look overgrown by comparison.

Race-day medication is legal in Argentina, but not as legal as it is in the United States. Lasix and Butazolidin are allowed in 4-year-olds and up, the idea being to keep juveniles and the classic generation drug free. Moreover, Bute is not allowed on race day for any horse running in a group or listed race.

Racing in Argentina is still dominated by a number of longstanding breeding farms, chief among them Haras La Quebrada, Haras La Biznaga, Haras Firmamento, Haras Vacacion, and Haras de la Pomme. Trainers to take note of are Juan Carlos Etchechoury, Juan Carlos Maldotti, Alfredo Gaitan Dassie, and Arturo Bullrich. Jockeys Pablo Falero, Juan Herrera, Julio Mendez, and Jorge Ricardo, the Brazilian now based in Argentina who has won more races than any jockey in history, are the country's most notable riders.

TRACK RECORDS

DISTANCE	RECORD TIME	HORSE	DATE
TURF			
4f	43.80	Megafog	Nov. 14, 1982
		Muladi	Nov. 27, 1983
5f	53.07	Locomotivo	May 17, 1997
6f	1:06.40	Cachateo	Oct. 7, 2000
7f	1:17.60	Vanguardia	Nov. 15, 2001
1m	1:31.00	Riton	Feb. 25, 1995
1⅛m	1:44.58	Ditch Digger	Dec. 24, 2000
1¼m	1:56.82	Storm Military	Feb. 11, 2007
1⅜m	2:10.10	Potro Rex	Nov. 20, 2004
1½m	2:21.80	Asidero	Dec. 11, 1999
DIRT			
5½f	1:01.80	Wally	Nov. 12, 1994
6f	1:07.28	Soy El Brujo	April 4, 2007
7f	1:20.22	Enriendado	July 30, 1997
1m	1:33.20	Menesteo	Nov. 23, 1994
1⅛m	1:45.60	Galileo	Nov. 9 1994
1¼m	1:58.86	Candy Gift	Aug. 1, 2007
1⅜m	2:13.19	Pulpy Marshal	July 30, 2003

MAJOR RACES (Alphabetical Order by Group)

RACE	CONDITIONS
CARRERAS DE LAS ESTRELLAS (Odd-numbered years on turf)	
Estrellas Classic-G1	1¼m (T) 3yo+
Estrellas Distaff-G1	1¼m (T) 3yo+ f&m
Estrellas Junior Sprint-G1	5f (T) 2yo
Estrellas Juvenile-G1	1m (T) 2yo c

Estrellas Juvenile Fillies-G I	I m (T) 2yo f
Estrellas Sprint-G I	5f (T) 3yo+

TURF GROUP I

Gran Premio Carlos Pellegrini*	I ½m 3yo+
Copa de Oro	I ½m 4yo+
Copa de Plata	I ¼m 3yo+ f&m
Polla de Potrancas	I m 2yo f
Dos Mil Guineas*	I m 3yo c
Gran Premio Eliseo Ramirez	7f 2yo f
Gran Premio Enrique Acebal	I ¼m 3yo f
Gran Premio Feliz de Alzega Unzue	5f 3yo+
Gran Criterium	I m 2yo
Gran Premio Joaquin de Anchorena	I m 3yo+
Gran Premio Jockey Club*	I ¼m 3yo
Gran Premio Miguel Alfredo Martinez de Hoz	I ¼m 3yo+
Mil Guineas	I m 3yo f
Gran Premio Raul e Raul E. Chevalier	7f 2yo c
Gran Premio San Isidro	I m 3yo+
Gran Premio Suipacha	5f 3yo+
Gran Premio 25 de Mayo	I ½m 3yo+

* San Isidro Triple Crown
 The Gran Premio del Jockey Club is also the second leg of the Argentine Triple Crown along with the Polla de Potrillos and the Gran Premio Nacional at the Hipodromo Argentino.

TURF GROUP 2

Clasico Abril	I ⅛m 3yo+ f&m
Clasico Capital	I m 3yo+
Clasico Carlos P. Rodriguez	I m 3yo+ f&m
Clasico Cyllene	5f 3yo+
Clasico Ecuador	I m 4yo+
Clasico Ensayo	I ⅛m 3yo c
Clasico General Pueyrredon	I ⅞m 4yo+
Clasico Juan Shaw	I ⅜m 3yo+ f&m
Clasico La Mission	I ¼m 4yo+ f&m
Clasico Los Haras	I ¼m 4yo+ f&m
Clasico 9 de Julio	I m 4yo+

RACE	CONDITIONS
Clasico Particula	1⅜m 3yo+ f&m
Clasico Pippermint	5f 4yo+
Clasico Provincia	
de Buenos Aires	1½m 3yo
Clasico Ricardo, Ezequiel e	
Ezequiel M. Fernandez Guerrico	1m 3yo+ f&m
Clasico Sibila	1m 4yo+ f&m
Clasico Tomas Lyon	5f 3yo+ f&m
TURF GROUP 3	
Clasico Condesa	5f 3yo+ f&m
Clasico Congreve	5f 2yo
Clasico Eudora J. Balsa	1m 4yo+ f&m
Clasico Gay Hermit	5f 3yo+
Clasico General Las Heras	7f 3yo+ f&m
Clasico General Viamonte	5f 3yo+
Clasico Horatio Bustillo	1m 3yo+
Clasico Ocurrencia	5f 4yo+ f&m
Clasico Olavarria	5f 3yo+ f&m
Clasico Omega	1m 4yo+ f&m
Clasico Pedro Chapar	7f 3yo+
Clasico Porteno	1m 3yo+
Clasico Progreso	1½m 4yo+
Clasico Santiago Lawrie	5f 3yo+
Clasico Velocidad	5f 2yo

All of the group races at San Isidro are run on turf. The best races run on the San Isidro dirt course are all listed races, of which there are 18.

DAYS OF RACING: San Isidro holds two or three days of racing per week. Days are split between turf and dirt. On turf days, all 12 to 14 races are run on turf. On dirt days, all 12 to 14 races are run on dirt. There are 10 meetings per month, 120 per year, split equally between turf and dirt meetings.

HOW TO GET THERE: From Buenos Aires' main Retiro Station it is a 20-minute ride to San Isidro. There is a free shuttle bus from the station to the main gate, which is about a 10-minute walk from the station.

SURROUNDING AREA: Headquarters of the Argentine Jockey Club, San

Isidro is a well-to-do suburb, population 291,000, built around the race-course and the training center, somewhat in the spirit of Newmarket. Virtually all of the horses that race at San Isidro, the Hipodromo Argentino, and La Plata train at the San Isidro facilities, which are separate from but adjacent to the racecourse. There are five training tracks—four dirt tracks and one turf course.

LA PLATA ☰

Hipodromo de la Plata
Calle 44 and 116
La Plata, Provincia de Buenos Aires
Argentina
Phone: 011-54-221-423-1071
Internet: www.loteria.gba.gov.ar/hplp

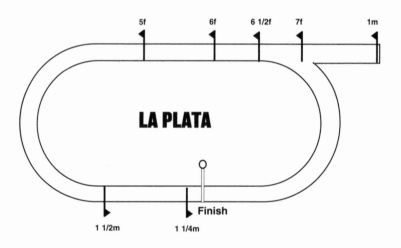

LOCATION: 50 miles southeast of Buenos Aires.

COURSE DESCRIPTION: La Plata is a level, left-handed oval 1¼ miles around. The stretch is two furlongs long.

HISTORY: There has been racing at La Plata since December 11, 1882. In 1904 it came under the auspices of the newly founded provincial Jockey Club. The first running of La Plata's premier race, the Gran Premio Dardo Rocha, was held in 1915.

ANALYSIS: While La Plata draws large fields, they are mostly of the ground-meat variety compared to the prime cuts on offer at Palermo and San Isidro. Group races here are generally at least one notch below their equivalents at the other two tracks, while allowance races are rarely better than low-level claimers at Belmont or Santa Anita.

When attempting to compare times at La Plata with those run on the dirt track at Palermo, remember that the track at La Plata is deeper than Palermo's. Times for equivalent distances at La Plata are not infrequently up to two seconds slower.

Generally speaking, a horse that has won a few allowances at La Plata will have great difficulty winning an allowance almost anywhere in America save the cheapest tracks. Horses that have won or placed in a La Plata Group 1 or Group 2 may be capable of placing in a decent American allowance race.

TRACK RECORDS

DISTANCE	RECORD TIME	HORSE	DATE
4f	45.56	Filis Parade	Dec. 8, 2005
5f	56.90	La Copera	Sept. 11, 1986
5½f	1:03.27	Chick Flick	April 11, 2008
6f	1:10.05	Maktub	March 30, 2006
6½f	1:15.84	Regrandote Yev	Oct. 2, 2004
7f	1:21.28	Suzzane	Nov. 7, 2006
7½f	1:29.49	The Haunted	June 8, 2006
1m	1:34.89	Don Lobizon	Nov. 2, 2006
1¹⁄₁₆m	1:43.09	Varonil	Aug. 4, 2005
1⅛m	1:51.40	Avriloy	Sept. 23, 1982
1¼m	2:02.97	Alkmaar	Feb. 4, 2007
1⁵⁄₁₆m	2:09.31	Black Humour	July 24, 2007
1⅜m	2:14.70	Black Humour	Sept. 9, 2007
1½m	2:29.92	Chevillard	Nov. 19, 1998

MAJOR RACES (Alphabetical Order by Group)

RACE	CONDITIONS
GROUP 1	
Gran Premio Dardo Rocha	1½m 3yo+
Gran Premio Joaquin V. Gonzalez	1m 3yo+
Gran Premio Provincia de Buenos Aires	1⅜m 3yo+
Seleccion de Potrancas	1¼m 3yo f

GROUP 2

Race	Conditions
Clasico Ciudad de La Plata	6f 3yo+
Clasico Clausura	1¼m 3yo+
Clasico General Manuel Belgrano	6f 3yo+
Clasico Isidoro Aramburu	1m 3yo c
Clasico Jockey Club del Provincia	
de Buenos Aires	1¼m 3yo
Clasico Los Criadores	1¼m 3yo+ f&m
Clasico Marcos Levalle	1m 3yo+ f&m
Clasico Miguel Luis Morales	1m 3yo f
Clasico Pedro Goenaga	7f 2yo c
Polla de Potrancas de La Plata	1m 3yo f
Polla de Potrillos de La Plata	1m 3yo c
Clasico Raul Aristegui	7f 2yo f
Clasico 25 de Mayo 1810	1m 3yo+
Clasico Uberto F. Vignart	6f 3yo+

GROUP 3

Race	Conditions
Clasico Agustin B. Gambier	6f 2yo c
Clasico Antonio Cane	1⅚m 3yo+
Clasico Arturo A. Bullrich	6f 3yo+ f&m
Clasico Bonaerense de Propietarios	
de Caballos de Carrera	6f 3yo+
Clasico Asociacion de Propietarios	
de Carrera de Buenos Aires	7½f 2yo c
Clasico Benito Lynch	6f 3yo+
Clasico Clemente Benavides	7½f 2yo f
Clasico Diego White	1¹⁄₁₆m 3yo f
Clasico Fortunato Damiani	5f 2yo f
Clasico General Jose de San Martin	7f 4yo+
Clasico Hipodromo de La Plata	1m 4yo+
Clasico Joaquin V. Maqueda	7f 3yo+ f&m
Clasico Jose Pedro Ramirez	1¹⁄₁₆m 3yo c
Clasico Latinoamerica	1m 3yo+
Clasico Luis Maria Doyhenard	5f 2yo c
Clasico Manuel e Emilio Gnecco	1m 4yo+ f&m
Clasico 9 de Julio	1m 4yo+

Clasico Organizacion Sudamericana	
de Fomento del Pura Sangre	
de Carrera	1⅜m 4yo+
Clasico Republica de Venezuela	6f 2yo f

DAYS OF RACING: Like San Isidro and Palermo, La Plata has 120 days of racing per year, two or three per week for a total of 12 per month.

HOW TO GET THERE: From the Constitucion train station in Buenos Aires, it is about a one-hour ride to La Plata. The racetrack is a five-minute walk from the station.

The train ride to La Plata is an introduction to the greater part of Argentina that is a third-world country. Unofficial vendors roam the aisles offering everything from *panchos* (hot dogs) to wristwatches. Until reaching La Plata, the stations outside Buenos Aires are little more than crumbling cinder-block lean-tos surrounded by what appear to American eyes as shantytowns. On a return trip to Buenos Aires one evening after racing, one witnessed a dog boarding the train at one station. It then walked up the aisle to the next car and disembarked two stations later, during which time it was not asked to present a ticket. Those seeking a more comfortable mode of travel to La Plata might consider departing from Buenos Aires' Retiro train terminal on the bus, but that won't provide half as much fun—or excitement—as the train.

SUROUNDING AREA: Argentina's second-largest city, with a population of 575,000, La Plata was founded by the governor of the Province of Buenos Aires, Dardo Rocha, the man after whom the track's most important race is named. The Cathedral de La Plata, the largest church in South America, is a 20-minute walk from the train station, and about 25 minutes back again to the racetrack. La Plata is twinned with both Louisville, Kentucky, and Liverpool, England; they are sister cities, engaged in cultural and social exchange programs. Unfortunately, there are no races run there that approach the quality of either the Kentucky Derby or the Grand National.

10

Brazil

GAVEA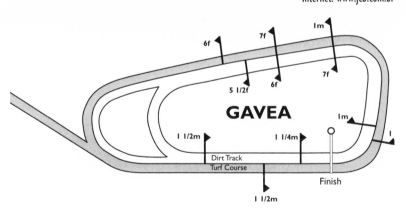

Hipodromo da Gavea
Praca Santos Dumont, 131
Rio de Janeiro 22470-060
Brazil
Phone: 011-55-21-2259-1596
Internet: www.jcb.com.br

LOCATION: Gavea is just a five-minute walk from the famed Ipanema Beach in Rio de Janeiro, 4,815 miles south of New York, 6,295 miles southeast of Los Angeles, and 1,230 miles northeast of Buenos Aires.

COURSE DESCRIPTION: Gavea is an irregularly shaped, left-handed oval with an outer 1⅜-mile turf course and an inner 1¼-mile, 44-yard dirt course. The stretch on both courses is three furlongs long. The turf course stretch extends to form a six-furlong course that makes a mild left-hand bend into the straight.

Gavea is structured along American lines in that horses, about 1,500 of them, are stabled on the backstretch. Inside of the dirt track used for racing, there is a 1¹⁄₁₆-mile dirt training track.

HISTORY: The first races at Gavea were run in 1926, six years after work had begun on the track. Although it has a capacity of 80,000, there are only 3,000 seats available to the public. Brazilian racing at both Gavea and in Sao Paulo at the Hipodromo da Cidade Jardim thrived domestically until 1961, when the capital of Brazil was moved to the new model city of Brasilia, 468 miles inland. With the capital went much of the country's political infrastructure and a good number of businessmen. It wasn't until 1992, when a forward-looking group of influential horsemen took over the Jockey Club Brasileiro, that Brazilian racing got back on track.

Throughout much of its history, racing in Brazil has played second fiddle to Argentina. The new administration quickly took up the chase. By the mid-1990s they were producing horses like Much Better, who was good enough to run in the Prix de l'Arc de Triomphe in 1994, finishing 14th. Two months later he proved that Brazilian racing had arrived as he won Argentina's best race, the Gran Premio Carlos Pellegrini.

Two Brazilian-breds who made a big splash in the United States at about the same time were Siphon and Sandpit. A son of Itajara, Siphon used victory in the 1⅜-mile, Group 2 Grande Premio Presidente as a springboard to a highly successful career in the States, where he won the Hollywood Gold Cup in 1996 and the Santa Anita Handicap a year later.

Sandpit, a turf specialist by an Irish-bred son of Sassafras, Baynoun, won the Caesars International at Atlantic City in 1995 and 1996, the 1994 Oak Tree, the 1995 San Luis Rey, and the 1996 Hollywood Turf Handicap.

In 1997 their mutual trainer, Dick Mandella, sent them both to Nad Al Sheba where Siphon, owned by leading Brazilian horseman Linneo de Paulo Machado, finished second and Sandpit, owned by Sierra Thoroughbreds, third behind Singspiel in the Dubai World Cup.

Brazilian success in North America hasn't been as great since those heady days. Stud TNT has, however, continued to fly the flag in America with Grade 2 winner Out of Control and Grade 3 winner Cagney.

ANALYSIS: With the exception of the well-intended types that hail from the big Brazilian stables like those of Stud TNT and the Machados, few Brazilian imports succeed in the U.S. at the graded-stakes level. The racing at Gavea is, however, half a cut above that at the Sao Paulo track, Cidade Jardim, at least at the maiden and allowance level. At the group-race level there is little to choose between them, as the best Brazilian horses frequently make the 220-mile trip from one track and its training center to another for the biggest races.

The overwhelming majority of the best races at Gavea—at every level—are run on turf. A glance at the track records confirms this, as all the track records on turf are two or three seconds faster than the dirt records.

Of late, one of the better Brazilian imports to run in America is Einstein. By Spend a Buck, he never ran in Brazil, but is a three-time Grade 1 winner on turf in the United States, an example of what can be found in South America—or any foreign land—by owners willing to test the untried waters of foreign yearling markets.

Out of Control, one of a number of fine horses sent by Stud TNT to Bobby Frankel, ran only three times in Brazil, the last his best when second in the one-mile, Group 1 Grande Premio Presidente da Republica on turf. In the U.S. he has won a pair of Grade 2 turf contests, an example of a lightly raced, improving South American import that improved again under a new regime.

Handicappers should be aware of the two tracks in Brazil that rate below Gavea and Cidade Jardim. These are Cristal and Taruma. The racing at both is strictly provincial. The racing there is so low-end that many maidens at Gavea and Cidade Jardim are written for horses that have never won a race in Rio de Janeiro or Sao Paulo, thus allowing maiden winners at Cristal and Taruma to run in such races.

TRACK RECORDS

DISTANCE	RECORD TIME	HORSE	DATE
TURF			
4f	45.20	Hay Que Dar	Jan. 17, 1987
5f	54.32	Requebra	Oct. 7, 2007
6f	1:08.00	Guascaco	March 25, 1984

DISTANCE	RECORD TIME	HORSE	DATE
6½f	1:14.22	Jaguarao	Aug. 25, 2007
7f	1:20.80	Rubio del Rio	Oct. 13, 2007
7½f	1:26.80	Round Hill	Feb. 24, 2001
1m	1:32.29	Jet	Aug. 19, 2007
1¼m	1:58.40	Falcon Jet	Feb. 15, 1992
1½m	2:23.52	Ivoire	April 15, 2007
2m	3:17.20	John Tess	Oct. 28, 2001
DIRT			
4½f	52.80	Flex Fortune	Dec. 17, 1988
5½f	1:03.10	Dollar Fighter	April 9, 1996
6f	1:09.00	Mensageiro Alado	Dec. 16, 1995
6½f	1:15.08	Sarissa	Nov. 6, 2007
7f	1:22.50	Groove	Dec. 16, 1995
7½f	1:29.40	Majd	Dec. 23, 1995
		Never Alone	Nov. 17, 1996
1m	1:34.70	Dancer Man	Oct. 20, 1996
1³⁄₁₆m	1:56.20	Autobelle	Dec. 20, 1996
1¼m	2:01.30	Natrix	Dec. 22, 1996
1½m	2:27.20	Quid Obscurum	Dec. 16, 1995
2m	3:30.30	Prime Asset	Nov. 29, 1998

MAJOR RACES (Chronological Order)

RACE	CONDITIONS
Grande Premio Roger Guedon-G3	1m (T) 3yo f
Grande Premio Jose Buarque de Macedo-G3	1m (T) 3yo c
Grande Premio Prefeitura da Cidade do Rio de Janeiro-G3	1¼m (D) 3yo+
Grande Premio Henrique Possolo-G1**	1m (T) 3yo f
Grande Premio Estado do Rio de Janeiro-G1*	1m (T) 3yo c
Grande Premio Presidente Arthur da Costa e Silva-G3	1¼m (T) 3yo+
Grande Premio Diana (Brazilian Oaks)-G1**	1¼m (T) 3yo f
Grande Premio Euvaldo Lodi-G3	1m (T) 3yo+ f&m
Grande Premio Francisco Eduardo* de Paula Machado-G1	1¼m (T) 3yo c&f
Grande Premio Presidente Emilio Garrastazu Medici-G2	1m (T) 3yo+

RACE	CONDITIONS
Grande Premio Zelia Gonzaga**	
Peixoto de Castro-G1	1½m (T) 3yo f
Grande Premio Antonio Joaquin	
Peixoto de Castro Junior-G2	1¼m (T) 3yo+
Grande Premio Cruzeiro do Sul-G1*	1½m (T) 3yo
Grande Premio Associacao de Criadores	
e Proprietarios de Cavalos de Corrida	
do Rio de Janeiro-G3	5f (T) 3yo+
Grande Premio Marciano de	
Aguiar Moreira-G2	1¼m (T) 3yo+ f&m
Grande Premio Joao Borges Filho-G2	1½m (T) 3yo+
Grande Premio Nestor Jost-G3	7½f (T) 3yo c
Grande Premio Antonio Carlos Amorim-G3	1m (T) 3yo+ f&m
Grande Premio Francisco Vilella	
de Paula Machado-G2	7½f (T) 2yo f
Grande Premio Conde de Herzberg-G2	7½f (T) 2yo c
Grande Premio Professor Nova Monteiro-G3	1¼m (D) 3yo
Grande Premio Henrique de Toledo Lara-G3	1¼m (T) 3yo+ f&m
Grande Premio Presidente Vargas-G2	1³⁄₁₆m (D) 4yo+
Grande Premio Associacao Brasileiro	
de Criadores e Proprietarios	
do Cavalo de Corrida-G1	1m (T) 2yo
Grande Premio OSAF-G2	1½m (T) 4yo+
Grande Premio Adayr Eiras de Araujo-G2	1¼m (T) 4yo+ f&m
Grande Premio 11 de Julho-G2	5f (T) 3yo+
Grande Premio Joao Adhemar e Nelson	
de Almeida Prado-G3	1m (T) 3yo f
Grande Premio Gervasio Seabra-G2	1m (T) 3yo+
Grande Premio Roberto e Nelson	
Grimaldi Seabra-G1 1¼m (T) 4yo+ f&m	
Grande Premio Major Suckow-G1	5f (T) 3yo+
Grande Premio Brasil-G1	1½m (T) 4yo+
Grande Premio Presidente da Republica-G1	1m (T) 3yo+
Grande Premio Costa Ferraz-G3	1m (T) 3yo c
Grande Duque de Caxias-G3	1¼m (T) 4yo+ f&m
Grande Premio Jose Carlos	
e Joao Jose de Figueiredo-G3	1m (T) 3yo+
Grande Premio Carlos Telles e	
Carlos Gilberto da Rocha Faria-G2	1¼m (T) 3yo f

RACE	CONDITIONS
Grande Premio Doutor Frontin-G2	1½m (T) 4yo+
Grande Premio Adhemar de Faria e	
Roberto Gabizo de Faria-G3	5f (T) 3yo+
Grande Premio Salgado Filho-G2	1m (D) 3yo+
Grande Premio Oswaldo Aranha-G2	1½m (T) 3yo+ f&m
Grande Mariano Procopio-G3	1m (T) 3yo f
Grande Premio Federico Lundgren-G3	1m (T) 3yo
Grande Premio Almirante Marques	
de Tamandare-G3	1½m (T) 3yo+

* Colts' Triple Crown
** Fillies' Triple Crown

DAYS OF RACING: Gavea conducts four days of racing per week, Friday through Monday, 52 weeks of the year. Fridays and Mondays are evening meetings, Saturdays and Sundays are afternoon meetings.

HOW TO GET THERE: Take the Linha 1 subway to the Flamengo station, then follow the crowds through the park to the racecourse.

SURROUNDING AREA: "The Girl from Ipanema" is one of pop music's most seductive songs for good reason. The Hipodromo da Gavea is just a stone's throw from Ipanema's sultry, golden beach. If you can tear your eyes away from the nearly naked bathers at Ipanema, you will be rewarded with a magnificent view of the statue of Christ Redemptor that stands atop Sugarloaf Mountain beyond Gavea's far turn, visible from almost every part of the racetrack.

CIDADE JARDIM ≡

Hipodromo da Cidade Jardim
Avenida Lineu de Paula Machado, 1263
Sao Paulo, Brazil
Phone: 011-55-11-2161-8325
Internet: www.jockeysp.com.br

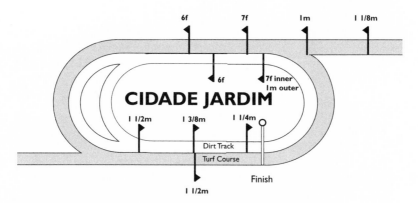

LOCATION: Sao Paulo is 220 miles southwest of Rio de Janeiro. Cidade Jardim is located in the western part of the city on the west bank of the Pinheiras River.

COURSE DESCRIPTION: Cidade Jardim has both an outer turf course and an inner dirt track. Both are perfectly level, left-handed ovals. The turf course is 1⅜ miles with a quarter-mile stretch. The dirt track measures 1¼ miles with a quarter-mile stretch. Inside the dirt course there is a dirt training track.

HISTORY: Cidade Jardim ("Garden City") opened its gates on January 25, 1941, although racing has been held in Sao Paulo, Brazil's "second city," under the auspices of the Jockey Club Sao Paulo since 1876.

ANALYSIS: As Sao Paulo is Brazil's second city, so too is Cidade Jardim Brazil's second racetrack behind Gavea. The difference between the two, however, is minimal, especially where the best stakes races are concerned. Horses that do well in good company at one track are well capable of duplicating their form at the other. At the maiden and allowance levels, however, there is a bit more quality at Gavea.

TRACK RECORDS

DISTANCE	RECORD TIME	HORSE	DATE
TURF			
5f	53.75	New Hampshire	June 24, 2006
6f	1:08.20	Napo	May 4, 1968
6½f	1:14.28	Zeitz	Oct. 6, 2007
7f	1:20.58	Annex Ridge	Dec. 5, 1999
7½f	1:26.45	Neleo	May 18, 2003
1m	1:32.26	Eyjur	May 15, 2005
1⅛m	1:45.15	Unipolar	May 3, 1997
1¼m	1:56.29	Top Hat	June 24, 2006
1½m	2:24.49	Dono da Raia	May 21, 2006
1¾m	2:54.19	Audacious	Dec. 22, 2007
DIRT			
5f	59.20	Egmont	March 3, 1977
		Riadhis	Jan. 25, 1978
5½f	1:02.43	Old Gipsy	Feb. 27, 2005
6f	1:07.69	Old Gipsy	Jan. 16, 2005
6½f	1:14.33	Blade Prospector	July 25, 1999
7f	1:20.65	Going Away	April 2, 2005
7½f	1:27.08	Park Ville	June 8, 2001
1m	1:33.37	Light It Up	June 23, 2001
1³⁄₁₆m	1:53.95	Naked Option	June 1, 2001
1¼m	1:58.66	Al Arz	Feb. 14, 2004
1⅜m	2:13.92	Gary Stevens	March 11, 2006
1½m	2:26.87	Horowicks	Sept. 7, 2000
1¾m	2:57.90	Black Jack	Jan. 31, 1992

MAJOR RACES (Chronological Order)

RACE	CONDITIONS
Grande Premio Presidente do Jockey Club-G3	1m (D) 3yo+
Grande Premio 25 de Janeiro-G2	1¼m (D) 3yo+ f&m
Grande Premio Presidente Joao Carlos Leite Penteado-G3	6f (D) 2yo c
Grande Premio Presidente Hernani Azevedo Silva-G2	1m (T) 3yo+ f&m
Grande Premio Linneo de Paula Machado-G3	1¼m (T) 3yo+

Grande Premio Presidente Augusto	
de Souza Queiroz-G3	6f (D) 2yo
Grande Presidente Guilherme Ellis-G2	7f (T) 2yo f
Grande Premio Pitatininga-G2	1⅜m (D) 3yo+
Grande Premio Presidente Jose	
de Souza Queiroz-G2	7f (T) 2yo c
Grande Premio Jacutinga-G3	7f (D) 2yo f
Grande Premio Presidente Fabio	
da Silva Prado-G3	1¼m (T) 3yo+ f&m
Grande Premio Oswaldo Aranha-G3	1½m (T) 3yo+
Grande Premio Presidente Antonio	
T. Assumpcao Netto-G3	1m (T) 3yo+
Grande Premio Joao Cecilio Ferraz-G1	7½f (T) 2yo f
Grande Premio Antenor de Lara Campos-G2	7½f (D) 2yo c
Grande Premio Presidente Julio Mesquita-G3	5f (T) 3yo+
Grande Premio Sao Paulo-G1	1½m (T) 3yo+
Grande Premio Presidente da Republica-G1	1m (T) 3yo+
Grande Premio Associacao Brasileira	
de Criadores e Proprietarios ao Pura Sangue	
do Cavalo de Corrida-G1	5f (T) 3yo+
Grande Premio Organizacao Sulamericana	
De Fomento ao Pura Sangue de Corrida-G1	1¼m (T) 3yo+ f&m
Grande Premio Juliano Martins-G1	1m (T) 2yo c
Grande Presidente Roberto Alves de Almeida-G2	1m (D) 2yo+ f&m
Grande Premio Jose Paulino Nogueiro-G3	1½m (T) 3yo+ f&m
Grande Premio Gal Couto de Magalhaes-G2	2m, 20y (T) 3yo+
Grande Premio ABCPCC	1¼m (T) 3yo+
Grande Premio J. Adhemar de Almeida Prado-G1	1m (T) 2yo c
Grande Premio Margarida Polak Lara-G1	1m (T) 2yo f
Grande Premio Velocidade-G3	5f (T) 2yo
Grande Premio Duplex-G2	1m (D) 2yo c
Grande Premio Luiz Fernando Cirne Lima-G3	1⅛m (T) 4yo+ f&m
Grande Premio Ministro da Agricultura-G3	1½m (T) 4yo+
Grande Premio ABCPCC-G3	1m (T) 3yo+
Grande Premio Immensity-G2	1m (D) 3yo+ f&m
Grande Premio Siphon-G2	1m (D) 3yo+
Grande Premio Barao de Piracicaba-G1**	1m (T) 3yo f
Grande Premio Paula Jose da Costa-G3	1³⁄₁₆m (D) 3yo f
Grande Premio Ipiranga-G1*	1m (T) 3yo c

Grande Premio Independencia-G3	5f (T) 3yo+ f&m
Grande Premio Henrique de Toledo Lara-G1**	1⅛m (T) 3yo f
Grande Premio Ricardo Lara Vidigal-G3	1¼m (D) 3yo c
Grande Premio Jockey Club de Sao Paulo-G1*	1¼m (T) 3yo c
Grande Premio Diana-G1**	1¼m (T) 3yo f
Grande Premio Presidente Antonio	
Correa Barbosa-G2	1⅜m (D) 3yo+
Copa dos Criadores-G3	1¼m (T) 3yo+ f&m
Derby Paulista-G1*	1½m (T) 3yo
Grande Premio Governador do Estado-G2	1m (T) 3yo+
Grande Premio Criadores e Proprietarios	
de Cavalos de Corrida de Sao Paulo-G3	1½m (T) 4yo+
Grande Premio Proclamacao da Republica-G2	5f (T) 3yo+
Grande Presidente Jose Bonifacio	
Coutinho Nogueira-G2	1½m (T) 3yo+ f&m
Grande Premio Consagracao-G2*	1¾m (T) 3yo+
Grande Premio Natal-G3	1⅛m (T) 3yo+

---

* Sao Paulo Quadruple Crown
** Sao Paulo Triple Crown for fillies

DAYS OF RACING: Cidade Jardim generally runs four days of racing per week, Friday through Monday. Virtually all stakes races are run at afternoon meetings on Saturdays and Sundays. Fridays and Mondays are evening meetings. The track will host the Gran Premio Internacional Asociacion Latinoamericana de Jockey Clubes e Hipodromos for the third time on March 14, 2009.

HOW TO GET THERE: As there is no subway system in Sao Paulo, the best way to get to Cidade Jardim is by bus. Use the route that leads to Avenida Joquei Clube.

11

Chile

CLUB HIPICO ▤

Club Hipico de Santiago
Avenida Blanco Encalada 2540
Santiago, Chile
Phone: 011-56-2-693-9600
Internet: www.clubhipico.cl

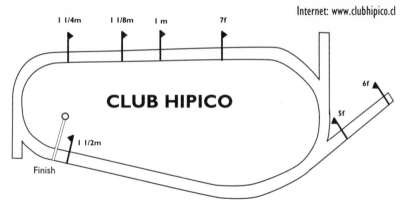

LOCATION: Santiago, Chile is 5,125 miles south of New York, 5,587 miles southeast of Los Angeles, 4,340 miles south of Miami, and 690 miles west of Buenos Aires.

COURSE DESCRIPTION: Designed to resemble Longchamp, Club Hipico is a level, right-handed turf course, 1½ miles around. The clubhouse turn is tighter than the far turn, the stretch is four furlongs long. A six-furlong straight joins the homestretch. There is a chute for seven-furlong races that makes a near 90-degree turn into the stretch.

HISTORY: The track opened in 1870 and is home to South America's oldest race, the Clasico El Ensayo. The Chilean turf equivalent of the Belmont Stakes, it is traditionally run the first Sunday in November.

Like the track itself, the Baroque-style grandstand was built to resemble the former Longchamp stand, but the racing here never approaches the fare at the famous Parisian racecourse. The current edifice dates from 1923.

Theodore Roosevelt visited during his post-presidential barnstorming days, as did the Prince of Wales, the future Edward VII, and his great granddaughter, Elizabeth II.

The exploits of the stallions Roy and Hussonet lent a touch of class to Chilean racing in the 1990s and during the early part of the new century, one that has not really been maintained of late.

ANALYSIS: All of the racing at Club Hipico is on turf. In interpreting Chilean form, a general rule of thumb might be to remember that Chile rates a close third in the South American Thoroughbred hierarchy behind Argentina and Brazil.

The Chilean turf Triple Crown for colts consists of the 1¹⁄₁₆-mile Polla de Potrillos (the equivalent of the 2000 Guineas) with a 2008 value of $53,650; the Premio Nacional Ricardo Lyon at $53,650; and the El Ensayo (turf Derby) worth $177,000. All three races were won in 1990 by one of Chile's best horses in recent years, Wolf. He would go on to win turf allowances at Santa Anita and Woodbine before finishing fourth behind Wiorno, Snurge, and Ghazi in the 1992 Canadian International. Wolf still holds the track record for 1½ miles at the Club Hipico, set in his 1990 El Ensayo victory.

Crystal House, winner of the Nacional (in which he set the track mark for 1¼ miles) and the El Ensayo in 1999, was later sent to Ron McAnally, for whom he was 0 for 6, largely in allowance company. The 2001 El Ensayo winner, Crisantemo, moved to California three years later and was 0 for 8 in allowance company there. Eres Magica, the 2006 El Ensayo winner, did little better under the care of Michael Matz, winning a 1⅜-mile ungraded stakes at Monmouth in nine North American tries.

The versatile Host, a son of Chile's leading sire, Hussonet, is much more of an American success story. In 2003 he won the Group 2 Gran Premio Criadores on the Club Hipico turf before winning in his first try on dirt at the crosstown Hipodromo Chile in the Dos Mil Guineas, the Chilean dirt equivalent of the 2000 Guineas. With Todd Pletcher he has won turf stakes at Keeneland, Calder, Aqueduct, Gulfstream, and Monmouth.

Generally speaking, a Group 2 or 3 winner at Club Hipico is probably going to be no more than a competitive allowance type in America, with the occasional Host popping up to become a stakes winner.

One exception to that rule was Pompeyo. The winner of the 1997 El Ensayo, he won just once in seven starts on the flat for Neil Drysdale before becoming America's champion steeplechaser under Sanna Neilson in 2001. He is a testament to the ability of his American owner, George Strawbridge, to recognize stamina, something for which the Chilean breeding industry is deservedly famous.

TRACK RECORDS

DISTANCE	RECORD TIME	HORSE	DATE
5f	55.25	Master Price	2001
5½f	1:01.91	Grace and Glory	2002
6f	1:06.88	Petit Galeon	2005
6½f	1:12.84	Spirit du Roi	2005
7f	1:20.68	Beisha	1988
7½f	1:26.00	Teseo	1993
1m	1:32.02	Stacatto	2008
1¹⁄₁₆m	1:38.18	Pel	2003
1⅛m	1:44.43	El Pardo	1997
1¼m	1:55.32	Crystal House	1999
1⅜m	2:10.84	Prince Albert II	1998
1½m	2:23.21	Wolf	1990

MAJOR RACES (Chronological Order)

RACE	CONDITIONS
Premio Verano-G2	1¼m 3yo+
Cotejo de Potrillos-G3	6½f 2yo c
Cotejo de Potrancas-G3	6½f 2yo f
Premio Club Hipico de Santiago-G1	1¼m 3yo+
Premio Alvaro Covarrubias-G3	1m 2yo c
Premio Carlos Campino-G2	1⅛m 3yo+ f&m
Premio Julio Subercaseaux-G3	1m 2yo f
Premio Alberto Vial-G1	1m 2yo c

RACE	CONDITIONS
Premio Francisco Baeza-G2	1¼m 3yo+
Premio Arturo Lyon-G1	1m 2yo f
Premio Raimundo Valdes-G3	1m 3yo c
Premio Invierno-G3	1¼m 3yo+
Premio Carlos Valdes-G3	1m 3yo+ f&m
Premio Criadores-G2	1m 3yo c
Premio Criadores-G2	1m 3yo f
Polla de Potrillos-G1*	1¹⁄₁₆m 3yo c
Copa de Oro-G2	1¼m 3yo+
Polla de Potrancas-G**	1¹⁄₁₆m 3yo f
Premio Nacional Ricardo Lyon-G1*	1¼m 3yo c&f
Premio El Ensayo-G1*	1½m 3yo c&f
Paddock Stakes-G3	1⅛m 3yo+
La Copa-G3	1½m 3yo+
Premio Velocidad-G2	5f 3yo+
Las Oaks-G1**	1¼m 3yo f
Gran Clasico Coronacion-G2	1¼m 3yo+

* Triple Crown
** Fillies' Triple Crown

DAYS OF RACING: Club Hipico conducts between six and eight days of racing per month, including every Friday, for a total of about 92 days per year. Race cards are day-long affairs with 18 races per day the norm. The classics and most other Group 1 contests are run on Sundays.

HOW TO GET THERE: Take the metro (subway) to station Union Latinoamerica or station Republica. The track is located immediately west of Parque O'Higgins.

HIPODROMO CHILE ≡

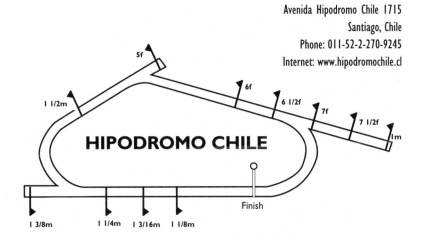

Avenida Hipodromo Chile 1715
Santiago, Chile
Phone: 011-52-2-270-9245
Internet: www.hipodromochile.cl

LOCATION: In Independencia, across town from Santiago's turf course, the Club Hipico.

COURSE DESCRIPTION: The Hipodromo Chile is a level, left-handed track. Shaped like a triangle similar to Nad Al Sheba, it measures 1¼ miles around with a quarter-mile stretch. Races of one mile and 1⅛ miles start from a chute on the backstretch.

HISTORY: Opened in 1906 as Chile's major dirt track, the Hipodromo Chile is the home of all of Chile's dirt classics. Like Argentina and Brazil, this South American country has two sets of classics, one on turf and one on dirt.

ANALYSIS: Whereas horses in Argentina are likely to be tried on both turf and dirt with a certain regularity, the same is not quite true of Chilean Thoroughbreds. While there is some crossover between the two surfaces, most horses concentrate on one or the other. If they fail in an attempt on the new surface, they are not likely to be tried on it again.

Dirt racing at the Hipodromo Chile is in much the same league as turf racing at the Club Hipico. Horses that take longer than two or three races to break their maidens, or those that flounder in the allowance ranks, are probably not going to win anything in America better than a very modest claiming race. Stakes winners at the Hipodromo will most likely find their American level in decent claimers or modest allowances at lesser tracks.

TRACK RECORDS

DISTANCE	RECORD TIME	HORSE	DATE
5f	55.63	Somariba	June 11, 2005
6f	1:08.80	Troyano	June 3, 1978
		El Ruco	May 23, 2002
6½f	1:15.00	Se Me Acabo	Nov. 3, 2001
7f	1:21.40	Marquisette	July 7, 2000
7½f	1:27.20	Gert	July 23, 1994
1m	1:33.20	Molto Vivace	July 18, 1998
1⅛m	1:49.80	Buen Paso	Dec. 7, 2000
1³⁄₁₆m	1:55.20	Puerto Madero	Oct. 4, 1997
1¼m	1:59.60	Prepo	Feb. 15, 1997
1⅜m	2:12.40	Gran Ducato	April 27, 1996
1½m	2:28.40	Franbulo	June 6, 2001

MAJOR RACES (Chronological Order)

RACE	CONDITIONS
Seleccion de Potrancas-G3	6f 2yo f
Seleccion de Potrillos-G3	6f 2yo c
Gran Handicap de Chile-G3	1m 3yo+
Premio Juan Cavieres-G3	6½f 2yo c
Gran Premio Hipodromo Chile-G1	1⅜m 3yo+
Premio Jose Saavedra-G3	7½f 2yo f
Premio Victor Matetic-G3	7½f 2yo c
Gran Premio de Honor-G2	1½m 3yo+
Tanteo de Potrancas-G1	7½f 2yo f
Tanteo de Potrillos-G1	7½f 2yo c
Premio Pedro del Rio-G2	1⅜m 3yo+
Premio Fernando Moller-G2	1m 3yo+
Gran Premio Criadores-G2	1m 3yo c
Premio Criadores Salvador Hess-G2	7½f 3yo f
Premio Carlos Allende-G3	7½f 3yo+ f&m
Premio Libertador Bernardo O'Higgins-G3	1¼m 3yo+
Premio Domingo Herrera-G2	7½f 3yo c
Mil Guineas-G1	1m 3yo f
Dos Mil Guineas-G1	1m 3yo c&f

RACE	CONDITIONS
Gran Criterium-G I	1¾₆m 3yo c&f
Premio Independencia-G2	1⅛m 3yo f
Premio Alberto Solari Magnasco-G I	1¼m 3yo f
Premio Haras de Chile-G2	1¼m 3yo+ f&m
Chilean St. Leger-G I	1⅜m 3yo c&f
Seleccion de Velocistas-G2	5f 3yo+
Premio General Jose Miguel	
Carrera Verdugo-G3	1⅛m 3yo+

DAYS OF RACING: Hipodromo Chile races 87 days per year, two or three Thursdays per month and every Saturday. As at Club Hipico, there are usually 18 races per day at the Hipodromo, with meetings lasting well into the evening hours.

HOW TO GET THERE: Take a micro (mini-bus) from Avenida Independencia to the racecourse, which is located on the outskirts of Santiago in the Independencia district.

Other Racecourses in Chile

VALPARAISO ▤

Valparaiso, which runs under the jurisdiction of the Valparaiso Sporting Club, is Chile's beach-resort track. Located in the city of the same name, it is a left-handed turf course and is the home of El Derby, a 1½-mile race for 3-year-olds that is more or less the Chilean turf equivalent of the Travers Stakes, as the real Chilean Derby is run at the Club Hipico.

Many of the better turf horses at the Club Hipico travel to Valparaiso for stakes races, the best of which are run during the summer months of January and February when Chileans flock to the Pacific coast and bay beaches in and around Valparaiso ("Paradise Valley") in much the same way that the French migrate en masse every August to Deauville and environs.

12

Australia

FLEMINGTON ☰

Flemington Racecourse
Victoria Racing Club
One Queens Road
Melbourne, Victoria 3004
Australia
Phone: 011-61-9-277-0777
Internet: www.vrc.net.au

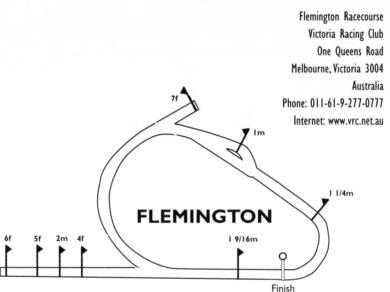

LOCATION: Situated in the southeast corner of Australia on Port Philip Bay, which itself is off the Bass Strait that separates Australia from Tasmania, Melbourne is 440 miles southwest of Sydney, 10,360 miles from New York, 7,918 miles from Los Angeles, 4,560 miles from Hong Kong, 5,068 miles from Tokyo, 7,450 miles from Dubai, 10,496 miles from London, and 1,630 miles from Auckland, New Zealand.

COURSE DESCRIPTION: Flemington is a level, pear-shaped, left-handed track 1½ miles around with a 2½-furlong stretch. The two-mile Melbourne Cup starts from a chute that extends from the homestretch. Cup runners travel a straight 4½ furlongs before making a sharp left-hand turn onto the three-furlong backstretch. There follows one of the world's widest sweeping turns, 5½ furlongs in length, which empties into the 2½-furlong stretch.

The full length of the straight course is six furlongs. There is also a chute on the wide far turn for seven-furlong races.

HISTORY: While they have been racing at Flemington since 1840, the Victoria Racing Club was founded in 1864. When gold was discovered in the area in 1851, the city, and its racing industry, went into boom mode.

The first Melbourne Cup, Flemington's world-famous race—the one that "stops a nation" in a way England's Epsom Derby and America's Kentucky Derby no longer do—was first run in 1861. Almost from the get-go, crowds of 100,000 became the norm. The 2006 Cup Day attendance of 129,089 set a record that may stand forever, since the Club invoked a 120,000 limit a year later.

Melbourne Cup Day is an official holiday in the state of Victoria and in the capital district of Canberra, but for the rest of Australia it is more like a semi-holiday, with people either calling in sick from work or taking an extended midafternoon lunch break to watch the big race, much as Americans did for weekday midafternoon World Series games before they were all switched to nighttime.

The first Melbourne Cup was won by Archer. It has been recorded that he walked 250 miles to get to Flemington for the big race, but that may be the stuff of legend. In any event, Archer proved his initial victory was no fluke by taking the Cup again the next year.

The tradition of running the Cup on the first Tuesday in November, the same day that Americans are engaged in the less serious business of electing their rulers, began in 1876. The first Tuesday in November has since been synonymous with our own first Saturday in May.

But the Melbourne Cup is not a classic race like the Kentucky Derby. Its place in the development of Thoroughbred racing is closer to that of those great old handicaps that we used to run in America, the ones in the early 20th century that were won by weight-carrying specialists like Whisk Broom II and Exterminator.

Perhaps the most famous of all Melbourne Cup winners is Phar Lap. The great gelding won it as a 4-year-old in 1930 after having won the AJC Derby, the Victoria Derby, and the Cox Plate. He was the target of

GLOBAL RACING

an assassination attempt that same year. A disgruntled bookmaker who must have grown weary of paying out huge sums on the short prices being offered tried to shoot him, but missed. Phar Lap won 32 of his last 35 starts, the very last of them coming when he took the Agua Caliente Handicap in Tijuana, Mexico. He was then sent to California while his owner, David Davis, negotiated for his next appearance.

Which never came. On April 5, 1932, Phar Lap died, the apparent victim of poisoning, some theorize at the hands of bookmakers who feared losing large sums to high-rolling favorites players.

In the modern era, the Melbourne Cup has gone from strength to strength. The great mare Makybe Diva became the first and only horse to win it three times, taking the race from 2003 through 2005. The Dermot Weld-trained Irish invaders Vintage Crop in 1993 and Media Puzzle in 2002, along with the Japanese one-two finishers Delta Blues and Pop Rock in 2006, established the Melbourne Cup as one of the most important races on the international calendar. In 2007 it ranked as the fourth-richest race in the world at $4,678,740, behind only the three big races at Nad Al Sheba: the Dubai World Cup, the Dubai Duty Free, and the Dubai Sheema Classic.

ANALYSIS: Due in part to geography, neither the Melbourne Cup nor any other race at Flemington (or any other Australian racecourse) has any bearing on racing in America. Only a dozen or so horses are imported to the United States from down under each year, and almost none of them have group-race form. A more important reason for the dearth of ex-Aussies in the States is Australian prize money, which, at the group-race level, is on a par with American graded stakes.

Those horses that are imported to America tend to be bleeders and so in need of Lasix. Their form in this country over the last 20 years has been spotty. Generally speaking, however, maidens, allowances, and stakes at Flemington and the other major Australian tracks at Randwick, Rosehill, Moonee Valley, Caulfield, and Doomben are more or less the equivalent of similar events at major American tracks.

One of the few truly grand Australian horses to arrive on these shores in the last 20 years was the New Zealand-bred mare Let's Elope. She won the Melbourne Cup in 1991, then returned to Flemington four months later to take the 1¼-mile Group 1 Australian Cup. Sent to America to be trained by Ron McAnally, she finished first by a nose in Arlington's Beverly D but was disqualified after a rodeo-like ride from Pat Valenzuela. No Australian horse of comparable ability has been seen in America since.

The Melbourne Cup is not the only important race run at Flemington. The track's prestigious Spring Racing Carnival, of which the Cup is the centerpiece, is a four-day festival of high-class racing. Ten Group 1 races are run during the Carnival, among them the Victoria Derby, the MacKinnon Stakes, and the VRC Oaks. The Carnival never fails to attract an average of 100,000 fans a day, making it the best-attended short meeting in the world.

TRACK RECORDS

DISTANCE	RECORD TIME	HORSE	DATE
5f	55.50	Special	Feb. 13, 1988
5½f	1:02.20	Don't Tell Tom	Dec. 18, 2004
6f	1:07.16	Iglesia	Jan. 1, 2001
7f	1:20.60	Lovey	Dec. 12, 1992
1m	1:33.49	Scenic Peak	Nov. 9, 2002
1¹⁄₁₆m	1:41.40	Knight's Word	March 9, 1998
1⅛m	1:47.05	Depeche Mode	Nov. 2, 1999
1¼m	1:58.73	Makybe Diva	March 12, 2005
1³⁄₁₆m	2:33.00	Kawtuban	Nov. 7, 1992
2m	3:16.30	Kingston Rule	Nov. 6, 1990

MAJOR RACES (Chronological Order)

RACE	CONDITIONS
Australian Guineas-G1	1m 3yo
Lightning Stakes-G1	5f 3yo+
Australian Cup-G1	1¼m 2yo+
SPRING RACING CARNIVAL	
Salinger Handicap-G1	6f 3yo+
Newmarket Handicap-G1	6f 3yo+
Turnbull Stakes-G1	1¼m 4yo+
Victoria Derby-G1	1³⁄₁₆m 3yo
Melbourne Cup-G1	2m 3yo+
Ascot Vale Stakes-G1	6f 3yo
LKS MacKinnon Stakes-G1	1¼m 3yo+
VRC Oaks-G1	1³⁄₁₆m 3yo f
Cantala Stakes-G1	1m 3yo+
Myer Classic-G1	1m 3yo+ f&m

DAYS OF RACING: Flemington runs 17 days a year with at least one meeting per month, save August. Australian Cup Day is the first or second Saturday in March, VRC St. Leger Day the last Wednesday in April, Melbourne Cup Preview Day the first Saturday in October. The four-day Spring Racing Carnival is centered around Melbourne Cup Day, the first Tuesday in November. The Victoria Derby is run on the Saturday preceding the Cup. VRC Oaks Day comes on the Thursday after Cup Day. The Carnival closes on the Saturday after Cup Day.

HOW TO GET THERE: From Flinders Street Station in Melbourne, take the train directly to the Flemington Racecourse station.

SURROUNDING AREA: With a population of 3.8 million, Melbourne is Australia's second most populous city after Sydney and is considered the country's sports capital. The Melbourne Cricket Ground is the home of both the national cricket team and the center for Australian-rules (some would say "no rules") football. In January the city hosts the Australian Open, the first stop of tennis's Grand Slam.

Melbourne is renowned for its numerous examples of Victorian architecture, not least the magnificent Flinders Street Station from which Melburnians depart the city for Flemington Racecourse.

Other Racecourses in Australia

CAULFIELD ≡

Like Flemington, Caulfield Racecourse is located in the state of Victoria. But whereas Flemington comes under the auspices of the Victoria Racing Club, Caulfield is run by the Melbourne Racing Club. Regional and local racing clubs were formed in Australia in the 19th century before any controlling authority could be formed nationally. The best remaining example of this in the United States occurs at Santa Anita, where the winter-spring meeting is run by the California Horse Racing Board, while the fall meeting is run by Oak Tree.

Caulfield is a left-handed, more or less triangular track with three very wide turns. Measuring 1¼ miles, 75 yards around, with a short 325-yard stretch (a little longer than Del Mar's), it has a chute at the turn farthest from the grandstand from which six-furlong races are run into a single 90-degree turn into the stretch.

Caulfield runs 23 days of racing per year with at least one day per month, but usually two or three, many of them on Saturdays. The track hosts 35 group races: 10 Group 1's, 10 Group 2's, and 15 Group 3's. Chief among them is the 1½-mile Caulfield Cup on the third Saturday in October, the centerpiece of Caulfield's Spring Carnival.

The C. F. Orr Stakes at seven furlongs in February and the Underwood Stakes at 1⅛ miles in September are two of the track's better races for 3-year-olds and up. The Caulfield Guineas at a mile for 3-year-old colts and the Thousand Guineas over the same distance for 3-year-old fillies are run in mid-October on days leading up to Caulfield Cup Day.

MOONEE VALLEY ≡

Located just outside Melbourne, Moonee Valley is a 1⅛-mile square-shaped, left-handed track with a very short one-furlong stretch.

While the Melbourne Cup is Australia's most famous and popular race, Moonee Valley is the home of the country's best race, the Cox Plate. First run in 1922 at a distance of 1¼ miles, 40 yards on the last Saturday in October (usually Breeders' Cup Day), the Cox Plate ranked as the world's 11th-richest race in 2007 at $2,798,070. Phar Lap won it in his Melbourne Cup year of 1930. More recently it has been taken by good ones such as Sunline, Northerly, and Makybe Diva. In 1954 it was won by the New Zealand-bred Rising Fast, who sandwiched it between victories in the Caulfield Cup and the Melbourne Cup. He remains the only horse to have pulled off a nearly impossible triple, as the three races are run within three weeks of one another.

Moonee Valley runs 31 times a year spread evenly throughout the calendar, nine of those at night under the lights. In addition to the Cox Plate, the track is home to two of Australia's most important sprints, the Australia Stakes and the Mankato Stakes, both Group 1 contests at six furlongs for 3-year-olds and up. Eleven Group 2's and six Group 3's complete the group-race schedule.

RANDWICK

Founded by the Australian Jockey Club (AJC), the nation's oldest racing body, Randwick is Australia's most important right-handed track and Sydney's leading racecourse. A squarish 1⅜-mile affair with a two-furlong, 12-yard stretch, it has chutes for races of six furlongs, seven furlongs, and a mile.

Among the 16 Group 1 races at Randwick are the country's two most important classics, the AJC (Australian) Derby and the AJC (Australian) Oaks, both run at 1½ miles. The Doncaster Handicap, one of Australia's top miles for 3-year-olds and up, and the All-Aged Stakes at seven furlongs are Randwick's other two Group 1 races. Ten Group 2's and 16 Group 3's also grace the Randwick calendar.

First run in 1861, 14 years before the first Kentucky Derby and 81 years after the first Epsom Derby, the AJC Derby takes place on either the last Saturday in March or the first Saturday in April. In 2007 it was worth $1,487,700, the same as the Doncaster Handicap. The Derby was won in 1929 by Phar Lap and in 1996 by Octagonal, who set a course record of 2:28.41 that still stands today.

ROSEHILL

Under the auspices of the Sydney Turf Club, Rosehill Racecourse, aka Rosehill Gardens, rates not far behind Randwick in prestige as Sydney's second track. A four-cornered, left-handed, squarish course of 1¼ miles, 50 yards, with a stretch of two furlongs, 12 yards, Randwick is the home of the world's most valuable race for juveniles, the six-furlong Golden Slipper Stakes, which in 2007 was the eighth-richest race in the world at $2,844,450. That purse also makes the Golden Slipper the world's richest sprint race for horses of any age, coming in well ahead of the $2 million Dubai Golden Shaheen.

The Golden Slipper is generally run on the Saturday one week before Easter, but in 2008 it was run on April 19, four weeks after Easter.

Rosehill conducts 41 days of racing per year, generally four to six days each during the warm months and two days per month during the winter. The Golden Slipper is one of five Group 1 contests at the track, along with 14 Group 2's and nine Group 3's.

13

New Zealand

ELLERSLIE ☰

Ellerslie Racecourse
Auckland Racing Club
80-100 Ascot Avenue
Greenlane East
Auckland, New Zealand
Phone: 011-64-9-524-4069
Internet: www.ellerslie.co.nz

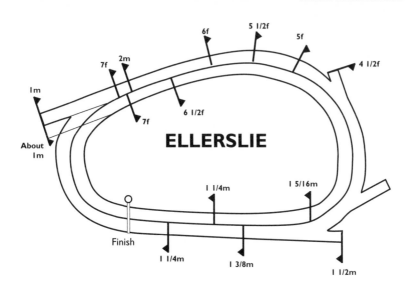

LOCATION: Ellerslie Racecourse is located in Auckland on New Zealand's North Island. Auckland is 1,630 miles from Melbourne, 1,338 miles from Sydney, 5,667 miles from Hong Kong, 5,474 miles from Tokyo, 8,826 miles from Dubai, 6,508 miles from Los Angeles, 8,815 miles from New York, and 11,387 miles from London.

COURSE DESCRIPTION: Ellerslie is a right-handed oval not dissimilar to Longchamp in that its first turn is much tighter than its wide, sweeping far turn. The outer old course is 1¾6 miles; the inner new course is 1⅛6 miles, 15 yards. The two courses share a two-furlong stretch.

HISTORY: Racing at Ellerslie falls under the auspices of the Auckland Racing Club, which was founded in 1874, although racing had begun in the New Zealand capital in 1842 at a racecourse that its British colonial founders had named Epsom Downs.

Ellerslie has long been the premier racetrack in New Zealand, where most of the best horses compete on the North Island. It is home to seven of the country's 23 Group 1 races, among them the New Zealand Derby, which had its inaugural running in 1875. The race at that time, and until 1973, was known as the Great Northern Derby, as the New Zealand Derby was run at Riccarton on the South Island. In 1973, the New Zealand Derby was switched to Ellerslie with its larger horse population. In its stead, Riccarton was granted both the New Zealand 1000 Guineas and the New Zealand 2000 Guineas.

It will be noted in the track-records section below that no new course mark has been set at Ellerslie since 1998. There are a number of reasons for this, most notably the fact that since the mid-nineties New Zealand-breds have become increasingly popular with Australian buyers. With their superior resources, the Aussies have been plundering some of the best New Zealand bloodstock in much the same way that Europeans and Arabs have been doing so for nearly 30 years at Keeneland and Saratoga.

Moreover, New Zealand races since 1998 have shifted away from front-to-back tactics that produce fast times, a la America, to back-to-front waiting tactics that produce slower times, a la Europe. Add increased watering of New Zealand tracks to provide easier racing surfaces and it is little wonder that it has been such a long time since a new track record has been set at Ellerslie.

ANALYSIS: As most of the two dozen or so New Zealand horses that are imported into the United States each year have never graduated beyond

GLOBAL RACING

the allowance or handicap ranks, it is difficult to compare graded-race form with that in America. At the same time, New Zealand allowance winners usually wind up running in American claimers, especially on the southern California circuit, which is where a majority of ex-New Zealanders are directed.

If, however, a horse has won decent allowances at Ellerslie, which rates as the country's major racecourse, or at tracks such as Riccarton, Te Rapa, Hastings, or Trentham, he may be well capable of competing in minor allowances anywhere in the States.

The major meeting at Ellerslie is the Auckland Cup Festival. A three-day fixture held during the first week of March, it includes the Derby, the Auckland Cup, and the Diamond Stakes. As a Southern Hemisphere country, New Zealand's month of March is the Northern Hemisphere equivalent of September, a rather late time of year for a country to be running its Derby.

Another feature race at the Auckland Cup Festival is the Karaka Million. Like the highly successful Goffs Million at the Curragh, the Karaka Million is a six-furlong juvenile event restricted to horses sold the previous year at New Zealand's Karaka Million Sale. At $795,500, it is the country's second-richest race, behind Hastings's Kelt Capital Stakes at $1,519,400 and ahead of the Auckland Cup and the New Zealand Derby, both of which were worth $556,850 in 2008.

New Zealand has long been more open-minded about the acceptance of women riders than most countries, a policy that led to Lisa Cropp becoming the first female to win a national riding title there during the 2006–07 season.

New Zealand-breds are a tough bunch, consistently hitting above their weight despite the relatively meager resources available to horsemen on the faraway island. With the exception of a handful of stakes races, purses in New Zealand are small, and pale before those in Australia. It is all the more remarkable, then, that New Zealand-breds have been so successful. Horses like the British-bred Sir Tristram and his best son, Zabeel, have made a deep impact not only in New Zealand racing circles but in Australia as well. Twenty-nine of the last 50 winners of the Melbourne Cup were bred in New Zealand. Seven of the 10 horses in history that have pulled off the Caulfield Cup-Melbourne Cup double—Rising Fast, Even Stevens, Galilee, Gurner's Lane, Let's Elope, Doriemus, and Might and Power—were bred in New Zealand.

These accomplishments have a great deal to do with the fact that New Zealand horsemen still breed for stamina. Ever the racing underdog down in the antipodes, the little kiwi enjoys taking a poke at the big kangaroo at every opportunity.

TRACK RECORDS

DISTANCE	RECORD TIME	HORSE	DATE
4f, 80y	48.00	Catamarca	1988
5½f	1:03.18	Nugget Bah	1984
6f	1:07.73	Diamond Lover	1987
6½f	1:14.45	High Regards	1985
7f	1:20.62	My Quota	1996
7½f	1:27.44	Dear John	1992
1m	1:32.08	Comdale	1993
1¼m	1:58.89	Tidal Light	1987
1⁵⁄₁₆m	2:07.04	Kotare Chief	1987
1⅜m	2:13.22	Miltak	1993
1½m	2:24.80	So Casual	1998
2m	3:15.66	Sea Swift	1988

MAJOR RACES (Chronological Order)

RACE	CONDITIONS
Railway Handicap-G1	6f 3yo+
New Zealand Derby-G1	1½m 3yo
Auckland Cup-G1	2m 3yo+
Diamond Stakes-G1	6f 2yo
New Zealand Stakes-G1	1¼m 3yo+
Easter Handicap-G1	1m 3yo+
Zabeel Classic-G1	1¼m 3yo

DAYS OF RACING: Ellerslie conducts 27 days of racing annually.

HOW TO GET THERE: Lacking a subway system, it is best to travel to Ellerslie by car or taxi.

SURROUNDING AREA: More than a quarter of New Zealand's citizens live in Auckland, a city of 1.4 million. New Zealanders are a sports-mad people, as attested by the exploits of their national teams, known as the All Blacks because of their all-black uniforms.

The national rugby team has an international reputation for ferocity, as exemplified by the All Blacks' performance of the *haka*, a Maori challenge dance, before each of their international matches, as well as by their victory rate, the highest of any national rugby team in the world. The All Blacks divide their home international test matches among Wellington, Christchurch, and Auckland, where they play at Eden Park, which is also the home stadium of the local professional rugby team, the Auckland Blues.

Other Racecourses in New Zealand

HASTINGS

Located on the southeast coast of New Zealand's North Island, Hastings is a left-handed rectangular course measuring 1¹⁄₁₆ miles with a two-furlong stretch. Run by the Hawke's Bay Racing Club, the track made history in 2007 when it ran New Zealand's first million-dollar race, the 1¼-mile, 44-yard Kelt Capital Stakes, originally known as the Ormond Gold Cup when it was first run in 1955.

Worth $NZ 2 million ($US 1,519,400), the race received its huge cash influx from Sam Kelt, the owner of Kelt Capital Ltd., and its debut as a million-dollar race was won by Princess Coup.

Hastings also hosts two other Group 1 races during its 19 days of racing per year, the seven-furlong Mudgway Stakes and the one-mile Stoney Bridge Stakes, both for 3-year-olds and up.

RICCARTON PARK

The most important track on New Zealand's South Island, Riccarton is the site of both the country's mile classics, the New Zealand 1000 Guineas and the New Zealand 2000 Guineas. An irregularly shaped left-handed oval with mild turns, Riccarton is a 1½-mile track with a 2½-furlong stretch. The Guineas are run from a chute at the head of the backstretch, similar to one-mile races on Belmont Park's main track.

Riccarton is located near Christchurch, and its 25 days of racing per year are run by the Canterbury Jockey Club.

TE RAPA ≣

Located in Hamilton, in the center of New Zealand's breeding country—about 50 miles south of Ellerslie—Te Rapa's 20 days of racing, two of them jump meetings, are conducted by the Waikato Racing Club. A 1⅛-mile left-handed track with a stretch of two furlongs, 20 yards, Te Rapa has two Group 1 races on its schedule, the 1¼-mile International Stakes and the seven-furlong Waikato Sprint.

TRENTHAM ≣

Trentham Racecourse is tucked away on the southern tip of New Zealand's North Island near the city of Wellington, where the Wellington Racing Club is in charge. The track is a 1¼-mile left-handed oval with a 2¼-furlong stretch. There is a curved chute leading into the stretch used for the start of five- and six-furlong races. The big race at Trentham is the 1½-mile New Zealand Oaks. Run in mid-March, the 2007 edition went to subsequent Kelt Capital Stakes winner Princess Coup. A second Group 1 contest, the one-mile Captain Cook Stakes for 3-year-olds and up, is run on the last Saturday of October.

The New Zealand Oaks came into prominence from an American point of view in 2008 when its 2007 fifth-place finisher, Black Mamba, achieved stardom in California via victories in the Beverly Hills Handicap and the John C. Mabee Handicap. Those triumphs came after five second-place finishes in California Grade 2's on turf. While this clearly marks the New Zealand Oaks as a race for American buyers to take note of in the future, Black Mamba's ascendancy probably has just as much to do with the improvement she showed on American racetracks and the training methods we employ here.

100 RICHEST THOROUGHBRED
FLAT RACES IN THE WORLD–2007

Race Rank/Name	Track	Conditions	Purse
1 Dubai World Cup (G1)	Nad Al Sheba (UAE)	1¼m (D) 4yo+	$6,000,000
2 Dubai Duty Free (G1)	Nad Al Sheba (UAE)	1⅛m (T) 4yo+	5,000,000
2 Dubai Sheema Classic (G1)	Nad Al Sheba (UAE)	1½m (T) 4yo+	5,000,000
4 Melbourne Cup Hcp (G1)	Flemington (Aus)	2m (T) 3yo+	4,678,740
5 Breeders' Cup Classic (G1)	**Monmouth Park (USA)**	**1¼m (D) 3yo+**	**4,580,000**
6 Japan Cup (G1)	Tokyo (Jpn)	1½m (T) 3yo+	4,434,175
7 Arima Kinen (G1)	Nakayama (Jpn)	1⁹⁄₁₆m (T) 3yo+	3,072,323
8 Golden Slipper Stakes (G1)	Rosehill (Aus)	6f (T) 2yo	2,844,450
9 Prix de l'Arc de Triomphe (G1)	Longchamp (Fr)	1½m (T) 3yo+ c&f	2,827,000
10 Tokyo Yushun-Jpn (G1) (Japanese Derby)	Tokyo (Jpn)	1½m (T) 3yo c&f	2,821,926
11 Cox Plate (G1)	Moonee Valley (Aus)	1¼m,44y (T) 3yo+	2,798,070
12 Breeders' Cup Turf (G1)	**Monmouth Park (USA)**	**1½m (T) 3yo+**	**2,748,000**
13 Hong Kong Cup (G1)	Sha Tin (HK)	1¼m (T) 3yo+	2,566,000
14 Caulfield Cup Hcp (G1)	Caulfield (Aus)	1½m (T) 3yo+	2,544,000
15 Epsom Derby (G1)	Epsom (GB)	1½m (T) 3yo c&f	2,478,125
16 Breeders' Cup Mile (G1)	**Monmouth Park (USA)**	**1m (T) 3yo+**	**2,409,080**
17 Kikuka Sho-Jpn G1 (Japanese St Leger)	Kyoto (Jpn)	1⅞m (T) 3yo c&f	2,359,460
18 Japan Cup Dirt (G1)	Tokyo (Jpn)	1⁵⁄₁₆m (D) 3yo+	2,331,856
19 Autumn Tenno Sho (G1)	Tokyo (Jpn)	1¼m (T) 3yo+	2,229,800
20 Goffs Million	Curragh (Ire)	7f (T) 2yo c&g	2,221,760
20 Goffs Fillies Million	Curragh (Ire)	7f (T) 2yo f	2,221,760
22 Kentucky Derby (G1)	**Churchill Downs (USA)**	**1¼m (D) 3yo**	**2,210,000**
23 Spring Tenno Sho (G1)	Kyoto (Jpn)	2m (T) 4yo+	2,139,347
24 Takarazuka Kinen (G1)	Hanshin (Jpn)	1⅜mm (T)	2,081,999
25 Canadian International (G1)	**Woodbine (Can)**	**1½m (T) 3yo+**	**2,073,698**

Bold-faced type indicates races in North America

Race Rank/Name	Track	Conditions	Purse
26 Breeders' Cup Distaff (G1)	**Monmouth Park (USA)**	**1 1/8m (D) 3yo+ f&m**	**2,070,160**
27 Hong Kong Mile (G1)	Sha Tin (HK)	1m (T) 3yo+	2,052,800
28 Hong Kong Derby-HK (G1)	Sha Tin (HK)	1 1/2m (T) 4yo	2,048,000
29 Irish Derby (G1)	Curragh (Ire)	1 1/2m (T) 3yo c&f	2,030,250
30 Prix du Jockey Club (G1) (French Derby)	Chantilly (Fr)	1 5/16m (T) 3yo c&f	2,017,050
31 Dubai Golden Shaheen (G1)	Nad Al Sheba (UAE)	6f (D) 3yo+	2,000,000
31 UAE Derby (G2)	Nad Al Sheba (UAE)	1 1/8m (D) 3yo	2,000,000
33 Satsuki Sho-Jpn G1 (Japanese 2000 Guineas)	Nakayama (Jpn)	1 1/4m (T) 3yo c&f	1,979,982
34 Singapore Airlines Intl Cup (G1)	Kranji (Sin)	1 1/4m (T) 3yo+	1,965,600
35 Breeders' Cup F&M Turf (G1)	**Monmouth Park (USA)**	**1 3/8m (T) 3yo+f&m**	**1,951,080**
36 Yushun Himba-Jpn G1 (Japanese Oaks)	Tokyo (Jpn)	1 1/2m (T) 3yo f	1,883,442
37 Breeders' Cup Juvenile (G1)	**Monmouth Park (USA)**	**1 1/16m (D) 2yo**	**1,832,000**
37 Breeders' Cup Juvenile Fillies (G1)	**Monmouth Park (USA)**	**1 1/16m (D) 2yo f**	**1,832,000**
37 Breeders' Cup Sprint (G1)	**Monmouth Park (USA)**	**6f (D) 3yo+**	**1,832,000**
40 BMW Classic (G1)	Rosehill (Aus)	1 1/2m (T) 3yo+	1,828,575
41 Hong Kong Vase (G1)	Sha Tin (HK)	1 1/2m (T) 3yo+	1,796,200
42 Queen Elizabeth II Cup (G1)	Sha Tin (HK)	1 1/4m (T) 3yo+	1,789,200
43 Mile Championship (G1)	Kyoto (Jpn)	1m (T) 3yo+	1,778,521
44 Oka Sho-Jpn (G1) (Japanese 1000 Guineas)	Hanshin (Jpn)	1m (T) 3yo f	1,756,443
45 Queen Elizabeth II Commemorative Cup (G1)	Kyoto (Jpn)	1 3/8m (T) 3yo+ f&m	1,612,465
46 Yasuda Kinen (G1)	Tokyo (Jpn)	1m (T) 3yo+	1,611,579
47 Sprinters Stakes (G1)	Nakayama (Jpn)	6f (T) 3yo+	1,601,101
48 Takamatsunomiya Kinen (G1)	Chukyo (Jpn)	6f (T) 4yo+	1,579,211
49 Hong Kong Sprint (G1)	Sha Tin (HK)	6f (T) 3yo+	1,539,600
50 February Stakes (G1)	Tokyo (Jpn)	1m (D) 4yo+	1,533,324
51 Kelt Capital Stakes (G1)	Hastings (NZ)	1 1/4m,44y (T) 3yo+	1,519,400
52 King George VI & Queen Elizabeth Stakes (G1)	Ascot (GB)	1 1/2m (T) 3yo+	1,519,050
53 NHK Mile Cup-Jpn G1	Tokyo (Jpn)	1m (T) 3yo c&f	1,508,308
54 JBC Classic-Jpn G1	Ohi (Jpn)	1 1/4m (D) 3yo+	1,504,500
55 Shuka Sho-Jpn G1	Kyoto (Jpn)	1 1/4m (T) 3yo f	1,493,576
56 AJC Derby (G1)	Randwick (Aus)	1 1/2m 3yo	1,487,700
56 Doncaster Handicap (G1)	Randwick (Aus)	1m (T) 3yo+	1,487,700
58 Victoria Mile-Jpn G1	Tokyo (Jpn)	1m (T) 4yo+ f&m	1,481,049
59 Irish Champion Stakes (G1)	Leopardstown (Ire)	1 1/4m (T) 3yo+	1,376,800
60 Victoria Derby (G1)	Flemington (Aus)	1 9/16m (T) 3yo	1,360,245
61 Tokyo Daishoten-Jpn G1	Ohi (Jpn)	1 1/4m (D) 3yo+	1,204,416

Bold-faced type indicates races in North America

Race Rank/Name	Track	Conditions	Purse
62 JBC Sprint-Jpn GI	Ohi (Jpn)	6f (D) 3yo+	1,203,600
63 Hanshin Cup (G2)	Hanshin (Jpn)	7f (T) 3yo+	1,201,206
64 Pacific Classic (G1)	**Del Mar (USA)**	**1¼m (S) 3yo+**	**1,120,000**
65 Stayers Stakes (G1)	Nakayama (Jpn)	2¼m (T) 3yo+	1,117,576
66 E.P. Taylor Stakes (G1)	**Woodbine (Can)**	**1¼m (T) 3yo+ f&m**	**1,087,983**
67 Sankei Sho All-Comers (G2)	Nakayama (Jpn)	1⅜m (T) 3yo+	1,078,169
68 Mainichi Okan (G2)	Tokyo (Jpn)	1⅛m (T) 3yo+	1,077,475
69 St Leger Stakes (G1)	Doncaster (GB)	1¾m,166y(T)3yo c&f	1,074,410
70 Kyoto Daishoten (G2)	Kyoto (Jpn)	1½m (T) 3yo+	1,074,021
71 Prix de Diane (G1) (French Oaks)	Chantilly (Fr)	1 5/16m (T) 3yo f	1,069,520
72 Hanshin Daishoten (G2)	Hanshin (Jpn)	1⅞m (T) 4yo+	1,061,007
73 Haskell Invitational (G1)	**Monmouth Park (USA)**	**1⅛m (D) 3yo**	**1,060,000**
74 Hanshin Juvenile Fillies-Jpn (G1)	Hanshin (Jpn)	1m (T) 2yo f	1,049,641
75 Nakayama Kinen (G2)	Nakayama (Jpn)	1⅛m (T) 4yo+	1,049,328
76 Nikkei Sho (G2)	Nakayama (Jpn)	1 9/16m (T) 4yo+	1,047,434
77 Juddmonte International (G1)	York (GB)	1¼m,88y (T) 3yo+	1,043,085
78 Futurity Stakes-Jpn (G1)	Nakayama (Jpn)	1m 2yo (T) c&f	1,035,567
79 Osaka Hai (G2)	Hanshin (Jpn)	1¼m (T) 4yo+	1,035,451
80 Breeders' Cup F&M Sprint	**Monmouth Park (USA)**	**6f (D) 3yo+, f&m**	**1,030,500**
81 Kyoto Kinen (G2)	Kyoto (Jpn)	1⅜m (T) 4yo+	1,026,370
82 Hong Kong Classic Mile	HK G1 Sha Tin (HK)	1m (T) 4yo	1,025,600
82 Stewards Cup-HK G1	Sha Tin (HK)	1m (T) 3yo+	1,025,600
84 Hong Kong Champions & Chater Cup-HK (G1)	Sha Tin (HK)	1½m (T) 3yo+	1,024,800
85 Hong Kong Gold Cup-HK G1	Sha Tin (HK)	1¼m (T) 3yo+	1,024,000
86 Copa Republica Argentina (G2)	Tokyo (Jpn)	1 9/16m (T) 3yo+	1,022,475
87 Champions Mile-HK G1	Sha Tin (HK)	1m (T) 3yo+	1,022,400
88 Kinko Sho (G2)	Chukyo (Jpn)	1¼m (T) 3yo+	1,014,183
89 Centaur Stakes (G2)	Hanshin (Jpn)	6f (T) 3yo+	1,012,606
90 Swan Stakes (G2)	Kyoto (Jpn)	7f (T) 3yo+	1,008,561
91 Topkapi Trophy (G2)	Veliefendi (Tur)	1m (T) 3yo+	1,007,261
92 Delaware Handicap (G2)	Delaware Park (USA)	1¼m (D) 3yo+ f&m	1,000,900
93 Arlington Million (G1)	**Arlington Park (USA)**	**1¼m (T) 3yo+**	**1,000,000**
93 Arkansas Derby (G2)	**Oaklawn Park (USA)**	**1⅛m (D) 3yo**	**1,000,000**
93 Belmont Stakes (G1)	**Belmont Park (USA)**	**1½m (D) 3yo**	**1,000,000**
93 CashCall Mile Invtl (G2)	**Hollywood Park (USA)**	**1m (T) 3yo+ f&m**	**1,000,000**
93 Delta Jackpot (G3)	**Delta Downs (USA)**	**1 1/16m (D) 2yo**	**1,000,000**

Bold-faced type indicates races in North America

Race Rank/Name	Track	Conditions	Purse
93 Florida Derby (G1)	**Gulfstream Park (USA)**	**1⅛m (D) 3yo**	**1,000,000**
93 Godolphin Mile (G2)	Nad Al Sheba (UAE)	1m (D) 3yo+	1,000,000
93 Pennsylvania Derby (G2)	Philadelphia Park (USA)	1⅛m (D) 3yo	1,000,000
93 Preakness Stakes (G1)	Pimlico (USA)	1³⁄₁₆m (D) 3yo	1,000,000
93 Santa Anita Handicap (G1)	Santa Anita (USA)	1¼m (D) 4yo+	1,000,000
93 Sunshine Millions Classic	Gulfstream Park (USA)	1⅛m (D) 4yo+	1,000,000
93 Travers Stakes (G1)	Saratoga (USA)	1¼m (D) 3yo	1,000,000
93 Virginia Derby (G2)	Colonial Downs (USA)	1¼m (T) 3yo	1,000,000

Bold-faced type indicates races in North America

Appendix A

Appendix B

RESULTS OF MAJOR FOREIGN STAKES RACES (1988-2007)

Australia

MELBOURNE CUP
HANDICAP. 2 Miles. 3-year-olds and upward.
(Flemington, Melbourne, Victoria)
First Run in 1851

Year	First	Age	Jockey	Wt	Second	Age	Wt	Third	Age	Wt	Time	Win Value
1988	Empire Rose	6	T Allan	118	Natski	5	121	Na Botto	4	112	03:19.9	879,986
1989	Tawrrific	5	R S Dye	119	Super Impose	5	123	Kudz	6	116	03:17.1	925,160
1990	Kingston Rule	5	D Breadman	117	The Phantom	5	120	Mr. Brooker	5	117	03:16.3	1,024,400
1991	Let's Elope	4	S King	112	Shiva's Revenge	4	118	Magnolia Hall	5	116	03:18.9	1,043,970
1992	Subzero	4	G Hall	120	Veandercross	3	120	Casteltown	7	126	3:243/5	904,670
1993	Vintage Crop	7	M J Kinane	122	Te Akau Nick	5	123	Mercator	7	119	3:252/5	870,408
1994	Jeune	6	W Harris	125	Paris Lane	4	122	Oompala	6	116	03:19.8	962,780
1995	Doriemus	5	D M Oliver	120	Nothin' Leica Dane	3	105	Vintage Crop	9	130	03:27.6	1,015,001
1996	Saintly	4	D Beadman	122	Count Chivas	5	126	Skybeau	4	110	03:18.8	1,152,955
1997	Might and Power	4	J Cassidy	123	Doriemus	7	127	Markham	4	116	03:18.3	1,030,774
1998	Jezabeel	6	C J Munce	112	Champagne	4	112	Persian Punch	6	125	03:18.6	1,070,503
1999	Rogan Josh	7	J Marshall	110	Central Park	5	127	Zazabelle	4	108	03:19.6	1,175,318
2000	Brew	6	K McEvoy	108	Yippyio	5	115	Second Coming	6	116	03:18.7	1,077,940
2001	Ethereal	3	S Seamer	114	Give The Slip	4	121	Persian Punch	8	126	03:21.1	944,656
2002	Media Puzzle	6	D M Oliver	116	Mr Prudent	8	115	Beekeeper	4	117	03:17.0	1,139,439
2003	Makybe Diva	4	G Boss	112	She's Archie	4	110	Jardines Lookout	6	122	03:19.9	1,655,844
2004	Makybe Diva	5	G Boss	123	Vinnie Roe	6	128	Zazzman	6	116	03:28.5	2,092,720
2005	Makybe Diva	6	G Boss	128	On A Jeune	5	112	Xcellent	4	119	03:19.2	2,380,018
2006	Delta Blues	5	Y Iwata	123	Pop Rock	5	117	Maybe Better	4	110	03:21.4	2,391,340
2007	Efficient	4	M Rodd	120	Purple Moon	4	119	Mahler	3	112	03:23.3	2,853,550

Britain

ASCOT GOLD CUP-G1
2½ miles, 4-year-olds & up, Royal Ascot
First run in 1807

Year	1st (Age)	Jockey	Trainer	Owner	2nd	3rd	Time
1988*	Sadeem (5)	G. Starkey	G. Harwood	Sheikh Mohammed	Sergeyevich	Chauve Souris	04:15.6
1989	Sadeem (6)	W. Carson	G. Harwood	Sheikh Mohammed	Mazzacano	Lauries Crusader	04:22.6
1990	Ashal (4)	R. Hills	H T Jones	H Al Maktoum	Tyrone Bridge	Thethingaboutitis	04:28.4
1991	Indian Queen (6f)	W. R. Swinburn	Lord Huntingdon	G. Brunton	Arazanni	Warm Feeling	04:23.8
1992	Drum Taps (6)	L. Dettori	Lord Huntingdon	Y. Asakawa	Arcadian Heights	Turgeon	04:18.2
1993	Drum Taps (7)	L. Dettori	Lord Huntingdon	Y. Asakawa	Assessor	Turgeon	04:32.6
1994	Arcadian Heights (6)	M. Hills	G. Wragg	J. Pearce	Vintage Crop	Sonus	04:27.7
1995	Double Trigger (4)	J. Weaver	M. Johnston	R. Huggins	Moonax	Admiral's Well	04:20.3
1996	Classic Cliche (4)	M. J. Kinane	S. bin Suroor	Godolphin	Double Trigger	Nononito	04:23.2
1997	Celeric (5)	Pat Eddery	D. Morley	C. Spence	Classic Cliche	Election Day	04:26.2
1998	Kayf Tara (4)	L. Dettori	S. bin Suroor	Godolphin	Double Trigger	Three Cheers	04:32.4
1999	Enzeli (4)	J. P Murtagh	J. Oxx	Aga Khan	Invermark	Kayf Tara	04:18.9
2000	Kayf Tara (6)	M J Kinane	S bin Suroor	Godolphin	Far Cry	Compton Ace	04:24.5
2001	Royal Rebel (5)	J P Murtagh	M Johnston	P D Savill	Persian Punch	Jardines Lookout	04:18.9
2002	Royal Rebel (6)	J P Murtagh	M Johnston	P D Savill	Vinnie Roe	Wareed	04:25.6
2003	Mr Dinos (4)	K Fallon	P Cole	C Shiacolas	Persian Punch	Pole Star	04:20.1
2004	Papineau (4)	L Dettori	S bin Suroor	Godolphin	Westerner	Darasim	04:20.9
2005*	Westerner (6)	O Peslier	E Lellouche	Ecurie Wildenstein	Distinction	Vinnie Roe	04:19.5
2006	Yeats (5)	K Fallon	A P O'Brien	Magnier & Nagle	Reefscape	Distinction	04:20.4
2007	Yeats (6)	M J Kinane	A P O'Brien	Magnier & Nagle	Geordieland	Le Miracle	04:20.8

* Run at York in 2005

CHAMPION STAKES-G1
1¼ miles, 3-year-olds & up, Newmarket (Rowley Mile Course)
First run in 1877

Year	1st (Age)	Jockey	Trainer	Owner	2nd	3rd	Time
1988	Indian Skimmer(4f)	M Roberts	H Cecil	Sheikh Mohammed	Persian Heights	Doyoun	02:10.4
1989	Legal Case (3)	W R Swinburn	L Cumani	G White	Dolpour	Ile de Chypre	02:02.8
1990	In The Groove (3f)	S Cauthen	D Elsworth	B Cooper	Linamix	Legal Case	02:05.6
1991	Tel Quel (3)	T Jarnet	A Fabre	Sheikh Mohammed	Cruachan	In The Groove	02:01.8
1992	Rodrigo de Triano(3)	L Piggott	P Chapple-Hyam	R Sangster	Lahib	Environment Friend	02:02.4
1993	Hatoof (4f)	W R Swinburn	C Head	M Al Maktoum	Ezzoud	Dernier Empereur	02:06.8
1994	Dernier Empereur(4)	S Guillot	A Fabre	G Tanaka	Grand Lodge	Muhtarram	02:05.6
1995	Spectrum (3)	J Reid	P Chapple-Hyam	Lord Weinstock	Riyadian	Montjoy	02:02.6
1996	Bosra Sham (3f)	Pat Eddery	H Cecil	W Said	Halling	Timarida	02:03.7
1997	Pilsudski (5)	M J Kinane	M Stoute	Lord Weinstock	Loup Sauvage	Bahhare	02:05.5
1998	Alborada (3f)	G Duffield	M Prescott	K Rausing	Insatiable	Daylami	02:03.7
1999*	Alborada (4f)	G Duffield	M Prescott	K Rausing	Shiva	Kabool	02:05.6
2000	Kalanisi (4)	J P Murtagh	J Oxx	HH Aga Khan	Montjeu	Distant Music	02:05.6
2001	Nayef (3)	R Hills	M Tregoning	H Al Maktoum	Tobougg	Indian Creek	02:07.7
2002	Storming Home (4)	M Hills	B Hills	M Al Maktoum	Moon Ballad	Noverre	02:01.4
2003	Rakti (4)	P Robinson	M Jarvis	G A Tanaka	Carnival Dancer	Indian Creek	02:03.3
2004	Haafhd (3)	R Hills	B Hills	H Al Maktoum	Chorist	Azamour	02:06.9

ear	1st (Age)	Jockey	Trainer	Owner	2nd	3rd	Time
005	David Junior (3)	J P Spencer	B Meehan	Roldvale Ltd	Pride	Maraahel	02:05.4
006	Pride (5m)	C-P Lemaire	A de Royer-Dupre	NP Bloodstock Ltd	Rob Roy	Hurricane Run	02:06.8
007	Literato (3)	C-P Lemaire	J-C Rouget	H Morin	Eagle Mountain	Doctor Dino	02:04.2

Run on the July Course

HEVELEY PARK STAKES-G1
furlongs, 2-year-old fillies, Newmarket (Rowley Mile Course)
First run in 1899

ear	1st	Jockey	Trainer	Owner	2nd	3rd	Time
988	Pass The Peace	T R Quinn	P Cole	B Bell	Dancing Tribute	Jaljuli	01:11.8
989	Dead Certain	C Asmussen	D Elsworth	G Marten	Line Of Thunder	Chimes Of Freedom	01:14.8
990	Capricciosa	J Reid	M V O'Brien	R Sangster	Imperfect Circle	Divine Danse	01:12.2
991	Marling	W R Swinburn	G Wragg	E Loder	Absurde	Basma	01:11.6
992	Sayyedati	W R Swinburn	C Brittain	M Obaida	Lyric Fantasy	Poker Chip	01:11.8
993	Prophecy	Pat Eddery	J Gosden	K Abdullah	Risky	Lemon Souffle	01:14.7
994	Gay Gallanta	Pat Eddery	M Stoute	Cheveley Park Stud	Tanami	Harayir	01:11.1
995	Blue Duster	M J Kinane	D Loder	Sheikh Mohammed	My Branch	Najiya	01:12.8
996	Pas de Reponse	F Head	C Head	Wertheimer & Frere	Moonlight Paradise	Ocean Ridge	01:11.2
997	Embassy	K Fallon	D Loder	Sheikh Mohammed	Crazee Mental	Royal Shyness	01:12.3
998	Wannabe Grand	Pat Eddery	J Noseda	B McAllister	Imperial Beauty	Subeen	01:12.4
999*	Seazun	T R Quinn	M Channon	J Breslin	Torgau	Crimplene	01:12.9
000	Regal Rose	L Dettori	M Stoute	Cheveley Park Stud	Toroca	Mala Mala	01:13.7
001	Queen's Logic	S Drowne	M Channon	Jaber Abdullah	Sophisticat	Good Girl	01:12.3
002	Airwave	C Rutter	H Candy	H Candy & Partners	Russian Rhythm	Danaskaya	01:10.7
003	Carry On Katie	L Dettori	J Noseda	Mohammed Rashid	Majestic Desert	Badminton	01:13.0
004	Magical Romance	R Winston	B Meehan	F C T Wilson	Suez	Damson	01:12.6
005	Donna Blini	M J Kinane	B Meehan	Mrs T S M Cunningham	Wake Up Maggie	Flashy Wings	01:10.9
006	Indian Ink	R Hughes	R Hannon	R Tooth	Dhanyata	Silca Chiave	01:14.8
007	Natagora	C-P Lemaire	P Bary	Stefan Friborg	Fleeting Spirit	Festoso	01:11.5

Run on the July Course

ORONATION CUP-G1
1/2 miles, 4-year-olds & up, Epsom
First run in 1902

ear	1st (Age)	Jockey	Trainer	Owner	2nd	3rd	Time
988	Triptych (6f)	S. Cauthen	P-L Biancone	P Brant	Infamy	Moon Madness	02:34.8
989	Sheriff's Star (4)	R. Cochrane	Lady Herries	Duchess of Norfolk	Ile de Chypre	Green Adventure	02:35.4
990	In the Wings (4)	C. Asmussen	A. Fabre	Sheikh Mohammed	Observation Post	Ibn Bey	02:36.4
991	In The Groove (4f)	S. Cauthen	D. Elsworth	B. Cooper	Terimon	Rock Hopper	02:36.2
992	Saddlers' Hall (4)	W. R. Swinburn	M. Stoute	Lord Weinstock	Rock Hopper	Terimon	02:35.6
993	Opera House (4)	M. Roberts	M. Stoute	Sheikh Mohammed	Environment Friend	Apple Tree	02:35.1
994	Apple Tree (5)	T Jarnet	A. Fabre	Sultan Al Kabeer	Environment Friend	Blush Rambler	02:35.4
995	Sunshack (4)	Pat Eddery	A. Fabre	K. Abdullah	Only Royale	Time Star	02:35.8
996	Swain (4)	L Dettori	A. Fabre	Sheikh Mohammed	Singspiel	De Quest	02:40.3
997	Singspiel (5)	L Dettori	M. Stoute	Sheikh Mohammed	Dushyantor	Le Destin	02:37.7

Year	1st (Age)	Jockey	Trainer	Owner	2nd	3rd	Time
1998	Silver Patriarch (4)	P. Eddery	J. Dunlop	P Winfield	Swain	Ebadiyla	02:37.6
1999	Daylami (5)	L Dettori	S. bin Suroor	Godolphin	Royal Anthem	Dream Well	02:40.3
2000	Daliapour (4)	K Fallon	M Stoute	HH Aga Khan	Fantastic Light	Border Arrow	02:41.6
2001	Mutafaweq (5)	L Dettori	S bin Suroor	Godolphin	Wellbeing	Millenary	02:36.7
2002	Boreal (4)	K Fallon	P Schiergen	Gestut Amerland	Storming Home	Zindabad	02:45.0
2003	Warrsan (5)	P Robinson	C E Brittain	S Manana	Highest	Black San Bellamy	02:35.7
2004	Warrsan (6)	D Holland	C E Brittain	S Manana	Doyen	Vallee Enchantee	02:36.0
2005	Yeats (4)	K Fallon	A P O'Brien	Magnier & Nagle	Alkaased	Reefscape	02:37.0
2006	Shirocco (5)	C Soumillon	A Fabre	Baron G von Ullmann	Ouija Board	Enforcer	02:37.6
2007	Scorpion (5)	M J Kinane	A P O'Brien	Mrs J Magnier	Septimus	Maraahel	02:40.8

CORONATION STAKES-G1
1 mile, 3-year-old fillies, Ascot
First run in 1840

Year	1st	Jockey	Trainer	Owner	2nd	3rd	Time
1988	Magic Of Life	Pat Eddery	J Tree	S Niarchos	Inchmurrin	Ravinella	
1989	Golden Opinion	C B Asmussen	A Fabre	Sheikh Mohammed	Magic Gleam	Guest Artiste	
1990	Chimes Of Freedom	S Cauthen	H Cecil	S Niarchos	Hasbah	Heart Of Joy	01:41.3
1991	Kooyonga	W J O'Connor	M Kauntze	M Haga	Shadayid	Gussy Marlowe	01:42.5
1992	Marling	W R Swinburn	G Wragg	E J Loder	Culture Vulture	Katakana	01:39.0
1993	Gold Splash	G Mosse	C Head	J Wertheimer	Elizabeth Bay	Zarani Sidi Anna	01:47.7
1994	Kissing Cousin	M J Kinane	H Cecil	Sheikh Mohammed	Eternal Reve	Mehthaaf	01:40.0
1995	Ridgewood Pearl	J P Murtagh	J Oxx	Anne Coughlan	Smolensk	Harayir	01:38.6
1996	Shake The Yoke	O Peslier	E Lellouche	S Brunswick	Last Second	Dance Design	01:40.5
1997	Rebecca Sharp	M Hills	G Wragg	A E Oppenheimer	Ocean Ridge	Sleepytime	01:42.0
1998	Exclusive	W R Swinburn	M R Stoute	Cheveley Park Stud	Zalaiyka	Winona	01:44.0
1999	Balisada	M Roberts	G Wragg	A E Oppenheimer	Golden Silca	Valentime Waltz*	01:41.4
2000	Crimplene	P Robinson	C E Brittain	Marwan Al Maktoum	Princess Ellen	Bluemamba	01:41.6
2001	Banks Hill	O Peslier	A Fabre	K Abdullah	Crystal Music	Tempting Fate	01:39.6
2002	Sophisticat	M J Kinane	A P O'Brien	Tabor & Magnier	Zenda	Dolores	01:41.7
2003	Russian Rhythm	K Fallon	M R Stoute	Cheveley Park Stud	Soviet Song	Mail The Desert	01:38.5
2004	Attraction	K Darley	M Johnston	Duke of Roxburghe	Majestic Desert	Red Bloom	01:38.5
2005	Maids Causeway	M Hills	B Hills	Martin S Schwartz	Karen's Caper	Mona Lisa	01:36.6
2006	Nannina	J Fortune	J Gosden	Cheveley Park Stud	Flashy Wings	Nasheej	01:39.1
2007	Indian Ink	R Hughes	R Hannon	Raymond Tooth	Mi Emma	Darjina	01:42.3

* In 1999 Valentine's Waltz finished in a deadheat for 3rd with Wannabe Grand

** Run at York in 2005

DEWHURST STAKES-G1

furlongs, 2-year-old colts & fillies, Newmarket (Rowley Mile Course)
irst run in 1875

Year	1st	Jockey	Trainer	Owner	2nd	3rd	Time
1988	Prince Of Dance*	W Carson	N Graham	M Sobell			
1988	Scenic*	M Hills	B Hills	Sheikh Mohammed	—	Saratogan	01:27.6
1989	Dashing Blade	J Matthias	I Balding	J C Smith	Call To Arms	Anshan	01:25.4
1990	Generous	T R Quinn	P Cole	Prince F Salman	Bog Trotter	Surrealist	01:28.4
1991	Dr Devious	W Carson	P Chapple-Hyam	L Gaucci	Great Palm	Thourios	01:23.4
1992	Zafonic	Pat Eddery	A Fabre	K Abdullah	Inchinor	Firm Pledge	01:23.6
1993	Grand Lodge	Pat Eddery	W Jarvis	H de Walden	Stonehatch	Nicolotte	01:28.3
1994	Pennekamp	T Jarnet	A Fabre	Sheikh Mohammed	Green Perfume	Eltish	01:25.4
1995	Alhaarth	W Carson	W R Hern	H Al Maktoum	Danehill Dancer	Tagula	01:24.6
1996	In Command	M Hills	B Hills	M Al Maktoum	Musical Pursuit	Air Express	01:25.9
1997	Xaar	O Peslier	A Fabre	K Abdullah	Tamarisk	Impressionist	01:24.8
1998	Mujahid	R Hills	J Dunlop	H Al Maktoum	Auction House	Stravinsky	01:25.3
1999*	Distant Music	M Hills	B Hills	K Abdullah	Brahms	Zentsov Street	01:26.8
2000	Tobougg	C Williams	M Channon	Ahmed Al Maktoum	Noverre	Tempest	01:27.9
2001	Rock Of Gibraltar	M J Kinane	A P O'Brien	Ferguson & Magnier	Landseer	Tendulkar	01:28.7
2002	Tout Seul	S Carson	R JhnsnHoughton	Eden Racing	Tomahawk	Trade Fair	01:24.0
2003	Milk It Mick	D Holland	J Osborne	P J Dixon	Three Valleys	Haafhd	01:25.2
2004	Shamardal	K Darley	M Johnston	Gainsborough Stud	Oratorio	Montgomery's Arch	01:27.2
2005	Sir Percy	M. Dwyer	M. Tergoning	A.E. Pakenham	Horatio Nelson	Opera Cape	01:26.5
2006	Teofilo	K J Manning	J S Bolger	Mrs J S Bolger	Holy Roman Emperor	Strategic Prince	01:26.1
2007	New Approach	K J Manning	J S Bolger	Mrs J S Bolger	Fast Company	Raven's Pass	01:25.3

Prince Of Dance and Scenic finished in a deadheat in 1988

ECLIPSE STAKES-G1

¼ miles, 3-year-olds & up, Sandown Park
irst run in 1886. Run at Kempton Park in 1973

Year	1st (Age)	Jockey	Trainer	Owner	2nd	3rd	Time
1988	Mtoto (5)	M Roberts	A Stewart	A Al Maktoum	Shady Heights	Triptych	2:06
1989	Nashwan (3)	W Carson	W R Hern	H Al Maktoum	Opening Verse	Indian Skimmer	02:07.2
1990	Elmaamul (3)	W Carson	W R Hern	H Al Maktoum	Terimon	Ile de Chypre	2:04
1991	Environment Friend (3)	G Duffield	J Fanshawe	W Gredley	Stagecraft	Sanglamore	02:07.6
1992	Kooyonga (4f)	W O'Connor	M Kauntze	M Haga	Opera House	Sapience	02:10.8
1993	Opera House (5)	M J Kinane	M Stoute	Sheikh Mohammed	Misil	Tenby	02:06.2
1994	Ezzoud (5)	W R Swinburn	M Stoute	M Al Maktoum	Bob's Return	Erhaab	02:04.7
1995	Halling (4)	W R Swinburn	S bin Suroor	Godolphin	Singspiel	Red Bishop	02:05.3
1996	Halling (5)	J Reid	S bin Suroor	Godolphin	Bijou d'Inde	Pentire	02:08.1
1997	Pilsudski (5)	M J Kinane	M Stoute	Lord Weinstock	Benny the Dip	Bosra Sham	02:12.5
1998	Daylami (5)	L Dettori	S bin Suroor	Godolphin	Faithful Son	Central Park	02:06.8
1999	Compton Admiral (3)	D Holland	G Butler	E Penser	Xaar	Fantastic Light	02:06.4
2000	Giant's Causeway (3)	G Duffield	A P O'Brien	Mrs J Magnier/M Tabor	Kalanisi	Shiva	02:05.3
2001	Medicean (4)	K Fallon	M Stoute	Cheveley Park Stud	Grandera	Bach	02:04.7
2002	Hawk Wing (3)	M J Kinane	A P O'Brien	Mrs J Magnier	Sholokhov	Equerry	02:13.3
2003	Falbrav (5)	D Holland	L Cumani	Scuderia Rencati	Nayef	Kaieteur	02:05.6
2004	Refuse To Bend (4)	L Dettori	S bin Suroor	Godolphin	Warrsan	Kalaman	02:08.3
2005	Oratorio (3)	K Fallon	A P O'Brien	Mrs J Magnier/M Tabor	Motivator	Altieri	02:07.0

Year	1st (Age)	Jockey	Trainer	Owner	2nd	3rd	Time
2006	David Junior (4)	J P Spencer	B Meehan	Roldvale Ltd	Notnowcato	Blue Monday	02:07.3
2007	Notnowcato (5)	R L Moore	M R Stoute	A & D de Rothschild	Authorized	GeorgeWashington	02:05.9

ENGLISH OAKS-G1
1½ miles, 3-year-old fillies, Epsom
First run in 1779

Year	1st	Jockey	Trainer	Owner	2nd	3rd	Time
1988	Diminuendo	S. Cauthen	H Cecil	Sheikh Mohammed	Sudden Love	Animatrice	2:35
1989	Snow Bride	S. Cauthen	H Cecil	M Al Maktoum	Roseate Tern	Mamaluna	2:34.2*
1990	Salsabil	W. Carson	J. Dunlop	H Al Maktoum	Game Plan	Knight's Baroness	02:38.6
1991	Jet Ski Lady	C. Roche	J. Bolger	M Al Maktoum	Shamshir	Shadayid	02:37.2
1992	User Friendly	G. Duffield	C. Brittain	W Gredley	All At Sea	Pearl Angel	02:39.6
1993	Intrepidity	M. Roberts	A. Fabre	Sheikh Mohammed	Royal Ballerina	Oakmead	02:34.2
1994	Balanchine	L Dettori	H Ibrahim	Godolphin	Wind In Her Hair	Hawajiss	02:40.4
1995	Moonshell	L Dettori	S. bin Suroor	Godolphin	Dance A Dream	Pure Grain	02:35.4
1996	Lady Carla	Pat Eddery	H Cecil	W. Said	Pricket	Mezzogiorno	02:35.5
1997	Reams Of Verse	K. Fallon	H Cecil	K. Abdullah	Gazelle Royale	Crown Of Light	02:35.6
1998	Shahtoush	M. J. Kinane	A P O'Brien	Nagle & Magnier	Bahr	Midnight Line	02:38.2
1999	Ramruma	K. Fallon	H Cecil	Prince F Salman	Noushkey	Zahrat Dubai	02:38.7
2000	Love Divine	T R Quinn	H Cecil	Lordship Stud	Kalypso Katie	Melikah	02:43.1
2001	Imagine	M J Kinane	A P O'Brien	Magnier & Nagle	Flight Of Fancy	RelishTheThought	02:36.7
2002	Kazzia	L Dettori	S bin Suroor	Godolphin	Quarter Moon	Shadow Dancing	02:44.5
2003	Casual Look	M Dwyer	A Balding	W S Farish III	Yesterday	Summitville	02:38.1
2004	Ouija Board	K Fallon	E Dunlop	Lord Derby	All Too Beautiful	Punctilious	02:35.4
2005	Eswarah	R Hills	M Jarvis	H Al Maktoum	Something Exciting	Pictavia	02:39.0
2006	Alexandrova	K Fallon	A P O'Brien	Magnier,Tabor & Smith	Rising Cross	Short Skirt	02:38.0
2007	Light Shift	T E Durcan	H Cecil	Niarchos Family	Peeping Fawn	All My Loving	02:40.4

* Aliysa finished first but was disqualified from purse money

DERBY STAKES (EPSOM DERBY)-G1
1½ miles, 3-year-old colts & fillies, Epsom
First run in 1780. Run at 1 mile 1780–1784
Run at Newmarket (July Course) as the New Derby 1915–1918 and 1940–1945

Year	1st	Jockey	Trainer	Owner	2nd	3rd	Time
1988	Kahyasi	R Cochrane	L Cumani	Aga Khan	Glacial Storm	Doyoun	02:33.8
1989	Nashwan	W Carson	W R Hern	H Al Maktoum	Terimon	Cacoethes	02:34.9
1990	Quest For Fame	Pat Eddery	R Charlton	K Abdullah	Blue Stag	Elmaamul	02:37.3
1991	Generous	A Munro	P Cole	Prince F Salman	Marju	Star Of Gdansk	2:34
1992	Dr Devious	J Reid	P Chapple-Hyam	S Craig	St. Jovite	Silver Wisp	02:36.2
1993	Commander In Chief	M J Kinane	H Cecil	K Abdullah	Blue Judge	Blues Traveller	02:34.5
1994	Erhaab	W Carson	J Dunlop	H Al Maktoum	King's Theatre	Colonel Collins	02:34.2
1995	Lammtarra	W R Swinburn	S bin Suroor	S M Al Maktoum	Tamure	Presenting	02:32.3
1996	Shaamit	M Hills	W Haggas	K A Dasman	Dushyantor	Shantou	02:35.0
1997	Benny The Dip	W Ryan	J Gosden	L Knight	Silver Patriarch	Romanov	02:35.8
1998	High-Rise	O Peslier	L Cumani	M O Al Maktoum	City Honours	Border Arrow	02:33.9
1999	Oath	K Fallon	H Cecil	The Thoroughbred Corp	Daliapour	Beat All	02:37.4

Year	1st	Jockey	Trainer	Owner	2nd	3rd	Time
2000	Sinndar	J P Murtagh	J Oxx	HH Aga Khan	Sakhee	Beat Hollow	02:36.7
2001	Galileo	M J Kinane	A P O'Brien	Magnier & Tabor	Golan	Tobougg	02:33.3
2002	High Chaparral	J P Murtagh	A P O'Brien	Tabor & Magnier	Hawk Wing	Moon Ballad	02:39.4
2003	Kris Kin	K Fallon	M R Stoute	S Suhail	The Great Gatsby	Alamshar	02:33.3
2004	North Light	K Fallon	M R Stoute	Ballymacoll Stud	Rule Of Law	Let The Lion Roar	02:33.7
2005	Motivator	J P Murtagh	M Bell	RoyalAscotRacingClub	Walk in the Park	Dubawi	02:35.7
2006	Sir Percy	M Dwyer	M Tregoning	A E Pakenham	Dragon Dancer	Dylan Thomas	02:35.2
2007	Authorized	L Dettori	P Chapple-Hyam	Al Homaizi & Al Sagar	Eagle Mountain	Aqaleem	02:34.8

FILLIES' MILE-G1

m, 2-year-old fillies, Ascot

First run in 1973.

Run as the Green Shield Stakes in 1973. Run as the Argos Stakes 1975–1977

Year	1st	Jockey	Trainer	Owner	2nd	3rd	Time
1988	Tessla	Pat Eddery	H Cecil	C St George	Pick Of The Pops	Rain Burst	01:44.0
1989	Silk Slippers	M Hills	B Hills	R Sangster	Moon Cactus	Fujaiyrah	01:42.5
1990	Shamshir	L Dettori	L Cumani	Sheikh Mohammed	Safa	Atlantic Flyer	01:43.3
1991	Midnight Air	Pat Eddery	P Cole	C Wright	Culture Vulture	Mystery Play	01:46.1
1992	Ivanka	M Roberts	C Brittain	A Saeed	Ajfan	Iviza	01:46.7
1993	Fairy Heights	C Asmussen	N Callaghan	F Golding	Dance To The Top	Kissing Cousin	01:44.4
1994	Aqaarid	W Carson	J Dunlop	H Al Maktoum	Jural	Snowtown	01:44.7
1995	Bosra Sham	Pat Eddery	H Cecil	W Said	Bint Shadayid	Matiya	01:43.1
1996	Reams Of Verse	M J Kinane	H Cecil	K Abdullah	Khassah	Sleepytime	01:44.3
1997	Glorosia	L Dettori	L Cumani	R H Smith	Jibe	Exclusive	01:42.3
1998	Sunspangled	M J Kinane	A P O'Brien	Tabor & Magnier	Calando	Edabiya	01:44.8
1999	Teggiano	L Dettori	C Brittain	A S Bul Hab	Britannia	My Hansel	01:49.7
2000	Crystal Music	L Dettori	J Gosden	A Lloyd-Webber	Summer Symphony	Hotelgenie Dot Com	01:44.4
2001	Gossamer	J P Spencer	L Cumani	G W Leigh	Maryinsky	Esloob	01:46.4
2002	Soviet Song	O Urbina	J Fanshawe	Elite Racing Club	Casual Look	ReachForTheMoon	01:42.3
2003	Red Bloom	K Fallon	M R Stoute	Cheveley Park Stud	Sundrop	Punctilious	01:40.8
2004	Playful Act	J Fortune	J Gosden	Sangster Family	Maids Causeway	Dash To The Top	01:42.2
*2005	Nannina	J Fortune	J Gosden	Cheveley Park Stud	Alexandrova	Nasheej	01:38.5
2006	Simply Perfect	D Holland	J Noseda	Smith,Tabor & Magnier	Treat	English Ballet	01:41.9
2007	Listen	J P Murtagh	A P O'Brien	Smith,Magnier & Tabor	Proviso	Saoirse Abu	01:43.3

Run at Newmarket in 2005

JUDDMONTE INTERNATIONAL STAKES-G1

mile, 2 furlongs, 85 yards, 3-year-olds & up, York

First run in 1972

Run as the Benson & Hedges Gold Cup through 1985

Matchmaker International 1986–7. International Stakes in 1988

Year	1st (Age)	Jockey	Trainer	Owner	2nd	3rd	Time
1988	Shady Heights (4)	W Carson	R Armstrong	G Tong	Indian Skimmer	Persian Heights	02:06.2
1989	Ile de Chypre (4)	A Clark	G Harwood	G Christodoulou	Cacoethes	Shady Heights	02:06.8
1990	In The Groove (3f)	S Cauthen	D Elsworth	B Cooper	Elmaamul	Batshoof	02:08.6

Year	1st (Age)	Jockey	Trainer	Owner	2nd	3rd	Time
1991	Terimon (5)	M Roberts	C Brittain	Lady Beaverbrook	Quest For Fame	Stagecraft	2:16
1992	Rodrigo de Triano (3)	L Piggott	P Chapple-Hyam	R Sangster	All At Sea	Seattle Rhyme	2:07
1993	Ezzoud (4)	W R Swinburn	M Stoute	M Al Maktoum	Sabrehill	Spartan Shareef	02:12.2
1994	Ezzoud (5)	W R Swinburn	M Stoute	M Al Maktoum	Muhtarram	King's Theatre	02:08.9
1995	Halling (4)	W R Swinburn	S bin Suroor	Godolphin	Bahri	Annus Mirabilis	02:06.4
1996	Halling (5)	L Dettori	S bin Suroor	Godolphin	First Island	Bijou d'Inde	02:06.9
1997	Singspiel (5)	L Dettori	M Stoute	Sheikh Mohammed	Desert King	Benny the Dip	02:12.1
1998	One So Wonderful (4)	Pat Eddery	L Cumani	Helena Springfield Ltd	Faithful Son	Chester House	02:06.5
1999	Royal Anthem (4)	G Stevens	H Cecil	Thoroughbred Corp	Greek Dance	Chester House	02:06.9
2000	Giants Causeway (3)	M J Kinane	A P O»Brien	Mrs J Magnier/M Tabor	Kalanisi	Lear Spear	02:09.1
2001	Sakhee (4)	L Dettori	S bin Suroor	Godolphin	Grandera	Medicean	02:08.3
2002	Nayef (4)	R Hills	M Tregoning	H Al Maktoum	Golan	Noverre	02:08.7
2003	Falbrav (5)	D Holland	L Cumani	Scuderia Rencati	Magistretti	Nayef	02:06.8
2004	Sulamani (5)	L Dettori	S bin Suroor	Godolphin	Norse Dancer	Bago	02:11.8
2005	Electrocutionist (4)	M J Kinane	V Valiani	Earle I Mack	Zenno Rob Roy	Maraahel	02:07.5
2006	Notnowcato (4)	R L Moore	M Stoute	A & D de Rothschild	Maraahel	Blue Monday	02:12.3
2007	Authorized (3)	L Dettori	P Chapple-Hyam	al Homeizi & Al Sagar	Dylan Thomas	Notnowcato	02:11.8

KING GEORGE VI AND QUEEN ELIZABETH DIAMOND STAKES-G1
1½ miles, 3-year-olds & up, Ascot
First run in 1951

Year	1st (Age)	Jockey	Trainer	Owner	2nd	3rd	Time
1988	Mtoto (5)	M Roberts	A Stewart	A Al Maktoum	Unfuwain	Tony Bin	02:37.3
1989	Nashwan (3)	W Carson	W R Hern	H Al Maktoum	Cacoethes	Top Class	02:32.3
1990	Belmez (3)	M J Kinane	H Cecil	Sheikh Mohammed	Old Vic	Assatis	02:30.8
1991	Generous (3)	A Munro	P Cole	Prince F Salman	Sanglamore	Rock Hopper	02:29.0
1992	St. Jovite (3)	S Craine	J Bolger	V K Payson	Saddlers' Hall	Opera House	02:30.9
1993	Opera House (5)	M Roberts	M Stoute	Sheikh Mohammed	White Muzzle	Commander In Chief	02:33.9
1994	King's Theatre (3)	M J Kinane	H Cecil	Sheikh Mohammed	White Muzzle	Wagon Master	02:28.9
1995	Lammtarra (3)	L Dettori	S bin Suroor	S M Al Maktoum	Pentire	Strategic Choice	02:31.0
1996	Pentire (4)	M Hills	G Wragg	Mollers Racing	Classic Cliche	Shaamit	02:28.1
1997	Swain (5)	J Reid	S bin Suroor	Godolphin	Pilsudski	Helissio	02:36.5
1998	Swain (6)	L Dettori	S bin Suroor	Godolphin	High-Rise	Royal Anthem	02:29.1
1999	Daylami (5)	L Dettori	S bin Suroor	Godolphin	Nedawi	Fruits Of Love	02:29.4
2000	Montjeu (4)	M J Kinane	J Hammond	M Tabor	Fantastic Light	Daliapour	02:30.0
2001	Galileo (3)	M J Kinane	A P O'Brien	Magnier & Tabor	Fantastic Light	Hightori	02:27.7
2002	Golan (4)	K Fallon	M Stoute	Est of Lord Weinstock	Nayef	Zindabad	02:29.7
2003	Alamshar (3)	J P Murtagh	J Oxx	H H Aga Khan	Sulamani	Kris Kin	02:33.3
2004	Doyen (4)	L Dettori	S bin Suroor	Godolphin	Hard Buck	Sulamani	02:33.2
2005*	Azamour (4)	M J Kinane	J Oxx	H H Aga Khan	Norse Dancer	Bago	02:28.7
2006	Hurricane Run (4)	C Soumillon	A Fabre	M Tabor	Electrocutionist	Heart's Cry	02:30.3
2007	Dylan Thomas (4)	J P Murtagh	A P O'Brien	Magnier & Tabor	Youmzain	Maraahel	02:31.1

* Run at Newbury in 2005

MIDDLE PARK STAKES-G1
furlongs, 2-year-old colts, Newmarket (Rowley Mile Course)
First run in 1866

Year	1st	Jockey	Trainer	Owner	2nd	3rd	Time
1988	Mon Tresor	M Roberts	R Boss	Mrs P Fitsall	Pure Genius	Northern Tryst	01:12.2
1989	Balla Cove	S Cauthen	R Boss	H Cohen	Rock City	Cordoba	1:11
1990	Lycius	C Asmussen	A Fabre	Sheikh Mohammed	Distinctly North	Majlood	1:10
1991	Rodrigo de Triano	W Carson	P Chapple-Hyam	R Sangster	Lion Cavern	River Falls	1:11
1992	Zieten	S Cauthen	A Fabre	Sheikh Mohammed	Pips Pride	Factual	01:11.2
1993	First Trump	M Hills	G Wragg	Mollers Racing	Owington	Redoubtable	01:13.7
1994	Fard	W Carson	D Morley	H Al Maktoum	Green Perfume	Fallow	01:11.4
1995	Royal Applause	W R Swinburn	B Hills	M Al Maktoum	Woodborough	Kahir Almaydan	01:11.4
1996	Bahamian Bounty	L Dettori	D Loder	M Al Maktoum	Muchea	In Command	01:11.9
1997	Hayil	R Hills	D Morley	H Al Maktoum	Carrowkeel	Designer	01:12.4
1998	Lujain	L Dettori	D Loder	Sheikh Mohammed	Bertolini	Vision Of Night	01:14.7
1999*	Primo Valentino	Pat Eddery	P Harris	Primo Donnas	Fath	Brahms	01:12.8
2000	Minardi	M J Kinane	A P O»Brien	Magnier & Tabor	Endless Summer	Red Carpet	01:12.7
2001	Johannesburg	M J Kinane	A P O'Brien	Tabor & Magnier	Zipping	Doc Holiday	01:11.7
2002	Oasis Dream	J Fortune	J Gosden	K Abdullah	Tomahawk	Elusive City	01:09.6
2003*	Balmont	Pat Eddery	J Noseda	S R Robertson	Holborn	Auditorium	01:10.7
2004	Ad Valorem	J P Spencer	A P O'Brien	Mrs John Magnier	Rebuttal	Iceman	01:12.2
2005	Amadeus Wolf	N Callan	K Ryan	J Duddy & B McDonald	Red Clubs	Always Hopeful	01:12.4
2006	Dutch Art	L Dettori	P Chapple-Hyam	Susan Roy	Wi Dud	Captain Marvelous	01:14.1
2007	Dark Angel	M Hills	B Hills	J Corbett & C Wright	Strike the Deal	Tajdeef	01:12.1

Run on the July Course

NUNTHORPE STAKES-G1
furlongs, 2-year-olds & up, York
First run in 1903

Year	1st (Age)	Jockey	Trainer	Owner	2nd	3rd	Time
1988	Handsome Sailor (5)	M Hills	B Hills	R Sangster	Silver Fling	Perion	:58.73
1989	Cadeaux Genereux(4)	Pat Eddery	A Scott	M Al Maktoum	Silver Fling	Statoblest	:57.67
1990	Dayjur (3)	W Carson	W R Hern	H Al Maktoum	Statoblest	Pharaoh's Delight	:56.16
1991	Sheikh Albadou (3)	Pat Eddery	A Scott	H Salem	Paris House	Blyton Lad	:58.21
1992	Lyric Fantasy (2f)	M Roberts	R Hannon	Lord Carnarvon	Mr Brooks	Diamonds Galore	:57.39
1993	Lochsong (5f)	L Dettori	I Balding	J C Smith	Paris House	College Chapel	:58.12
1994	Blue Siren (3)	M Hills	M Channon	J Mitchell	Piccolo	Mistertopogigo	:57.61
1995	So Factual (5)	L Dettori	S bin Suroor	Godolphin	Ya Malak	Hever Golf Rose	:57.47
1996	Pivotal (3)	G Duffield	M Prescott	Cheveley Park Stud	Eveningperformance	Hever Golf Rose	:56.53
1997	Coastal Bluff (5)	K Darley	T Barron	Mrs D Sharp	Ya Malak	Averti	:59.58
1998	Lochangel (4f)	L Dettori	I Balding	J C Smith	Sainte Marine	Dashing Blue	:56.83
1999	Stravinsky (3)	M J Kinane	A P O'Brien	Tabor & Magnier	Sainte Marine	Proud Native	:59.33
2000	Nuclear Debate (5)	G Mosse	J Hammond	J R Chester	Bertolini	Pipalong	:57.83
2001	Mozart (3)	M J Kinane	A P O'Brien	Tabor & Magnier	Nuclear Debate	Bishops Court	:57.27
2002	Kyllachy (4)	J P Spencer	H Candy	Thurloe Thrghbrds	Malhub	Indian Prince	:58.10
2003	Oasis Dream (3)	R Hughes	J Gosden	K Abdullah	The Tatling	Acclamation	:56.20
2004	Bahamian Pirate (9)	S Sanders	D Nicholls	Lucayan Stud	The Tatling	One Cool Cat	:58.89
2005	La Cucaracha (4f)	M Hills	B Hills	Guy Reed	The Tatling	Majestic Missile	:56.82
2006	Reverence (5)	K Darley	E Alston	Mr&Mrs G Middlebrook	Amadeus Wolf	Pivotal Flame	01:00.7
2007	Kingsgate Native (2)	J Quinn	J Best	John Mayne	Desert Lord	Dandy Man	:58.14

In 1983 Soba finished first but was disqualified and placed last

1000 GUINEAS STAKES-G1
1 mile, 3-year-old fillies, Newmarket (Rowley Mile Course)
First run in 1814

Year	1st	Jockey	Trainer	Owner	2nd	3rd	Time
1988	Ravinella	G Moore	C Head	Ecurie Aland	Dabaweyaa	Diminuendo	01:40.9
1989	Musical Bliss	W R Swinburn	M Stoute	Sheikh Mohammed	Kerrera	Aldbourne	01:42.7
1990	Salsabil	W Carson	J Dunlop	H Al Maktoum	Heart Of Joy	Negligent	01:38.1
1991	Shadayid	W Carson	J Dunlop	H Al Maktoum	Kooyonga	Crystal Gazing	01:38.2
1992	Hatoof	W R Swinburn	C Head	M Al Maktoum	Marling	Kenbu	01:39.5
1993	Sayyedati	W R Swinburn	C Brittain	M Obaida	Niche	Ajfan	01:37.3
1994	Las Meninas	J Reid	T Stack	R Sangster	Balanchine	Coup de Genie	01:36.7
1995	Harayir	R Hills	W R Hern	H Al Maktoum	Aqaarid	Moonshell	01:36.7
1996	Bosra Sham	Pat Eddery	H Cecil	W Said	Matiya	Bint Shadayid	01:37.8
1997	Sleepytime	K Fallon	H Cecil	Greenbay Stables Ltd	Oh Nellie	Dazzle	01:37.7
1998	Cape Verdi	L Dettori	S bin Suroor	Godolphin	Shahtoush	Exclusive	01:37.9
1999*	Wince	K Fallon	H Cecil	K Abdullah	Wannabe Grand	Valentine Waltz	01:37.9
2000	Lahan	R Hills	J Gosden	Hamdan Al Maktoum	Princess Ellen	Petrushka	01:36.4
2001	Ameerat	P Robinson	M Jarvis	A Al Maktoum	Muwakleh	Toroca	01:38.4
2002	Kazzia	L Dettori	S bin Suroor	Godolphin	Snowfire	Alasha	01:37.8
2003	Russian Rhythm	K Fallon	M R Stoute	Cheveley Park Stud	Six Perfections	Intercontinental	01:38.4
2004	Attraction	K Darley	M Johnston	Duke of Roxburghe	Sundrop	Hathrah	01:36.8
2005	Virginia Waters	K Fallon	A P O'Brien	Mrs J Magnier	Maids Causeway	Vista Bella	01:36.5
2006	Speciosa	M Fenton	Pamela Sly	Sly, Davies & Sly	Confidential Lady	Nasheej	01:40.5
2007	Finsceal Beo	K J Manning	J S Bolger	M A Ryan	Arch Swing	Simply Perfect	01:39.9

* Run on the July Course

QUEEN ELIZABETH II STAKES-G1
1 mile, 3-year-olds & up, Ascot
First run in 1955

Year	1st (Age)	Jockey	Trainer	Owner	2nd	3rd	Time
1988	Warning (3)	Pat Eddery	G Harwood	K Abdullah	Salse	Persian Heights	01:40.5
1989	Zilzal (3)	W R Swinburn	M Stoute	M Al Maktoum	Polish Precedent	Distant Relative	01:40.6
1990	Markofdistinction (4)	L Dettori	L Cumani	G Leigh	Distant Relative	Green Line Express	01:39.7
1991	Selkirk (3)	R Cochrane	I Balding	G Strawbridge	Kooyonga	Shadayid	01:44.3
1992	Lahib (4)	W Carson	J Dunlop	H Al Maktoum	Brief Truce	Selkirk	01:44.5
1993	Bigstone (3)	Pat Eddery	E Lellouche	D Wildenstein	Barathea	Kingmambo	01:42.9
1994	Maroof (3)	R Hills	R Armstrong	H Al Maktoum	Barathea	Bigstone	01:42.8
1995	Bahri (3)	W Carson	J Dunlop	H Al Maktoum	Ridgewood Pearl	Soviet Line	01:40.5
1996	Mark Of Esteem (3)	L Dettori	S bin Suroor	Godolphin	Bosra Sham	First Island	01:41.0
1997	Air Express (3)	O Peslier	C Brittain	M Obaida	Rebecca Sharp	Faithful Son	01:40.6
1998	Desert Prince (3)	O Peslier	D Loder	Lucayan Stud	Dr Fong	Second Empire	01:39.6
1999	Dubai Millennium (3)	L Dettori	S bin Suroor	Godolphin	Almushtarak	Gold Academy	01:46.2
2000	Observatory (3)	K Darley	J Gosden	K Abdullah	Giants Causeway	Best Of The Bests	01:41.4
2001	Summoner (4)	R Hills	S bin Suroor	Godolphin	Noverre	Hawkeye	01:44.5
2002	Where Or When (3)	K Darley	T G Mills	John Humphreys Ltd	Hawk Wing	Tillerman	01:41.4
2003	Falbrav (5)	D Holland	L Cumani	Scuderia Rencati	Russian Rhythm	Tillerman	01:39.0
2004	Rakti (5)	P Robinson	M Jarvis	G A Tanaka	Lucky Story	Refuse To Bend	01:39.8
*2005	Starcraft (5)	C-P Lemaire	L Cumani	Australian Syndicate	Dubawi	Blatant	01:37.9
2006	George Washington (3)	M J Kinane	A P O'Brien	Magnier,Tabor & Smith	Araafa	Court Masterpiece	01:40.1
2007	Ramonti (5)	L Dettori	S bin Suroor	Godolphin	Excellent Art	DukeOfMarmalade	01:42.4

* Run at Newmarket in 2005

RACING POST TROPHY-G1
1 mile, 2-year-old colts & fillies, Doncaster
First run in 1961
Run as the Timeform Gold Cup 1961–1964. Run as the Observor Gold Cup 1965–1975
Run as the William Hill Futurity 1976–1988. Run at Newcastle in 1989

Year	1st	Jockey	Trainer	Owner	2nd	3rd	Time
1988	Al Hareb	W Carson	N Graham	H Al Maktoum	Zalazi	Frequent Flyer	01:40.6
1989	Be My Chief	S Cauthen	H Cecil	P Burrell	Baligh	Qathil	01:43.0
1990	Peter Davies	S Cauthen	H Cecil	C St George	Mukaddamah	Marcham	01:46.0
1991	Seattle Rhyme	C Asmussen	D Elsworth	H J Senn	Mack The Knife	Assessor	01:39.6
1992	Armiger	Pat Eddery	H Cecil	K Abdullah	Ivanka	Zind	01:39.7
1993	King's Theatre	W Ryan	H Cecil	M Poland	Fairy Heights	Bude	01:41.0
1994	Celtic Swing	K Darley	Lady Herries	P Savill	Annus Mirabilis	Juyush	01:40.0
1995	Beauchamp King	J Reid	J Dunlop	E Penser	Even Top	Mons	01:38.9
1996	Medaaly	G Hind	S bin Suroor	Godolphin	Poteen	Benny The Dip	01:41.1
1997	Saratoga Springs	M J Kinane	A P O'Brien	Tabor & Magnier	Mudeer	Mutamam	01:40.4
1998	Commander Collins	J Fortune	P Chapple-Hyam	Sangster & Collins	Magno	Housemaster	01:47.8
1999	Aristotle	G Duffield	A P O'Brien	Mrs J Magnier	Lermontov	Ekraar	01:45.6
2000	Dilshaan	J P Murtagh	M Stoute	S Suhail	Tamburlaine	Bonnard	01:45.9
2001	High Chaparral	K Darley	A P O'Brien	Tabor & Magnier	Castle Gandolfo	Redback	01:45.4
2002	Brian Boru	K Darley	A P O'Brien	Mrs J Magnier	Powerscourt	Illustrator	01:46.0
2003	American Post	C Soumillon	C Head-Maarek	K Abdullah	Fantastic View	Magritte	01:39.6
2004	Motivator	K Fallon	M Bell	RylAscotRacingClub	Albert Hall	Henrik	01:42.6
2005	Palace Episode	N. Callan	K. Ryan	Mrs T Marnane	Winged Cupid	Septimus	01:45.1
2006*	Authorized	L Dettori	P Chapple-Hyam	Al Homaizi & Al Sagar	Charlie Farnsbarns	Medicine Path	01:43.7
2007	Ibn Khaldun	K McEvoy	S bin Suroor	Godolphin	City Leader	Feared In Flight	01:37.6

* Run at Newbury in 2006

ST. JAMES'S PALACE STAKES-G1
1 mile, 3-year-old colts, Royal Ascot
First run in 1833

Year	1st	Jockey	Trainer	Owner	2nd	3rd	Time
1988	Persian Heights	Pat Eddery	G A Huffer	HH Prince Yazid Saud	Raykour	Caerwent	01:39.6
1989	Shaadi	W R Swinburn	M R Stoute	Sheikh Mohammed	Greensmith	Scenic	01:39.3
1990	Shavian	S Cauthen	H Cecil	Lord H de Walden	Rock City	Lord Florey	01:41.5
1991	Marju	W Carson	J Dunlop	H Al Maktoum	Second Set	Hokusai	01:42.0
1992	Brief Truce	M J Kinane	D K Weld	Moyglare Stud Farms	Zaadi	Ezzoud	01:39.3
1993	Kingmambo	C B Asmussen	F Boutin	S Niarchos	Needle Gun	Ventiquattrofogli	01:44.1
1994	Grand Lodge	M J Kinane	W Jarvis	Lord H de Walden	Distant View	Turtle Island	01:38.8
1995	Bahri	W Carson	J Dunlop	H Al Maktoum	Charnwood Forest	Vettori	01:40.2
1996	Bijou d'Inde	J Weaver	M Johnston	J S Morrison	Ashkalani	Sorbie Tower	01:39.7
1997	Starborough	L Dettori	D Loder	Sheikh Mohammed	Air Express	Daylami	01:39.2
1998	Dr Fong	K Fallon	H Cecil	The ThoroughbredCorp	Desert Prince	Duck Row	01:41.3
1999	Sendawar	G Mosse	A de Royer-Dupre	HH Aga Khan	Aljabr	Gold Academy	01:40.0
2000	Giant's Causeway	M J Kinane	A P O'Brien	Magnier & Tabor	Valentino	Medicean	01:42.6
2001	Black Minnaloushe	J P Murtagh	A P O'Brien	Magnier & Tabor	Noverre	Olden Times	01:41.4
2002	Rock Of Gibraltar	M J Kinane	A P O'Brien	Ferguson & Magnier	Landseer	Aramram	01:40.9
2003	Zafeen	D Holland	M Channon	J Abdullah	Kalaman	Martillo	01:39.9

Year	1st	Jockey	Trainer	Owner	2nd	3rd	Time
2004	Azamour	M J Kinane	J Oxx	HH Aga Khan	Diamond Green	Antonius Pius	01:39.0
2005	Shamardal	K McEvoy	S bin Suroor	Godolphin	Ad Valorem	Oratorio	01:37.2
2006	Araafa	A Munro	J Noseda	Al Homaizi & Al Sagar	Stormy River	Ivan Denisovich	01:39.6
2007	Excellent Art	J P Spencer	A P O'Brien	Magnier,Smith,Tabor	Duke of Marmalade	Astronomer Royal	01:39.3

* Run at York in 2005

ST LEGER STAKES-G1
I mile, 6 furlongs, 132 yards, 3-year-old colts & fillies, Doncaster
First run in 1776
Run at Ayr in 1989

Year	1st	Jockey	Trainer	Owner	2nd	3rd	Time
1988	Minster Son	W Carson	N Graham	Lady Beaverbrook	Diminuendo	Sheriff's Star	03:06.8
1989	Michelozzo	S Cauthen	H Cecil	C St George	Sapience	Roseate Tern	03:20.7
1990	Snurge	T R Quinn	P Cole	M Arbib	Hellenic	River God	03:08.8
1991	Toulon	Pat Eddery	A Fabre	K Abdullah	Saddlers' Hall	Micheletti	03:03.1
1992	User Friendly (f)	G Duffield	C Brittain	W Gredley	Sonus	Bonny Scot	03:05.5
1993	Bob's Return	P Robinson	M Tompkins	Mrs G Smith	Armiger	Edbaysaan	03:07.9
1994	Moonax	Pat Eddery	B Hills	Sheikh Mohammed	Broadway Flyer	Double Trigger	03:04.2
1995	Classic Cliche	L Dettori	S bin Suroor	Godolphin	Minds Music	Istidaad	03:09.7
1996	Shantou	L Dettori	J Gosden	Sheikh Mohammed	Dushyantor	Samraan	03:05.1
1997	Silver Patriarch	Pat Eddery	J Dunlop	P Winfield	Vertical Speed	The Fly	03:06.9
1998	Nedawi	J Reid	S bin Suroor	Godolphin	High And Low	Sunshine Street	03:05.6
1999	Mutafaweq	R Hills	S bin Suroor	Godolphin	Ramruma	Adair	03:02.8
2000	Millenary	T R Quinn	J Dunlop	L N Jones	Air Marshall	Chimes At Midnight	03:02.6
2001	Milan	M J Kinane	A P O'Brien	Tabor & Magnier	Demophilos	Mr Combustible	03:05.2
2002	Bollin Eric	K Darley	T Easterby	N Westbrook	Highest	Bandari	03:02.9
2003	Brian Boru	J P Spencer	A P O'Brien	Mrs J Magnier	High Accolade	Phoenix Reach	03:04.6
2004	Rule Of Law	K McEvoy	S bin Suroor	Godolphin	Quiff	Tycoon	03:06.3
2005	Scorpion	L Dettori	A P O'Brien	M Tabor/Mrs J Magnier	The Geezer	Tawqeet	03:19.0
2006*	Sixties Icon	L Dettori	J Noseda	Susan Roy	The Last Drop	Red Rocks	02:57.3
2007	Lucarno	J Fortune	J Gosden	George Strawbridge	Mahler	Honolulu	03:03.0

* Run at York in 2006

SUSSEX STAKES-G1
I mile, 3-year-olds & up, Goodwood
First run in 1878

Year	1st (Age)	Jockey	Trainer	Owner	2nd	3rd	Time
1988	Warning (3)	Pat Eddery	G Harwood	K Abdullah	Then Again	Most Welcome	01:39.8
1989	Markofdistinction	R Cochrane	L Cumani	Mana Al Maktoum	Most Welcome	Opening Verse	01:36.8
1990	Distant Relative (4)	W Carson	B Hills	W Said	Green Line Express	Shavian	01:36.0
1991	Second Set (3)	L Dettori	L Cumani	R Duchossois	Shadayid	Priolo	01:40.4
1992	Marling (3f)	Pat Eddery	G Wragg	E Loder	Selkirk	Second Set	01:36.6
1993	Bigstone (3)	D Boeuf	E Lellouche	D Wildenstein	Sayyedati	Inchinor	01:40.2
1994	Distant View (3)	Pat Eddery	H Cecil	K Abdullah	Barathea	Grand Lodge	01:35.7
1995	Sayyedati (5f)	B Doyle	C Brittain	M Obaida	Bahri	Darnay	01:36.2

Year	1st (Age)	Jockey	Trainer	Owner	2nd	3rd	Time
1996	First Island (4)	M Hills	G Wragg	Mollers Racing	Charnwood Forest	Alhaarth	01:37.8
1997	Ali-Royal (4)	K Fallon	H Cecil	Greenbay Stables Ltd	Starborough	Allied Forces	01:38.0
1998	Among Men (4)	M J Kinane	M Stoute	Tabor & Magnier	Almushtarak	Lend A Hand	01:40.2
1999	Aljabr (3)	L Dettori	S bin Suroor	Godolphin	Docksider	Almushtarak	01:35.7
2000	Giants Causeway (3)	M J Kinane	A P O>Brien	Mrs J Magnier/M Tabor	Dansili	Medicean	01:38.7
2001	Noverre (3)	L Dettori	S bin Suroor	Godolphin	No Excuse Needed	Black Minnaloushe	01:37.1
2002	Rock Of Gibraltar (3)	M J Kinane	A P O'Brien	Ferguson & Magnier	Noverre	Reel Buddy	01:38.3
2003	Reel Buddy (5)	Pat Eddery	R Hannon	Speedlith Group	Statue Of Liberty	Norse Dancer	01:40.0
2004	Soviet Song (4f)	J P Murtagh	J Fanshawe	Elite Racing Club	Nayyir	Le Vie dei Colori	01:37.0
2005	Proclamation (3)	M J Kinane	J Noseda	PrincessHayaOfJordan	Soviet Song	Ad Valorem	01:40.2
2006	Court Masterpiece (6)	J Fortune	EDunlop	Gainsborough Stud	Soviet Song	Rob Roy	01:36.1
2007	Ramonti (5)	L Dettori	S bin Suroor	Godolphin	Excellent Art	Jeremy	01:37.3

2000 GUINEAS STAKES-G1
1 mile, 3-year-old colts & fillies, Newmarket (Rowley Mile Course)
First run in 1809

Year	1st	Jockey	Trainer	Owner	2nd	3rd	Time
1988	Doyoun	W R Swinburn	M Stoute	Aga Khan	Charmer	Bellefella	01:41.7
1989	Nashwan	W Carson	W R Hern	H Al Maktoum	Exbourne	Danehill	01:36.4
1990	Tirol	M J Kinane	R Hannon	J Horgan	Machiavellian	Anshan	01:35.8
1991	Mystiko	M Roberts	C Brittain	Lady Beaverbrook	Lycius	Ganges	01:37.8
1992	Rodrigo de Triano	L Piggott	P Chapple-Hyam	R Sangster	Lucky Lindy	Pursuit Of Love	01:38.4
1993	Zafonic	Pat Eddery	A Fabre	K Abdullah	Barathea	Bin Ajwaad	01:35.3
1994	Mister Baileys	J Weaver	M Johnston	G R Bailey Ltd	Grand Lodge	Colonel Collins	01:35.1
1995	Pennekamp	T Jarnet	A Fabre	Sheikh Mohammed	Celtic Swing	Bahri	01:35.2
1996	Mark Of Esteem	L Dettori	S bin Suroor	Godolphin	Even Top	Bijou d'Inde	01:37.6
1997	Entrepreneur	M J Kinane	M Stoute	Tabor & Magnier	Revoque	Poteen	01:35.6
1998	King Of Kings	M J Kinane	A P O'Brien	Tabor & Magnier	Lend A Hand	Border Arrow	01:39.3
1999*	Island Sands	L Dettori	S bin Suroor	Godolphin	Enrique	Mujahid	01:37.1
2000	Kings Best	K Fallon	M Stoute	S Suhail	Giants Causeway	Barathea Guest	01:37.8
2001	Golan	K Fallon	M Stoute	Lord Weinstock	Tamburlaine	Frenchmans Bay	01:37.5
2002	Rock Of Gibraltar	J P Murtagh	A P O'Brien	Ferguson & Magnier	Hawk Wing	Redback	01:36.5
2003	Refuse To Bend	P J Smullen	D K Weld	Moyglare Stud Farm	Zafeen	Norse Dancer	01:38.0
2004	Haafhd	R Hills	B Hills	H Al Maktoum	Snow Ridge	Azamour	01:36.6
2005	Footstepsinthesand	K Fallon	A P O>Brien	M Tabor/Mrs J Magnier	Rebel Rebel	Kandidate	01:36.1
2006	George Washington	K Fallon	A P O>Brien	Magnier,Tabor & Smith	Sir Percy	Olympian Oddyssey	01:36.9
2007	Cockney Rebel	O Peslier	G Huffer	Phil Cunningham	Vital Equine	Dutch Art	01:35.3

* Run on the July Course

France

CRITERIUM DE SAINT-CLOUD-G1

2000 meters (1¼ miles), 2-year-old colts & fillies, Saint-Cloud

Year	1st	Jockey	Trainer	Owner	2nd	3rd	Time
1988	Miserden	Pat Eddery	A Fabre	K Abdullah	Louis Cyphre	Plein d'Esprit	02:16.4
1989	*Intimiste	G Mosse	F Boutin	I della Rochetta	Snurge	Guiza	02:19.3
1990	Pistolet Bleu	D Boeuf	E Lellouche	D Wildenstein	Pigeon Voyageur	Fortune's Wheel	02:17.8
1991	Glaieul	D Boeuf	E Lellouche	D Wildenstein	Calling Collect	Contested Bid	02:20.3
1992	Marchand de Sable	D Boeuf	E Lellouche	L De Angeli	Infrasonic	Arinthod	02:19.4
1993	Sunshack	T Jarnet	A Fabre	K Abdullah	Zindari	Tikkanen	02:15.2
1994	Poliglote	F Head	C Head	J Wertheimer	Solar One	Highest Cafe	02:19.4
1995	Polaris Flight	J Reid	P Chapple-Hyam	R Kaster	Ragmar	Oliviero	02:13.7
1996	Shaka	J-R Dubosc	J-C Rouget	R Bousquet	Daylami	Sendoro	02:15.8
1997	Special Quest	O Doleuze	C Head	Wertheimer & Frere	Asakir	Daymarti	02:11.9
1998	Spadoun	D Boeuf	C Laffon-Parias	J Gonzalez	Bienamado	Cupid	02:21.5
1999	Goldamix (f)	D Boeuf	C Laffon-Parias	Wertheimer & Frere	Petroselli	Cosmographe	02:15.7
2000	Sagacity	O Peslier	A Fabre	J-L Lagardere	Reduit	Sligo Bay	02:17.8
2001	Ballingarry	J P Spencer	A P O'Brien	Magnier & Tabor	Castle Gandolfo	Black Sam Bellamy	02:24.6
2002	Alberto Giacometti	M J Kinane	A P O'Brien	Mrs J Magnier	Summerland	Marshall	02:25.9
2003	Voix du Nord	D Boeuf	D Smaga	Zuylen de Nyevelt	Simplex	Day or Night	02:16.0
2004	Paita (f)	A Suborics	Mario Hofer	Manfred Hofer	Yehudi	Laverock	02:19.0
2005	Linda's Lad	C Soumillon	A Fabre	S Mulryan	Fauvelia	Flashing Numbers	02:23.3
2006	Passage of Time (f)	R Hughes	H Cecil	K Abdullah	Soldier of Fortune	Empire Day	02:08.9
2007	Full of Gold	T Gillet	C Head-Maarek	Alec Head	Hannouma	Putney Bridge	02:18.1

* Snurge finished first but was disqualified and placed second.

PRIX JEAN-LUC LAGARDERE-G1

1400 meters (7 furlongs), 2-year-old colts & fillies, Longchamp
Run at 1600 meters (1 mile) through 2000
Run as the Grand Criterium through 2002

Year	1st	Jockey	Trainer	Owner	2nd	3rd	Time
1988	Kendor	M Phillipperon	R Touflan	A Bader	Along All	Ecossais	01:40.8
1989	Jade Robbery	C Asmussen	A Fabre	Z Yoshida	Linamix	Honor Rajana	01:40.6
1990	Hector Protector	F Head	F Boutin	S Niarchos	Masterclass	Beau Sultan	01:41.1
1991	Arazi	G Mosse	F Boutin	A E Paulson	Rainbow Corner	Seattle Rhyme	01:41.4
1992	Tenby	Pat Eddery	H Cecil	K Abdullah	Blush Rambler	Basim	01:46.9
1993	Lost World	O Peslier	E Lellouche	D Wildenstein	Signe Divin	Psychobabble	01:45.9
1994	Goldmark	S Guillot	A Fabre	Sheikh Mohammed	Walk on Mix	Montjoy	01:43.4
1995	Loup Solitaire	O Peslier	A Fabre	D Wildenstein	Manninamix	Eternity Range	01:37.6
1996	Revoque	J Reid	P Chapple-Hyam	R Sangster	Majorien	King Sound	01:37.7
1997	Second Empire	M J Kinane	A P O'Brien	Tabor & Magnier	Charge d'Affaires	Alboostan	01:47.8
1998	Way of Light	C Asmussen	P Bary	Niarchos Family	Red Sea	Glamis	01:52.5
1999	Ciro*	M J Kinane	A P O'Brien	Tabor & Magnier	Barathea Guest	Ocean of Wisdom	01:50.5
2000	Okawango	O Doleuze	C Head	Wertheimer & Frere	Kings County	Honours List	01:41.6
2001	Rock Of Gibraltar	M J Kinane	A P O'Brien	Ferguson & Magnier	Bernebeau	Dobby Road	01:23.0
2002	Hold That Tiger	K Fallon	A P O'Brien	Tabor & Magnier	Le Vie dei Colori	Intercontinental	01:20.4
2003	American Post	R Hughes	C Head-Maarek	K Abdullah	Charming Prince	Ximb	01:24.5
2004	Oratorio	J P Spencer	A P O'Brien	Magnier & Tabor	Early March	Layman	01:19.3

Year	1st	Jockey	Trainer	Owner	2nd	3rd	Time
2005	Horatio Nelson	K Fallon	A P O'Brien	Magnier & Nagle	Opera Cape	Mauralakana	1;20.60
2006	Holy Roman Emperor	K Fallon	A P O'Brien	Mrs J Magnier	Battle Paint	Vital Equine	01:18.6
2007	Rio de la Plata	L Dettori	S bin Suroor	Godolphin	Declaration of War	Shediak	01:21.5

* Barathea Guest finished first but was disqualified and placed second.

GRAND PRIX DE PARIS-G1

2400 meters (1½ miles), 3-year-old colts & fillies, Longchamp

First run in 1863

Run at 3000 meters (1⅞ miles) through 1986

Run at 2000 meters (1¼ miles) from 1987 to 2004

Year	1st	Jockey	Trainer	Owner	2nd	3rd	Time
1988	Fijar Tango	A Cruz	G Mikhalides	M Fustok	Pasakos	Welkin	02:05.8
1989	Dancehall	C Asmussen	A Fabre	T Wada	Norberto	Creator	02:03.6
1990	Saumarez	S Cauthen	N Clement	B McNall	Priolo	Tirol	02:07.5
1991	Subotica	T Jarnet	A Fabre	O Lecerf	Sillery	Kotashaan	02:05.2
1992	Homme de Loi	T Jarnet	A Fabre	P de Moussac	Kitwood	Guislaine	02:03.9
1993	Fort Wood	S Guillot	A Fabre	Sheikh Mohammed	Bigstone	Siam	02:01.6
1994	Millkom	J-R Dubosc	J-C Rouget	J-C Gour	Solid Illusion	Celtic Arms	02:04.4
1995	Valanour	G Mosse	A de Royer-Dupre	Aga Khan	Singspiel	Diamond Mix	02:02.2
1996	Grape Tree Road	T Jarnet	A Fabre	M Tabor	Glory of Dancer	Android	02:02.3
1997	Peintre Celebre	O Peslier	A Fabre	D Wildenstein	Ithaki	Shaka	02:08.4
1998	Limpid	O Peslier	A Fabre	Sheikh Mohammed	Almutawakel	Croco Rouge	02:03.2
1999	Slickly	T Jarnet	A Fabre	J-L Lagardere	Indian Danehill	Sardaukar	02:03.9
2000	Beat Hollow	T R Quinn	H Cecil	K Abdullah	Premier Pas	Rhenium	02:03.7
2001	Chichicastenango	A Junk	P Demercastel	Mme B Brunet	Mizzen Mast	Bonnard	02:01.0
2002	Khalkevi	C Soumillon	A de Royer-Dupre	HH Aga Khan	Shaanmer	WithoutConnexion	02:02.4
2003	Vespone	C-P Lemaire	N Clement	Ecurie Mister Ess A S	Magistretti	Look Honey	02:01.1
2004	Bago	T Gillet	J Pease	Niarchos Family	Cacique	Alnitak	02:05.6
2005	Scorpion	K Fallon	A P O'Brien	Mrs J Magnier	Desideratum	Orion Star	02:24.3
2006	Rail Link	C Soumillon	A Fabre	K Abdullah	Red Rocks	Sudan	02:26.4
2007	Zambezi Sun	S Pasquier	P Bary	K Abdullah	Axxos	Sagara	02:31.6

GRAND PRIX DE SAINT-CLOUD-G1

2400 meters (1½ miles), 4-year-olds & up, colts & fillies, Saint-Cloud

Run for 3-year-olds & up, colts & fillies, through 2004

First run in 1903

Year	1st (Age)	Jockey	Trainer	Owner	2nd	3rd	Time
1988	Village Star (5)	C Asmussen	A Fabre	A J Richards	Saint Andrews	Frankly Perfect	02:36.3
1989	Sheriff's Star (4)	T Ives	Lady Herries	Duchess of Norfolk	Golden Pheasant	Boyatino	02:35.8
1990	In the Wings (4)	C Asmussen	A Fabre	Sheikh Mohammed	Ode	Zartota	02:29.6
1991	Epervier Bleu (4)	D Boeuf	E Lellouche	D Wildenstein	Rock Hopper	Passing Sale	02:28.1
1992	Pistolet Bleu (4)	D Boeuf	E Lellouche	D Wildenstein	Magic Night	Subotica	02:30.3
1993	User Friendly (4f)	G Duffield	C Brittain	W Gredley	Apple Tree	Modhish	02:28.5
1994	Apple Tree (5)	T Jarnet	A Fabre	Sultan Al Kabeer	Muhtarram	Zimzalabim	2:30
1995	Carnegie (4)	T Jarnet	A Fabre	Sheikh Mohammed	Luso	Only Royale	02:35.2

Year	1st (Age)	Jockey	Trainer	Owner	2nd	3rd	Time
1996	Helissio (3)	O Peslier	E Lellouche	E Sarasola	Swain	Poliglote	02:27.4
1997	Helissio (4)	C Asmussen	E Lellouche	E Sarasola	Magellano	Riyadian	02:29.5
1998	Fragrant Mix (4)	O Peslier	A Fabre	J-L Lagardere	Romanov	Gazelle Royale	02:31.3
1999	El Condor Pasa (4)	M Ebina	Y Ninomiya	T Watanabe	Tiger Hill	Dream Well	02:28.8
2000	Montjeu (4)	C Asmussen	J Hammond	M Tabor	Daring Miss	Sagamix	02:31.4
2001	Mirio (4)	C Soumillon	J de Choubersky	E Soderberg	Perfect Sunday	Egyptband	02:29.3
2002	Ange Gabriel (4)	T Jarnet	E Libaud	Mme H Devin	Polish Summer	Aquarelliste	02:28.6
2003	Ange Gabriel (5)	T Jarnet	E Libaud	Mme H Devin	Polish Summer	Loxias	02:30.9
2004	Gamut (5)	K Fallon	M R Stoute	Mrs G Smith	Policy Maker	Visorama	02:36.1
2005	Alkaased (5)	L Dettori	L Cumani	M Charlton	Policy Maker	Bago	02:31.3
2006	Pride (6m)	C-P Lemaire	A de Royer-Dupre	qNP Bloodstock Ltd	Hurricane Run	Laverock	02:35.9
2007	Mountain High (5)	K Fallon	M R Stoute	Magnier & Tabor	Mandesha	Prince Flori	02:29.7

POULE D'ESSAI DES POULAINS (French 2000 Guineas)-G1
1600 meters (1 mile), 3-year-old colts, Longchamp
First run in 1883

Year	1st	Jockey	Trainer	Owner	2nd	3rd	Time
1988	Blushing John	F Head	F Boutin	A E Paulson	French Stress	Tay Wharf	01:37.2
1989	Kendor	M Philipperon	R Touflan	A Bader	Goldneyev	Ocean Falls	01:36.1
1990	Linamix	F Head	F Boutin	J-L Lagardere	Zoman	Funambule	01:35.9
1991	Hector Protector	F Head	F Boutin	S Niarchos	Acteur	Francais Sapieha	01:37.6
1992	Shanghai	F Head	F Boutin	S Niarchos	Rainbow Corner	Lion Cavern	01:38.2
1993	Kingmambo	C Asmussen	F Boutin	S Niarchos	Bin Ajwaad	Hudo	01:39.1
1994	Green Tune	O Doleuze	C Head	J Wertheimer	Turtle Island	Psychobabble	01:37.4
1995	Vettori	L Dettori	S bin Suroor	Godolphin	Atticus	Petit Poucet	01:40.4
1996	Ashkalani	G Mosse	A de Royer-Dupre	Aga Khan	Spinning World	Tagula	01:37.6
1997	Daylami	G Mosse	A de Royer-Dupre	Aga Khan	Loup Sauvage	Visionary	01:42.6
1998	Victory Note	J Reid	P Chapple-Hyam	Magnier & Sangster	Muhtathir	Desert Prince	01:34.5
1999	Sendawar	G Mosse	A de Royer-Dupre	Aga Khan	Dansili	Kingsalsa	01:36.2
2000	Bachir	L Dettori	S bin Suroor	Godolphin	Beriness Son	Valentino	01:39.4
2001*	Vahorimix	C Soumillon	A Fabre	J-L Lagardere	Clearing	Denon	01:35.4
2002	Landseer	M J Kinane	A P O'Brien	Tabor & Magnier	Medecis	Bowman	01:36.8
2003	Clodovil	C Soumillon	A Fabre	Famille Lagardere	Catcher In The Rye	Krataios	01:36.4
2004	American Post	R Hughes	C Head-Maarek	K Abdullah	Diamond Green	Byron	01:36.5
2005	Shamardal	L Dettori	S bin Suroor	Godolphin	Indesatchel	Gharir	01:39.2
2006	Aussie Rules	K Fallon	A P O'Brien	Magnier,Tabor,Salman	Marcus Andronicus	Stormy River	01:37.0
2007	Astronomer Royal	C O'Donoghue	A P O'Brien	Derrick Smith	Creachadoir	Honoured Guest	01:37.1

* Noverre finished first but was disqualified from purse money

POULE D'ESSAI DES POULICHES (French 1000 Guineas)-G1
1600 meters (1 mile), 3-year-old fillies, Longchamp
First run in 1883

Year	1st	Jockey	Trainer	Owner	2nd	3rd	Time
1988	Ravinella	G Moore	C Head	Ecurie Aland	Duckling Park	Sacre Look	01:38.3
1989	Pearl Bracelet	A Gibert	R Wojtowiez	Ecurie Fustok	Pass the Peace	Golden Opinion	01:37.1
1990	Houseproud	Pat Eddery	A Fabre	K Abdullah	Pont Aven	Gharam	01:38.5

Year	1st	Jockey	Trainer	Owner	2nd	3rd	Time
1991	Danseuse du Soir	D Boeuf	E Lellouche	D Wildenstein	Sha-Tha	Caerlina	01:38.6
1992	Culture Vulture	T R Quinn	P Cole	C Wright	Hydro Calido	Guislaine	01:37.0
1993	Madeleine's Dream	C Asmussen	F Boutin	A E Paulson	Ski Paradise	Gold Splash	01:36.4
1994	East of the Moon	C Asmussen	F Boutin	S Niarchos	Agathe	Bella Argentine	01:37.1
1995	Matiara	F Head	C Head	Ecurie Aland	Carling	Shaanxi	01:42.4
1996	Ta Rib	W Carson	E Dunlop	H Al Maktoum	Shake the Yoke	Sagar Pride	01:38.7
1997	Always Loyal	F Head	C Head	M Al Maktoum	Seebe	Red Camellia	01:40.2
1998	Zalaiyka	G Mosse	A de Royer-Dupre	Aga Khan	Cortona	La Nuit Rose	01:35.7
1999	Valentine Waltz	R Cochrane	J Gosden	Kirby Maher Synd	Karmifira	Calando	01:36.0
2000	Bluemamba	S Guillot	P Bary	Ecurie Skymarc Farm	Peony	Alshakr	01:40.2
2001	Rose Gypsy	M J Kinane	A P O'Brien	Magnier & Tabor	Banks Hill	Lethals Lady	01:36.7
2002	Zenda	R Hughes	J Gosden	K Abdullah	Firth of Lorne	Sophisticat	01:37.0
2003	Musical Chimes	C Soumillon	A Fabre	M Al Maktoum	Maiden Tower	Etoile Montante	01:36.0
2004	Torrestrella	O Peslier	F Rohaut	B Bargues	Grey Lilas	Miss Mambo	01:35.7
2005	Divine Proportions	C-P Lemaire	P Bary	Niarchos Family	Toupie	Ysoldina	01:38.5
2006*	Tie Black	J-B Eyquem	F Rohaut	J Gispert	Impressionnante	Price Tag	01:36.6
2007	Darjina	C Soumillon	A de Royer-Dupre	PrincessZahraAgaKhan	Finsceal Beo	Rahiyah	01:37.2

* In 2006 Price Tag finished first but was disqualified and placed third.

PRIX DE DIANE (French Oaks)-G1
2100 meters (1⁵/₁₆ miles), 3-year-old fillies, Chantilly
First run in 1843

Year	1st	Jockey	Trainer	Owner	2nd	3rd	Time
1988	Resless Kara	G Mosse	F Boutin	J-L Lagardere	Riviere d'Or	Raintree Renegade	02:07.5
1989	Lady in Silver	A Cruz	R Wojtowiez	A Karim	Louveterie	Premier Amour	02:10.6
1990	Rafha	W Carson	H Cecil	Prince A Faisal	Moon Cactus	Air de Rien	02:11.7
1991	Caerlina	E Legrix	J de Roualle	K Nitta	Magic Night	Louve Romaine	02:10.5
1992	Jolypha	Pat Eddery	A Fabre	K Abdullah	Sheba Dancer	Verveine	02:09.5
1993	Shemaka	G Mosse	A de Royer-Dupre	Aga Khan	Baya	Dancienne	02:16.0
1994	East of the Moon	C Asmussen	F Boutin	S Niarchos	Her Ladyship	Agathe	02:07.9
1995	Carling	T Thulliez	C Barbe	Ecurie Delbart	Matiara	Tryphosa	02:07.7
1996	Sil Sila	C Asmussen	B Smart	L Alvarez-Cervera	Miss Tahiti	Matiya	02:07.3
1997	Vereva	G Mosse	A de Royer-Dupre	Aga Khan	Mousse Glace	Brilliance	02:08.2
1998	Zainta	G Mosse	A de Royer-Dupre	Aga Khan	Abbatiale	Insight	02:11.2
1999	Daryaba	G Mosse	A de Royer-Dupre	Aga Khan	Star of Akkar	Visionnaire	02:16.1
2000	Egyptband	O Doleuze	C Head	Wertheimer & Frere	Volvoreta	Goldamix	02:08.5
2001	Aquarelliste	D Boeuf	E Lellouche	D Wildenstein	Nadia	Time Away	02:09.5
2002	Bright Sky	D Boeuf	E Lellouche	Ecurie Wildenstein	Dance Routine	Ana Marie	02:07.6
2003	Nebraska Tornado	R Hughes	A Fabre	K Abdullah	Time Ahead	Musical Chimes	02:08.1
2004	Latice	C Soumillon	J-M Beguigne	E Ciampi	Millionaia	Grey Lilas	02:07.0
2005	Divine Proportions	C-P Lemaire	P Bary	Niarchos Family	Argentina	Paita	02:06.3
2006	Confidential Lady	S Sanders	M Prescott	Cheveley Park Stud	Germance	Queen Cleopatra	02:05.9
2007	West Wind	L Dettori	H-A Pantall	Sheikh Mohammed	Mrs. Lindsay	Diyakalanie	02:06.3

PRIX DE L'ABBAYE DE LONGCHAMP-GI

1000 meters (5 furlongs), 2-year-old & up, colts & fillies, Longchamp

Year	1st (Age)	Jockey	Trainer	Owner	2nd	3rd	Time
1988	Handsome Sailor (5)	M Hills	B Hills	R Sangster	Caerwent	Silver Fling	:57.00
1989	Silver Fling (4f)	J Matthias	I Balding	G Strawbridge	Zadracarta	Nabeel Dancer	:59.90
1990	Dayjur (3)	W Carson	W R Hern	H Al Maktoum	Lugana Beach	Pharaoh's Delight	:58.70
1991	Keen Hunter (4)	S Cauthen	J Gosden	Sheikh Mohammed	Sheikh Albadou	Magic Ring	:59.40
1992	Mr Brooks (5)	L Piggott	R Hannon	P C Greem	Keen Hunter	Elbio	01:02.3
1993	Lochsong (5f)	L Dettori	I Balding	J C Smith	Stack Rock	Monde Bleu	:59.70
1994	Lochsong (6f)	L Dettori	I Balding	J C Smith	Mistertopogigio	Spain Lane	:57.20
1995	Hever Golf Rose (4f)	J Weaver	T J Naughton	M Hanson	Cherokee Rose	Eveningperformance	:57.70
1996	Kistena (3f)	O Doleuze	C Head	Wertheimer & Frere	Anabaa	Hever Golf Rose	:59.30
1997	Carmine Lake (3f)	J Reid	P Chapple-Hyam	R Sangster	Pas de Reponse	Royal Applause	:56.90
1998	My Best Valentine(8)	R Cochrane	V Soane	The Valentines	Averti	Sainte Marine	:58.90
1999	Agnes World (4)	Y Take	H Mori	T Watanabe	Imperial Beauty	Keos	01:01.4
2000	Namid (4)	J P Murtagh	J Oxx	Lady Clague	Superstar Leo	Pipalong	:55.10
2001	Imperial Beauty (5f)	Y Take	J Hammond	Mrs J Magnier	Bahamian Pirate	Pipalong	:58.88
2002	Continent (5)	D Holland	D Nicholls	Lucayan Stud	Slap Shot	Zipping	:57.20
2003	Patavellian (5)	S Drowne	R Charlton	D J Deer	The Trader	The Tatling	:59.30
2004	Var (5)	L Dettori	C E Brittain	M Rashid	The Tatling	Royal Millennium	:55.00
2005	Avonbridge (5)	S Drowne	R Charlton	D J Deer	Striking Ambition	Fire Up The Band	:56.90
2006	Desert Lord (6)	J P Spencer	K Ryan	Bull & Bell Partnership	Reverence	Moss Vale	:54.80
2007	Benbaun (6)	P J Smullen	M Wallace	Ransley,Birks,Hillen	Kingsgate Native	Desert lord	:56.70

PRIX DE L'ARC DE TRIOMPHE-GI

2400 meters (1½ miles), 3-year-olds & up colts & fillies, Longchamp

First run in 1920

Year	1st (Age)	Jockey	Trainer	Owner	2nd	3rd	Time
1988	Tony Bin (5)	J Reid	L Camici	Mme V Gaucci del Bono	Mtoto	Boyatino	02:27.3
1989	Carroll House (4)	M J Kinane	M Jarvis	A Balzarini	Behera	Saint Andrews	02:30.8
1990	Saumarez (3)	G Mosse	N Clement	B McNall	Epervier Bleu	Snurge	02:29.8
1991	Suave Dancer (3)	C Asmussen	J Hammond	H Chalhoub	Magic Night	Pistolet Bleu	02:31.4
1992	Subotica (4)	T Jarnet	A Fabre	O Lecerf	User Friendly	Vert Amande	02:39.0
1993	Urban Sea (4f)	E Saint-Martin	J Lesbordes	D Tsui	White Muzzle	Opera House	02:37.9
1994	Carnegie (3)	T Jarnet	A Fabre	Sheikh Mohammed	Hernando	Apple Tree	02:31.1
1995	Lammtarra (3)	L Dettori	S bin Suroor	S M Al Maktoum	Freedom Cry	Swain	02:31.8
1996	Helissio (3)	O Peslier	E Lellouche	E Sarasola	Pilsudski	Oscar Schindler	02:29.9
1997	Peintre Celebre (3)	O Peslier	D Wildenstein	A Fabre	Pilsudski	Borgia	02:24.6
1998	Sagamix (3)	O Peslier	A Fabre	J-L Lagardere	Leggera	Tiger Hill	02:34.5
1999	Montjeu (3)	M J Kinane	J Hammond	M Tabor	El Condor Pasa	Croco Rouge	02:38.5
2000	Sinndar (3)	J P Murtagh	J Oxx	HH Aga Khan	Egyptband	Volvoreta	02:25.8
2001	Sakhee (4)	L Dettori	S bin Suroor	Godolphin	Aquarelliste	Sagacity	02:35.9
2002	Marienbard (5)	L Dettori	S bin Suroor	Godolphin	Sulamani	High Chaparral	02:26.7
2003	Dalakhani (3)	C Soumillon	A de Royer-Dupre	HH Aga Khan	Mubtaker	High Chaparral	02:32.3
2004	Bago (3)	T Gillet	J Pease	Niarchos Family	Cherry Mix	Ouija Board	02:25.0
2005	Hurricane Run (3)	K Fallon	A Fabre	M Tabor	Westerner	Bago	02:27.4
2006	Rail Link (3)	S Pasquier	A Fabre	K Abdullah	Pride	Hurricane Run	02:31.7
2007	Dylan Thomas (4)	K Fallon	A P O'Brien	Magnier & Tabor	Youmzain	Sagara	02:28.5

* Deep Impact finished third in 2006 but was disqualified and placed last

CRITERIUM INTERNATIONAL-GI

1600 meters (1 mile), 2-year-old colts & fillies, Saint-Cloud

Replaced the Prix de la Salamandre (7 furlongs, Longchamp) in 2001

Year	1st	Jockey	Trainer	Owner	2nd	3rd	Time
1988	Oczy Czarnie (f)	G Moore	J-M Beguigne	G de Rothschild	Kendor	Star Touch	01:25.0
1989	Machiavellian	F Head	F Boutin	S Niarchos	Qirmazi	Ernani	01:24.8
1990	Hector Protector	F Head	F Boutin	S Niarchos	Lycius	Booming	01:20.8
1991	Arazi	G Mosse	F Boutin	A E Paulson	Made of Gold	Silver Kite	01:20.9
1992	Zafonic	Pat Eddery	A Fabre	K Abdullah	Kingmambo	Splendent	01:23.3
1993	Coup de Genie (f)	C Asmussen	F Boutin	S Niarchos	Majestic Role	Volochine	01:23.1
1994	Pennekamp	T Jarnet	A Fabre	Sheikh Mohammed	Montjoy	Bin Nashwan	01:22.9
1995	Lord Of Men	L Dettori	J Gosden	Sheikh Mohammed	With Fascination	Woodborough	01:27.0
1996	Revoque	J Reid	P Chapple-Hyam	R Sangster	The West	Zamindar	01:20.9
1997	Xaar	O Peslier	A Fabre	K Abdullah	Charge d'Affaires	Speedfit Too	01:21.6
1998	Aljabr	L Dettori	S bin Suroor	Godolphin	Kingsalsa	Zirconi	01:24.0
1999	Giant's Causeway	M J Kinane	A O'Brien	Tabor & Magnier	Race Leader	Bachir	01:22.9
2000	Tobougg	C Williams	M Channon	Ahmed Al Maktoum	Honours List	Wooden Doll	01:22.2
2001	Act One	T Gillet	J Pease	G W Leigh	Landseer	Guys And Dolls	01:47.1
2002	Dalakhani	C Soumillon	A de Royer-Dupre	HH Aga Khan	Chevalier	Governor Brown	01:52.0
2003	Bago	T Gillet	J Pease	Niarchos Family	Top Seed	Acropolis	01:47.0
2004	Helios Quercus	A Roussel	C Diard	T Maudet	Dubai Surprise	Walk in the Park	01:45.3
2005	Carlotamix	C Soumillon	A Fabre	H H Aga Khan	Stormy River	Porto Santo	01:45.4
2006	Mount Nelson	J A Heffernan	A P O'Brien	Smith,Tabor & Magnier	Spirit One	Yellowstone	01:41.3
2007	Thewayyouare	S Pasquier	A Fabre	Sean Mulryan	Hello Morning	Redolent	01:45.3

PRIX DU JOCKEY-CLUB (French Derby)-GI

2100 meters (1 5/16 miles), 3-year-old colts & fillies, Chantilly

Run at 2400 meters (1 ½ miles), 3-year-old colts & fillies through 2004

First run in 1836

Year	1st	Jockey	Trainer	Owner	2nd	3rd	Time
1988	Hours After	Pat Eddery	P-L Biancone	Marquise de Moratalla	Ghost Buster's	Emmson	02:33.4
1989	Old Vic	S Cauthen	H Cecil	Sheikh Mohammed	Dancehall	Galetto	02:28.7
1990	Sanglamore	Pat Eddery	R Charlton	K Abdullah	Epervier Bleu	Erdelistan	02:24.6
1991	Suave Dancer	C Asmussen	J Hammond	H Chalhoub	Subotica	Cudas	02:27.4
1992	Polytain	L Dettori	A Spanu	Mme Houillion	Marignan	Contested Bid	02:30.3
1993	Hernando	C Asmussen	F Boutin	S Niarchos	Dernier Empereur	Hunting Hawk	02:27.2
1994	Celtic Arms	G Mosse	P Bary	J-L Bouchard	Solid Illusion	Alriffa	02:31.3
1995	Celtic Swing	K Darley	Lady Herries	P Savill	Poliglote	Winged Love	02:32.8
1996	Ragmar	G Mosse	P Bary	J-L Bouchard	Polaris Flight	Le Destin	02:27.2
1997	Peintre Celebre	O Peslier	A Fabre	D Wildenstein	Oscar	Astarabad	02:29.6
1998	Dream Well	C Asmussen	P Bary	Niarchos Family	Croco Rouge	Sestino	02:39.3
1999	Montjeu	C Asmussen	J Hammond	M Tabor	Nowhere to Exit	Rhagaas	02:33.5
2000	Holding Court	P Robinson	M Jarvis	J R Good	Lord Flasheart	Circus Dance	02:31.8
2001	Anabaa Blue	C Soumillon	C Lerner	C Mimouni	Chichicastenango	Grandera	02:27.9
2002	Sulamani	T Thulliez	P Bary	Niarchos Family	Act One	Simeon	02:25.0
2003	Dalakhani	C Soumillon	A de Royer-Dupre	HH Aga Khan	Super Celebre	Coroner	02:26.7
2004	Blue Canari	T Thulliez	P Bary	Jean-Louis Bouchard	Prospect Park	Valixir	02:25.2
2005	Shamardal	L Dettori	S bin Suroor	Godolphin	Hurricane Run	Rocamadour	02:09.0
2006	Darsi	C Soumillon	A de Royer-Dupre	HH Aga Khan	Best Name	Arras	02:05.8
2007	Lawman	L Dettori	J-M Beguigne	C Marzocco	Literato	Shamdinan	02:05.9

PRIX DU MOULIN DE LONGCHAMP-G1

1600 meters (1 mile), 3-year-olds & up, colts & fillies, Longchamp

Year	1st (Age)	Jockey	Trainer	Owner	2nd	3rd	Time
1988	Soviet Star (4)	C Asmussen	A Fabre	Sheikh Mohammed	Miesque	Gabina	01:40.3
1989	Polish Precedent (3)	C Asmussen	A Fabre	Sheikh Mohammed	Squill	Cadeaux Genereux	01:38.5
1990	Distant Relative (4)	Pat Eddery	W Said	B Hills	Linamix	Priolo	01:38.4
1991	Priolo (4)	G Mosse	F Boutin	Ecurie Skymarc Farm	Mukaddamah	Lycius	01:38.4
1992	All At Sea (3f)	Pat Eddery	H Cecil	K Abdullah	Brief Truce	Hatoof	01:40.7
1993	Kingmambo (3)	C Asmussen	S Niarchos	F Boutin	Ski Paradise	Bigstone	01:37.6
1994	Ski Paradise (4f)	Y Take	A Fabre	T Yoshida	East of the Moon	Green Tune	01:37.8
1995	Ridgewood Pearl (3f)	J P Murtagh	J Oxx	A Coughlan	Shaanxi	Missed Flight	01:36.9
1996	Ashkalani (3)	G Mosse	A de Royer-Dupre	Aga Khan	Spinning World	Shake the Yoke	01:37.2
1997	Spinning World (4)	C Asmussen	J Pease	Niarchos Family	Helissio	Daylami	01:37.1
1998	Desert Prince (3)	O Peslier	D Loder	Lucayan Stud	Gold Away	Second Empire	01:40.9
1999	Sendawar (3)	G Mosse	A de Royer-Dupre	Aga Khan	Gold Away	Dansili	01:35.2
2000	Indian Lodge (4)	C Asmussen	A Perrett	S Cohn & E Parker	Kingsalsa	Diktat	01:40.8
2001	Slickly (5)	L Dettori	S bin Suroor	Godolphin	Banks Hill	Hawkeye	01:39.0
2002	Rock Of Gibraltar (3)	M J Kinane	A P O'Brien	Ferguson & Magnier	Banks Hill	Gossamer	01:39.3
2003	Nebraska Tornado(3f)	R Hughes	A Fabre	K Abdullah	Lohengrin	Bright Sky	01:38.7
2004	Grey Lilas (3f)	E Legrix	A Fabre	Gestut Amerland	Diamond Green	Antonius Pius	01:37.5
2005	Starcraft (5)	C-P Lemaire	L Cumani	Australian Syndicate	Gorella	Majors Cast	01:36.1
2006	Librettist (4)	L Dettori	S bin Suroor	Godolphin	Stormy River	Manduro	01:38.1
2007	Darjina (3f)	C Soumillon	A de Royer-Dupre	PrincessZahraAgaKhan	Ramonti	GeorgeWashington	01:36.8

PRIX GANAY-G1

2100 meters (1⁵⁄₁₆ miles), 4-year-olds & up, colts & fillies, Longchamp

Year	1st (Age)	Jockey	Trainer	Owner	2nd	3rd	Time
1988	Saint Andrews (4)	A Badel	J-M Beguigne	Mme Volterra	Grand Fleuve	Triptych	
1989	Saint Andrews (5)	A Badel	J-M Beguigne	Mme Volterra	Star Lift	Mansonnien	02:20.8
1990	Creator (4)	C Asmussen	A Fabre	Sheikh Mohammed	In the Wings	Ibn Bey	2:13
1991	Kartajana (4f)	W Mongil	A de Royer-Dupre	Aga Khan	Passing Sale	Dear Doctor	02:18.4
1992	Subotica (4)	T Jarnet	A Fabre	O Lecerf	Pistolet Bleu	Suave Dancer	02:09.3
1993	Vert Amande (5)	D Boeuf	E Lellouche	E Sarasola	Opera House	Misil	02:02.1
1994	Marildo (7)	G Guignard	D Smaga	D Smaga	Intrepidity	Urban Sea	02:11.9
1995	Pelder (5)	L Dettori	P Kelleway	O Pedroni	Alderbrook	Richard of York	02:20.7
1996	Valanour (4)	G Mosse	A de Royer-Dupre	Aga Khan	Luso	Swain	02:10.9
1997	Helissio (4)	O Peslier	E Lellouche	E Sarasola	Le Destin	Pilsudski	02:12.1
1998	Astarabad (4)	G Mosse	A de Royer-Dupre	Aga Khan	Que Belle	Taipan	02:21.5
1999	Dark Moondancer (4)	G Mosse	A de Royer-Dupre	B Arbib	Dream Well	Croco Rouge	02:11.3
2000	Indian Danehill (4)	O Peslier	A Fabre	Baron E de Rothschild	Greek Dance	Chelsea Manor	02:27.2
2001	Golden Snake (5)	Pat Eddery	J Dunlop	The National Stud	Egyptband	With the Flow	02:16.7
2002	Aquarelliste (4f)	D Boeuf	E Lellouche	Ecurie Wildenstein	Execute	Sensible	02:11.4
2003	Fair Mix (5)	O Peslier	M Rolland	Ecurie Week-End	Execute	Falbrav	02:13.0
2004	Execute (7)	T Gillet	J Hammond	Ecurie Chalhoub	Vespone	Fair Mix	02:14.6
2005	Bago (4)	T Gillet	J Pease	Niarchos Family	Reefscape	Ace	02:17.7
2006	Corre Caminos (4)	T Jarnet	M Delzangles	Marquise de Moratalla	Royal Highness	Manduro	02:17.1
2007	Dylan Thomas (4)	C Soumillon	A P O'Brien	Magnier & Tabor	Irish Wells	Doctor Dino	02:07.9

PRIX JACQUES LE MAROIS-G1

1600 meters (1 mile), 3-year-olds & up, colts & fillies, Deauville

Year	1st (Age)	Jockey	Trainer	Owner	2nd	3rd	Time
1988	Miesque (4f)	F Head	F Boutin	S Niarchos	Warning	Gabina	01:38.6
1989	Polish Precedent (3	C Asmussen	A Fabre	Sheikh Mohammed	French Stress	Magic Gleam	01:37.3
1990	Priolo (3)	A Lequeux	F Boutin	Ecurie Skymarc Farm	Linamix	Distant Relative	01:38.2
1991	Hector Protector (3)	F Head	F Boutin	S Niarchos	Lycius	Danseuse du Soir	01:39.4
1992	Exit to Nowhere (4)	C Asmussen	F Boutin	S Niarchos	Lahib	Cardoun	01:40.8
1993	Sayyedati (3f)	W Swinburn	C Brittain	M Obaida	Ski Paradise	Kingmambo	01:39.8
1994	East of the Moon (3f)	C Asmussen	F Boutin	S Niarchos	Sayyedati	Mehthaaf	01:35.7
1995	Miss Satamixa (3f)	S Guillot	A Fabre	J-L Lagardere	Sayyedati	Shaanxi	01:35.7
1996	Spinning World (3)	C Asmussen	J Pease	Niarchos Family	Vetheuil	Shaanxi	01:39.1
1997	Spinning World (4)	C Asmussen	J Pease	Niarchos Family	Daylami	Neuilly	01:34.4
1998	Taiki Shuttle (4)	Y Okabe	K Fujisawa	Taiki Farm Inc	Among Men	Cape Cross	01:37.4
1999	Dubai Millennium (3)	L Dettori	S bin Suroor	Godolphin	Slickly	Dansili	01:44.3
2000	Muhtathir (5)	L Dettori	S bin Suroor	Godolphin	Sendawar	Kingsalsa	01:34.6
2001*	Vahorimix (3)	O Peslier	A Fabre	J-L Lagardere	Banks Hill	Noverre	01:38.8
2002	Banks Hill (4f)	O Peslier	A Fabre	K Abdullah	Domedriver	Best Of The Bests	01:35.2
2003	Six Perfections (3f)	T Thulliez	P Bary	Niarchos Family	Domedriver	Telegnosis	01:38.3
2004	Whipper (3)	C Soumillon	Robert Collet	R C Strauss	Six Perfections	My Risk	01:38.4
2005	Dubawi (3)	K McEvoy	S bin Suroor	Godolphin	Whipper	Valixir	01:37.1
2006	Librettist (4)	L Dettori	S bin Suroor	Godolphin	Manduro	Peeress	01:43.1
2007	Manduro (5)	S Pasquier	A Fabre	Baron G von Ullmann	Holocene	Turtle Bowl	01:37.4

PRIX MARCEL BOUSSAC-G1

1600 meters (1 mile), 2-year-old fillies, Longchamp

Year	1st	Jockey	Trainer	Owner	2nd	3rd	Time
1988	Mary Linoa	A Lequeux	D Smaga	D Smaga	Rose de Crystal	Reine du Ciel	01:41.2
1989	Salsabil	W Carson	J Dunlop	H Al Maktoum	Houseproud	Alchi	01:40.3
1990	Shadayid	W Carson	J Dunlop	H Al Maktoum	Caerlina	Sha-Tha	01:40.7
1991	Culture Vulture	T R Quinn	P Cole	C Wright	Hatoof	Verveine	01:40.6
1992	Gold Splash	G Mosse	C Head	J Wertheimer	Kindergarten	Love of Silver	01:44.9
1993	Sierra Madre	G Mosse	P Bary	J-L Bouchard	Flagbird	Mehthaaf	01:45.4
1994	Macoumba	F Head	C Head	Haras d'Etreham	Piquetnol	Chrysalu	01:43.8
1995	Miss Tahiti	O Peslier	A Fabre	D Wildenstein	Shake the Yoke	Solar Crystal	01:40.2
1996	Ryafan	L Dettori	J Gosden	K Abdullah	Yashmak	Family Tradition	01:39.8
1997	Loving Claim	O Doleuze	C Head	M Al Maktoum	Isle de France	Plaisir des Yeux	01:37.6
1998	Juvenia	O Doleuze	C Head	Wertheimer & Frere	Crystal Downs	Blue Cloud	01:43.0
1999	Lady of Chad	O Peslier	R Gibson	J D Martin	New Story	Lady Vettori	01:44.9
2000	Amonita	T Jarnet	P Bary	Mme P de Moussac	Karasta	Choc Ice	01:36.3
2001	Sulk	L Dettori	J Gosden	J Wigan	Danseuse d'Etoile	Kournakova	01:42.0
2002	Six Perfections	T Thulliez	P Bary	Niarchos Family	Etoile Montante	Luminata	01:37.9
2003	Denebola	C-P Lemaire	P Bary	Niarchos Family	Green Noon	Tulipe Royale	01:40.9
2004	Divine Proportions	C-P Lemaire	P Bary	Niarchos Family	Titian Time	Fraloga	01:36.7
2005	Rumplestiltskin	K Fallon	A P OₕBrien	Mrs J Magnier	M TaborQuiet Royal	Deveron	01:37.3
2006	Finsceal Beo	K J Manning	J S Bolger	M A Ryan	Darrfonah	Legerete	01:34.9
2007	Zarkava	C Soumillon	A de Royer-Dupre	H H Aga Khan	Conference Call	Mad About You	01:37.0

PRIX MORNY-GI

1200 meters (6 furlongs), 2-year-old colts & fillies, Deauville

Year	1st	Jockey	Trainer	Owner	2nd	3rd	Time
1988	Tersa (f)	G Mosse	F Boutin	Ecossais	A E Paulson	Money Movers	01:15.6
1989	Machiavellian	F Head	F Boutin	S Niarchos	Qirmazi	Mill Lady	01:12.8
1990	Hector Protector	F Head	F Boutin	S Niarchos	Divine Danse	Acteur Francais	01:14.4
1991	Arazi	G Mosse	F Boutin	A E Paulson	Kenbu	Lion Cavern	01:13.3
1992	Zafonic	Pat Eddery	A Fabre	K Abdullah	Secrage	Marina Park	01:14.8
1993	Coup de Genie (f)	C Asmussen	F Boutin	S Niarchos	Psychobabble	Spain Lane	01:13.1
1994	Hoh Magic (f)	M Hills	M Bell	D Allport	Bruttina	Tereshkova	01:11.7
1995	Tagula	W R Swinburn	I Balding	Mr & Mrs R Hitchens	With Fascination	Barricade	01:11.6
1996	Bahamian Bounty	L Dettori	D Loder	Lucayan Stud Ltd	Zamindar	Pas de Reponse	01:11.0
1997	Charge d'Affaires	G Mosse	A de Royer-Dupre	Marquise de Moratalla	Xaar	Heeremandi	01:12.7
1998	Orpen	M J Kinane	A P O'Brien	Tabor & Magnier	Exeat	Golden Silca	01:10.5
1999	Fasliyev	M J Kinane	A P O'Brien	Tabor & Magnier	Warm Heart	Bachir	01:11.0
2000	Bad As I Wanna Be	G Mosse	B Meehan	J Allbritton	Endless Summer	Noverre	01:10.3
2001	Johannesburg	M J Kinane	A P O'Brien	Tabor & Magnier	Zipping	Meshaheer	01:10.4
2002	Elusive City	K Fallon	G Butler	Thoroughbred Corp	Zafeen	Loving Kindness	01:10.4
2003	Whipper	S Maillot	Robert Collet	E Zaccour	Much Faster	Denebola	01:14.0
2004	Divine Proportions(f)	C-P Lemaire	P Bary	Niarchos Family	Layman	Russian Blue	01:12.8
2005	Silca's Sister (f)	T E Durcan	M Channon	Aldridge Racing Ltd	Ivan Denisovich	Always Hopeful	01:12.0
2006	Dutch Art	C Soumillon	P Chapple-Hyam	Susan Roy	Magic America	Excellent Art	01:13.6
2007	Myboycharlie	K Fallon	T Stack	Mrs J Magnier	Natagora	Alexandros	01:13.1

PRIX VERMEILLE-GI

2400 meters (1½ miles), 3-year-olds & up, fillies & mares, Longchamp
(3 & 4-year-old fillies, 2004-5)
(3-year-old fillies only through 2003)

Year	1st (Age)	Jockey	Trainer	Owner	2nd	3rd	Time
1988	Indian Rose	A Cruz	J-M Beguigne	G de Rothschild	Sudden Love	Light the Lights	02:28.8
1989	Young Mother	A Badel	J-M Beguigne	J-M Beguigne	Sierra Roberta	Colorado Dancer	02:33.1
1990	Salsabil	W Carson	J Dunlop	H Al Maktoum	Miss Alleged	In The Groove	02:29.6
1991	Magic Night	A Badel	P Demercastel	Mme P Demercastel	Pink Turtle	Crnagora	02:27.8
1992	Jolypha	Pat Eddery	A Fabre	K Abdullah	Cunning	Urban Sea	02:32.8
1993	Intrepidity	T Jarnet	A Fabre	Sheikh Mohammed	Wemyss Bight	Bright Moon	02:36.8
1994	Sierra Madre	G Mosse	P Bary	J-L Bouchard	Yenda	State Crystal	02:35.3
1995	Carling	T Thulliez	C Barbe	Ecurie Delbart	Valley of Gold	Larrocha	02:32.8
1996	My Emma	C Asmussen	R Guest	Matthews Breeding&Racng	Papering	Miss Tahiti	02:31.3
1997	Queen Maud	O Peslier	J de Roualle	G Tanaka	Gazelle Royale	Brilliance	02:28.2
1998	Leggera	T R Quinn	J Dunlop	Mrs A Focke	Cloud Castle	Zainta	02:41.4
1999	Daryaba	G Mosse	A de Royer-Dupre	Aga Khan	Etizaaz	Cerulean Sky	02:30.6
2000	Volvoreta	M J Kinane	C Lerner	Mme M S Vidal	Reve d›Oscar	Egyptband	02:26.3
2001	Aquarelliste	D Boeuf	E Lellouche	D Wildenstein	Diamilina	Mare Nostrum	02:28.0
2002	Pearly Shells	C Soumillon	F Rohaut	6C Racing Ltd	Ana Marie	Bright Sky	02:26.0
2003	Mezzo Soprano	L Dettori	S bin Suroor	Godolphin	Yesterday	Fidelite	02:26.1
2004	Sweet Stream (4)	T Gillet	J Hammond	Team Valor	Royal Fantasy	Pride	02:29.5
2005	Shawanda (3)	C Soumillon	A de Royer-Dupre	H H Aga Khan	Royal Highness	Paita	02:32.0
2006	Mandesha (3)	C Soumillon	A de Royer-Dupre	Prncss Zahra Aga Khan	Montare	Royal Highness	02:29.2
2007	Mrs. Lindsay (3)	J P Murtagh	F Rohaut	Bettina Jenney	West Wind	Passage of Time	02:27.0

Ireland

IRISH CHAMPION STAKES-G1
1¼ miles, 3-year-olds & up, Leopardstown
First run in 1984
Run as the Phoenix Champion Stakes at Phoenix Park prior to 1991

Year	1st (Age)	Jockey	Trainer	Owner	2nd	3rd	Time
1988	Indian Skimmer (4f)	M Roberts	H Cecil	Sheikh Mohammed	Shady Heights	Triptych	02:06.5
1989	Carroll House (4)	M J Kinane	M Jarvis	A Balzarini	Citidancer	Petrullo	02:04.0
1990	Elmaamul (3)	W Carson	W R Hern	H Al Maktoum	Sikeston	Kostroma	02:02.9
1991	Suave Dancer (3)	C Asmussen	J Hammond	H Chalhoub	Environment Friend	Stagecraft	02:06.8
1992	Dr Devious (3)	J Reid	P Chapple-Hyam	S Craig	St. Jovite	Alflora	2:10
1993	Muhtarram (4)	W Carson	J Gosden	H Al Maktoum	Opera House	Lord Of The Field	02:06.1
1994	Cezanne (5)	M J Kinane	M Stoute	Godolphin	Del Deya	Grand Lodge	02:07.9
1995	Pentire (3)	M Hills	G Wragg	Mollers Racing	Freedom Cry	Flagbird	02:04.4
1996	Timarida (4f)	J P Murtagh	J Oxx	Aga Khan	Dance Design	Glory Of Dancer	02:06.2
1997	Pilsudski (5)	M J Kinane	M Stoute	Lord Weinstock	Desert King	Alhaarth	02:04.7
1998	Swain (6)	L Dettori	S bin Suroor	Godolphin	Alborada	Xaar	02:10.2
1999	Daylami (5)	L Dettori	S bin Suroor	Godolphin	Dazzling Park	Dream Well	02:08.4
2000	Giant's Causeway (3)	M J Kinane	A P O'Brien	Mrs J Magnier/M Tabor	Greek Dance	Best Of The Bests	02:03.1
2001	Fantastic Light (5)	L Dettori	S bin Suroor	Godolphin	Galileo	Bach	02:01.8
2002	Grandera (4)	L Dettori	S bin Suroor	Godolphin	Hawk Wing	Best Of The Bests	02:04.7
2003	High Chaparral (4)	M J Kinane	A P O'Brien	M Tabor/Mrs J Magnier	Falbrav	Islington	02:03.3
2004	Azamour (3)	M J Kinane	J Oxx	H H Aga Khan	Norse Dancer	Powerscourt	02:02.0
2005	Oratorio (3)	K Fallon	A P O'Brien	Mrs J Magnier	Motivator	Alexander Goldrun	02:03.9
2006	Dylan Thomas (3)	K Fallon	A P O'Brien	Mrs J Magnier	Ouija Board	Alexander Goldrun	02:02.9
2007	Dylan Thomas (4)	K Fallon	A P O'Brien	Mrs J Magnier	Duke of Marmalade	Red Rock Canyon	02:02.3

IRISH DERBY-G1
1½ miles, 3-year-old colts & fillies, The Curragh
First run in 1866

Year	1st	Jockey	Trainer	Owner	2nd	3rd	Time
1988	Kahyasi	R Cochrane	L Cumani	Aga Khan	Insan	Glacial Storm	02:32.4
1989	Old Vic	S Cauthen	H Cecil	Sheikh Mohammed	Observation Post	Ile de Nisky	02:29.8
1990	Salsabil (f)	W Carson	J Dunlop	H Al Maktoum	Deploy	Belmez	02:33.0
1991	Generous	A Munro	P Cole	Prince Fahd Salman	Suave Dancer	Star Of Gdansk	02:33.3
1992	St. Jovite	C Roche	J Bolger	V K Payson	Dr Devious	Contested Bid	02:25.6
1993	Commander In Chief	Pat Eddery	H Cecil	K Abdullah	Hernando	Foresee	02:31.2
1994	Balanchine (f)	L Dettori	H Ibrahim	Godolphin	King's Theatre	Colonel Collins	02:32.7
1995	Winged Love	O Peslier	A Fabre	Sheikh Mohammed	Definite Article	Annus Mirabilis	02:30.1
1996	Zagreb	P Shanahan	D K Weld	A E Paulson	Polaris Flight	His Excellence	02:30.6
1997	Desert King	C Roche	A O'Brien	Tabor & Magnier	Dr Johnson	Loup Sauvage	02:32.5
1998	Dream Well	C Asmussen	P Bary	Niarchos Family	City Honours	Desert Fox	02:44.3
1999	Montjeu	C Asmussen	J Hammond	M Tabor	Daliapour	Tchaikovsky	02:30.1
2000	Sinndar	J P Murtagh	J Oxx	HH Aga Khan	Glyndebourne	Ciro	02:33.9
2001	Galileo	M J Kinane	A P O'Brien	Magnier & Tabor	Morshdi	Golan	02:27.1
2002	High Chaparral	M J Kinane	A P O'Brien	Tabor & Magnier	Sholokhov	Ballingarry	02:32.2
2003	Alamshar	J P Murtagh	J Oxx	HH Aga Khan	Dalakhani	Roosevelt	02:28.2
2004	Grey Swallow	P J Smullen	D K Weld	Rochelle Quinn	North Light	Tycoon	02:28.7

Year	1st	Jockey	Trainer	Owner	2nd	3rd	Time
2005	Hurricane Run	K Fallon	A Fabre	Gestut Ammerland	Scorpion	Shalapour	02:29.4
2006	Dylan Thomas	K Fallon	A P O'Brien	Mrs J Magnier	Gentlewave	Best Alibi	02:29.8
2007	Soldier of Fortune	J A Heffernan	A P O'Brien	Magnier,Smith,Tabor	Alexander of Hales	Eagle Mountain	02:36.0

IRISH OAKS-G1
1½ miles, 3-year-old fillies, The Curragh
First run in 1895

Year	1st	Jockey	Trainer	Owner	2nd	3rd	Time
1988	Diminuendo*	S Cauthen	H Cecil	Sheikh Mohammed			
1988	Melodist*	W R Swinburn	M Stoute	Sheikh Mohammed	—	Silver Lane	02:36.4
1989	Alydaress	M J Kinane	H Cecil	Sheikh Mohammed	Aliysa	Petite Ile	2:31..0
1990	Knight's Baroness	T R Quinn	P Cole	Prince F Salman	Atoll	Assertion	02:31.6
1991	Possessive Dancer	S Cauthen	A Scott	A Al Maktoum	Jet Ski Lady	Eileen Jenny	02:31.0
1992	User Friendly	G Duffield	C Brittain	W Gredley	Market Booster	Arrikala	02:33.7
1993	Wemyss Bight	Pat Eddery	A Fabre	K Abdullah	Royal Ballerina	Oakmead	02:35.8
1994	Bolas	Pat Eddery	B Hills	K Abdullah	Hawajiss	Gothic Dream	02:37.6
1995	Pure Grain	J Reid	M Stoute	R Barnett	Russian Snows	Valley Of Gold	02:33.6
1996	Dance Design	M J Kinane	D K Weld	Moyglare Stud Farm	Shamadara	Key Change	02:29.7
1997	Ebadiyla	J P Murtagh	J Oxx	HH Aga Khan	Yashmak	Brilliance	02:33.7
1998	Winona	J P Murtagh	J Oxx	Lady Clague	Kitza	Bahr	02:39.8
1999	Ramruma	K Fallon	H Cecil	Prince F Salman	Sunspangled	Sister Bella	02:33.0
2000	Petrushka	J P Murtagh	M Stoute	Highclere Thor. Racing	Melikah	Inforapenny	02:31.2
2001	Lailani	L Dettori	E Dunlop	M Al Maktoum	Mot Juste	Karsavina	02:30.5
2002	Margarula	K J Manning	J Bolger	Mrs J Bolger	Quarter Moon	Lady's Secret	02:37.4
2003	Vintage Tipple	L Dettori	P Mullins	P J O'Donovan	L'Ancresse	Casual Look	02:28.3
2004	Ouija Board	K Fallon	E Dunlop	Lord Derby	Punctilious	Hazarista	02:28.2
2005	Shawanda	C Soumillon	A de Royer-Dupre	H H Aga Khan	Playful Act	Mona Lisa	02:27.1
2006	Alexandrova	K Fallon	A P O'Brien	Mrs J Magnier	Scottish Stage	Rising Cross	02:29.7
2007	Peeping Fawn	J P Murtagh	A P O'Brien	Michael Tabor	Light Shift	All My Loving	02:39.1

* Diminuendo and Melodist finished in a deadheat in 1988

IRISH 1000 GUINEAS-G1
1 mile, 3-year-old fillies, The Curragh
First run in 1922

Year	1st	Jockey	Trainer	Owner	2nd	3rd	Time
1988	Trusted Partner	M J Kinane	D K Weld	Moyglare Stud	Dancing Goddess	Jingle Gold	01:39.8
1989	Ensconse	R Cochrane	L Cumani	Sheikh Mohammed	d Aldbourne	Run To Jenny	01:38.4
1990	In The Groove	S Cauthen	D Elsworth	B Cooper	Heart Of Joy	Performing Arts	01:41.2
1991	Kooyonga	W O'Connor	M Kauntze	M Haga	Julie La Rousse	Umniyatee	01:37.2
1992	Marling	W R Swinburn	G Wragg	E Loder	Market Booster	Tarwiya	01:41.4
1993	Nicer	M Hills	B Hills	Mrs J Corbett	Goodnight Kiss	Danse Royale	01:44.2
1994	Mehthaaf	W Carson	J Dunlop	H Al Maktoum	Las Meninas	Relatively Special	1:49
1995	Ridgewood Pearl	C Roche	J Oxx	A Coughlan	Warning Shadows	Khaytada	01:43.9
1996	Matiya	W Carson	B Hanbury	H Al Maktoum	Dance Design	My Branch	01:39.8
1997	Classic Park	S Craine	A P O'Brien	S Burns	Strawberry Roan	Caiseal Ros	01:42.2
1998	Tarascon	J P Spencer	T Stack	Mrs J Rowlinson	Kitza	La Nuit Rose	01:38.4

Year	1st	Jockey	Trainer	Owner	2nd	3rd	Time
1999	Hula Angel	M Hills	B Hills	J R Fleming	Golden Silca	Dazzling Park	01:38.8
2000	Crimplene	P Robinson	C E Brittain	Marwan Al Maktoum	Amethyst	Storm Dream	01:39.8
2001	Imagine	J A Heffernan	A P O'Brien	Magnier & Nagle	Crystal Music	Toroca	01:41.1
2002	Gossamer	J P Spencer	L Cumani	G Leigh-Cancerbacup	Quarter Moon	Starbourne	01:45.5
2003	Yesterday	M J Kinane	A P O'Brien	Mrs J Magnier	Six Perfections	Dimitrova	01:40.8
2004	Attraction	K Darley	M Johnston	Duke of Roxburghe	Alexander Goldrun	Illustrious Miss	01:37.6
2005	Saoire	M J Kinane	F Crowley	Joseph Joyce	Penkenna Princess	Luas Line	01:41.5
2006	Nightime	P J Smullen	D K Weld	Mrs C L Weld	Ardbrae Lady	Queen Cleopatra	01:48.4
2007	Finsceal Beo	K J Manning	J S Bolger	M A Ryan	Dimenticata	Peeping Fawn	01:39.3

IRISH 2000 GUINEAS-GI
1 mile, 3-year-old colts & fillies, The Curragh
First run in 1921

Year	1st	Jockey	Trainer	Owner	2nd	3rd	Time
1988	Prince Of Birds	D Gillespie	M V O'Brien	R Sangster	Caerwent	Intimidate	01:39.8
1989	Shaadi	W R Swinburn	M Stoute	Sheikh Mohammed	Great Commotion	Distant Relative	01:37.4
1990	Tirol	Pat Eddery	R Hannon	John Horgan	Royal Academy	Lotus Pool	01:39.2
1991	Fourstars Allstar	M E Smith	L O'Brien	R Bomze	Star Of Gdansk	Lycius	01:38.6
1992	Rodrigo de Triano	L Piggott	P Chapple-Hyam	R Sangster	Ezzoud	Brief Truce	01:41.6
1993	Barathea	M Roberts	L Cumani	Sheikh Mohammed	Fatherland	Massyar	1:43
1994	Turtle Island	J Reid	P Chapple-Hyam	R Sangster	Guided Tour	Ridgewood Ben	01:50.1
1995	Spectrum	J Reid	P Chapple-Hyam	Lord Weinstock	Adjareli	Bahri	01:40.3
1996	Spinning World	C Asmussen	J Pease	Niarchos Family	Rainbow Blues	Beauchamp King	01:38.8
1997	Desert King	C Roche	A P O'Brien	M Tabor	Verglas	Romanov	01:38.3
1998	Desert Prince	O Peslier	D Loder	Lucayan Stud	Fa-Eq	Second Empire	01:36.2
1999	Saffron Walden	O Peslier	A P O'Brien	Tabor & Magnier	Enrique	Orpen	01:38.1
2000	Bachir	L Dettori	S bin Suroor	Godolphin	Giant's Causeway	Cape Town	01:39.8
2001	Black Minnaloushe	J P Murtagh	A P O'Brien	Magnier & Tabor	Mozart	Minardi	01:41.4
2002	Rock Of Gibraltar	M J Kinane	A P O'Brien	Ferguson & Magnier	Century	Della Frnacesca	01:47.2
2003	Indian Haven	J F Egan	P D'Arcy	Gleeson/Smith/Conway	France	Tout Seul	01:41.5
2004	Bachelor Duke	S Sanders	J Toller	Est/Duke of Devonshire	Azamour	Grey Swallow	01:40.0
2005	Dubawi	L Dettori	S bin Suroor	Godolphin	Oratorio	Democratic Deficit	01:41.7
2006	Araafa	A Munro	J Noseda	Al Homaizi & Al Sagar	George Washington	Decado	01:49.9
2007	Cockney Rebel	O Peslier	G Huffer	Phil Cunningham	Creachadoir	He's A Decoy	01:36.1

Germany
GROSSER PREIS VON BADEN-GI
1½ miles, 3-year-olds & up, Baden-Baden (Ger)

Year	1st (Age)	Jockey	Trainer	Owner	2nd	3rd	Time
1988	Carroll House (3)	B Raymond	M Jarvis	A Balzarini	Helikon	Boyatino	02:52.7
1989	Mondrian (3)	K Woodburn	U Stoltefuss	Stall Hanse	Per Quod	Summer Trip	02:29.6
1990	Mondrian (4)	M Hofer	U Stoltefuss	Stall Hanse	Ibn Bey	Per Quod	02:34.6
1991	Lomitas (3)	P Schiergen	A Wohler	Gestut Fahrhof	Temporal	Wajd	02:28.8
1992	Mashaallah (4)	J Reid	J Gosden	A Al MAktoum	Platini	Sapience	02:37.8
1993	Lando (3)	A Tylicki	H Jentzsch	Gestut Haus Ittlingen	Platini	George Augustus	02:28.2

Year	1st (Age)	Jockey	Trainer	Owner	2nd	3rd	Time
1994	Lando (4)	P Schiergen	H Jentzsch	Gestut Haus Ittlingen	Monsun	Kornado	02:27.3
1995	Germany (4)	L Dettori	B Schutz	J Abdullah	Lecroix	Right Win	02:37.7
1996	Pilsudski (4)	W R Swinburn	M Stoute	Lord Weinstock	Germany	Sunshack	02:26.7
1997	Borgia (3f)	K Fallon	B Schutz	Gestut Ammerland	Luso	Predappio	02:28.5
1998	Tiger Hill (3)	A Suborics	P Schiergen	Baron G von Ullmann	Caitano	Public Purse	02:40.1
1999	Tiger Hill (4)	T Hellier	P Schiergen	Baron G von Ullmann	Flamingo Road	Belenus	02:29.9
2000	Samum (3)	A Starke	A Schutz	Stall Balnkenese	Catella	Fruits Of Love	02:39.0
2001	Morshdi (3)	P Robinson	M Jarvis	Darley Stud Mngmnt	Boreal	Sabiango	02:31.3
2002	Marienbard (5)	L Dettori	S bin Suroor	Godolphin	Salve Regina	Noroit	02:34.9
2003	Mamool (4)	L Dettori	S bin Suroor	Godolphin	Black Sam Bellamy	Dano-Mast	02:32.8
2004	Warrsan (6)	K McEvoy	C E Brittain	S Manana	Egerton	Shirocco	02:32.8
2005	Warrsan (7)	K McEvoy	C E Brittain	S Manana	Gonbarda	Westerner	02:34.4
2006	Prince Flori (3)	F Minarik	S Smrczek	Stall Reni	Oriental Tiger	Saddex	02:33.9
2007	Quijano (5)	A Starke	P Schiergen	Gestut Fahrhof	Adlerflug	Egerton	02:28.2

Premier Asian Stakes

DUBAI WORLD CUP-G1

2000 meters (1¼ miles) (Dirt), 4-year-olds & up, Nad Al Sheba

First run in 1996

Year	1st (Age)	Jockey	Trainer	Owner	2nd	3rd	Time
1996	Cigar (6)	J D Bailey	W I Mott	A E Paulson	Soul of the Matter	L'Carriere	02:03.8
1997	Singspiel (5)	J D Bailey	M Stoute	Sheikh Mohammed	Siphon	Sandpit	02:01.9
1998	Silver Charm (4)	G Stevens	B Baffert	R & B Lewis	Swain	Loup Sauvage	02:04.3
1999	Almutawakel (4)	R Hills	S bin Suroor	H Al Maktoum	Malek	Victory Gallop	02:00.7
2000	Dubai Millennium (4)	L Dettori	S bin Suroor	Godolphin	Behrens	Public Purse	01:59.5
2001	Captain Steve (4)	J D Bailey	B Baffert	M E Pegram	To The Victory	Hightori	02:00.4
2002	Street Cry (4)	J D Bailey	S bin Suroor	Godolphin	Sei Mi	Sahkee	02:01.2
2003	Moon Ballad (4)	L Dettori	S bin Suroor	Godolphin	Harlan's Holiday	Nayef	02:00.5
2004	PleasantlyPerfect(6)	A Solis	R Mandella	Diamond A Racing Corp	Medaglia d'Oro	Victory Moon	02:00.2
2005	Roses in May (5)	J R Velazquez	D L Romans	K & S Ramsey	Dynever	Choctaw Nation	02:02.2
*2006	Electrocutionist (5)	L Dettori	S bin Suroor	Godolphin	Wilko	Magna Graduate	02:01.3
2007	Invasor (5)	F Jara	K P McLaughlin	Hamdan Al Maktoum	Premium Tap	Bullish Luck	02:00.0

In 2006 Brass Hat finished second but was disqualified and placed last

HONG KONG CUP-G1

2000 meters (1¼ miles), 3-year-olds & up, Sha Tin

First run in 1990

Run twice in 1993, in April and December.

Run as Hong Kong International Cup at 1800 meters (1-1/8 miles) 1990-1998.

Year	1st (Age)	Jockey	Trainer	Owner	2nd	3rd	Time
1990	Kessem (5)	K Moses	B J Smith	Durcan & Smith	Livistona Lane	Colonial Chief	01:48.4
1991	River Verdon (4)	G Mosse	D Hill	O Cheung	Prudent Manner	Majestic Boy	01:49.8
1992	RACE NOT RUN						
1993	Romanee Conti (4)	G Childs	L K Laxson	P J & P M Vela	Fraar	Charmonnier	01:48.2

Year	1st (Age)	Jockey	Trainer	Owner	2nd	3rd	Time
1993	Motivation (5)	J Marshall	J Moore	S Hui	Verveine	Stark South	01:49.2
1994	State Taj (5)	D Oliver	J Riley	H & Mrs L Croll	River Majesty	Volochine	01:48.4
1995	Fujiyama Kenzan (7)	M Ebina	H Mori	T Fujimoto	Ventquattrofogli	Jade Age	01:47.0
1996	First Island (4)	M Hills	G Wragg	Mollers Racing	Seascay	Kingston Bay	01:48.2
1997	Val's Prince (5)	C J Asmussen	J Picou	Martin & Weiner	Oriental Express	Wixim	01:47.2
1998	Midnight Bet (4)	H Kawachi	H Nagahama	Shadai Racehorse Co	Johan Cruyff	Almushtarak	01:46.9
1999	Jim and Tonic (5)	G Mosse	F Doumen	J D Martin	Running Stag	Lear Spear	02:01.4
2000	Fantastic Light (4)	L Dettori	S bin Suroor	Godolphin	Greek Dance	Jim and Tonic	02:02.2
2001	Agnes Digital (4)	H Shii	T Shirai	T Watanabe	Tobougg	Terre a Terre	02:02.8
2002	Precision (4)	M J Kinane	D Oughton	Wu Sai Wing	Paolini	Dano-Mast	02:07.1
2003	Falbrav (5)	L Dettori	L Cumani	Scuderia Rencati	Rakti	Elegant Fashion	02:00.9
2004	AlexanderGoldrun(3f)	K J Manning	J S Bolger	Mrs N O'Callaghan	Bullish Luck	Touch of Land	02:03.3
2005	Vengeance OfRain(5)	A Delpech	D Ferraris	R Gianco/C H Man	Pride	Maraahel	02:04.5
2006	Pride (6m)	C-P Lemaire	A de Royer-Dupre	NP Bloodstocl Ltd	Admire Moon	Vengeance Of Rain	02:01.6
2007	Ramonti (5)	L Dettori	S bin Suroor	Godolphin	Viva Pataca	Musical Way	02:02.8

JAPAN CUP-G1

2400 meters (1½ miles), 3-year-olds & up, Tokyo

First run in 1981

Year	1st (Age)	Jockey	Trainer	Owner	2nd	3rd	Time
1988	Pay the Butler (4)	C McCarron	R Frankel	E Gann	Tamamo Cross	Oguri Cap	02:25.5
1989	Horlicks (6f)	L O'Sullivan	D O'Sullivan	G de Gruchy	Oguri Cap	Pay the Butler	02:22.2
1990	Better Loosen Up (5)	M Clarke	D Hayes	G Farrah	Ode	Cacoethes	02:23.2
1991	Golden Pheasant (5)	G Stevens	C Whittingham	B McNall	Magic Night	Shaftesbury Avenue	02:24.7
1992	Tokai Teio (4)	Y Okabe	S Matsumoto	M Uchimura	Naturalism	Dear Doctor	02:24.6
1993	Legacy World (4)	H Kawachi	H Mori	Y Souma	Kotashaan	Winning Ticket	02:24.4
1994	Marvelous Crown(4)	K Minai	M Osawa	S Sasahara	Paradise Creek	Royce And Royce	02:23.6
1995	Lando (5)	M Roberts	H Jentzsch	Gestut Ittlingen	Hishi Amazon	Hernando	02:24.6
1996	Singspiel (4)	L Dettori	M Stoute	Sheikh Mohammed	Fabulous la Fouine	Strategic Choice	02:23.8
1997	Pilsudski (5)	M J Kinane	M Stoute	Lord Weinstock	Air Groove	Bubble Gum Fellow	02:25.8
1998	El Condor Pasa (3)	M Ebina	Y Ninomiya	T Watanabe	Air Groove	Special Week	02:25.9
1999	Special Week (4)	Y Take	T Shirai	H Usuda	Indigenous	High-Rise	02:25.5
2000	T.M. Opera O (4)	R Wada	I Iwamoto	M Takezono	Meisho Doto	Fantastic Light	02:26.1
2001	Jungle Pocket (3)	O Peslier	S Watanabe	Y Saito	T.M. Opera O	Narita Top Road	02:23.8
*2002	Falbrav (4)	L Dettori	L Brogi	Scuderia Rencati	Sarafan	Symboli Kris S	02:12.2
2003	Tap Dance City (6)	T Sato	S Sasaki	Yushun Horse	That's The Plenty	Symboli Kris S	02:28.7
2004	Zenno Rob Roy (4)	O Peslier	K Fujisawa	S Oosako	Cosmo Bulk	Delta Blues	02:24.2
2005	Alkaased (5)	L Dettori	L Cumani	M Charlton	Heart's Cry	Zenno Rob Roy	02:22.1
2006	Deep Impact (4)	Y Take	Y Ikee	Kaneko Makoto Hldngs	Dream Passport	Ouija Board	02:25.1
2007	Admire Moon (4)	Y Iwata	H Matsuda	Japan Darley Famr Co	Pop Rock	Meisho Samson	02:24.7

* Run at Nakayama at 1¼ miles.

Appendix B

Major Jump Races

CHAMPION HURDLE-G1

2¹⁄₁₆ miles (8 hurdles), 5-year-old & up, Cheltenham (GB)

First run in 1927

Year	1st (Age)	Jockey	Trainer	Owner	2nd	3rd	Time
1988	Celtic Shot (6)	P Scudamore	F Winter	D Horton	Classical Charm	Celtic Chief	04:14.4
1989	Beech Road (7)	R Guest	G Balding	A Geake	Celtic Chief	Celtic Shot	04:02.1
1990	Kribensis (6)	R Dunwoody	M Stoute	Sheikh Mohammed	Nomadic Way	Past Glories	03:50.7
1991	Morley Street (7)	J Frost	G Balding	M Jackson	Nomadic Way	Ruling	03:54.6
1992	Royal Gait (9)	G McCourt	J Fanshawe	Sheikh Mohammed	Oh So Risky	Ruling	03:57.2
1993	Granville Again (7)	P Scudamore	M Pipe	E Scarth	Royal Derbi	Halkopous	03:51.6
1994	Flakey Dove (8)	M Dwyer	R Price	J Price	Oh So Risky	Large Action	04:02.0
1995	Alderbrook (6)	N Williamson	K Bailey	E Pick	Large Action	Danoli	04:03.0
1996	Collier Bay (6)	G Bradley	J Old	W Stuart	Alderbrook	Pridwell	03:59.0
1997	Make A Stand (6)	A P McCoy	M Pipe	P A Deal	Theatreworld	Space Trucker	03:48.4
1998	Istabraq (6)	C Swan	A P O'Brien	J P McManus	Theatreworld	I'm Supposin	03:49.1
1999	Istabraq (7)	C Swan	A P O'Brien	J P McManus	Theatreworld	French Holly	03:56.8
2000	Istabraq (8)	C Swan	A P O'Brien	J P McManus	Hors La Loi III	Blue Royal	03:48.1
2001	RACE NOT RUN						
2002	Hors La Loi III (7)	D Gallagher	J Fanshawe	P Green	Marble Arch	Bilboa	03:53.8
2003	Rooster Booster (9)	R Johnson	P J Hobbs	T Warner	Westender	RhinestoneCowboy	03:54.7
2004	Hardy Eustace (7)	C O'Dwyer	D Hughes	L Byrne	Rooster Booster	Intersky Falcon	03:54.5
2005	Hardy Eustace (8)	C O'Dwyer	D Hughes	L Byrne	Harchibald	Brave Inca	03:51.5
2006	Brave Inca (8)	A P McCoy	C A Murphy	D W Macauley	Macs Joy	Hardy Eustace	03:50.0
2007	Sublimity (7)	P Carberry	J Carr	W Hennessy	Brave Inca	Afsoun	03:55.7

CHELTENHAM GOLD CUP STEEPLECHASE-G1

3¼ miles (22 fences), 6-year-olds & up, Cheltenham (GB)

First run in 1924

Year	1st (Age)	Jockey	Trainer	Owner	2nd	3rd	Time
1988	Charter Party (10)	R Dunwoody	D Nicholson	Mrs C Smith	Cavvies Clown	Beau Ranger	06:58.9
1989	Desert Orchid (10)	S Sherwood	D Elsworth	R Burridge	Yahoo	Charter Party	07:17.6
1990	Norton's Coin (9)	G McCourt	S Griffiths	S Griffiths	Toby Tobias	Desert Orchid	06:30.9
1991	Garrison Savannah (8)	M Pitman	J Pitman		The Fellow	Desert Orchid	06:49.8
1992	Cool Ground (10)	A Maguire	G Balding	Whitcombe Manor	The Fellow	Docklands Express	06:47.5
1993	Jodami (8)	M Dwyer	P Beaumont	J Yeardon	Rushing Wild	Royal Athlete	06:34.4
1994	The Fellow (9)	A Kondrat	F Doumen	Marquise de Moratalla	Jodami	Young Hustler	06:40.6
1995	Master Oats (9)	N Williamson	K Bailey	P Matthews	Dubacilla	Minnehoma	06:56.1
1996	Imperial Call (7)	C O'Dwyer	F Sutherland	Lisselan Farm	Rough Quest	Couldnt Be Better	06:42.5
1997	Mr Mulligan (9)	A P McCoy	N Chance	M & G Worcester	Barton Bank	Dorans Pride	06:35.5
1998	Cool Dawn (10)	A Thornton	R Alner	Miss D Harding	Strong Promise	Dorans Pride	06:39.5
1999	See More Business (9)	M FitzGerald	P Nicholls	Barber & Keighley	Go Ballistic	Florida Pearl	06:41.9
2000	Looks Like Trouble	R Johnson	N Chance	T Collins	Florida Pearl	Strong Promise	06:30.3
2001	RACE NOT RUN						
2002	Best Mate (7)	J Culloty	H C Knight	J Lewis	Commanche Court	See More Business	06:50.1
2003	Best Mate (8)	J Culloty	H C Knight	J Lewis	Truckers Tavern	Harbour Pilot	06:39.0
2004	Best Mate (9)	J Culloty	H C Knight	J Lewis	Sir Rembrandt	Harbour Pilot	06:42.6

Year	1st (Age)	Jockey	Trainer	Owner	2nd	3rd	Time
2005	Kicking King (7)	B J Geraghty	T Taafe	C Clarkson	Take The Stand	Sir Rembrandt	06:42.9
2006	War Of Attrition (7)	C O'Dwyer	M F Morris	GigginstownHouseStud	Hedgehunter	Forget The Past	06:31.7
2007	Kauto Star (7)	R Walsh	P Nicholls	Clive D Smith	Exotic Dancer	Turpin Green	06:40.5

GRAND NATIONAL STEEPLECHASE HANDICAP-G3
4½ miles (30 fences), 7-year-olds & up, Aintree (GB)
First run in 1839

Year	1st (Age)	Jockey	Trainer	Owner	2nd	3rd	Time
1988	Rhyme N' Reason (9)	B Powell	D Elsworth	Miss J Reed	Durham Edition	Monanore	09:53.5
1989	Little Polveir (12)	J Frost	G Balding	E Harvey	West Tip	The Thinker	10:06.8
1990	Mr Frisk (11)	Mr M Armytage	K Bailey	Mrs H Duffey	Durham Edition	Rinus	08:47.8
1991	Seagram (11)	N Hawke	D Barons	E Parker	Garrison Savannah	Auntie Dot	09:29.9
1992	Party Politics (8)	C Llewellyn	N Gaselee	Mrs D Thompson	Romany King	Laura's Beau	09:06.3
1993	RACE VOID						
1994	Minnehoma (11)	R Dunwoody	M Pipe	F Starr	Just So	Moorcroft Boy	10:18.8
1995	Royal Athlete (12)	J F Titley	J Pitman	G & L Johnson	Party Politics	Over the Deel	09:04.1
1996	Rough Quest (10)	M Fitzgerald	T Casey	A Wates	Encore Un Peu	Superior Finish	09:00.8
1997	Lord Gyllene (9)	A Dobbin	S Brookshaw	S Clarke	Suny Bay	Camelot Knight	09:05.9
1998	Earth Summit (10)	C Llewellyn	N Twiston-Davies	Summit Prtnrshp	Suny Bay	Samlee	10:51.4
1999	Bobby Jo (9)	P Carberry	T Carberry	R Burke	Blue Charm	Call It A Day	09:14.1
2000	Papillon (9)	R Walsh	T M Walsh	Mrs B Moran	Mely Moss	Niki Dee	09:09.7
2001	Red Marauder (11)	R Guest	N B Mason	N B Mason	Smarty	Blowing Wind	11:00.1
2002	Bindaree (8)	J Culloty	N Twiston-Davies	H R Mould	What's Up Boys	Blowing Wind	09:08.6
2003	Monty's Pass (10)	B J Geraghty	J J Mangan	Dee Racing Syndicate	Supreme Glory	Amberleigh House	09:21.7
2004	AmberleighHouse(12)	G Lee	D McCain	Halewood Intl Ltd	Clan Royal	Lord Atterbury	09:20.3
2005	Hedgehunter (8)	R Walsh	W Mullins	T Hemmings	Royal Auclair	Simply Gifted	09:20.8
2006	Numbersixvalverde (10)	N P Madden	M Brassil	O B P Carroll	Hedgehunter	Clan Royal	09:41.0
2007	Silver Birch (10)	R M Power	G Elliott	Brian Walsh	McKelvey	Slim Pickings	09:13.6

GRAND STEEPLECHASE DE PARIS-G1
5800 meters (3⅗ miles) (23 obstacles), 6-year-olds & up, Auteuil (Fr)

Year	1st (Age)	Jockey	Trainer	Owner	2nd	3rd	Time
1988	Katko (5)	D Vincent	B Secly	Comte de Montesson	Nupsala	Cyborg	07:09.0
1989	Katko (6)	J-Y Beaurain	B Secly	Comte de Montesson	Oteuil	Ouragan Collonges	07:09.0
1990	Katko (7)	J-Y Beaurain	B Secly	Comte de Montesson	Sabre d'Estruval	The Fellow	07:15.0
1991	The Fellow (6)	D Vincent	F Doumen	Marquise de Moratalla	Sabre d'Estruval	Oteuil	07:14.0
1992	El Triunfo (6)	D Vincent	F Rohaut	Mme M Montauban	Ucello II	Ubu III	07:20.0
1993	Ucello II (7)	C Aubert	F Doumen	Marquise de Moratalla	Al Capone II	Vorentin	07:16.0
1994	Ucello II (8)	C Aubert	F Doumen	Marquise de Moratalla	Venus de Mirande	Arenice	07:07.0
1995	Ubu III (9)	P Chevalier	F Doumen	Marquise de Moratalla	Val d'Alene	Bannkipour	07:20.0
1996	Arenice (8)	P Sourzac	G Macaire	Mme M Montauban	Al Capone II	Bannkipour	07:07.0
1997	Al Capone II (9)	J-Y Beaurain	B Secly	R Fougedoire	Cand'Or	Gracky	07:42.0
1998	First Gold (5)	T Doumen	F Doumen	Marquise de Moratalla	Saint-Quenin	Chamberko	07:10.0
1999	Mandarino (6)	P Chevalier	M Rolland	Mme D Ricard	Al Capone II	Chant Royal	07:43.0
2000	Vieux Beaufai (7)	P Bigot	F Danloux	Ecurie Siklos	Or Jack	First Gold	07:19.0
2001	Kotkijet (6)	T Majorcryk	J-P Gallorini	D Wildenstein	Ilare	El Paso III	07:13.0

Year	1st (Age)	Jockey	Trainer	Owner	2nd	3rd	Time
2002	Double Car (6)	C Cheminaud	B de Watrigant	J Biraben	El Paso III	Batman Senora	07:31.0
2003	Line Marine (6f)	C Pieux	C Aubert	Mme G Vuillard	Batman Senora	Urga	07:37.0
2004	Kotkijet (9)	T Majorcryk	J-P Gallorini	Ecurie Wildenstein	Kamillo	Majadal	07:21.0
2005	Sleeping Jack (6)	C Pieux	J Ortet	R Temam	Ma Royale	Lord Carmont	07:03.0
2006	Princesse d'Anjou(5m)	P A Carberry	F M Cottin	J-P Senechal	Rigoureux	Kotkijet	07:08.0
2007	Mid Dancer (6)	C Gombeau	A Chaille-Chaille	Sean Mulryan	Lord Carmont	Golden Flight	07:32.0

GRANDE COURSE DE HAIES D'AUTEUIL (French Champion Hurdle)-G1
5100 meters (3³⁄₁₆ miles) (16 obstacles), 5-year-olds & up, Auteuil (Fr)

Year	1st (Age)	Jockey	Trainer	Owner	2nd	3rd	
1988	Goodea (8)	B Marie	J-P Gallorini	P Elmoznino	Marly River	Rocarvin	
1989	Sire Rochelais (5)	L Manceau	G Cherel	J-C Evain	Frappeuse	Afkal	
1990	Tongan (7)	D Vincent	G Collet	W Nikolic	Isabey	Ma Puce	
1991	Rose Or No (7)	V Sartori	P Demercastel	Ecurie Ouaki	Ubu III	March On	
1992	Ubu III (6)	A Kondrat	F Doumen	Marquise de Moratalla	Roi d'Ecajeul	Crystal Spirit	
1993	Ubu III (7)	A Kondrat	F Doumen	Marquise de Moratalla	True Brave	Gabarret	
1994	Le Roi Thibault (5)	Y Fouin	G Doleuze	Haras du Reuilly	Ubu III	Bog Frog	
1995	Matchou (6)	D Mescam	J Lesbordes	Mlle Montauban	Royal Chance	Chinese Gordon	
1996	Earl Grant (7)	J-Y Beaurain	B Secly	L Gautier	Mysilv	Montperle	
1997	Bog Frog (8)	J-Y Beaurain	B Secly	Mme Scarisbrick	Alpha Tauri	Royal Chance	
1998	Mantovo (6)	F Benech	M Rolland	F A McNulty	Earl Grant	Nononito	
1999	Vaporetto (6)	T Majorcryk	J-P Gallorini	D Wildenstein	Mon Romain	Asolo	06:25.0
2000	Le Sauvignon (6)	T Majorcryk	J Bertran de Balanda	D J Jackson	Full of Ambition	Vaporetto	06:09.0
2001	Le Sauvignon (7)	D Bressou	J Bertran de Balanda	D J Jackson	Gilder	Bounce Back	06:19.0
2002	Laveron (7	T Doumen	F Doumen	D Grauert	Vic Toto	Galant Moss	06:19.0
2003	Nobody Told Me (5f)	D J Casey	W Mullins	Amber Syndicate	Karly Flight	Katiki	06:25.0
2004	Rule Supreme (8)	D J Casey	W Mullins	J Fallon	Great Love	Kotkijet	06:20.0
2005	Lycaon de Vauzelle(6)	B Chameraud	J Bertran de Balanda	F Wintz	Rule Supreme	Double Car	06:31.0
2006	Mid Dancer (5)	C Pieux	A Chaille-Chaille	Sean Mulryan	Princesse d'Anjou	Lycaon de Vauzelle	06:07.9
2007	Zaiyad (6)	J Ricou	A Chaille-Chaille	Sean Mulryan	Mister Gyor	Monoalco	06:22.

Acknowledgments

GRATEFUL THANKS TO Nick Smith of Ascot Racecourse, Dominique Gabel-Litny of France-Galop, Peter Brauer of the Direktorium fur Vollblutzucht und Rennen, Winifried Engelbrecht-Bresges and Julia Tsang of the Hong Kong Jockey Club, Nobitushi Mochizuki, Junichi Hasegawa and Takeshi Kodama of the Japan Racing Association, Kevin Robertson of Ellerslie Racecourse, Chris Williams of *Timeform,* David Ashforth of *The Racing Post,* Bernard Barouche of *Paris-Turf,* and Tom Tribolet.

Special thanks to Adrian Beaumont, Robert Carter, James Crisp, and Alastair Donald of the International Racing Bureau.

Photo Credits

Bibliography

Ascot: The History, by Sean Magee with Sally Aird. Methuen Publishing Ltd. United Kingdom, 2002

The Breedon Book of Horse Racing Records, by Edward Abelson and John Tyrrel. Breedon Books Publishing Company, Derby. United Kingdom, 1993

The Derby Stakes, by Michael Church. Racing Post Ltd. United Kingdom, 1997

Favourite Racehorses. A Timeform Publication. Portway Press Ltd. 1997

The Grand History of the Prix de l'Arc de Triomphe, by Arthur FitzGerald. Genesis Publications Limited. United Kingdom, 1997

Headquarters: A History of Newmarket and Its Racing, by Richard Onslow. Great Ouse Press. United Kingdom, 1971

Les Heures Mouvements de la Societe d'Encouragement: 1933–1991, by Guy Thibault, incorporating *Centenaire de la Societe d'Encouragement: 1833–1933,* by Rene Romanet-Riondet. Editions Castelet. France, 1993

Les Hippodromes, by Marc Gaillard. Editions de La Palatine-Bibliotheque des Arts, Paris. France, 1984

The History of Thoroughbred Racing in America, by William H. P. Robertson. Bonanza Books. United States, 1964

Horse Racing Records, Facts and Champions, by Tony Morris and John Randall. Guinness Books. United Kingdom, 1988

The Irish Derby, by Guy St. John Williams and Francis P. M. Hyland. J. A. Allen & Co. Ltd. United Kingdom,1980

Irish Horseracing: An Illustrated History, by John Welcome. Gill and Macmillan. Republic of Ireland, 1982

A Race Apart: The History of the Grand National, by Reg Green. Hodder & Stoughton. United Kingdom, 1988

Racecourses on the Flat, by John Tyrrel. The Crowood Press. United Kingdom, 1989

Royal Ascot: A History of Royal Ascot from Its Founding by Queen Anne to the Present Time, by Dorothy Laird. Hodder & Stoughton. United Kingdom, 1976

Un Siecle de Galop: 1900–2000, by Guy Thibault. Editions Filipacchi. France, 2001

The World Atlas of Horse Racing, by Julian Bedford. The Hamlyn Publishing Group Limited. United Kingdom, 1989